Forensic Facial Identification

Wiley Series in

The Psychology of Crime, Policing and Law

Series Editors

Graham M. Davies and **Ray Bull**

University of Leicester, UK

The Wiley Series in the Psychology of Crime, Policing and Law publishes concise and integrative reviews on important emerging areas of contemporary research. The purpose of the series is not merely to present research findings in a clear and readable form, but also to bring out their implications for both practice and policy. In this way, it is hoped the series will not only be useful to psychologists but also to all those concerned with crime detection and prevention, policing, and the judicial process.

For other titles in this series please see www.wiley.com/go/pcpl

Forensic Facial Identification

Theory and Practice of Identification from Eyewitnesses, Composites and CCTV

Edited by

Tim Valentine
Goldsmiths, University of London

Josh P. Davis
University of Greenwich

WILEY Blackwell

This edition first published 2015
© 2015 John Wiley & Sons, Ltd.

Registered Office
John Wiley & Sons, Ltd, The Atrium, Southern Gate, Chichester, West Sussex, PO19 8SQ, UK

Editorial Offices
350 Main Street, Malden, MA 02148-5020, USA
9600 Garsington Road, Oxford, OX4 2DQ, UK
The Atrium, Southern Gate, Chichester, West Sussex, PO19 8SQ, UK

For details of our global editorial offices, for customer services, and for information about how to apply for permission to reuse the copyright material in this book please see our website at www.wiley.com/wiley-blackwell.

The right of Tim Valentine and Josh P. Davis to be identified as the authors of the editorial material in this work has been asserted in accordance with the UK Copyright, Designs and Patents Act 1988.

Library of Congress Cataloging-in-Publication Data

Forensic facial identification : theory and practice of identification from eyewitnesses, composites and CCTV / edited by Tim Valentine, Josh P. Davis.
     pages   cm
   Includes bibliographical references and index.
   ISBN 978-1-118-46911-8 (cloth) – ISBN 978-1-118-46958-3 (pbk.)   1. Eyewitness identification.   2. Face perception.   I. Valentine, Tim, 1959–   II. Davis, Josh P.
   HV8073.F572 2015
   363.25′8–dc23

                                        2014047946

A catalogue record for this book is available from the British Library.

Cover image: © Peter Stroh / Alamy
              © mauro grigollo / iStockphoto

Set in 10/12pt Century Schoolbook by SPi Publisher Services, Pondicherry, India
Printed and bound in Malaysia by Vivar Printing Sdn Bhd

1   2015

Contents

Contributors

Neil Brewer

School of Psychology, Flinders University, Adelaide, Australia
e-mail: neil.brewer@flinders.edu.au

Charity Brown

Institute of Psychological Sciences, University of Leeds, Leeds,
United Kingdom
e-mail: psccbr@leeds.ac.uk

Steven E. Clark

Professor of Psychology, Director, Presley Center for Crime and
Justice Studies, University of California, Riverside, United States
e-mail: steven.clark@ucr.edu

Josh P. Davis (Editor)

Senior Lecturer, Psychology and Counselling Department, University
of Greenwich, London, United Kingdom
e-mail: j.p.davis@gre.ac.uk

Jennifer E. Dysart

Associate Professor, Department of Psychology, John Jay College of
Criminal Justice, New York, United States
e-mail: jdysart@jjay.cuny.edu

Gary Edmond

School of Law, University of New South Wales, Sydney, Australia
e-mail: g.edmond@unsw.edu.au

Heather D. Flowe
School of Psychology, University of Leicester, Leicester, United
Kingdom
e-mail: hf49@leicester.ac.uk

Charlie Frowd

University of Winchester, Winchester, United Kingdom
e-mail: Charlie.Frowd@winchester.ac.uk

Fiona Gabbert

Department of Psychology, Goldsmiths, University of London, London,
United Kingdom
e-mail: f.gabbert@gold.ac.uk

Victoria Z. Lawson

Research Associate, CUNY Institute of State and Local Governance,
New York, United States
e-mail: Victoria.Lawson@islg.cuny.edu

Molly B. Moreland

Psychology, University of California, Riverside, United States
e-mail: molly.moreland@email.ucr.edu

Alice O'Toole

The University of Texas at Dallas, School of Behavioral and Brain
Sciences, Richardson, United States
e-mail: otoole@utdallas.edu

P. Jonathon Phillips

Electrical Engineer, National Institute of Standards and Technology,
United States
e-mail: jonathon.phillips@nist.gov

Andrew Roberts

Senior Lecturer, Melbourne Law School, Melbourne, Australia
e-mail: arob@unimelb.edu.au

Ryan A. Rush

Visiting Assistant Professor of Psychology, Wabash College,
United States
e-mail: rushr@wabash.edu

Hannah Ryder

School of Psychology, University of Leicester, Leicester, United
Kingdom
e-mail: hr98@le.ac.uk

James D. Sauer

School of Medicine (Psychology), University of Tasmania, Hobart,
Australia
e-mail: jim.sauer@utas.edu.au

Harriet M.J. Smith

Division of Psychology, Nottingham Trent University, Nottingham,
United Kingdom
e-mail: harriet.smith2011@my.ntu.ac.uk

Tim Valentine (Editor)

Professor of Psychology, Department of Psychology, Goldsmiths,
University of London, London, United Kingdom
e-mail: t.valentine@gold.ac.uk

Caroline Wilkinson

Director of Face Lab, Liverpool School of Art & Design, Liverpool
John Moores University, Liverpool, United Kingdom
c.m.wilkinson@ljmu.ac.uk

Foreword

The criminal justice system involves a pantheon of values, and it is not always easy to figure out the best course of action when one of those values appears to clash with another. And so it is the case with our value about avoiding the wrongful prosecution of innocent people and our value about ensuring the correct prosecution of guilty people. *Forensic Facial Identification* is a superb edited volume whose contributors collectively worry about both of these values, how to balance them, and how scientific evidence on facial identification can help us think about the legal structures that should exist in a world that has a good balance.

Forensic Facial Identification is primarily about the problem of distinguishing accurate eyewitness testimony from mistaken testimony. It is broader than most books on eyewitness testimony in that it concerns not only identification of eyewitnesses who might have actually seen the robbery, or been a victim of the rape, but also the identification of perpetrators from closed-circuit television images, as is becoming increasingly common with the proliferation of cameras throughout our society. And it also concerns the identification of deceased individuals by reconstructions of their faces as they appeared in real life, as happened, for example, when Osama bin Laden was captured and killed. How do you think we know for sure that the man who was shot and killed on May 2, 2011, inside a private residential compound in Pakistan was really the Saudi Arabian bin Laden? The introductory chapter does a splendid job of briefly reviewing these topics – and ones not mentioned – that readers will find in each chapter so there is no need to repeat this review here.

Forensic Facial Identification is broader than most books on eyewitness testimony in other ways. Each chapter begins with a specific case that is used by the chapter authors to guide discussion. The cases, and discussions, cover many regions of the world, mostly the UK and US, but also Australia and New Zealand in particular. The cases are sometimes famous, as is that of the murder of the foreign minister Anna Lindh in Sweden in 2003, and sometimes not famous, as in the case of a fast food worker in Manchester, UK, who was accused of rapes in 2009 and 2010. The cases are historical, as in the case of Adolf Beck who was convicted in 1896 in London for defrauding women. Most are more modern, as in the numerous cases of wrongful conviction uncovered by the New York-based Innocence Project.

One case that is mentioned frequently (in several chapters) is a recent case that was decided by the New Jersey Supreme Court (*State v. Henderson*). Since the present authors did not go into much detail about this case, and it has been so significant in the US, I thought I would use my "forward platform" to say a bit more about it. In that murder case, the defendant Larry Henderson was accused of being involved in a shooting in an apartment in Camden, New Jersey. About two weeks after the murder, a surviving witness who had been in the apartment identified Henderson from a set of photos. A subsequent identification at trial resulted in Henderson's conviction. It might seem like an open and shut case, but actually there were serious problems with the initial identification. It turns out that the witness only picked Henderson's photo after the investigating officers put on some "pressure" and did some "nudging", as the behaviour of those officers would later be characterized. More specifically, it appears that when the key witness first looked at the photos, he did not see anyone he recognized. He finally narrowed things down to two photos but was indecisive. Pressure and nudging cracked the indecisiveness. On top of this, it turned out that the witness himself had, during the day and just prior to the shooting, consumed large amounts of alcohol and crack cocaine. Henderson appealed his conviction, and when that appeal was heard by the New Jersey Supreme Court in 2011, the criminal justice world paid attention. That decision showed a deep appreciation of the eyewitness problems in the case and a sophisticated appreciation of the science of eyewitness testimony, and the ruling rather dramatically changed the legal standard for how eyewitness evidence is assessed in a criminal case.

What now happens in New Jersey is this. A defendant who can show some evidence of suggestive influences on witness testimony is entitled to a court hearing in which all the psychological factors bearing on the testimony are reviewed and analysed. After this scrutiny, if the judge still decides to admit the testimony at trial, then the judge must also provide to the jury a set of instructions that can guide them on how to think about the eyewitness evidence. Over the next year or so, those instructions were crafted by a committee, which produced a 26-page document that can be found on the internet at: www.judiciary.state.nj. us/criminal/ModelCrimJuryChargeCommHENDERSONREPORT.pdf

Curious as to what happened to Henderson after his successful appeal, psychology professor John Wixted found a prosecutor who gave him an update. According to this source, another hearing was held in which it was determined that proper procedure had been followed during Henderson's initial trial, which meant that his original guilty verdict was upheld. Of course the procedure might have been "proper" during the trial, but that does not mean that the early identification "activities" shouldn't make us suspicious about whether the identification of Henderson was truly accurate. For now, we have to live with that uncertainty.

The Henderson decision changed the way eyewitness evidence is handled not only in cases where there are questions about the role of law enforcement in producing an identification, but in cases where law enforcement played little or no role. There was a companion case to Henderson that has not received nearly the same attention, but is important because it extends these safeguarding procedures to a wide array of cases. The companion case (*New Jersey v. Chen*) involved some titillating facts. One Sunday in 2005, Mr Kim got a phone call from his ex-girlfriend, Cecilia Chen, the first such call since they had ended their relationship in 2000. Kim told Chen he was happily married and expecting a child; Chen told Kim she was not doing well and wondered about what would have happened had they not broken up. Three days later, Kim's wife Helen was home alone, five months pregnant, and recovering from surgery. A woman came to the Kim home, said her car had broken down and she needed to use the bathroom and phone. The intruder then stabbed Helen with a kitchen knife. Soon thereafter, in discussions with his wife, Kim thought the intruder might be Chen. They accessed Chen's website and looked at photos of her, and Helen became "ninety percent positive" after viewing one particular photo. So we have a case in which key aspects of the identification process were independent of any law enforcement, but nonetheless rather suggestive. Cases with such facts would also, after Henderson, be entitled to the same legal safeguards, namely the hearing and the judicial warnings.

The policy innovations resulting from the Henderson case will hopefully reduce the likelihood of mistaken identification and wrongful conviction that can result. It remains to be seen whether subsequent research confirms the effectiveness of this bold direction.

Forensic Facial Identification not only presents the basic science in each chapter, but also discusses other policy recommendations. There are recommendations concerning the procedures used to obtain an identification in the first place, such as double-blind testing. There are recommendations concerning the interviewing process, such as taking steps to avoid allowing errors to creep into the early descriptions of witnesses. There are recommendations about the use of composites, mugshot searches, showups, and street identifications, face matching and more. Collectively these authors express their appreciation of procedures that will provide some protection for a suspect who is innocent. But what about catching the guilty? Sadly, some of the reforms may come with a cost, because they reduce correct identifications. So what to do? The editors of *Forensic Facial Identification* came to a resolution that I very much appreciated: (spoiler alert; skip if you don't want to know yet)

> ...the potential disadvantage from adopting these recommendations is no reason to abandon the more important duty to avoid wrongfully prosecuting innocent suspects. Indeed a mistaken identification may result in an investigation being terminated because an innocent person has been charged, leaving the guilty free to commit further offences. The justice obtained from maximizing the rate of suspect identifications from unfair procedures would give a false sense of security.

Forensic Facial Identification should be applauded for its heroic efforts to offer society a true sense of security. Hopefully its messages will be read by many who care about fairness, and how psychological science can help us achieve it.

Elizabeth F. Loftus
University of California, Irvine

Series Preface

The Wiley Series in the Psychology of Crime, Policing and the Law publishes both single and multi-authored monographs and edited reviews of important and emerging areas of contemporary research. The purpose of this series is not merely to present research findings in a clear and readable form, but also to bring out their implications for both practice and policy. Books in this series are useful not only to psychologists, but also to all those involved in crime detection and prevention, child protection, policing and judicial processes.

As the originator of this book series, it has always been my ambition to have a volume devoted to issues surrounding facial identification. It was an early interest of both myself and the co-editor of the series, Professor Ray Bull. Each of us was involved in research into the vagaries of facial identification and we were responsible, with our co-authors, for some of the earliest books and papers published in the UK on this topic (see Clifford & Bull, 1978; Davies, Ellis, & Shepherd, 1981; Shepherd, Ellis, & Davies, 1982). However, we readily acknowledge the primacy of the pioneering work of Elizabeth Loftus (Loftus, 1979), who has provided a forward for this new book.

While research in the UK and the US into facial identification and misidentification stemmed from a common concern over miscarriages of justice based on confident but unreliable witnesses, the drivers and direction which research then took in the two countries was rather different. In the US, a wider range of offences result in jury trials, and the courts have traditionally shown a liberal approach to the admission of testimony by experts which might inform the jury on issues relevant to the evidence (Cutler & Penrod, 1995). Defence attorneys were not slow to grasp the significance of early research by psychologists on eyewitness reliability, but Elizabeth Loftus and another pioneer, the late

Robert Buckhout, still faced considerable resistance to the admission of their testimony in cases where issues of identification formed an important element in the prosecution case. Despite reverses, research on the vagaries of identification has gained in credibility as a growing number of American State Courts now admit evidence from suitably qualified psychologists in cases of disputed identification (Loftus, Doyle, & Dysart, 2013). For Loftus, this courtroom experience helped to highlight issues of concern which subsequently became the subject of research (Loftus, 1986)

In the UK, the interest of psychologists in facial identification did not stem from the adversarial cockpit of the courtroom. British courts have traditionally taken a more conservative view on the admissibility of experts in criminal trials, particularly in relation to the credibility of witnesses, where the *Turner* ruling (Mackay, Colman, & Thornton, 1999) effectively prevents psychologists from commenting on the accuracy or reliability of witnesses in the criminal court: this is a matter for counsel to explore and juries alone to decide. However, miscarriages of justice based on mistaken identification have a long history in the British courts (Davies & Griffiths, 2008), culminating in a Government enquiry led by the distinguished judge, Lord Devlin. Among the recommendations of his report (Devlin, 1976) was that "research should be directed to establishing ways in which the insights of psychology can be brought to bear on the conduct of parades and the practice of the courts" (p.149). Devlin's recommendation helped to ensure that state funding and support flowed toward psychologists involved in improving police procedures and practices, in order to minimize the risk of misidentification, rather than dealing with its consequences in the courts.

Since those early days, the study of facial memory has matured and spread across the globe, raising new issues, and there has been much cross-fertilisation as *Forensic Facial Identification* amply demonstrates. However, those early origins can still be discerned. The North American tradition can be seen in research on such issues as the relationship between confidence and accuracy and the composition and fairness of lineups, while the UK approach is reflected in studies of witness interviewing for identification, facial composite techniques and identification from closed-circuit television.

The editors, Tim Valentine and Josh Davis, both have established reputations in the field. Tim has played a crucial role in the development of video identification procedures, a technique which appears to offer a fairer and more accurate test for establishing a positive identification compared with traditional methods, while Josh has contributed important insights into identification from CCTV. Through their standing, they have been able to call upon a range of distinguished international contributors, to offer authoritative perspectives on all aspects of human facial identification. This handbook will be read with profit and interest by practitioners and researchers in law, psychology and policing, who seek safe and effective methods of prosecuting the guilty and safeguarding the innocent.

Graham M. Davies
University of Leicester

REFERENCES

Clifford, B.R., & Bull, R. (1978). *The Psychology of Person Identification*. London: Routledge & Kegan Paul.

Cutler, B.L., & Penrod, S.D. (1995). *Mistaken Identification: The Eyewitness, Psychology and the Law*. New York: Cambridge University Press.

Davies, G.M., Ellis, H.D., & Shepherd, J.W.(1981). *Perceiving and Remembering Faces*. London: Academic Press.

Davies, G.M., & Griffiths, L. (2008). Eyewitness identification and the English courts: A century of trial and error. *Psychiatry, Psychology and Law, 15*, 435–449.

Devlin, Lord P. (1976). *Report to the Secretary of State for the Home Department on the Departmental Committee on Evidence of Identification in Criminal Cases*. London: HMSO.

Loftus, E.F. (1979). *Eyewitness Testimony*. Cambridge, MA: Harvard University Press.

Loftus, E.F. (1986). Ten years in the life of an expert witness. *Law and Human Behavior, 10*, 241–263.

Loftus, E.F., Doyle, J.M., & Dysart, J. (2013). *Eyewitness Testimony: Civil and Criminal* (5th ed.). Charlottesville, VA: Lexis Law Publishing.

Mackay, R.D., Colman, A.M., & Thornton, P. (1999). The admissibility of expert psychological and psychiatric testimony. In A. Heaton-Armstrong, E. Shepherd, & D. Wolchover (Eds.), *Analysing Witness Testimony: A Guide for Legal Practitioners and Other Professionals* (pp. 321–334). Oxford: Oxford University Press.

Shepherd, J.W., Ellis, H.D., & Davies, G.M. (1982). *Identification Evidence: A Psychological Evaluation*. Aberdeen:Aberdeen University Press.

Part 1

Introduction

1

Identification and Surveillance of Facial Images: Progress and Problems

TIM VALENTINE AND JOSH P. DAVIS

Eyewitness testimony is older than the law. Even today, with sophisticated forensic science, eyewitness testimony forms the bedrock of many criminal cases. Whenever a witness gives testimony in court, jurors, judge(s) or magistrate(s) are faced with two basic questions: Is this witness giving an honest account? If so, can their account be relied upon as accurate? There are many reasons why a witness may deliberately give false testimony or identify a defendant they know to be innocent. The witness may be seeking revenge, have been intimidated into giving a false account, or be motivated to deflect blame away from the true culprit. Legal procedure is designed to expose a dishonest witness. In an adversarial system, for example in the UK, US, Canada, Australia and New Zealand, the defence have the right to test the testimony of prosecution witnesses through cross-examination. Equally the prosecution cross-examines witnesses for the defence. Cross-examination has been described as "the greatest legal engine ever invented for the

Forensic Facial Identification: Theory and Practice of Identification from Eyewitnesses, Composites and CCTV, First Edition. Edited by Tim Valentine and Josh P. Davis.
© 2015 John Wiley & Sons, Ltd. Published 2015 by John Wiley & Sons, Ltd.

Case study

"George Davis is innocent" daubed on walls and bridges was a familiar sight around London in the late 1970s. The graffiti referred to a man convicted for an armed robbery, which targeted a wages delivery at the office of London Electricity Board (LEB), Ilford, on April 4, 1974. Acting on information received, two plain-clothed policemen were watching the building. Two guns were carried by the robbers, and as they made a desperate getaway, one of the policemen at the scene was shot in the leg, and several motorists were hijacked at gunpoint.

At trial in March 1975 the prosecution primarily relied upon identification evidence by the police officers at the scene, and by police and other witnesses at other locations as the robbers switched vehicles during a dramatic car chase. Blood samples, recovered from the scene of a crashed getaway car, did not match any of the defendants. George Davis was the only one of four defendants to be convicted. He was sentenced to 20 years in prison. The conviction was upheld by the Court of Appeal in December 1975.

There was a high-profile campaign against George Davis' conviction, which involved much graffiti around London. The campaign gained notoriety when the Headingley cricket pitch was dug up during an England v. Australia test match, preventing play from continuing. In May 1976 the Home Secretary took the exceptional step of exercising the Royal Prerogative of Mercy to release Davis without referring the case back to the Court of Appeal. The Home Secretary deemed the conviction to be unsafe because of doubts over the police evidence, but Davis was not held to be innocent.

In 1977, George Davis was caught in the act of an armed robbery on the Bank of Cyprus. He pleaded guilty and was sentenced to 15 years in prison. He was released in 1984 but convicted of armed robbery for a third time in 1987.

George Davis' conviction for the armed robbery of the LEB wages office was quashed by the Court of Appeal on May 24, 2011 – 37 years after the original conviction. The principal grounds were concerns about the reliability of the identification of Davis from a live identity parade (lineup) by the two police officers who witnessed the robbery. Most notably the prosecution had not disclosed that one officer, PC Grove, had previously identified a different man from police photographs. Prior to the identity parade in which George Davis was identified, the investigating officer had told PC Grove that he had been mistaken in his identification of the photograph. Confidential government papers are normally subjected to a 30-year embargo, after which the papers are held by the Public Record Office. In 2006 the embargo of the papers relating to the Home Secretary's 1976 decision to free George Davis was extended by 20 years.

Sources:
Davis v R. (2011) EWCA Crim 1258 (24 May 2011). Retrieved from http:// www.bailii.org/ew/cases/EWCA/Crim/2011/1258.html
Wikipedia entry for George Davis (robber). Retrieved from http://en.wikipedia. org/wiki/George_Davis_(robber)

discovery of truth".[1] It is intended as a method to expose a dishonest witness, but psychological science shows that cross-examination is ineffective in distinguishing reliable eyewitnesses from those who are honest but mistaken (e.g., Valentine & Maras, 2011; Zajac & Hayne, 2003, 2006).

Courts have long acknowledged that a mistaken eyewitness may give convincing identification evidence. The extraordinary case of Adolf Beck, twice wrongly convicted on the basis of mistaken eyewitness identification, described in the case study in Chapter 6, resulted in the Criminal Appeal Act (1907) which established the Court of Criminal Appeal in London (Bogan & Roberts, 2011). Widespread concern about the reliability of eyewitness identification evidence in a number of English cases during the 1970s led the British government to set up an enquiry into eyewitness identification evidence (Devlin, 1976; see case study). Despite legal reforms in the UK since the 1970s, studies of police identification procedures have shown that a third of all identifications from live parades (Valentine, Pickering, & Darling, 2003; Wright & McDaid, 1996) and 40% of all positive identifications from video lineups are known to be mistaken, as the witness selected an innocent volunteer foil or filler (Horry, Memon, Wright, & Milne, 2012). The Innocence Project (2013) in New York has produced incontrovertible evidence of the devastating impact of mistaken eyewitness identification in the US. Over the last 20 years more than 300 prisoners have been exonerated by DNA evidence that proved they were actually innocent of the crimes of which they were convicted. The crimes were serious, mostly rape and murder, because physical evidence from which a DNA profile can be obtained is most likely to be available and collected in serious violent crimes. Mistaken eyewitness identification was the leading cause of wrongful conviction, and occurred in nearly 75% of cases.

[1] J. Wigmore, Evidence §1367 (J. Chadbourn rev. 1974).

In addition to the strong evidence of the high risk of mistaken eyewitness identification, research also demonstrates that approximately 40% of witnesses fail to identify anyone from a lineup. In many cases the witness may not have an adequate memory of the culprit. It may be that in an unknown proportion of these cases, the culprit was not included and the witness was making the correct decision. However, justice is served by developing procedures that both reduce the likelihood of an innocent suspect being identified, and enhance the likelihood that the actual perpetrator will be identified. Identification failures may leave a guilty suspect free to offend again.

The problem of distinguishing accurate from inaccurate identification is at the heart of *Forensic Facial Identification*. In the chapters that follow, distinguished scholars grapple with the problems of identification of suspects by eyewitnesses, from CCTV imagery, and identification of deceased victims from reconstructions of their facial appearance in life.

In many criminal investigations, the first problem the police may face is to identify a suspect. This issue is addressed in Part 2. If an eyewitness is available, the first step will be to interview the witness and in the course of that interview obtain a description of the offender. In Chapter 2 Fiona Gabbert and Charity Brown evaluate the relationship between the completeness and accuracy of a witness' description of the perpetrator and the likelihood that a subsequent identification from a lineup will be accurate. This is a difficult issue for the psychology of eyewitness identification because research findings are contradictory. Most researchers accept that, contrary to common-sense expectations, there is little relationship between the quality of a witness' verbal description of the perpetrator and their identification accuracy. On balance, laboratory research shows that a witness who gives a detailed description is no more likely to be able to identify the offender than a witness who can provide only a brief description. From their analysis of the literature Gabbert and Brown show that it is the inclusion of incorrect details in a verbal description that adversely affects identification accuracy. Therefore interview procedures that produce detailed descriptions by encouraging witnesses to provide details of which they are unsure are likely to impair eyewitness memory for the perpetrator and may increase the risk of a mistaken identification. Informed by this analysis, Gabbert and Brown provide practical advice for the employment of appropriate procedures most likely to obtain accurate descriptions from witnesses. These guidelines should help to safeguard the quality of any subsequent eyewitness identification.

Having obtained a description of the offender(s), in the absence of other evidence, the police may ask a witness to create a facial composite or likeness from memory. The image can then be publicized in the hope that somebody will recognize it as an individual they know and will provide a name to the police. In Chapter 3, Charlie Frowd reviews the development of techniques and methods used to construct facial composite images. This field has shown remarkable development in recent years. In 2007 the best recognized images were facial sketches produced by skilled police artists, and these were recognized by only 8% of people who knew the depicted person (Davies & Valentine, 2007). Since then, new systems that evolve a facial composite using artificial but highly realistic facial images have become much more effective. In addition, a range of techniques have been developed that considerably improve the quality of facial composites after production. These include a new interview technique, construction of the composites with the external features of the face occluded, viewing the composite under circumstances of either perceptual distortion or caricatured animation, and morphing composites produced by multiple witnesses, or indeed, multiple composites produced by the same witness. In the most recent research, Frowd reports recognition of facial composites by 74% of people who were familiar with the individual depicted.

If the police attend a street crime, after taking a description from the witness, they may drive the witness around the area, or allow them to view a suspect who has been stopped on the basis of the description. The aim is to secure an identification of that suspect or to eliminate them from the investigation. This procedure, known as a street identification or showup, is inherently suggestive. In Chapter 4, Victoria Lawson and Jennifer Dysart review research that shows a showup is not as reliable as a lineup, but the outcomes can be surprisingly similar. Showups are widely used, and may often be the only practical means of investigating a street robbery. Therefore, the procedure is likely to remain an essential investigative tool, but its use does need to be regulated appropriately.

If no suspect is identified from a showup, the witness may be asked to view large numbers of mugshot images of known offenders. Lawson and Dysart also review the literature on mugshot viewings, which perhaps not surprisingly, given the large numbers of images that are viewed, results in very different outcomes from that of a showup.

If a witness does identify a suspect from a showup or a mugshot, it is common practice in both the UK and the US for the witness to view the same suspect in a lineup at a later date to collect "formal" identification evidence. The psychological science shows very clearly that repeated identification procedures with the same suspect and witness are very prone to mistaken identification. If a witness has made a mistake in a showup or mugshot, they are highly likely to repeat the same mistaken identification from a lineup. Analysis of the Innocence Project (2013) cases show that mistaken identifications often arise when the victim identified the innocent suspect in repeated identification procedures. For example, Ronald Cotton and Johnnie Briscoe were both identified from police photographs prior to being identified from a lineup procedure by the same witness.

When human remains are found, the police may be faced with the problem of identifying the victim. A DNA profile can only identify somebody who is already on a database. In Chapter 5, Caroline Wilkinson reviews the methods used to reconstruct facial appearance, so that somebody who knew the victim may provide a name. Once the police have a possible identity, physical evidence (e.g. DNA, dental records) may be used to confirm the identification. Traditionally facial reconstruction is a highly skilled process that requires detailed anthropological knowledge and artistic skills, although computer technology now makes a substantial contribution. Using computational methods similar to those used to construct facial composites under the guidance of a witness, reconstructed facial appearances can be rotated and have global changes applied (e.g. ageing) to enhance the likelihood of identification.

Formal identification evidence from eyewitnesses is considered in Part 3. Recently there has been major reform of the identification procedures used in the UK. Until 2003, live identity parades remained the standard procedure. The Police and Criminal Evidence Act (1984) gave any suspect who disputes their identification the right to test the evidence in a formal procedure. Live parades were frequently held in purpose-built identification suites in which the witness viewed the lineup through a one-way mirror to shield the witness from the view of the lineup members. The use of such mirrors was not universal, and some witnesses were required to make their decision in full view of the suspect. The procedure was costly and difficult to administer. Half of all parades were cancelled because a bailed suspect did not attend or suitable volunteer foils could not be found (Pike, Brace, & Kyman, 2002). A police complaint was that the procedure was subject to manipulation by the defence, causing long delays. From the perspective of the witness, the procedure could be intimidating, especially for vulnerable witnesses, such as children, elderly witnesses and victims of sexual assaults.

Video identification procedures were introduced gradually in the UK between 2003, when video became an option, and 2008 when video became mandatory, unless it could be argued that a live parade was more suitable. The effect has been that video lineups have become universal. A major impact of the introduction of the video lineup has been to dramatically increase the number of procedures held. Devlin (1976) reported that 2143 live parades were held in the UK in 1973. This had increased to 14,000 by 1994 (Slater, 1994). This increase was attributed to the effect of the Police and Criminal Evidence Act (1984). At the time of writing, current estimates are that 110,000 video lineups are held annually.[2]

Approximately 20% of all witnesses make a known mistaken identification of volunteer foils or distracters from live parades organized by the British police (Valentine, Pickering, & Darling, 2003; Wright & McDaid, 1996). A recent study found that 26% of all witnesses mistakenly identify a volunteer from video lineups organized in England and Wales (Horry et al., 2012). This increase is difficult to interpret. Perhaps proportionally more foils are identified because video lineups are of better quality. Foils for video lineups are selected from large databases of around 25,000 video clips. Therefore foils in video lineups may be more plausible than the foils in live lineups. Alternatively, because it is now easier to run an identification procedure, there may be a greater tendency to ask witnesses who had little opportunity to view the culprit to attend an identification procedure. Whatever the explanation behind these data, it is a cruel irony that there has been a huge increase in reliance on eyewitness identification evidence, in spite of Devlin's warning of the particular risks of this form of evidence. As a result of efforts to improve eyewitness identification procedures there are, almost certainly, more mistaken eyewitness identifications presented in court than in Devlin's day.

Reform of eyewitness identification procedures in the US has followed a very different path. Identification from an array of photographs has always been widely used for formal identification evidence in the US and Canada, but has never been permissible in the UK. In the US, research effort and procedural reform has focused on the issue of whether it is more effective if the photographs are presented all at the same time (simultaneously) or one at a time (sequentially) with the witness asked to make a decision to each photograph as it is presented. Steven Clark, Molly Moreland and Ryan Rush skilfully set out in Chapter 6 the essential issues from the complicated literature on methods of identification procedures, drawing from practice in both the US and the UK.

When a jury or judge hears testimony of eyewitness identification in court, it is necessary to make a judgement of whether the identification is reliable. The only information available to the court is the description of the event, the demeanour of the witness and any evidence of the witness' character that may be given in evidence. In Chapter 7, Hannah Ryder, Harriet Smith and Heather Flowe consider the effect that the circumstances of the event, and the characteristics of the offender and of

---

[2]Two systems provide video lineups for the British police. The estimate of 110,000 is the sum of procedures claimed to have been conducted using each system on their websites (www.viper.com; www.promat.com).

the witness, have on the accuracy of eyewitness identification evidence. To what extent can these estimator factors be used to judge whether any given identification is accurate or not? The approach adopted by the courts in the US and the UK to address these issues is also discussed.

In Chapter 8, James Sauer and Neil Brewer evaluate the relationship between the level of confidence expressed by a witness and the quality of his or her memory for the perpetrator. These authors note that a positive identification of the suspect does not guarantee that the suspect is the culprit. Instead, an identification indicates that, of the lineup members presented, the suspect is the best match to the witness' memory of the culprit. They explain how cognitive and social factors can make a witness more or less likely to pick someone from the lineup. These influences on the witness' decision-making renders the identification less informative about the quality of the witness' memory. Basing their argument on the theoretical relationship between confidence and memory quality, Sauer and Brewer describe how, when appropriately measured, confidence can be indicative of the degree of a witness' recognition. They argue it would be foolish not to consider confidence when evaluating identification evidence. The protocols for collecting measures of confidence in the UK and the US are considered, and practical advice is given for collecting appropriate measures of confidence. Sauer and Brewer also discuss a radical new approach to collecting eyewitness identification evidence, which entirely excludes the necessity for the witness to make binary yes–no decisions, which are normally required when a witness chooses to identify one person from a lineup.

In view of the fragility of human memory, CCTV imagery appears to offer a valuable opportunity to avoid the need for eyewitnesses. At first sight, CCTV provides an irrefutable record of the appearance of the offender, and one important advantage is that when confronted with such imagery many offenders confess. But when the identification is disputed, verifying the identity of an offender caught on camera can be more difficult than expected. Identification from CCTV imagery or photographs is considered in Part 4. Josh Davis and Tim Valentine review the evidence on the human ability to match images of faces in Chapter 9. When the images are of people who are unfamiliar to the observer, 20–30% of judgements are mistaken even under ideal conditions. Using good quality images, in which the viewpoints of the images to be compared are similar, people make frequent simultaneous matching errors of judgement even under no time pressure. Two images of different people can appear very similar; and two images of the same person taken with different cameras can look very different. Both false positive and false negative errors are common. Unexpectedly, it turns out that the need to remember the appearance of an offender is not necessary for identification to be unreliable! CCTV images available in criminal cases in court are often of poor or very poor quality. The development of high-definition cameras and video systems is often portrayed as a solution to this problem. However the science is very clear. Even with the highest quality images, people often make mistakes. High definition will no doubt improve the quality of images and be useful for many reasons, but it will not solve the problem of human face-matching error.

The effectiveness of border and other security checks is critical to security. Realization that human face-matching of unfamiliar faces is so error-prone calls into question the effectiveness of passport checks at international borders. Perhaps border guards can be trained to be more reliable? Unfortunately, so far the results of research on the effectiveness of face-matching training have been disappointing. Training border guards to spot the rare event of a potential terrorist with a false passport is likely to be challenging.

There are two bright prospects in this generally rather bleak picture. First, we are rather good at identifying faces of people we know well, even in low-quality CCTV imagery. Therefore, if the potential "remote witness" knows the depicted person well, identification is usually reliable. This phenomenon is effectively exploited by TV and other media who regularly display videos and stills captured from crime scenes. The hope is that somebody who knows the person well will provide a name, and therefore a lead for the police to investigate further. A good example is the case of David Copeland, the London nail-bomber, who was identified from CCTV shown on national TV by a work colleague.[3]

The second bright prospect is selection. If it is not possible to train border guards, staff who are naturally talented at matching faces can be selected for these roles. There are strong individual differences in face recognition and matching abilities. A few people show exceptional prowess at recognizing unfamiliar faces. Davis and Valentine describe how the London Metropolitan Police have capitalized on this approach. With a large number of offenders to identify from hours of CCTV imagery of the 2011 London riots, the Metropolitan Police realized that a small number of officers are talented "super-recognizers" and were astonishingly proficient at identifying suspects from the imagery.

The widespread availability of CCTV imagery has posed a new problem for the courts. In the UK, if an image is of sufficient quality, the jury can be invited to compare it to the appearance of the defendant in the dock. As people, generally, are rather error-prone in matching unfamiliar faces, this procedure might carry some risk of wrongful conviction. Another approach, reviewed by Josh Davis, Gary Edmonds and Tim

[3]http://en.wikipedia.org/wiki/David_Copeland

Valentine in Chapter 10, is to admit opinion evidence from an expert in facial image comparison. Such experts come from varied backgrounds. In the UK, expert evidence from anthropologists, psychologists, medical artists and medical imaging experts, computer and video experts, and military intelligence experts has been admitted. These experts employ a number of methods to analyse facial images. The scientific literature on these methods is limited, but studies that are available demonstrate limitations and weaknesses in all of them. It may be the case that work of this nature attracts people who are naturally very good face recognizers and their judgements are often accurate, but there is no scientific evidence that the methods advocated by facial comparison experts are reliable.

As human face-matching is error-prone, perhaps computers can do a better job. The latest research on automatic face recognition is reviewed by Alice O'Toole and Jonathon Phillips in Chapter 11. There has been a steady improvement in the proficiency of automatic face recognition systems. In ideal environmental conditions, computers can now match facial identities more effectively than most humans can match unfamiliar faces. However, automatic recognition systems cannot yet achieve the proficiency of the human ability to match images of familiar faces in environmentally challenging conditions (e.g., from external CCTV images captured from above head height). In a practical application, such as checking passport images, automatic face-matching systems are likely to be used to support human decision-making, with the final decision being made by a human operator. O'Toole and Phillips address the issue of how automatic processing of facial images can be integrated with human judgements.

In the final part of the book the implications for the criminal justice system of the psychological science of facial identification is considered in detail. In Chapter 12, Andrew Roberts applies a legal analysis to many of the issues discussed by the authors of the previous chapters. Sequential presentation of lineup images, blind administration of lineups and recording of witness confidence are considered in detail. He reviews legal procedure and case law on identification by eyewitnesses, evidence of recognition from images, and facial image comparison, in the UK, the US, Australia and New Zealand. Roberts considers how investigatory procedures can mitigate risks of mistaken identification, and the extent to which appropriate procedures have been adopted. He argues that the legal response to the risk of mistaken identification from images has been slow and suggests that, compared with the well-known risk of mistaken identification by eyewitnesses, without legal and procedural safeguards the risk of mistaken identification from images may be consequently greater.

In the final chapter Tim Valentine and Josh Davis draw upon the extensive research considered by the authors of this volume to recommend best practice for a wide range of forensic applications. In recent years there has been very significant progress in the practical application of science to interviewing witnesses, constructing facial composites and automatic face recognition. In other areas, extensive research has led to better theoretical understanding of the issues and, as a result, clear recommendations can be made to mitigate against the risks of mistaken identification; examples include understanding the effects of repeated identification procedures, construction and administration of lineups, recording of witness confidence, and selection of personnel for security tasks involving face-matching. Expert analysis of facial comparison has attracted comparatively little research activity, but much critical analysis. It remains one of the most difficult problems to address. Valentine and Davis also consider "confirmation bias", a ubiquitous psychological phenomenon in which human judgement, memory and perception is interpreted in a way that is consistent with prior beliefs. Many areas of forensic science rely on subjective evaluation of evidence to determine whether there is a match (e.g., analysis of latent fingerprints, analysis of CCTV imagery), and therefore can be subject to bias derived from expectations due to an awareness of the background of information or other evidence. The US National Research Academy (2009) has identified confirmation bias as an issue that needs to be addressed by the forensic science community.

Scientific research and technological development have made identification of a suspect's face more available as a potential source of evidence during a criminal investigation. The fallibility of human facial identification has been acknowledged by scientists and in the legal system since early in the 20th century (Munsterberg, 1908; Bogan & Roberts, 2011). A hundred years later, development of photographic, video and computer technology has resulted in many more suspects being identified by eyewitnesses or from an image. Undoubtedly many more offenders have been convicted as a result. However, technology has had hardly any impact on reducing the risk of mistaken identification. Over the years there have been very clear warnings of the effect of mistaken identification. The risk was very clearly acknowledged in the UK by Devlin (1976). There have been over 300 DNA exonerations in the US, three-quarters of which convictions were a result of mistaken eyewitness identification. Because we have allowed technology to facilitate wider use of identification evidence, which has well-known flaws, innocent citizens are more at risk of wrongful conviction caused by mistaken identification than they have ever been.

REFERENCES

Bogan, P., & Roberts, A. (2011). *Identification: Investigation, Trial and Scientific Evidence* (2nd ed.). Bristol: Jordan.

Davies, G.M., & Valentine, T. (2007). Facial composites: Forensic utility and psychological research. In R.C.L. Lindsay, D.F. Ross, J.D. Read, & M.P. Toglia (Eds.), *Handbook of Eyewitness Psychology: Volume 2 – Memory for People* (pp. 59–83). Mahwah: LEA.

Devlin, P. (1976). *Report to the Secretary of State for the Home Department on the Departmental Committee on Evidence of Identification in Criminal Cases.* London: HMSO.

Horry, R., Memon, A., Wright, D.B., & Milne, R. (2012). Predictors of eyewitness identification decisions from video lineups in England: A field study. *Law and Human Behavior, 36,* 257–265. doi:10.1037/h0093959

Munsterberg, H. (1908/1925). *On the Witness Stand: Essays on Psychology and Crime.* Retrieved from http://psychclassics.yorku.ca/Munster/Witness

Pike, G., Brace, N., & Kyman, S. (2002). *The visual identification of suspects: procedures and practice. Briefing note 2/02.* Policing and Reducing Crime Unit, Home Office Research Development and Statistics Directorate. Retrieved from http://library.npia.police.uk/docs/hoprcbrf/brf202.pdf

Slater, A. (1994). *Identification Parades: A Scientific Evaluation.* Police Research Award Scheme. London: Police Research Group, Home Office.

US National Research Academy (2009). *Strengthening forensic science in the United States: A path forward.* Retrieved from https://www.ncjrs.gov/pdffiles1/nij/grants/228091.pdf

Valentine, T., & Maras, K. (2011). The effect of cross-examination on the accuracy of adult eyewitness testimony. *Applied Cognitive Psychology, 25,* 554–561. doi:10.1002/acp.1768

Valentine, T., Pickering, A., & Darling, S. (2003). Characteristics of eyewitness identification that predict the outcome of real lineups. *Applied Cognitive Psychology, 17,* 969–993. doi:10.1002/acp.939

Wright, D.B., & McDaid, A.T. (1996). Comparing system and estimator variables using data from real lineups. *Applied Cognitive Psychology, 10,* 75–84. doi:10.1002/(SICI)1099-0720(199602)10:1<75::AID-ACP364>3.0.CO;2-E

Zajac, R., & Hayne, H. (2003). I don't think that's what really happened: the effect of cross-examination on the accuracy of children's reports. *Journal of Experimental Psychology: Applied, 9,* 187–195. doi:10.1037/1076-898X.9.3.187

Zajac, R., & Hayne, H. (2006). The negative effect of cross-examination style on questioning on children's accuracy: older children are not immune. *Applied Cognitive Psychology, 20,* 3–16. doi:10.1002/acp.1169

Part 2

Searching for Suspects and the Identification of Victims

2

Interviewing for Face Identification

FIONA GABBERT AND CHARITY BROWN

Forensic investigations are all about collecting evidence of what happened and who was involved, so that the police can apprehend the correct perpetrators, and the courts can convict them appropriately for the crimes they committed. Perpetrator descriptions are considered by many police officers to be a source of evidence that can provide major leads for an investigation (Brown, Lloyd-Jones, & Robinson, 2008; Kebbell & Milne, 1998). Perhaps because of this, person descriptions are normally requested more than once during the course of an investigation: typically during the initial emergency call, then by the responding officer at the scene or during the course of initial enquiries, followed by the investigating officer assigned to formally interview the witness. The witness might then be approached throughout the investigation to clarify details concerning the description (Brown et al., 2008).

Person descriptions are often vital in the immediate stages of an investigation, especially when a search is initiated for an unknown suspect who might still be in close proximity to the crime scene. Descriptions are also important in later stages, for example, a description is typically

Forensic Facial Identification: Theory and Practice of Identification from Eyewitnesses, Composites and CCTV, First Edition. Edited by Tim Valentine and Josh P. Davis.
© 2015 John Wiley & Sons, Ltd. Published 2015 by John Wiley & Sons, Ltd.

Case study

The following case studies provide striking demonstrations of how eyewitnesses are able to influence one another's memories of a perpetrator's appearance.

The first concerns the high-profile murder investigation of the Swedish foreign minister, Anna Lindh, in September 2003. The attack took place in a busy shopping centre. Witnesses were placed together in a small room to prevent them leaving the scene of the crime prior to being interviewed. When in the room, the witnesses admitted to talking with one another (Granhag, Ask, & Rebelius, 2005). During these discussions, one witness mentioned to others present in the room that the perpetrator wore a camouflage patterned military jacket. As a result, a number of witnesses subsequently reported this clothing detail to the investigating officers. This description was used in an immediate search for the perpetrator in the surrounding area, and also featured in the release of a national police alert. The detail, however, was later revealed to be incorrect. Footage from surveillance cameras showed that the perpetrator, Mijailo Mijailovic, was in fact wearing a grey hooded sweatshirt. Given that witnesses were free to discuss the incident with each other at some length, it is reasonable to conclude that the discussion that had taken place amongst the witnesses was the source of error in the immediate stages of this investigation (Granhag *et al.*, 2005).

A second example from the UK also illustrates how witnesses' recognition decisions can be vulnerable to suggestion. Here, a witness central to the Jill Dando murder investigation (April 2001) became increasingly confident that the main suspect, Barry George, was responsible for the crime after discussing the identification parade with another witness who had identified George. This witness, who had not felt confident enough to make an identification originally, subsequently revealed that following discussions with the other witness, they now felt "95% sure" that George was the man she had seen at the crime scene (Cathcart, 2001; *R v. George*, 2002). Barry George's conviction for murder was subsequently quashed by the Court of Appeal (*R v. George*, 2007). In a re-trial he was acquitted (BBC, 2008).

These examples illustrate how recall and recognition are vulnerable to the suggestions of others. When this occurs in the context of a forensic investigation there can be serious and costly implications. In such cases, consistent statements obtained from witnesses might

> be seized upon as valuable corroborative evidence from independent witnesses, when in fact the evidence might be contaminated if the witnesses had discussed their memories prior to being interviewed by the police. This can lead to misdirected lines of enquiry, and has the potential to lead to miscarriages of justice.

obtained prior to a witness constructing a facial composite (see Chapter 3). The Police and Criminal Evidence Act (PACE) 1984 Code of Practice (Code D, 2011) for England and Wales requires that a record must be made of the suspect's description as first given by a witness. Thus, person descriptions may also afford some protection against misidentification where a suspect does not match the description first given. Interestingly, lineups in the UK are not constructed with reference to a witness' description. Instead, the PACE Code D specifies that "the set of images must include the suspect and at least eight other people who, so far as possible, resemble the suspect in age, general appearance and position in life" (Home Office, 2011, p. 47). In Scotland, the Lord Advocate's Guidelines on identification procedures are even more specific, stating that "it is more important that the other persons resemble the suspect or accused than that they should be like any descriptions previously given by witness(es)" (Lord Advocate's Guidelines to Chief Constables, 2007, p. 8). Thus, a "match to suspect" strategy is implemented when constructing a lineup rather than a "match to description" strategy (see Chapter 6 for more information). Furthermore, before viewing a lineup, PACE Code D states that witnesses should not be reminded of any description given of the culprit.

Despite there being a distinction between use of a witness' description and identification evidence in an investigation, it seems intuitive to expect there to be a relationship between the two. Indeed, in some legal settings the quality of a witness' description of the perpetrator is recommended as an indicator of the reliability of the witness' identification decision. For example, under English law (*R v. Turnbull and others*, 1976) the judge must caution the jury to consider (amongst other things) whether there is "any material discrepancy between the description of the accused given to the police by the witness when first seen by them and his actual appearance." The US Supreme Court (*Neil v. Biggers*, 1972) similarly advocates that the congruence between a witness's initial recall of the perpetrator, and the physical characteristics of the suspect, is an indicator of the validity of eyewitness testimony.

This chapter will examine the relationship between person descriptions and identification accuracy. Specifically it will consider questions such as:

1. How are person descriptions elicited from witnesses, and how reliable are they?
2. What is the relationship between the amount or accuracy of information reported in a description, and subsequent identification accuracy?
3. Is describing a face detrimental to subsequent identification performance?
4. What advice can be given to practitioners based upon a review of the literature?

HOW ARE PERSON DESCRIPTIONS ELICITED FROM WITNESSES, AND HOW RELIABLE ARE THEY?

The accuracy and completeness of a person description elicited from a witness can be influenced by a great many factors, including those that the police have no control over (age of the witness, lighting, proximity, intoxication, stress, etc.), and those that they do (the delay between an incident being reported and when the witness is interviewed, etc.). These factors are referred to as *estimator* and *system* variables respectively in the eyewitness literature (Wells, 1978; chapters 6 and 7 respectively).

Psychological research has been effectively incorporated into guidance on interviewing witnesses (Ministry of Justice, 2011; see also British Psychological Society, 2010). For example, the *cognitive interview* (CI; Fisher & Geiselman, 1992) is a well-established procedure that has been incorporated into police training in England and Wales since 1992. Founded on robust principles of memory, the CI is generally recognized as the "gold-standard" in achieving best evidence. It emerged from the psychological literature on how best to retrieve episodic information from memory, and centres around two principles: (1) a memory trace consists of several elements of related information; and (2) there are several possible ways of retrieving an encoded event, so information that cannot be retrieved in one way may be accessible using another method. Based on these theoretical assumptions, Fisher and Geiselman (1992) developed several mnemonic components that are now proven to facilitate the accurate retrieval of witnessed episodes (*report everything, mental reinstatement of context, change temporal order,* and *change perspective*). In addition, several strategies aimed at optimizing both the retrieval process and the social and communication aspects of an investigative interview were incorporated (e.g., *rapport building, transferring control of the interview to the witness, focused retrieval* and *witness compatible questioning*). When used appropriately, by skilled interviewers who fully understand and engage with the key principles, the CI increases the amount of information provided and reduces the use of inappropriate questioning. This interview technique currently underpins the dominant approach to investigative interviewing training and practice in the UK and other countries with developed procedures. Despite the success of the CI as an interview technique, it is not always effective in eliciting person descriptions. The current guidance on interviewing victims and witnesses (Ministry of Justice, 2011) recognizes that witnesses tend not to realize that the interviewer requires detailed descriptions of perpetrators, and as a result person descriptions tend to be short and incomplete. Furthermore, the difficulties that people have in translating a visual image into words are specifically acknowledged, and a few techniques are offered to help interviewers elicit specific details about people involved in the event (see p.201).

Brown, Lloyd-Jones, and Robinson (2008) surveyed 72 UK police officers about the methods they generally use to elicit person descriptions, and found that an encouraging 89% reported using techniques to facilitate free-recall, thus demonstrating the effectiveness of their interview training. Forty-seven percent said they would follow free-recall with specific probes to elicit more detail about the person's physical characteristics (including height, build, age, race, sex, gait, hairstyle and colour, clothing, accessories, distinguishing characteristics, and accent). Fifteen percent reported explicitly directing the witness to describe the person's facial features. While examples of actual instructions and questions given to witnesses were not collected in this study, psychological research shows that, in general, open questions that encourage free-recall elicit more accurate responses than closed questions that demand specific information and can be leading (e.g., "what colour was his hair?" or "was he wearing glasses?").

One reason why officers resort to using specific questions is because witnesses often don't provide enough information regarding person descriptions. For example, Kebbell and Milne (1998) surveyed 159 police officers and found that 76% of respondents agreed with the statement that witnesses "rarely" or "never" provide as many specific details about persons as they would like. Ten years later, Brown *et al.*'s (2008) survey revealed that an even higher percentage of officers (90.3%) agreed with this statement. Indeed, archival data from real-world witness statements support this general consensus of opinion amongst officers, showing that the content of person descriptors is typically limited and tends to focus upon general characteristics such as gender, age, race, build and height, rather than more specific information concerning individual facial features or unique details. For example, van Koppen and Lochun (1997) analysed the descriptions that witnesses provided of offenders involved in commercial robberies. The descriptions were typically given on the same day as the incident or on the following day. The total number of descriptors reported by witnesses ranged from 1 to 23 (out of a possible 43 that could be mentioned), and only 200 out of the 2299 descriptions analysed included over 15 descriptors. Moreover, specific facial features (eye colour, nose, mouth, eye shape, teeth, chin, ears) were mentioned in less than 5% of the descriptions. Laboratory studies have also shown that even under more optimum conditions, description completeness can be poor. For example, Sporer (2007) found participants to report an average of only 4.46 person details even when they gave their descriptions immediately after viewing the target in a filmed event.

Analysis of archival data by van Koppen and Lochun (1997) provides some insights into the accuracy of witness descriptions in real-world settings. They compared the person descriptions given by witnesses to the descriptions of the convicted offenders as recorded by police officers at the time of arrest. There are limitations to this methodology as some aspects of the offender's appearance may change over time (e.g., with loss of weight, illness) and it is unknown whether there were some instances where an offender was falsely convicted. Nevertheless, their data indicate that, in general, person characteristics are accurately reported. Gender, hair colour, age, race, height, and face shape were correctly reported in over 60% of descriptions (see also Fahsing, Ask, & Granhag, 2004). However, witness descriptions were also prone to error, particularly with regard to descriptors of individual facial features. Reports of the type of hair, nose, mouth, complexion, teeth, chin and ears were incorrect in over 60% of descriptions.

WHAT IS THE RELATIONSHIP BETWEEN DESCRIPTION QUALITY AND SUBSEQUENT IDENTIFICATION ACCURACY?

What can be said about the relationship between description quality and subsequent identification accuracy? Are witnesses who report a higher number of person, or facial, descriptors more likely to make a correct decision when viewing an identity parade or video lineup? Despite seeming intuitive, research examining eyewitness memory shows the relationship between description quality and identification accuracy to be complex. The description quality–identification accuracy relationship is not consistently observed, and when a relationship has been found it is generally small to moderate in size (for a review, see Meissner, Sporer, & Susa, 2008). This may be partially explained by evidence showing that factors associated with witnessing the event, and subsequently retaining and retrieving the person memory, can influence the strength of the description quality–identification accuracy relationship. However, there are also some methodological difficulties that need to be taken into account when evaluating research concerning the description quality–identification accuracy relationship as highlighted below. The situation is further complicated by the fact that a substantial body of research has shown that the act of providing a description of a face in itself can sometimes hinder and sometimes help subsequent face identification.

The weak, variable and complex nature of the relationship between description quality and identification accuracy is perhaps not surprising if we consider that the tasks of recalling information about a person and recognizing a person are likely to rely on different underlying psychological processes (e.g., Schooler, 2002; Wells, 1985). *Recall* requires the witness to translate their visual experience into a verbal description. Thus there is a mismatch between the modality in which the face was encoded (visual) and how the face is retrieved from memory (verbal). In contrast, *recognition* is predominantly a visual task. Successful recognition decisions are made on the basis of the match between the visual information originally encoded about the face and the visual information contained within each of the faces appearing in the lineup.

With regards to recall, in general it is difficult to capture information about a face in words, and our vocabulary for expressing the physical aspects of faces is limited (e.g., Ellis, Shepherd, & Davies, 1980). Descriptions of faces tend to emphasize the individual features of the face (e.g., broad nose, small eyes) (Wells & Turtle, 1987), whereas it appears to be the subtle configural information concerning the spacing and relationships between individual facial features that is best suited to the process of face recognition (e.g., Diamond & Carey, 1986). Furthermore, at the time of retrieval, recall and recognition tasks also differ in the extent to which retrieval cues are available in the environment (see Fisher & Schreiber, 2006, for a discussion). When the perpetrator appears in a lineup the witness makes their recognition decision in the presence of the strongest possible cue to retrieval (i.e., the perpetrator). If the witness has a good memory for the perpetrator then this process of successful recognition is likely to be automatic and rapid (e.g., Sporer, 1992). In contrast, during an interview witnesses are asked to generate retrieval cues themselves, for example, in the CI this is by mentally reinstating the context in which they viewed the perpetrator. Thus, successful recall in general is a more effortful process than recognition, and in comparison is supported by relatively weaker retrieval cues.

Researchers have assessed the quality of person descriptions in terms of the *quantity* or *accuracy* of the information they contain. Description quantity simply refers to the number of physical descriptors contained within a description, regardless of their accuracy. Accuracy can be assessed by separately counting the number of correct and incorrect details about the person, or by creating a composite measure whereby the number of correct details is divided by the quantity of information in the description (i.e., number of correct plus incorrect descriptors). Typically, these measures focus upon physical descriptors and exclude subjective judgements made about the person (e.g., judgements of personality or occupation; Meissner *et al.*, 2008). Even so, the measures vary considerably in terms of the types of physical descriptors they include (see Meissner *et al.*, 2008). For example, some researchers have focused specifically upon facial features and hair (e.g., Brown & Lloyd-Jones, 2002, 2003), whereas others have included assessments of the whole body such as height, build, weight, posture and sometimes clothes (van Koppen & Lochun, 1997). This variability in how descriptions are coded has added an additional complexity when researchers have attempted to compare measures of description quality across different studies (Meissner *et al.*, 2008). Future research should fully report and attempt to standardize these measures. Nevertheless, some common conclusions can be drawn.

Sporer (1992) examined the success of description *quantity* as a potential predictor of identification accuracy. He found a positive correlation between the number of descriptors and identification accuracy whereby participants providing more person descriptors were more likely to make an accurate identification decision. Valentine, Pickering, and Darling (2003) also examined this issue in an archival analysis including information from 640 identification attempts by eyewitnesses across 314 identity parades viewed during investigations by the Metropolitan Police in London. Investigating officers judged the completeness of the witness description as containing few details, average or detailed. Whilst it is not certain that the suspect appearing in each of these identity parades was always the actual culprit, they did find that witnesses who were judged as giving a detailed description of the suspect were more likely to positively identify the suspect (66%) than witnesses who were judged as giving an average description (40%) or only a few details (14%).

More recently a meta-analysis including a total of 2578 participants across 33 experiments failed to provide support for these findings (Meissner *et al.*, 2008). Overall, a small, marginally significant *negative* relationship between description quantity and identification accuracy was found, whereby participants providing more complete descriptions were more likely to make inaccurate identification decisions. Interestingly, across the studies, more complete descriptions tended to contain less accurate information about the face. This mirrors findings from the analysis of archival data undertaken by van Koppen and Lochun (1997), who also found a negative correlation between description quantity and description accuracy, whereby more detailed descriptions contained a smaller proportion of accurately reported details.

This pattern of findings is consistent with the conclusion that measures of description accuracy rather than quantity are more strongly associated with face identification performance. Indeed, Meissner *et al.* (2008) found a small but significant *positive* correlation between description accuracy and identification accuracy whereby more accurate descriptions were associated with better accuracy in a subsequent face identification test. The number of errors in a description proved to be an important factor; specifically, there was no relationship between the number of correct details and identification accuracy. However, a greater number of errors in the facial description was associated with worse accuracy in the face identification test.

Of course, in a forensic investigation the accuracy of a witness's description cannot be determined, as it is not known whether the suspect is the culprit while the accumulation of evidence is still in progress. The *quantity* of descriptors can of course be assessed, but based upon the available literature discussed above, this is not an informative method for predicting identification accuracy. Drawing upon current empirical knowledge of the description–accuracy relationship, it is unlikely that we will reach a point where the reliability of a single witness's identification decision can be successfully predicted on the basis of the quality of their description (Meissner *et al.*, 2008). Instead, the value of examining this research will be in identifying interviewing practices that can minimize the negative influence and maximize the positive influence of eliciting face descriptions on subsequent face identification performance.

IS DESCRIBING A FACE DETRIMENTAL TO SUBSEQUENT IDENTIFICATION PERFORMANCE?

Research in the laboratory has shown that describing a face can have negative consequences for a person's memory for that face. This finding, named the *verbal overshadowing* effect was first demonstrated in a series of experiments by Schooler and Engstler-Schooler (1990). They presented participants with a video of a bank robbery following which half the participants were instructed to spend five minutes describing the facial features of the bank robber in as much detail as possible. The remaining participants engaged in a no-description control activity (a reading comprehension task). All participants were then shown a simultaneous photo lineup including the face of the bank robber alongside seven foils who matched a similar description. The bank robber was correctly identified by 64% of the participants that did not describe his face, but by only 38% of participants who did.

This negative consequence of describing a face on its subsequent recognition has since been replicated many times, although there have been instances where researchers have reported a failure to obtain the effect (for a review, see Chin & Schooler, 2008). Generally however, evidence points to verbal overshadowing being a genuine and reliable phenomenon. Meissner and Brigham (2001) conducted a meta-analysis including 2018 participants across 15 research articles reporting verbal overshadowing studies. They compared the identification accuracy of groups of participants who had described, or not, a previously seen target face prior to viewing a target-present photo lineup. There was a reliable negative effect of describing faces on subsequent face identification across the 29 effect size comparisons included in the analysis (Fisher's $Zr = -0.12$). However, this effect of verbal overshadowing was small, accounting for 1.44% of variability across studies, which may explain why verbal overshadowing effects are not always reliably observed. Nevertheless, this does not detract from the fact that across the studies reviewed, participants describing the target face were 1.27 times more likely to make an inaccurate identification decision when subsequently viewing the photo lineup.

The Meissner meta-analysis suggests that the strongest effects of verbal overshadowing (i.e., description condition impaired compared with controls) are if the identification test takes place less than 10 minutes after the description is given. At longer delays (>30 min) they found no significant effect of verbal overshadowing. However, this was because the longer delay led to a reduction in correct identifications by participants in the no-description conditions, indicating that a significant degree of forgetting had taken place when participants had not described the face. In contrast, description participants' identification performance was similar across the shorter (<10 min) and longer (>30 min) delays. This raises an interesting possibility: that when there is a longer delay between describing a face and attempting identification, previously describing the face may actually be of benefit by providing some protection from forgetting. More research is clearly needed, as other studies have shown that the negative effects of describing a face can sometimes persist across longer timeframes.

For example, it has been evident on delays of 30 minutes (Meissner, Brigham, & Kelley, 2001) and two days (Schooler & Engstler-Schooler, 1990) between the description and identification test. Again, it appears that the influence of description on subsequent identification accuracy is complex. The following literature review will examine when and why verbal overshadowing occurs both immediately and following a delay, paying particular attention to factors that moderate when descriptions help or hinder face identification.

To date, the search for a single theoretical account to accommodate all verbal overshadowing findings within the literature has been unsuccessful. In fact, three broad accounts have been proposed, each of which is supported by favourable evidence. It seems that different underlying mechanisms may similarly give rise to negative effects of face descriptions on face identification accuracy. Furthermore, one or more of these mechanisms may come into play depending upon the conditions under which a face is described and subsequently recognized. We will examine the three accounts and supporting evidence in turn.

The *recoding interference* (or *retrieval based interference*) *account* proposes that when a participant describes a face they translate, or recode, visual information about that face into a new verbally-based memory (e.g., Meissner *et al.*, 2001; Schooler & Engstler-Schooler, 1990). This verbal memory competes with the original visual memory of the face. If the verbal memory contains imprecise or inaccurate information, and is relied upon during the identification test, then the participant will be less likely to identify the target correctly. In fact, people in the lineup other than the target may more adequately match the new verbal memory and this may lead to incorrect identification decisions. A key prediction therefore arising from this account is that there will be a relationship between the quality of the face descriptions given by participants and the accuracy of their identification performance. Critically, verbal overshadowing should be most apparent when participants' descriptions are low in accuracy.

Some verbal overshadowing studies have found a significant correlation to exist between participants' description accuracy and their identification performance. However, others have failed to demonstrate such a relationship (for a review, see Meissner *et al.*, 2008). In addition, as will be discussed later, there are instances where verbal overshadowing effects are evident, but where a recoding interference account clearly cannot apply (e.g., Brown & Lloyd-Jones, 2003). Such evidence highlights the limited generalizability of a recoding interference account of verbal overshadowing. Nevertheless, a relationship between description accuracy and identification accuracy can sometimes arise and there is evidence that this relationship is more apparent when certain retrieval conditions apply.

Supporting the recoding interference account is work by Meissner and colleagues, who manipulated the stringency of recall instructions to influence the quantity and accuracy of descriptors provided by participants. For example, Meissner *et al.* (2001) showed participants a photograph of a target face for 10 seconds, after which they engaged in a five-minute filler activity and then either described the target or engaged in a no-description filler activity. Participants who described the face were given one of three types of instructions. In a forced condition, participants were instructed to report everything that they could remember about the face even if they thought it was not important or if they started to feel they were guessing, thereby increasing the chance of self-generated errors being reported. In a warning condition, participants were instructed to strive for accuracy, to only report details they were confident they remembered and not to attempt to guess at any particular feature. In a standard condition, participants were instructed to describe the face in as much detail as possible, and were allowed to establish their own reporting criterion. Participants were then asked to identify the target face from a lineup consisting of the target and five foils of similar appearance. Participants forced to provide an elaborative description made significantly fewer correct identifications and instead more often mistakenly identified a foil from the lineup, compared with participants in the warning and standard instruction conditions, and in the no-description control (thus demonstrating an effect of verbal overshadowing). In contrast, warning participants to provide an accurate description led to significantly more correct identifications and fewer false identifications than the forced instruction condition or the no-description control, demonstrating that descriptions can in some instances be of benefit to subsequent identification. This same pattern of results was found to occur both when the identification task took place immediately after the description or following a 30-minute delay. In a follow-up study, Meissner (2002) found that using forced description instructions, compared with warning description instructions, not only led to a reduction in correct identifications when the target was present in the lineup, but an increase in mistaken identifications when the target was absent from the lineup.

The meta-analytic review of verbal overshadowing studies of face identification carried out by Meissner and Brigham (2001) provided further support for the importance of description instructions. They classified studies into two groups based on the description instructions given to participants. Those that encouraged participants to continue describing the face for the whole time period the experimenters had set (thus increasing the chance of self-generated errors being reported) were classified as using "elaborative instructions". These studies were compared with those that allowed participants to establish their own reporting criterion. It was found that verbal overshadowing was more likely to be observed in those studies using elaborative description instructions.

Taken together, these studies illustrate that the instructions given to a witness when eliciting a face description can influence the quantity and quality of the information recalled. In particular, it seems that *errors* in the description can interfere with a witness' later ability to make an accurate identification decision. Meissner's work has shown that while there is little relationship between the number of *correct* details and identification accuracy, participants reporting fewer *errors* are more likely to correctly identify a target from a lineup, and to correctly reject a target-absent lineup (Meissner, 2002; Meissner *et al.*, 2001). Whilst a witness may generate errors about the face in the course of giving their own description, erroneous information can also be introduced by other external sources (see the case studies presented in the boxed section).

In summary, there is considerable support for the recoding interference account, and much can be gleaned from the research findings when extracting advice for practitioners (see below). However, there are findings in the verbal overshadowing literature that are problematic for a recoding interference account. As previously indicated, the lack of a consistent relationship between description accuracy and identification performance is at odds with this account. Furthermore, this account predicts that the negative effect of description should be restricted to the face that is initially described, yet there are instances in the literature where describing one face has been found to more generally interfere with the recognition of other previously encountered faces that were not described (Brown & Lloyd-Jones, 2002, 2003). These findings have led researchers to identify an alternative account of verbal overshadowing that predicts that describing faces will more generally interfere with face recognition ability.

The *processing account* of verbal overshadowing focuses upon the general processes that are more or less beneficial to face recognition. Generally, it is agreed that successful face recognition typically relies upon the application of holistic processing (Valentine, 1988). However, describing a face encourages participants to focus on the featural aspects of that face that are more easily described. Describing a face therefore leads to a shift from the use of holistic processing to the use of featural processing. The use of featural processing reduces the ability of participants to perceive holistic information in faces that would be most beneficial for successfully recognizing them. This would explain why describing one face can interfere with the recognition of other previously seen faces that were not described. Furthermore, as face recognition does not rely upon the precise contents of the description, a relationship between description accuracy and identification accuracy would not be expected.

Nevertheless, the nature of the description may still be important under a processing shift account. There is evidence that explicitly directing participants to describe each facial feature (such as eyes, nose, mouth, and so on) appears to elicit more robust effects of verbal overshadowing (Brown & Lloyd-Jones, 2002), presumably because encouraging participants to focus on individual features elicits a strong shift to featural processing.

There are, however, some instances in which featural processing may be successfully applied to a face recognition task. In particular, there is evidence that other-ethnicity faces, compared with own-ethnicity faces, tend to be processed more featurally (Rhodes, Brake, Taylor, & Tan, 1989) and so should be less prone, if at all, to verbal overshadowing. Consistent with this, Fallshore and Schooler (1995) found that describing, compared to not describing, an own-ethnicity face impaired later memory for that face, but when describing an other-ethnicity face the participants' later ability to recognize that other-ethnicity face was unaffected. However, further research is needed to replicate these findings.

It is likely that the shift in processing elicited by a description will be short-lived, and so the negative effects of verbalization attributed to this shift will diminish over a short timeframe. It seems reasonable to assume that time, or other intervening activities between the description and identification test, may allow an individual to revert back to a form of processing that is more efficient for face recognition (cf. Brown et al., 2008; Chin & Schooler, 2008). Finger (2002) found that the negative effect of describing a target face on subsequent face identification was alleviated when participants undertook a non-verbal task (completing a series of mazes or listening to music) prior to making their identification decision. Finger and Pezdek (1999) also found that inserting a 24-minute delay between the description and identification task produced a similar effect. The non-verbal task or delay is believed to encourage a shift back to holistic from featural processing.

Evidence from other studies shows that engaging in tasks that encourage attention to the global characteristics of a stimulus prior to viewing a lineup can improve identification accuracy. In their study, Macrae and Lewis (2002) showed participants a video of a simulated robbery, and later these participants attempted to identify the robber from a target-present photo lineup. Prior to viewing the lineup participants were presented with a series of Navon figures. Each figure consisted of a large letter composed of many smaller letters (e.g., a large T made up of many smaller Ss, see below).

```
SSSSSSSSSSSSSSSSSSSSSSSSSSS
SSSSSSSSSSSSSSSSSSSSSSSSSSS
SS          SSSSS          SS
            SSSSS
            SSSSS
            SSSSS
            SSSSS
            SSSSS
            SSSSS
           SSSSSSS
        SSSSSSSSSSSS
```

Participants who identified the larger letters, assumed to be a global task, were significantly *better* able to identify the target face from the lineup than participants who under took no prior Navon letter-naming task. In contrast, those participants who identified the smaller letters, assumed to be a featural task, exhibited *worse* face recognition. Encouragingly, a number of studies using similar lineup methodologies have reliably replicated these results (Darling, Martin, Hellman, & Memon, 2009; Perfect, 2003; Perfect, Dennis, & Snell, 2007; Wickham & Lander, 2008). However, studies using other measures of recognition, for example, testing memory for multiple faces, have found the effects of the Navon task to be less reliably observed (e.g., Lawson, 2007). Encouraging participants to attribute personality characteristics to faces during their encoding has also been found to improve subsequent recognition of those faces in comparison to rating those faces on the basis of their features (Berman & Cutler, 1998; Wells & Hryciw, 1984; Winograd, 1981). It is proposed that personality attributions encourage participants to attend to the *whole* face (facial features and interrelations between features), and thus engage in holistic processing more so than featural processing. Frowd and colleagues have shown this method to benefit facial composite construction (see Chapter 2). In addition, a study by Wickham and Lander (2008) presents some preliminary evidence that describing faces holistically may improve face identification from a lineup. They found that describing faces in terms of the kind of person they looked like (e.g., their personality or occupation) led to better identification than providing a description that focused on facial features.

The third account put forward for verbal overshadowing effects is the *criterion shift account*. It relies neither upon the content of the memory associated with the face or the processing undertaken at recognition. Instead, describing a face leads participants to become less willing to make a positive identification from a lineup (Clare & Lewandowsky,

2004). This results in participants more frequently deciding not to choose anyone from the lineup. When the target is not present in the lineup this will actually lead to better identification accuracy as the correct decision is to say 'not present'. In this case it would appear that describing the perpetrator may be an advantage in a forensic situation as it may later protect an "innocent suspect" from being falsely identified. However, participants are not correctly rejecting the lineup on the basis of their memory for the perpetrator, but on the basis of a general bias not to choose anyone from the lineup. Thus when the perpetrator is present in the lineup, they are more often missed and the lineup rejected. For example, Clare and Lewandowsky (2004) found that compared with participants who provided no description, those that had described a target face were more likely to subsequently correctly reject a lineup that did not contain the target, but were also more likely to incorrectly reject a lineup that did contain the target.

Whilst some evidence for the criterion shift account has been found (Clare & Lewandowsky, 2008; Sauerland *et al.*, 2008), there are circumstances where a criterion account does not seem to apply. Notably, verbal overshadowing has been found to occur when participants are forced to choose an individual from the lineup and are not given the option of saying "not present" (Fallshore & Schooler, 1995). Furthermore, those studies requesting elaborative descriptions from participants have been less likely to show a pattern of findings consistent with the criterion shift account (Clare & Lewandowsky, 2004).

ADVICE FOR PRACTITIONERS

Based upon the literature reviewed here, there are certain recommendations that can be given to practitioners whose role it is to interview witnesses to elicit a person description and/or administer a lineup. It is perhaps useful to summarize what we have learned about when providing a description of a perpetrator is most likely to have a *negative* effect on subsequent identification accuracy. The main factors identified include:

- when witnesses report errors in their description (self-generated or those suggested to them);
- when witnesses engage in featural processing.

Steps can be taken to avoid, or offer some protection against, these factors. Below we list some recommendations for practitioners, based upon empirical psychological research.

Minimize Errors in Facial Descriptions by Avoiding Delays Prior to Interviewing Witnesses

Ideally witnesses should be interviewed as soon as possible after a report of an incident. However, delays between witnessing an incident and being formally interviewed by police are commonplace (Kebbell, Milne, & Wagstaff, 1999; Kebbell & Wagstaff, 1999). Within the psychological research literature it has long been observed that delay systematically reduces the amount of information that can be recalled (Ebbinghaus, 1885/1913; Kassin, Tubb, Hosch, & Memon, 2001). This is because items of information in memory become less accessible with increased time (see Anderson, 1983). In a forensic context, both the completeness and accuracy of eyewitness evidence has been shown to decrease as the delay between witnessing an incident and recall increases (see Penrod, Loftus, & Winkler, 1982; Turtle & Yuille, 1994). Van Koppen and Lochun (1997), in their archival analysis of witness descriptions of robbers, found that a shorter delay between the crime and providing a description (measured as 0, 1, 2, 3 or more days following the crime) was associated with more complete descriptions of both physical attributes (general physical and facial appearance), and descriptions of clothes, while accuracy was unaffected by delay. However, the relationship between retention interval and the completeness of person descriptions is not always evident in archival data (Fahsing et al., 2004). Nevertheless, in the laboratory, similar findings are reported in relation to identification accuracy. A meta-analysis of 128 studies of face recognition suggests there is a linear decline in the correct identification of previously seen faces after a delay (Deffenbacher, Bornstein, McGorty, & Penrod, 2008; Shapiro & Penrod, 1986).

Any delay prior to interview also increases the risk of memory contamination as witnesses have more time in which to encounter items of new and/or misleading post-event information. For example, co-witnesses could discuss their memories for the perpetrator and encounter misleading suggestions about what that person looked like (see Zajac & Henderson, 2009). Any misleading information encountered after witnessing an incident can be errantly and persistently reported in requests for information (Lane, Mather, Villa, & Morita, 2001).

In sum, interviewing witnesses as soon as possible after an incident has occurred would be a simple and effective way to minimize the problems associated with delay, and thus obtain more reliable statements and person descriptions. Of course this recommendation is not always easy to achieve, as delays are often unavoidable due to the increasing demands placed upon police resources and time. One potential solution is to use a tool designed specifically to assist investigators in such circumstances: the Self-Administered Interview (SAI©, Gabbert, Hope, & Fisher, 2009; Hope, Gabbert, & Fisher, 2011). The SAI© is a recall tool designed to obtain high-quality information from witnesses quickly and efficiently at the scene of an incident or shortly afterwards in a more convenient location. It takes the form of a booklet containing information about what is expected of the witness, instructions to facilitate the use of memory retrieval techniques and open questions about the incident. It enables witnesses to provide and capture, in their own words, a full account of what they have just witnessed, and does not require a trained interviewer to be present during this process.

The current version of the SAI© comprises seven sections containing information and instructions designed to facilitate both recall and reporting of memories for a witnessed event. One of these sections focuses specifically on eliciting detailed person descriptor information by asking witnesses to provide as much detail as possible about the perpetrator's appearance (e.g., hair, complexion, build, distinguishing features, etc.). This section also incorporates the use of non-leading prompts to cue recall. Gabbert, Hope, Fisher, and Jamieson (2012) found that participants who had completed an SAI© after viewing a mock crime reported significantly more accurate information in a subsequent recall test (one week later), in comparison with the performance of control participants who had no early recall opportunity. Furthermore, SAI© participants were significantly more resistant to post-event suggestions, one of which was a deliberate attempt to mislead the participant about the appearance of the main perpetrator (a false newspaper report suggested that he had light stubble when he was clean-shaven). A number of studies have now demonstrated that the SAI© can protect both the quantity and quality of information about a previously witnessed event. The recall tool is currently in use by an increasing number of police forces across the UK, as well as the Netherlands and Norway, and has already achieved practical and evidential benefits during investigations (see Hope *et al.*, 2011). However, while it is positive that the SAI© has been proven to protect memory overall, and for person descriptors in particular (Gabbert *et al.*, 2009, study 2), it remains to be seen whether there is a relationship between person descriptions elicited via use of the SAI© and subsequent identification accuracy; more research is necessary.

Minimize Errors in Facial Descriptions by Facilitating Recall and Helping Witnesses Regulate their Accuracy

Person descriptions are often elicited in the context of a cognitive interview (CI). In Brown *et al.*'s (2008) survey, 83.3% of officers reported that they "usually" or "always" use the "report everything" instruction from the CI to obtain person descriptions. This instruction asks witnesses to report everything that they can remember, regardless of how peripheral it may seem. It is an effective component because otherwise witnesses might withhold information that they don't deem important, and secondly because recalling partial details may lead to subsequent recall of additional relevant information. As such, this technique has been proven to significantly increase the amount of information reported (Milne & Bull, 2002). However, because the instruction suggests to witnesses that they should adopt a "lenient response criterion", it is often found that the CI produces an increase in the amount of accurate information, but also an increase in the amount of errant information reported. This is supported by a meta-analysis by Memon, Meissner, and Fraser (2010; see also Köhnken, Milne, Memon, & Bull, 1999).

In light of the association between errors in facial descriptions and subsequent identification accuracy, it is reasonable to suggest that this particular instruction should be omitted when asking witnesses to provide a facial description of a perpetrator. The aim should be to minimize the number of erroneous person-descriptor details reported. Thus, when eliciting descriptions interviewers should prompt witnesses to adopt a stricter response criterion by requesting that they are particularly careful when reporting person descriptions; strive for accuracy, avoid guesses, and only report information that they confidently remember themselves.

Retrieval can still be facilitated by the interviewer using other components of the CI, in particular the Mental Reinstatement of Context instruction. This technique is based upon the "encoding specificity" principle proposed by Tulving and Thomson (1973), which states that cues presented at the time of retrieval will be more effective in facilitating recall when there is some degree of contextual overlap with cues that were present at the time of encoding. Thus, instructing witnesses how to *mentally* recreate the context in which they had the clearest view of the perpetrator can help to generate cues to the target memory (the perpetrator's face), which can then be described. However, prior to reporting their description of the perpetrator, witnesses should be instructed to consider the likely accuracy of any information they volunteer.

There is evidence that people have some type of conscious access to memory strength, and can regulate their responses and monitor confidence to demonstrate a reasonable degree of confidence–accuracy calibration (Luna & Martín-Luengo, 2012). In other words, people can often distinguish between memories that are likely to be accurate (he definitely had black hair), and those that might be in error

(I think his hair was brown). Insight into one's own memory is termed "metacognitive awareness" and can be used to regulate what is reported based upon confidence judgements about the likely accuracy of the recalled information (Goldsmith, Koriat, & Weinberg-Eliezer, 2002; Weber & Brewer, 2008). Koriat and Goldsmith (1996) were one of the first to demonstrate that when answering a question from memory, an individual first assesses the likely accuracy of the answer; that is, a metacognitive or confidence judgment is made. This confidence judgment then provides the basis for (a) the individual's decision to withhold or volunteer that answer (assuming free-report conditions), and (b) the level of detail to provide in the answer (assuming that there is freedom to vary the level of detail). An extensive body of empirical evidence provides support for this model of the regulation of memory reporting, and demonstrates how individuals are able to trade off the amount of information reported, and the quality or accuracy of that information, in order to meet the strategic demands placed upon them, for example, "Tell me everything" versus "Only tell me things you are sure about" (Goldsmith *et al.*, 2002; Koriat & Goldsmith, 1996; Weber & Brewer, 2008). Therefore, with appropriate instructions about the importance of accuracy, there is supporting evidence that people are able to regulate their accuracy by deciding whether they are confident enough to report a memory. If confidence is above a certain threshold then the detail will be reported; if not, the detail will be withheld.

One consequence of changing a person's response criterion from "lenient" to "strict" is that the overall amount of accurate information reported is restricted. Wright, Gabbert, Memon, and London (2008) reported a study that sought to overcome the negative effects of encountering misleading post-event information in the context of people witnessing a crime and discussing it together prior to a police interview. Participants were presented with some misleading information from a co-witness after the encoding phase, and were subsequently given either strict or lenient instructions to "Only report what you are sure about" or "Report everything you can" respectively. It was found that using the strict instructions lowered the number of times that people erroneously reported what the other person suggested. However, the manipulation had a similar effect on recall of things that were actually seen.

Given the association between errors in facial descriptions and subsequent identification accuracy, perhaps this is one occasion where the completeness of a description should be compromised in favour of fewer, but more accurate, facial descriptors.

Minimize Potential Verbal Overshadowing Effects by Facilitating Holistic Processing

It is difficult to capture in words information about a face. Our vocabulary for expressing the physical aspects of a face is limited. Furthermore, people tend to describe individual features rather than configural information relating to the relationship between these features. The processing account of verbal overshadowing posits that this featural processing can be detrimental for successful face recognition, which is a task that requires holistic processing. Thus, any measures that help shift witnesses from featural to holistic processing are likely to be advantageous. Promising areas for future research discussed already in this chapter include (a) the use of a "holistic interview"; (b) engaging in a global Navon task prior to undertaking the identification tasks; and (c) inserting a delay between the description and identification tasks. These techniques would be simple to implement, and may help witnesses to revert back to a form of processing that is more efficient for face recognition.

REFERENCES

Anderson, J.R. (1983). A spreading activation theory of memory. *Journal of Verbal Learning and Verbal Behavior*, *22*, 261–295. doi:10.1016/S0022-5371(83)90201-3

BBC (2008). George not guilty of Dando murder. Retrieved from http://news.bbc.co.uk/1/hi/uk/7536815.stm

Berman, G.L., & Cutler, B.L. (1998). The influence of processing instructions at encoding and retrieval on face recognition accuracy. *Psychology, Crime & Law*, *4*, 89–106. doi:10.1080/10683169808401751

British Psychological Society (2010). *Guidelines on Memory and the Law: Recommendations from the Scientific Study of Human Memory*. Leicester: British Psychological Society. Retrieved from http://www.academia.edu/2326108/Guidelines_On_Memory_And_The_Law_Recommendations_From_The_Scientific_Study_Of_Human_Memory

Brown, C., & Lloyd-Jones, T.J. (2002). Verbal overshadowing in a multiple face presentation paradigm: Effects of description instruction. *Applied Cognitive Psychology*, *16*, 873–885. doi:10.1002/acp.919

Brown, C., & Lloyd-Jones, T.J. (2003). Verbal overshadowing of multiple face and car recognition: Effects of within- versus across-category verbal descriptions. *Applied Cognitive Psychology*, *17*, 183–201. doi:10.1002/acp.861

Brown, C., Lloyd-Jones, T.J., & Robinson, M. (2008). Eliciting person descriptions from eyewitnesses: A survey of police perceptions of eyewitness performance and reported use of interview techniques. *European Journal of Cognitive Psychology*, *20*, 529–560. doi:10.1080/09541440701728474

Cathcart, B. (2001). *Jill Dando: Her Life and Death*. London: Penguin.

Chin, J.M., & Schooler, J.W. (2008). Why do words hurt? Content, processes, and criterion shift accounts of verbal overshadowing. *European Journal of Cognitive Psychology*, *20*, 396–413. doi:10.1080/09541440701728623

Clare, J., & Lewandowsky, S. (2004). Verbalizing facial memory: Criterion effects in verbal overshadowing. *Journal of Experimental Psychology: Learning, Memory & Cognition*, *30*, 739–755. doi:10.1037/0278-7393.30.4.739

Darling, S., Martin, D., Hellman, J.H., & Memon, A. (2009). Some witnesses are better than others. *Personality and Individual Differences*, *47*, 369–373. doi:10.1016/j.paid.2009.04.010

Deffenbacher, K.A., Bornstein, B.H., McGorty, K., & Penrod, S.D. (2008). Forgetting the once-seen face: Estimating the strength of an eyewitness's memory representation. *Journal of Experimental Psychology: Applied*, *14*, 139–150. doi:10.1037/1076-898X.14.2.139

Diamond, R., & Carey, S. (1986) Why faces are and are not special: An effect of expertise. *Journal of Experimental Psychology: General*, *115*, 107–117. doi:10.1037/0096-3445.115.2.107

Ebbinghaus, H. (1913). *Memory: A Contribution to Experimental Psychology*. New York: Teachers College, Columbia University. (Original work published 1885).

Ellis, H.D., Shepherd, J.W., & Davies, G.M. (1980). The deterioration of verbal descriptions of faces over different delay intervals. *Journal of Police Science & Administration*, *8*, 101–106.

Fahsing, I.A., Ask, K., & Granhag, P.A. (2004). The man behind the mask: accuracy and predictors of eyewitness offender descriptions. *Journal of Applied Psychology*, *89*, 722–729. doi:10.1037/0021-9010.89.4.722

Fallshore, M., & Schooler, J.W. (1995). The verbal vulnerability of perceptual expertise. *Journal of Experimental Psychology: Learning, Memory & Cognition*, *21*, 1608–1623. doi:10.1037/0278-7393.21.6.1608

Finger, K. (2002). Mazes and music: Using perceptual processing to release verbal overshadowing. *Applied Cognitive Psychology*, *16*, 887–896. doi:10.1002/acp.922

Finger, K., & Pezdek, K. (1999). The effect of verbal description on face identification accuracy: Release from verbal overshadowing. *Journal of Applied Psychology*, *84*, 340–348. doi:10.1037/0021-9010.84.3.340

Fisher, R.P., & Geiselman, R.E. (1992). *Memory-Enhancing Techniques for Investigative Interviewing: The Cognitive Interview*. Springfield, IL: Charles C. Thomas.

Fisher, R.P., & Schreiber, N. (2006). Interview protocols for improving eyewitness memory. In R. Lindsay, D. Ross, J. Read, & M. Toglia (Eds.), *Handbook of Eyewitness Psychology: Memory for Events* (pp. 53–80). Mahwah, NJ: Lawrence Erlbaum.

Gabbert, F., Hope, L., & Fisher, R.P. (2009). Protecting eyewitness evidence: Examining the efficacy of a self-administered interview tool. *Law and Human Behavior*, *33*, 298–307. doi:10.1007/s10979-008-9146-8

Gabbert, F., Hope, L., Fisher, R.P., & Jamieson, K. (2012). Protecting against susceptibility to misinformation with a self-administered interview. *Applied Cognitive Psychology*, *26*, 568–575. doi:10.1002/acp.2828

Goldsmith, M., Koriat, A., & Weinberg-Eliezer, A. (2002). Strategic regulation of grain size memory reporting. *Journal of Experimental Psychology: General*, *131*, 73–95. doi:10.1037/0096-3445.131.1.73

Granhag, P., Ask, K., & Rebelius, A. (2005). *"I saw the man who killed Anna Lindh": A case study of eyewitness descriptions*. Presented at the 15th European Conference on Psychology & Law, Vilnuis, Lithuania.

Home Office (2011). *Police and Criminal Evidence Act (1984) Code D of Practice for the Identification of Persons by Police Officers*. Retrieved from http://homeoffice. gov.uk/publications/police/operational-policing/pace-codes/pace-code-d-2011

Hope, L., Gabbert, F., & Fisher, R.P. (2011). From laboratory to the street: Capturing witness memory using a Self-Administered Interview. *Legal and Criminological Psychology, 16*, 211–226. doi:10.1111/j.2044-8333.2011.02015.x

Kassin, S.M., Tubb, V.A., Hosch, H.M., & Memon, A. (2001). On the "general acceptance" of eyewitness testimony research: A new survey of the experts. *American Psychologist, 56*, 405–416. doi:10.1037/0003-066X.56.5.405

Kebbell, M., & Milne, R. (1998). Police officers' perception of eyewitness factors in forensic investigations. *Journal of Social Psychology, 138*, 323–330. doi:10.1080/00224549809600384

Kebbell, M.R., Milne, R., & Wagstaff, G.F. (1999). The cognitive interview: A survey of its forensic effectiveness. *Psychology, Crime & Law, 5*, 101–115. doi:10.1080/10683169908414996

Kebbell, M.R., & Wagstaff, G.F. (1999). The cognitive interview: An analysis of its forensic effectiveness. In D.V. Canter (Ed.), *Interviewing and Deception* (pp. 25–39). Aldershot: Dartmouth.

Köhnken, G., Milne, R., Memon, A., & Bull, R. (1999). A meta-analysis on the effects of the Cognitive Interview. *Psychology, Crime, & Law, 5*, 3–27. doi:10.1080/10683169908414991

Koriat, A., & Goldsmith, M. (1996). Monitoring and control processes in the strategic regulation of memory accuracy. *Psychological Review, 103*, 490–517. doi:10.1037/0033-295X.103.3.490

Lane, S.M., Mather, M., Villa, D., & Morita, S.K. (2001). How events are reviewed matters: Effects of varied focus on eyewitness suggestibility. *Memory & Cognition, 29*, 940–947.

Lawson, R. (2007). Local and global processing biases fail to influence face, object, and word recognition. *Visual Cognition, 15*, 710–740. doi:10.1080/13506280601112519

Lord Advocate's Guidelines to Chief Constables (2007). *Guidelines on the Conduct of Visual Identification Procedures*. Retrieved from http://www. copfs.gov.uk/Resource/Doc/13547/0000269.pdf

Luna, K., & Martín-Luengo, B. (2012). Confidence–accuracy calibration with general knowledge and eyewitness memory cued recall questions. *Applied Cognitive Psychology, 26*, 289–295. doi:10.1002/acp.1822

Macrae, C.N., & Lewis, H.L. (2002). Do I know you? Processing orientation and face recognition. *Psychological Science, 13*, 194–196. doi:10.1111/1467-9280.00436

Memon, A., Meissner, C.A., & Fraser, J. (2010). The Cognitive Interview: A meta-analytic review and study space analysis of the past 25 years. *Public Policy and Law, 16*, 340–372. doi:10.1037/a0020518

Meissner, C.A. (2002). Applied aspects of the instructional bias effect in verbal overshadowing. *Applied Cognitive Psychology, 16*, 911–928. doi:10.1002/acp.918

Meissner, C.A., & Brigham, J.C. (2001). A meta-analysis of the verbal overshadowing effect in face identification. *Applied Cognitive Psychology, 15*, 603–616. doi:10.1002/acp.728

Meissner, C.A., Brigham, J.C., & Kelley, C.M. (2001). The influence of retrieval processes in verbal overshadowing. *Memory & Cognition, 29*, 176–186.

Meissner, C.A., Sporer, S.L., & Susa, K.J. (2008). A theoretical review and meta-analysis of the description–identification relationship in memory for faces. *European Journal of Cognitive Psychology, 20*, 414–455. doi:10.1080/09541440701728581

Milne, R., & Bull, R. (2002). Back to basics: A componential analysis of the original cognitive interview mnemonics with three age groups. *Applied Cognitive Psychology*, *16*, 743–753. doi:10.1002/acp.825

Ministry of Justice (2011). *Achieving Best Evidence: Guidance on Interviewing Victims and Witnesses and Guidance on Using Special Measures*. London: Ministry of Justice. Retrieved from http://www.justice.gov.uk/downloads/victims-and-witnesses/vulnerable-witnesses/achieving-best-evidence-criminal-proceedings.pdf

Neil v. Biggers (1972). 409 US 188.

Penrod, S.D., Loftus, E.F., & Winkler, J. (1982). The reliability of eyewitness testimony: A psychological perspective. In N.L. Kerr, & R.M. Bray (Eds.), *The Psychology of the Courtroom* (pp. 119–168). Orlando, FL: Academic Press.

Perfect, T.J. (2003). Local processing bias impairs lineup performance. *Psychological Reports*, *93*, 393–394. doi:10.2466/pr0.2003.93.2.393

Perfect, T.J., Dennis, I., & Snell, A. (2007). The effects of local and global processing orientation on eyewitness identification performance. *Memory*, *15*, 784–798. doi:10.1080/09658210701654627

R v. George (2002). *EWCA Crim 1923*. Retrieved from http://www.bailii.org/ew/cases/EWCA/Crim/2002/1923.html

R v. George (2007). *EWCA Crim 2722*. Retrieved from http://www.bailii.org/ew/cases/EWCA/Civ/2007/2722.html

R v. Turnbull and others (1976). 3 All ER 549.

Rhodes, G., Brake, S., Taylor, K., & Tan, S. (1989). Expertise and configural coding in face recognition. *British Journal of Psychology*, *80*, 313–331. doi:10.1111/j.2044-8295.1989.tb02323.x

Sauerland, M., Holub, F.E., & Sporer, S.L. (2008). Person descriptions and person identifications: Verbal overshadowing or recognition criterion shift? *European Journal of Cognitive Psychology*, *20*, 497–528. doi:10.1080/09541440701728417

Schooler, J.W. (2002). Verbalization produces a transfer inappropriate processing shift. *Applied Cognitive Psychology*, *16*, 989–997. doi:10.1002/acp.930

Schooler, J.W., & Engstler-Schooler, T.Y. (1990). Verbal overshadowing of visual memories: Some things are better left unsaid. *Cognitive Psychology*, *22*, 36–71.

Shapiro, P.N., & Penrod, S.D. (1986). A meta-analytic analysis of facial identification studies. *Psychological Bulletin*, *100*, 139–156.

Sporer, S.L. (1992). Postdicting eyewitness identification accuracy: Confidence, decision times and person descriptions among choosers and non-choosers. *European Journal of Social Psychology*, *22*, 157–180. doi:10.1002/ejsp.2420220205

Sporer, S.L. (2007). Person description as retrieval cues: do they really help? *Psychology, Crime & Law*, *13*, 591–609. doi:10.1080/10683160701253986

Tulving, E., & Thomson, D.M. (1973). Encoding specificity and retrieval processes in episodic memory. *Psychological Review*, *80*, 352–373. doi:10.1037/h0020071

Turtle, J.W., & Yuille, J.C. (1994). Lost but not forgotten details: Repeated eyewitness recall leads to reminiscence but not hyperamnesia. *Journal of Applied Psychology*, *79*, 260–271. doi:10.1037/0021-9010.79.2.260

Valentine, T. (1988). Upside down faces: A review of the effect of inversion upon face recognition. *British Journal of Psychology*, *79*, 471–491. doi:10.1111/j.2044-8295.1988.tb02747.x

Valentine, T., Pickering, A., & Darling, S. (2003). Characteristics of eyewitness identification that predict the outcome of real lineups. *Applied Cognitive Psychology, 17,* 969–993. doi:10.1002/acp.939

Van Koppen, P.J., & Lochun, S.K. (1997). Portraying perpetrators: The validity of offender descriptions by witnesses. *Law and Human Behavior, 21,* 661–685. doi:10.1023/A:1024812831576

Weber, N., & Brewer, N. (2008). Eyewitness recall: Regulation of grain size and the role of confidence. *Journal of Experimental Psychology: Applied, 14,* 50–60. doi:10.1037/1076-898X.14.1.50.

Wells, G.L. (1978). Applied eyewitness-testimony research: System variables and estimator variables. *Journal of Personality and Social Psychology, 36,* 1546–1557. doi:10.1037/0022-3514.36.12.1546

Wells, G.L. (1985). Verbal descriptions of faces from memory: Are they diagnostic of identification accuracy? *Journal of Applied Psychology, 70,* 619–626. doi:10.1037/0021-9010.70.4.619

Wells, G.L., & Hryciw, B. (1984). Memory for faces: Encoding and retrieval operations. *Memory & Cognition, 12,* 338–344.

Wells, G.L., & Turtle, J.W. (1987). Eyewitness testimony: Current knowledge and emergent controversies. *Canadian Journal of Behavioural Science, 19,* 363–388. doi:10.1037/h0080000

Wickham, L.H.V., & Lander, K. (2008). The effect of verbal description and processing type on face identification. *European Journal of Cognitive Psychology, 20,* 577– 586. doi:10.1080/09541440701728433

Winograd, E. (1981). Elaboration and distinctiveness in memory for faces. *Journal of Experimental Psychology: Human Learning & Memory, 7,* 181-190. doi:10.1037/0278-7393.7.3.181

Wright, D.B., Gabbert, F., Memon, A., & London, K. (2008). Changing the criterion for memory conformity in free-recall. *Memory, 16,* 137–148. doi:10.1080/09658210701836174

Zajac, R., & Henderson, N. (2009). Don't it make my brown eyes blue: Co-witness misinformation about a target's appearance can impair target-absent lineup performance. *Memory 17,* 266–278. doi:10.1080/09658210802623950

3

Facial Composites and Techniques to Improve Image Recognizability

CHARLIE FROWD

There are various types of evidence that can help to bring a criminal to justice. Some are valuable at the early stages of an investigation, for instance when a suspect is named from CCTV footage by a member of the public (see Chapter 9). Other evidence is important later and can be used to confirm or refute whether a suspect is likely to have committed a particular offence. A suspect may, for instance, be picked out of an identity parade (Chapter 6), or an expert may be called upon to qualify the match between the suspect's face and a CCTV image (Chapter 10). In some investigations, however, the available evidence does not result in a suspect being identified. In these situations, the police may ask eyewitnesses to construct a likeness or *facial composite* of the offender's face. Facial composites have played a significant role in policing for about four decades. They are primarily used as an investigative tool, to enable a person familiar with the offender (e.g., a police officer or member of the public) to put a name to the face. Until recently, composites had very low correct naming rates (5%), suggesting that few offenders

Forensic Facial Identification: Theory and Practice of Identification from Eyewitnesses, Composites and CCTV, First Edition. Edited by Tim Valentine and Josh P. Davis.
© 2015 John Wiley & Sons, Ltd. Published 2015 by John Wiley & Sons, Ltd.

Case study

Greater Manchester Police were at a loss to locate a rapist who attacked at least two young women in 2009 and 2010. This was in spite of considerable police effort, construction of a composite by one of the victims, and public appeals for information.

The final victim in this case constructed an EvoFIT seven days after the attack. The internal-features first method was used, and the resulting image is shown in Figure 3.1. Greater Manchester Police used the animated composite in a public appeal for information (see Glendinning, 2010, for a description of the original police appeal and accompanying YouTube video link). Officers were inundated with calls from members of the public identifying the composite as Asim Javed, a worker in a local fast-food restaurant. As can be seen (Figure 3.1), the visual match between the composite and Javed is striking. Javed confessed to committing two rapes and commented that further crimes would have been committed had he not been stopped. He was sentenced to at least eight years in prison. The case, which received considerable media attention (see, for instance, Narain, 2011), illustrates the ideal use of composites: to provide an effective method of suspect identification for serious crime.

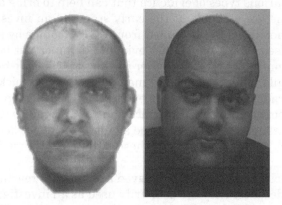

Figure 3.1 On the left is an EvoFIT composite constructed by a rape victim. On the right is a photograph of the convicted person in this case (Asim Javed).

were identified, although this level of performance is arguably better than the alternative of not utilizing composites at all.

More recently, a better understanding of the problems associated with accessing facial memory has led to substantial improvements in composite construction, and facilitated the development of "holistic" systems, which use methods designed to match closely with the way faces are processed. Better, more effective interview techniques have also been developed, as well as post-construction image manipulations that improve identification. This extensive research effort has been worthwhile: it is now possible to construct an unfamiliar face from long-term memory that other people can name with a high level of success.

FORENSIC USE OF COMPOSITES: POLICE PRACTICE

If a criminal investigation does not produce a suspect, the police may invite witnesses to construct a composite. Very occasionally, composite construction takes place on the day of the crime, but more usually it occurs a day or two afterwards – although this period can also be much longer. Victims, for example, may require time to overcome some of the trauma to be ready to externalize the face. If a composite is to be created, it is good practice for police practitioners to know little about the relevant case, so as not to be influenced by case information (which, of course, may be incorrect). It is also good practice to make initial contact with witnesses (who may be victims) prior to interview, normally over the telephone. While this more informal interaction has the obvious advantage of starting to build rapport with witnesses (which in itself should facilitate face recall), practitioners can check that the offender's face was clearly seen and gauge how well witnesses are likely to recall facial details. Witnesses can be advised that several hours of undisturbed time will be necessary to create a composite and a time/place agreed (usually at the witness' home or a police station). This procedure also allows practitioners to be prepared for the interview and to decide which type of facial composite system is likely to be required.

The witness and police practitioner then meet to construct a composite. Practitioners explain the process and typically administer an interview to recover a good description of the face (see below for details of different interview types). Practitioners take witnesses through the process of constructing the face with the relevant system and, once a composite is complete, statements are prepared that describe the process. The composite is also printed and put into secure storage, for potential use as evidence in court.

It is normal for composites to be passed on to the investigating officer in the case. These images are usually circulated within the relevant force so that police officers and support staff can identify them. Circulating composites in this way is good practice due to recidivism (i.e., offenders tend to be known to the police already). Names put forward can be used to generate potential suspects, and each person can then be eliminated from the investigation, or, given supporting evidence, interviewed and possibly arrested. In the absence of a suspect, investigating officers can release the composite to the media as part of a public appeal for information. For a case to go to court, however, there needs to be sufficient evidence that the suspect had committed the relevant offence. Note that the composite itself is treated as evidence but, the same as for other types of identification procedures (e.g., via identity parades), they are not sufficiently reliable to secure conviction. This is entirely sensible since human observers make errors when constructing composites and making judgements based on identity. In addition, Charman, Gregory, and Carlucci (2009) have found that the likeness of a composite to a defendant is related to whether (participants acting as) jurors believe the defendant to be guilty or not, suggesting that composites may not provide independent evidence and that their use in court is questionable. This issue is likely to be confounded by the fact that the newer holistic systems allow production of images that tend to be better than "type" likeness, as illustrated by the case study.

"TRADITIONAL" MECHANICAL FEATURE-BASED SYSTEMS

The first established method to create composites in criminal investigations was the sketch. An artist trained in portraiture would work with witnesses to draw the offender's face by hand, using pencils or crayons. The approach has flexibility, and the potential to create drawings in great detail, but is limited to practitioners with artistic skill. Alternative methods were created in the 1960s and 1970s to enable greater use by police professionals. In the UK, the main system was Photofit (see Figure 3.2). It contained photographs of facial parts (eyes and brows, nose, hair and ears, and chin and jawline) printed onto rigid card. Witnesses would search through example parts, a page of noses for instance, with the aim of selecting the best matches; choices were slotted into a mechanical frame to create the face. An artistic pencil was made available for adding moles, scars, wrinkles, etc. Practitioners in the US employed a similar system called Identikit, which contained drawings of facial elements printed on transparent slides.

The effectiveness of these traditional systems has been the subject of considerable research. This body of work has indicated that these composites tended to be a poor match with the intended face (e.g., Ellis, Shepherd, & Davies, 1975; Laughery & Fowler, 1980), even under the favourable (and unrealistic) condition where the target's face was

Figure 3.2 Facial composites of England international footballer, David Beckham (constructed in Frowd *et al.*, 2005b). Each image was created by a different constructor, unfamiliar with the face, and three-to-four hours after having seen a facial photograph. From left to right are composites from E-FIT, PRO-fit, Sketch and Photofit. For copyright reasons, the actual photograph used in the study cannot be reproduced here.

visible during construction (Ellis, Davies, & Shepherd, 1978a). Also, Photofit contained omissions in the range of available features (Davies, 1983), thus limiting the system's capability, and the presence of "demarcation" lines separating individual features interfered with subsequent recognition of the face (Ellis, Davies, & Shepherd, 1978b).

SECOND-GENERATION SOFTWARE-BASED FEATURE-BASED SYSTEMS

These deficiencies were largely overcome in the 1990s with the development of second-generation software systems in the UK (e.g., CD-FIT, E-FIT and PRO-fit) and the US (e.g., Mac-a-Mug Pro, FACES and Identikit 2000). These applications contained a greater range of features, which could be sized and positioned freely on the face, vastly improving the likeness to a target. Computer-graphics technology could blend features together, avoid demarcation lines, and produce a more realistic-looking face. Additional artistic-enhancement techniques were also possible using software painting tools.

A "cognitive" approach was now used to build the face, in order to maximize image accuracy. This approach involved two main developments. The first was necessary due to the much larger databases of facial features, and so "cognitive-type" interviewing (CI) techniques (see Chapter 2) were administered to recover a detailed description of the offender's face, allowing operatives to locate appropriately matching features. For example, PRO-fit's white-male database contains 283 pairs of eyes, with a more manageable set of 25 categorized as "round" and "light". So, composite construction evolved into a two-stage process: a face-recall interview, followed by selection of facial features.

The second development concerned the way in which facial features were presented. With the traditional systems, witnesses selected from pages of isolated features. However, research emerging at the time suggested that this strategy was unlikely to be optimal. Facial recognition requires processing of the appearance of features as well as their spatial arrangement or *configuration* on the face. Recognition of an individual feature (e.g., a mouth) is facilitated when seen embedded in a complete face rather than as an isolated part (e.g., Tanaka & Farah, 1993; Tanaka & Sengco, 1997). Consequently, these systems were designed so that example features were placed within an intact whole face.

"GOLD STANDARD" PROTOCOL FOR TESTING COMPOSITE SYSTEMS

To compare the effectiveness of composite systems, Frowd *et al.* (2005b) proposed a gold-standard protocol for laboratory evaluations, although for practical and theoretical reasons, not all research replicated this ideal. The protocol imitated the manner in which composites are used in the real world and required two groups of participants. Participants in one group ("constructors") would be shown a target individual, a celebrity such as a footballer or TV soap character with whom they were *unfamiliar*. Next, after a specified delay, a properly trained researcher or police operative would use interviewing techniques to collect the constructor's description of the target face. Finally, with the assistance of the operative, constructors would create a single composite using the full capabilities of the composite system.

Participants in the second group ("evaluators") would be recruited on the basis of being *familiar* with the relevant targets (e.g., football fans), although they should not be primed beforehand with the actual names of composites they would see. Instead, evaluators would usually be told that the composites were of a particular type (e.g., footballers) and asked to name them. Valentine, Davis, Thorner, Solomon, and Gibson (2010) indicate the value of providing this type of background (contextual) information, as might be the case in a police investigation. In their research, spontaneous naming was found to be only 0.8% correct before evaluators were told that the composites were constructed of actors from two TV soaps (*EastEnders* and *Neighbours*); once aware of this context, naming rates were approximately 20%. As constructors typically produce rather different-looking images for a given target (as illustrated in Figure 3.5), the protocol also recommends that at least eight constructors be recruited per system. Similarly, evaluators vary in recognition ability and so at least eight evaluators should attempt to name each composite. This design allows a stable measure of system performance to be calculated, and has the power to detect a forensically useful, medium-to-large effect size if repeated for each condition in an experiment.

SYSTEM EVALUATIONS

Using the gold-standard protocol and a three-to-four hour delay between constructors seeing a target and then creating a composite of it, Frowd *et al.* (2005b) found that the "second-generation" E-FIT and PRO-fit feature-based systems performed equivalently, producing composites with fairly-good mean correct naming rates of 18% (when the background context was known, as is the usual case). In contrast, mean correct naming was only 6% for composites created from the traditional Photofit system, and 9% for sketches produced by constructors working with a forensic artist. Overall, correct naming was about three times higher for composites of a distinctive face than a more average-looking face, a distinctiveness effect found generally for face recognition (e.g., Shapiro & Penrod, 1986). Example composites constructed in the study are shown in Figure 3.2.

In a forensic setting, witnesses usually create composites after a longer interval than three-to-four hours. Frowd *et al.* (2005a) replicated their gold-standard 2005 study (using E-FIT, PRO-fit and Sketch systems) but extended it with a two-day delay between target encoding and composite construction. Occasionally a recognizable image was created, but in general performance was very poor: mean correct naming of composites was only 1% overall, and sketch was the best method, at 8%. Also included was a computerized second-generation feature-based system called FACES (McQuiston-Surrett, Topp, & Malpass, 2006) that is popular in police investigations outside of the UK, but naming rates were similarly low at 3%. This poor performance was in spite of the usual procedure of evaluators being instructed that the composites were of celebrities and also verifying that they were familiar with the relevant identities. Ineffective composite naming following long delays has been replicated (Frowd *et al.*, 2007b, 2010b; Frowd, McQuiston-Surrett, Anandaciva, Ireland, & Hancock, 2007d; Frowd, McQuiston-Surrett, Kirkland & Hancock, 2005c), and found to extend to Identikit 2000 (Frowd *et al.*, 2007d). The overall implication is that offenders are unlikely to be identified reliably using these methods.

Similarly, police field trials have indicated low identification of composites from feature-based systems (e.g., Frowd *et al.*, 2011a, 2012b).

Why should this be the case? One reason is that the basic method to construct a composite – via the selection of individual facial features, irrespective of whether this is carried out in the context of a complete face – is at variance with the natural way we recognize faces, as *wholes* (e.g., Davies, Shepherd, & Ellis, 1978; Tanaka & Farah, 1993).

In spite of practitioners using appropriate interviewing techniques, many witnesses are still unable to recall facial details. They may be able to estimate age and race, but only give a brief description of hair and perhaps a single facial feature (e.g., "he had a large nose"). This situation of limited face recall tends to occur following longer delays, since recall reduces markedly with time (Ellis, Shepherd, & Davies, 1980). In contrast, with a small-to-medium effect size, recognition of an unfamiliar face declines much-less rapidly as a function of increasing delay (see Deffenbacher, Bornstein, McGorty, & Penrod, 2008, for a meta-analysis).

Poor face recall frequently occurs when victims do not realize that a crime is taking place. Bogus officials, for example, can appear to be genuine, and aggrieved persons may only realize later that they have been a victim of crime. The elderly are often targeted, and many UK police forces have dedicated units to deal with such distraction-burglary offences, supported by a national intelligence unit (Operation Liberal). Victims may themselves be distracted by the crime and so may not intentionally encode (learn) an offender's face. In any case, following sketchy recall, practitioners have little to go on to constrain the number of features to present to witnesses, and, even if a composite is attempted, witnesses may find it difficult to identify which features match the offender's face. This situation is similar for artists, since a facial description is still an important part of creating a sketched composite.

This issue was deemed serious enough that police guidelines in the UK advise against construction of feature-based composites (including sketch) in situations where face recall is limited (ACPO, 2003, 2009). What is required is a different approach to construct the face, one that depends neither on witness descriptions nor on selection of facial features, but on recognition of the face as a whole. The result is a new breed of composite systems.

HOLISTIC COMPOSITE SYSTEMS

The newer "holistic" systems are computerized and have a similar user interface to each other. There are three commercial systems in existence, each one the result of extensive development over the last decade.

The systems are EFIT-V and EvoFIT in the UK, and ID in South Africa. With each system, witnesses are presented with arrays of complete faces and are asked to select candidates that resemble the offender; the software takes selected faces and combines ("breeds") them together to produce more faces for selection, and this selection and breeding procedure is repeated a few times. The result is a search of the space of possible faces and, ideally, evolution towards the relevant identity. It is no longer necessary to describe an offender's face in detail, although there is considerable benefit for using the holistic cognitive interview in some cases (see below).

Fundamental Properties of a Holistic System

At the heart of a holistic system is a face generator capable of producing a large number of synthetic yet realistic-looking faces (e.g. Frowd, Hancock, & Carson, 2004). Rather than a database of individual features, mathematical modelling techniques are used (e.g., principal components analysis, PCA) that capture the way in which faces change in terms of (a) the contour and placement of features on the face, collectively referred to as *shape* information, and (b) pixel intensity of individual features and overall skin tone, or *texture*. PCA produces a set of reference faces that represent a different global property of a face (Hancock, Bruce, & Burton, 1997). One reference may, for example, capture the weight or pleasantness of a face, while another may change apparent age. PCA is sometimes used for data-compression applications (e.g., Sirovich & Kirby, 1987), by combining reference images scaled by a small set of coefficients (numbers) to reconstitute the original dataset. However, when these coefficients are given random values, a novel face is created. These coefficients can be conceptualized as face *genes*.

The face generator is called upon repeatedly, each time with different random face genes, to create an array of novel faces. Holistic systems have traditionally combined items selected from the array by copying the process of *sexual selection* found in nature. There are various schemes available to do this (e.g., Goldberg, 1989), but a popular one is to use a genetic algorithm (GA); this would pick a pair of faces ("parents") and mix their genes by taking a random half from each, known as *uniform crossover*, to realize an "offspring". Genetic mutation can also be applied, an operation that replaces genes with a random value, the aim of which is to maintain variability in the population of faces. The resulting face has characteristics of both parents, with some variation. The procedure is repeated, using different pairs of randomly selected faces, to repopulate the array. The breeding process is iterated using faces that witnesses have selected from the (evolved) array. Note that this approach inherently involves chance due to the random nature of selecting (a) breeding pairs and (b) individual genes taken from each parent. The consequence is that sometimes a good likeness emerges early on, but at other times the evolution takes longer. In any case, when the same person uses the system more than once, face arrays are different from the start, as are evolved composites (for an example, see Frowd, Bruce, Plenderleith, & Hancock, 2006b). Research has also indicated that, for both lab- and field-work, creating a composite usually takes less time with holistic than modern feature-based systems (e.g., Frowd *et al.*, 2011a).

Some research has been published on ID (e.g., Tredoux, Nunez, Oxtoby & Prag, 2006) and EFIT-V (e.g., Gibson, Solomon, Maylin, & Clark, 2009; Solomon, Gibson, & Mist, 2013). Research by Valentine *et al.* (2010) indicates that, as for the feature-based systems, fairly good performance (20% correct naming) is possible for EFIT-V when construction follows immediately after encoding. Identification following longer (more forensically relevant) intervals appears to be unknown, although in a recent evaluation, EFIT-V composites were appropriately assigned higher ratings of likeness (by participants familiar with the targets) when produced on the same day than after two days (Davis, Sulley, Solomon, & Gibson, 2010). In contrast to EvoFIT, ID and EFIT-V are capable of rendering composites in colour – although there is evidence to suggest that colour composites are not more identifiable in general than greyscale composites (Frowd *et al.*, 2006b).

Within EvoFIT, a set of *holistic scales* have been developed for a user to manipulate not just age, but other overall aspects of a face including attractiveness, health, masculinity, honesty and weight (Frowd, Bruce, McIntyre, Ross, & Hancock, 2006a). The accumulated effect of these 14 or so holistic scales can substantially improve the likeness of an evolved face. The EFIT-V system also includes holistic scales.

Research and development have been extensive for EvoFIT, with some 30 academic papers published in the previous decade (for a fairly detailed review, see Frowd, 2012). For instance, using the gold-standard procedure, constructors in Frowd *et al.* (2007b) created composites (after a two-day delay), using an early version of EvoFIT, that were correctly named at 12%. In comparison, composites from a second-generation modern feature-based system were correctly named at 5%.

Improving the Effectiveness of Composites

As noted, the majority of recent research included in the following section has been conducted on EvoFIT. However, since the general approach and software tools used for all three holistic systems are similar, the techniques discussed below are likely to generalize to holistic systems in general.

One reason for inaccurate face construction is a consequence of biases by which we process faces. When we recognize a face only seen once (an unfamiliar face), the *external facial features* such as the hair, ears and neck are highly salient. However, when recognizing people with whom we are familiar, the *internal facial features* are relatively more important (Ellis, Shepherd, & Davies, 1979). Our cognitive system learns the structure of this inner region – the eyes, brow, nose and mouth – when we acquire familiarity with a specific face (e.g., Clutterbuck & Johnston, 2002). When witnesses construct a composite, usually they have only seen the target once; that is, the face is unfamiliar. Therefore, the focus of attention for constructor-witnesses tends to be on external features, in particular hair. In contrast, as familiar face recognition is engaged when a composite is named by evaluator-witnesses, greater importance is placed on internal features (e.g., Frowd, Bruce, McIntyre, & Hancock, 2007a; Frowd, Skelton, Butt, Hassan, & Fields, 2011b). In summary, poor naming is a consequence of inaccurately constructed internal features. Fortunately, techniques that promote more accurate construction of internal features should also promote composites that are more identifiable. There have been several successful attempts to achieve this objective, as outlined below.

Blurring the external features Some users of an early version of EvoFIT complained that faces in the arrays were too similar to one another and this made selection difficult. With this software, the same external features (hair, ears and neck) were used throughout – these were selected at the start – but this design choice turned out to increase facial similarity. The issue was initially addressed by applying a Gaussian (blur) filter to the external features (Frowd, Park, McIntyre, *et al.*, 2008b), to reduce their salience. Based on research that the context in which a face is perceived is beneficial to recognition (e.g., Ellis *et al.*, 1979), external features were not removed entirely. Constructors still selected external features at the start, but this region was blurred during face selection and then restored to normal prior to holistic-scale use. The main advantage of blur was that constructors could now base face selection more easily on internal features.

The effectiveness of both blurring and holistic scales was confirmed in a gold-standard evaluation with a two-day delay (Frowd *et al.*, 2010b). EvoFIT composites created by constructors using both blur and holistic scales were named with a mean of 25% correct, compared with a mean of 4% for composites constructed using a modern feature-based system.

Obscuring the external features and "internal-features-first" The level of external-features blurring used by Frowd *et al.* (2010b) was selected to make recognition difficult if extended across the entire face. However, higher levels of blur yielded more identifiable composites and, unexpectedly, best performance emerged when external features were not shown at all (Frowd, Skelton, Atherton, et al., 2012e). Furthermore, the presence of external features inhibited effective use of holistic scales (e.g., age, face weight). Taken together, the implication was that face construction would be facilitated by evolving internal features first, using arrays as shown in Figure 3.3a, and then by adding the external features after holistic-scale use. Using the gold-standard protocol and a 24-hour delay to construction, composite naming success doubled from 23% using external-features blur to 46% using this novel "internal-features-first" method.

These experiments demonstrate that the mere presence of external features is a distraction to the person constructing the face. This is not to say that external features have no value, but their importance relates to naming: composites are much easier to recognize as a complete image than from internal features alone (e.g., Frowd et al., 2011b). This situation is also true for recognition of facial photographs (e.g., Ellis et al., 1979). Figure 3.3b illustrates the main stages of the optimized construction procedure.

The negative and positive impact of interviewing It is good practice for police practitioners to administer cognitive-type interviewing (CI) to obtain a detailed description of the face (see Chapter 2). In brief, witnesses are asked to try to recreate the scene of the crime (environmental context) in their memory; they are encouraged to report all details about the offender's face, no matter how trivial, but without guessing; this free-recall procedure can be repeated, to facilitate recall of new information, and further details can be elicited in a question-and-answer format (cued recall). The resulting description can facilitate feature search within a composite system, but there is evidence to suggest that this kind of extensive recall can interfere with recognition – a mechanism known as the *verbal overshadowing effect* (see Chapter 2). For a modern feature-based system, the knock-on effect appears to be interference to selection of facial features and a small reduction in composite quality (Frowd & Fields, 2011). There is even evidence (Wells, Charman, & Olson, 2005) to suggest that composite construction itself may result in a recognition deficit for witnesses taking part in a lineup, at least for the FACES feature-based system, especially if the resulting composite is a poor match to the target. Equally, there is evidence to support a facilitative effect on recognition from creating a composite (Davis, Gibson, & Solomon, 2014; see also the meta-analysis in Meissner & Brigham, 2001). Overall, the effect of face construction

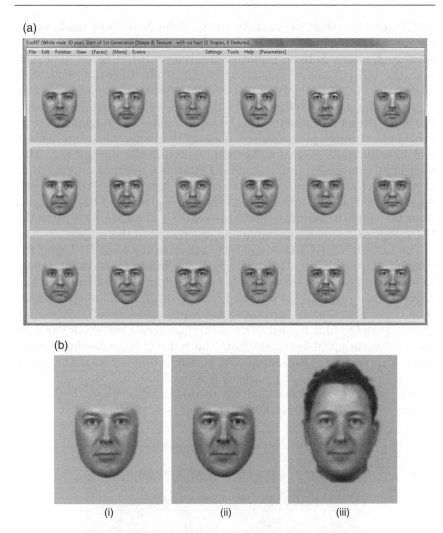

Figure 3.3 (a) EvoFIT composites are more accurately constructed when external features are omitted in the face arrays, as shown here. External features are added at the end, once internal features have been constructed in their entirety (i.e., after evolving and holistic-scale use). (b) Stages in the face construction of UK Prime Minister, David Cameron. Images are (i) best face at the end of generation 1, (ii) best face at the end of generation 2 and (iii) after use of holistic-scales and the addition of external features.

on eyewitness identification appears to be a complex issue and is not yet fully understood.

One account of the verbal overshadowing effect is that focusing on the local features of a face impairs face recognition. Therefore, such an effect may be overcome by a global mode of processing (e.g., MacLin,

2002), such as when personality (trait) judgements are made about another person's face (e.g., Berman & Cutler, 1998). This idea was developed into a holistic cognitive interview (H-CI) in collaboration with the UK police advisory group on facial identification. Following administration of the normal face-recall cognitive interview (CI), constructors are asked to think about the perceived character (personality) of the target face and then make seven whole-face judgements (e.g., heath, masculinity, pleasantness, honesty, distinctiveness, intelligence and likeability). A composite is then created in the normal way. This additional component to the standard interview requires only a couple of minutes to administer, but the result is striking. In Frowd, Bruce, Smith, and Hancock (2008a), correct naming of PRO-fits increased from 9% constructed after the face-recall CI alone, to 41% after the H-CI. Figure 3.4 shows example images created in the project.

The holistic CI (H-CI) is similarly effective for EvoFIT. Using the gold-standard protocol, 24-hour delay and external-features blur, more EvoFIT composites were correctly named after the H-CI (39%) than after the face-recall CI (24%; Frowd *et al.*, 2012a). For a holistic system, then, face selection is facilitated following recovery of information about (a) individual features (from the face-recall interview) and (b) the configuration of features (from the holistic interviewing component). This finding is consistent with research that shows that naming of photographs of faces (e.g., Cabeza & Kato, 2000) and composite faces (Frowd *et al.*, 2013a) is sensitive to information about both local features and their configuration (placement) on the face.

Figure 3.4 Example composites constructed following a traditional face-recall cognitive interview (left) and the holistic–cognitive interview (right). Two different people created these composite images using PRO-fit after having watched a video clip of EastEnders' character Billy Mitchell. (EastEnders is a popular, long-running British TV soap.)

One curious research finding is that components of the interview do not appear to be effective on their own. In Frowd *et al.* (2012a), EvoFITs were equally identifiable when the interview contained (a) free recall only, (b) holistic only and (c) neither free recall nor holistic components. Benefit was only observed when holistic prompts followed free recall (the H-CI). This research indicates that the free-recall interviewing component activates the memory trace for each facial feature, while the holistic component organizes these memories in such a way as to be conducive with composite construction and thus production of an identifiable image.

Since its introduction in 2007, police feedback indicates that the H-CI works effectively for witnesses with good recall of an offender's face. It should also work well with composite systems in regular use by UK police (E-FIT, EFIT-V, EvoFIT and PRO-fit). However, some holistic prompts may not be suitable to use all of the time. Likeability, for example, may be fine to use in a confidence crime but not in an assault case. It seems that the exact prompts used are not important for the H-CI to be effective, and so police can use them sensitively according to the crime.

Improving Composite Recognition Following Construction

Morphed composites A further area of research has considered the situation where several observers have seen the same target face. In Bruce, Ness, Hancock, Newman, and Rarity (2002), constructors created a single composite from memory using a feature-based system. Sets of two or four individual composites of the same identity were then averaged together, giving an equal contribution (weighting) to each image, to produce a *morphed* composite. Morphed composites were found to be more identifiable than an individual composite on average, and were at least as identifiable as the best image in the set. These effects are the result of individual constructors making errors in the selection and placement of facial features, but as these errors by different constructors tend to be independent of each other, they cancel out in the averaging process. In the example shown in Figure 3.5, notice how mouths are similar in appearance in three out of the four composites (same for hair in three different composites); the morphed image provides a sensible way to combine such differences and similarities. The research also indicated that morphed composites are more effective when composed of four rather than two individual composites. The superiority of morphed over individual feature-based composites has been replicated (Davis *et al.*, 2010; Frowd, Bruce, Ross, McIntyre, & Hancock, 2007c; Frowd *et al.*, 2012d; Hasel & Wells, 2007) and found to

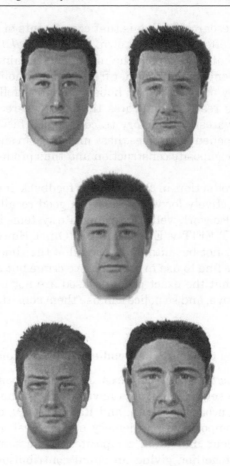

Figure 3.5 Feature-based composites of England footballer, John Terry, created in Frowd *et al.* (2012d, Experiment 2). Composites along the top and bottom rows were constructed by different people from memory. In the centre is the average of these four individual composites, an image known as a morphed composite.

extend to composites from a holistic system (Davis *et al.*, 2010; Valentine *et al.*, 2010). There is also evidence to suggest that a morphed composite should be effective in a police investigation (Frowd, Bruce, Storås, Spick, and Hancock, 2006c).

Police policy in the UK has been revised to accommodate multiple witnesses and morphed composites (in guidelines published by the Association of Chief Police Officers, ACPO, in 2003 and 2009). Previously, the guidelines only permitted one composite to be produced in an investigation, which itself caused the problem of determining which witness would produce the superior composite – of which there is no known reliable test. Now, each witness can work independently to produce an image of the same offender, for the purpose of creating a morph. In evidential terms, a composite image is referred to as an original or *primary* exhibit, to be referred to by the witness should the case go to trial, while a morphed image is a *secondary* exhibit that is created with the aim of enhancing identification (ACPO, 2009). As such, a morphed composite, but *not* any individual composite of which it comprises, may be released in a public appeal for information. The work has proved useful in another way since sometimes crimes are committed at different times but only later linked together (e.g., by DNA), thus enabling production of a morphed composite and a fresh appeal for information. Research also suggests that morphed composites produced by different systems in a police investigation should improve suspect identification (Frowd *et al.*, 2010a).

Nevertheless, criminal investigations usually only involve a single witness and thus a single composite, and so the morphing procedure is not applicable in general. However, there is promising research that has involved (a) one person constructing more than one composite of the same identity (Davis *et al.*, 2010; Frowd *et al.*, 2006b; Valentine *et al.*, 2010), and (b) morphing images taken from different stages in composite construction (Ness, 2003).

Dynamic caricature Another successful tactic (Frowd, *et al.*, 2007c) is to artificially inflate the level of distinctiveness in a composite, to create a caricature, which can improve recognition in much the same way as it can for a facial photograph (e.g., Benson & Perrett, 1994). Caricature is achieved by exaggerating the shape and placement of features with respect to an average. For example, caricaturing will result in a large nose expanding, and close-set eyes being located even closer together (see Figure 3.6).

The research actually found that no single level of caricature was effective for improving composite naming. People differ in the degree of caricature that is a best probe to their memory (Frowd *et al.*, 2007c). The solution is to present a range of caricature levels, from mild to extreme, but also in the opposite direction, making a composite appear more average (anti-caricature). Presented as an animated sequence of 21 frames that repeat every 6 seconds, dynamic caricature is extremely effective regardless of the initial quality of the composite (see YouTube link in case study reference: Glendinning, 2010).

This moving-image format also enhances the performance of morphed composites (an average of two or more individual composites), to yield better naming rates than using either morphing or dynamic

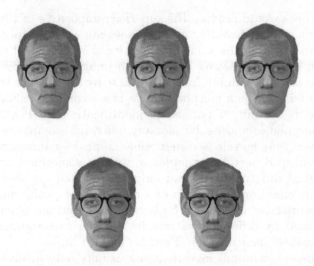

Figure 3.6 Caricaturing feature composite of US actor/director Woody Allen (Frowd *et al.*, 2005b). From left to right, images are at −50%, −25%, 0% (unaltered original composite), +25% and +50% caricature. Positive values exaggerate distinctive shape information, while negative values de-emphasize this information to make the face appear more average.

caricature alone (Frowd, *et al.*, 2012d). This recent research on caricature also reveals that, as we forget detail of facial features (e.g., Ellis *et al.*, 1980), there is a tendency for constructors to create composites with features that are less exaggerated than the target face.

Dynamic caricature is usually implemented as an animated GIF image, a standard internet format, and is effective for a range of systems (feature, sketch and holistic). In a police investigation, it is referred to as a *secondary* exhibit for court purposes, the same as for a morphed composite (ACPO, 2003, 2009). Dynamic caricature has been in police use since 2007 for releasing composites on TV, online newspapers and wanted-persons webpages. For example, it was used to help identify the serial rapist described in the case study.

Image stretching techniques An alternative technique that is also effective for publishing composites in newspapers involves a *physical linear stretch*. Frowd *et al.* (2013a) found that doubling the image height or width substantially improved correct naming (from 30% to 42%). As with morphing, this image technique appears to reduce the appearance of error: best results were found if the H-CI was also employed during composite construction (Frowd *et al.*, 2013b). However, stretched images look distorted and inappropriate for the serious application for which they are used. As illustrated in Figure 3.7, two solutions have emerged: (a) to look at an unaltered (unstretched) composite from the side, to create a *perceptual* rather than a *physical* stretch; and (b) to provide a relevant context to evaluator-witnesses. The latter, perceptual-backdrop image (PBI) format is a practical solution for police work. Both formats are accompanied by appropriate instructions, and were introduced into police use following a press release (Astbury, 2011).

Interactions between methods As discussed above, two recent advancements in the field relate to composite construction: H-CI (vs. CI) and internal-features-first method (vs. external-features blur). A third development relates to composite naming: dynamic caricature and image stretch. Frowd *et al.* (2013b) examined whether these techniques would have an additive effect if they were combined and, if so, what would be the overall performance? Constructors followed the gold-standard procedure and were interviewed 24 hours after viewing a target video using either a face-recall CI or an H-CI; they then constructed a single EvoFIT using either external-features blur or internal-features

(a)   (b)

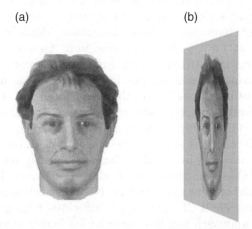

Figure 3.7 Image (a) is a composite of former UK Prime Minister, Tony Blair. To use the perceptual-stretch format, the composite would be shown (to police staff and the public) accompanied by the following written statement: "Viewing the composite sideways may help you to recognise the face". Image (b) is an example of the perceptual-backdrop image (PBI) format applied to the same composite of Blair. The image has been vertically stretched and displayed against a grey perceptual backdrop. Example wording to accompany the image format is: "Viewing the composite as shown should help you to recognise the face".

(a)   (b)   (c)   (d)

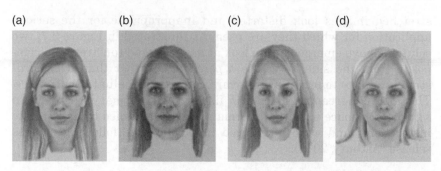

Figure 3.8 Composites produced of EastEnders's character, Roxy Mitchell, in Frowd *et al.* (2013b). Each image was created by a different person 24 hours after having watched a video depicting this character (an unfamiliar target). The study manipulated the interview (face-recall CI and H-CI) and the method used to construct the composite (external-features blur and internal-features-first). Composites were produced (a) using a CI and external-features blur, (b) CI and internal-features-first, (c) H-CI and external-features blur, and (d) H-CI and internal-features-first. Composites were least identifiable in (a) when they were viewed front-on, but most identifiable in (d) when viewed using perceptual stretch.

first (see Figure 3.8). Composite naming was carried out initially from the frontal view, the normal way to observe the face, and then by looking at the composite sideways, the perceptual-stretch technique. It was found that each technique reliably increased identification. Naming was 24% correct for the baseline condition (face-recall CI, blurred external-features construction and front-on naming), which is also very similar to past research, but increased to 74% when all three techniques were used together in the same condition (H-CI, internal-features-first and perceptual-stretch naming). Naming in the latter condition was reliably higher than that predicted by the sum of the main effects. New results suggest that these three developments, when applied in the same way in a modern feature-based system, also produce highly identifiable composites (also that the internal-features-first procedure should only be used with an H-CI: use full-face construction following a face-recall CI). This work indicates both generalizability of this holistic approach and best practice for feature-based systems.

Field Research on Facial Composites

Performance of composites in the real world The effectiveness of composites in the UK has been the subject of internal police audit (e.g., Bennett, 1986). In general, results indicate that suspects are occasionally identified from traditional feature-based composites. EFIT-V and

EvoFIT have also been the subject of formal police audit. The main measure of performance is identification of suspects arising from names put forward (by police staff and the public). For instance, an audit of EFIT-V over an 18-month period and a sample of 1000 composites constructed in police investigations revealed identification of suspects in 40% of cases (Solomon, Gibson, & Maylin, 2012).

EvoFIT was initially audited by three constabularies in the UK, as well as in Romania, over a two-year period from autumn 2007. The crimes ranged from minor theft to sexual assault and violent robbery, although the vast majority related to serious crime. There were a total of 111 witnesses and victims, and their ages ranged from 10 years to the very elderly. Construction interviews were conducted from one day to a month or so after the crime; the mode was two days. Results from Lancashire and Derbyshire constabularies indicated that suspect identification rates (arrests) for EvoFITs were 23% – a level of identification that was considerably higher than from the forces' previous (feature-based) systems (Frowd et al., 2010a). A further field trial with Devon and Cornwall Police and in Romania using a less detailed face recall interview found a higher level of suspect identification, at 40% (Frowd et al., 2011a).

However, there is an issue of ground truth with this type of audit: it is impossible to establish whether the correct suspect was identified. A more valid dependent variable is the number of convictions, since these outcomes involve evidence from a number of sources; they are simply more likely to be correct. The most recent audit (Frowd et al., 2012b) was carried out by Humberside police using EvoFIT and the internal-features-first approach. Suspect identification rates were 60%. However, this assessment also found that 29% of these identifications, or about one-in-six of all composites constructed, led to conviction. Examples are shown in the case study and these published field trials.

IMPLICATIONS FOR POLICY

For practitioners still using the second-generation *feature-based systems*, it is important that individual features are selected in the context of a complete face. This procedure is intrinsic with CD-FIT, E-FIT and PRO-fit, but not for all systems. Further, in cases where face recall is good and the H-CI is administered, best results are obtained when constructing the internal features first (without visible external features) – although this is only available with PRO-fit at present. Practitioners using other systems could consider manually concealing areas of the computer screen to give the same effect. Cognitive interviewing techniques should be used to elicit a free description of the offender's face, and in situations where witnesses have good face recall, the H-CI should be administered. The evidence is that the H-CI facilitates accurate selection of facial features and promotes identifiable composites. Nevertheless, when face recall is sketchy, practitioners should consider using a holistic system (without employing the holistic interview).

For practitioners who use *holistic composite systems*, constructing the face using the internal-features-first technique (without the presence of external features) is superior to construction with the whole face present, and so, ideally, systems should be used in this way. Also, the H-CI should be used whenever possible following good face recall. In addition, there is evidence indicating the benefit of a holistic system for witnesses with a mild intellectual disability (mID). Gawrylowicz, Gabbert, Carson, Lindsay, and Hancock (2012) found that while constructors with mID recalled significantly fewer details of a face than non-mID controls, they produced a more effective composite using EvoFIT than a feature system.

For the three basic methods to construct the face – feature, sketch and holistic – there is good evidence that dynamic caricature is a suitable format to increase composite naming. An animated composite can be produced ergonomically from EvoFIT, EFIT-V and PRO-fit; the caricaturing function within PRO-fit and EvoFIT can be used for sketch composites. Alternatively, practitioners can prepare a perceptual-stretch or perceptual backdrop image composite as illustrated in Figure 3.7. These two recent methods appear to be particularly effective if an H-CI has been administered, and obviously do not require software to create them (although both are standard output formats for EvoFIT).

SUMMARY AND THE FUTURE

Feature-based methods have dominated face construction for decades. They appear to work fairly well when delay to construction is very short, and when a cognitive approach is used to construct the face (context-based feature selection). In contrast, when deployed under normal longer delays, performance remains disappointing. Research has improved their success rate by augmenting the interview, changing the way that witnesses construct the face (internals first), combining composites of the same identity, and presenting composites in such a way to facilitate naming (dynamic caricature and stretch). Feature systems are clearly beneficial to police forces that continue to use this type of technology. However, under UK guidelines (ACPO, 2003, 2009), witnesses who cannot recall an offender's face in detail should not construct a feature-based composite; instead, a holistic system should be used.

Considerable effort has produced a much more effective method to access facial memory. The aim of these holistic systems is for construction to be based upon face recognition ability rather than on face recall, principally via repeated selection and breeding from arrays of whole faces. There are three main holistic systems and, although the research focus has been mainly on EvoFIT, the expectation is that techniques developed for this system will generalize to any other. Face construction is best achieved by witnesses working on internal features before they see external features. As with feature systems, the type of interview administered also impacts upon accuracy of holistic construction, and the H-CI, which recovers featural and configural information, is highly effective. Further, three techniques have facilitated recognition of a finished composite: dynamic caricature, and perceptual or physical image stretch.

Looking to the future, there are indications of how performance could be improved even further. For instance, composites are normally rendered from a front view in two dimensions and, while this may be fine for many crimes, for others there may be benefit for construction at a non-frontal view. An offender's face seen through the side window of a car, for example, may be more accurately reproduced at a view that matches that seen by the witness. Recent research already indicates that construction is not optimal when users are required to mentally rotate the face (Frowd et al., 2014), a principle that applies to recognition of unfamiliar faces (e.g., Liu, Chai, Shan, Honma, & Osada, 2009). Development of a 3D user-defined model is a sensible solution. In fact, images of faces change with viewing distance, and such changes in perception can interfere with unfamiliar face recognition (Liu & Chaudhuri, 2002). A multi-view model should be able to accurately render differences in perspective, so that the image at construction is a better match to the image seen at the crime scene. Therefore, memory should be facilitated by the greater overlap of cues seen that are available at recall (the encoding specificity principle; Tulving & Thompson, 1973). The same principle may be applicable to other factors such as lighting and facial expression. Promising signs are also on the horizon for augmenting the manual sketch method of face production, for example by combining the H-CI with context-based feature selection.

REFERENCES

ACPO (Association of Chief Police Officers) (2003). *National working practices in facial imaging.* Unpublished document.

ACPO (Association of Chief Police Officers) (2009). *Facial Identification Guidance.* Produced by the National Policing Improvement Agency. Retrieved from www.acpo.police.uk/documents/crime/2009/200911CRIFIG01.pdf

Astbury, R. (2011). Another side to fighting crime. *Lancashire Evening Post,* 2 November 2011, pp. 17.

Bennett, P. (1986). Face recall: A police perspective. *Human Learning, 5,* 197–202.

Benson, P.J., & Perrett, D.I. (1994). Visual processing of facial distinctiveness. *Perception, 23,* 75–93.

Berman, G.L., & Cutler, B.L. (1998). The influence of processing instructions at encoding and retrieval on face recognition accuracy. *Psychology, Crime & Law, 4,* 89–106. doi:10.1080/10683169808401751

Bruce, V., Ness, H., Hancock, P.J.B, Newman, C., & Rarity, J. (2002). Four heads are better than one. Combining face composites yields improvements in face likeness. *Journal of Applied Psychology, 87,* 894–902. doi:10.1037/0021-9010.87.5.894

Cabeza, R., & Kato, T. (2000). Features are also important: Contributions of featural and configural processing to face recognition. *Psychological Science, 11,* 429–433. doi:10.1111/1467-9280.00283

Charman, S.D., Gregory, A.H., & Carlucci, M. (2009). Exploring the diagnostic utility of facial composites: Beliefs of guilt can bias perceived similarity between composite and suspect. *Journal of Experimental Psychology: Applied, 15,* 76–90. doi:10.1037/a0014682

Clutterbuck, R., & Johnston, R.A. (2002). Exploring levels of face familiarity by using an indirect face-matching measure. *Perception, 31,* 985–994.

Davies, G.M. (1983). Forensic face recall: the role of visual and verbal information. In S.M.A. Lloyd-Bostock, & B.R. Clifford (Eds.), *Evaluating Witness Evidence* (pp. 103–123). Chichester: John Wiley & Sons, Ltd.

Davies, G.M., Shepherd, J.W., & Ellis, H.D. (1978). Remembering faces: Acknowledging our limitations. *Journal of Forensic Science, 18,* 19–24.

Davis, J.P., Gibson, S., & Solomon, C. (2014). The positive influence of creating a holistic facial composite on video lineup identification. *Applied Cognitive Psychology, 28,* 634–639. doi:10.1002/acp.3045

Davis, J.P., Sulley, L. Solomon, C. & Gibson, S. (2010). A comparison of individual and morphed facial composites created using different systems. In G. Howells, K. Sirlantzis, A. Stoica, T. Huntsberger, & A.T. Arslan (Eds.), *2010 IEEE International Conference on Emerging Security Technologies* (pp. 56–60). doi:10.1109/EST.2010.29

Deffenbacher, K.A., Bornstein, G.H., McGorty, E.K., & Penrod, S.D. (2008). Forgetting the once-seen face: Estimating the strength of an eyewitness's memory representation. *Journal of Experimental Psychology: Applied, 14,* 139–150. doi:10.1037/1076-898X.14.2.139

Ellis, H.D., Davies, G.M., & Shepherd, J.W. (1978a). A critical examination of the photofit system for recalling faces. *Ergonomics, 21,* 297–307.

Ellis, H.D., Davies, G.M., & Shepherd, J.W. (1978b). Remembering pictures of real and 'unreal' faces: Some practical and theoretical considerations. *British Journal of Psychology, 69,* 467–474.

Ellis, H.D., Shepherd, J.W., & Davies, G.M. (1975). An investigation of the use of Photofit for recalling faces. *British Journal of Psychology, 66,* 29–37.

Ellis, H.D., Shepherd, J.W., & Davies, G.M. (1979). Identification of familiar and unfamiliar faces from internal and external features: Some implications for theories of face recognition. *Perception, 8,* 431–439.

Ellis, H.D., Shepherd, J.W., & Davies, G.M. (1980). The deterioration of verbal descriptions of faces over different delay intervals. *Journal of Police Science and Administration, 8,* 101–106.

Frowd, C.D. (2012). Facial recall and computer composites. In C. Wilkinson, & C. Rynn (Eds.), *Craniofacial Identification* (pp. 42–56). New York: Cambridge University Press.

Frowd, C.D., Bruce, V., McIntyre, A., & Hancock, P.J.B. (2007a). The relative importance of external and internal features of facial composites. *British Journal of Psychology, 98,* 61–77. doi:10.1348/000712606X104481

Frowd, C.D., Bruce, V., McIntyre, A., Ross, D., & Hancock, P.J.B. (2006a). Adding holistic dimensions to a facial composite system. *Proceedings of the Seventh International Conference on Automatic Face and Gesture Recognition* (pp. 183–188). Los Alamitos, CA.

Frowd, C.D., Bruce, V., Ness, H., Bowie, L., Thomson-Bogner, C., Paterson, J., McIntyre, A., & Hancock, P.J.B. (2007b). Parallel approaches to composite production. *Ergonomics, 50,* 562–585. doi:10.1080/00140130601154855

Frowd, C.D., Bruce, V., Plenderleith, Y., & Hancock, P.J.B. (2006b). Improving target identification using pairs of composite faces constructed by the same person. *IEE Conference on Crime and Security* (pp. 386–395). London: IET.

Frowd, C.D., Bruce, V., Ross, D., McIntyre, A., & Hancock, P.J.B. (2007c). An application of caricature: how to improve the recognition of facial composites. *Visual Cognition, 15,* 1–31. doi:10.1080/13506280601058951.

Frowd, C.D., Bruce, V., Smith, A., & Hancock, P.J.B. (2008a). Improving the quality of facial composites using a holistic cognitive interview. *Journal of Experimental Psychology: Applied, 14,* 276–287. doi:10.1037/1076-898X.14.3.276

Frowd, C.D., Bruce, V., Storås, K., Spick, P., & Hancock, P.J.B. (2006c). An evaluation of morphed composites constructed in a criminal investigation. *Proceedings of the 16th Conference of the European Association of Psychology and Law* (pp. 59–66). London: IP-PA Publishing.

Frowd, C.D., Carson, D., Ness, H., McQuiston, D., Richardson, J., Baldwin, H., & Hancock, P.J.B. (2005a). Contemporary composite techniques: The impact of a forensically-relevant target delay. *Legal and Criminological Psychology, 10,* 63–81. doi:10.1348/135532504X15358

Frowd, C.D., Carson, D., Ness, H., Richardson, J., Morrison, L., McLanaghan, S., & Hancock, P.J.B. (2005b). A forensically valid comparison of facial composite systems. *Psychology, Crime & Law, 11,* 33–52. doi:10.1080/1068316030 10001634313

Frowd, C.D., & Fields, S. (2011). Verbalisation effects in facial composite production. *Psychology, Crime & Law, 17,* 731–744. doi:10.1080/10683161003623264

Frowd, C.D., Hancock, P.J.B., Bruce, V., McIntyre, A., Pitchford, M., Atkins, R., … Sendrea, G. (2010a). Giving crime the 'evo': catching criminals using EvoFIT facial composites. In G. Howells, K. Sirlantzis, A. Stoica, T. Huntsberger, & A.T. Arslan (Eds.), *2010 IEEE International Conference on Emerging Security Technologies* (pp. 36–43).

Frowd, C.D., Hancock, P.J.B., Bruce, V., Skelton, F.C., Atherton, C., Nelson, L., ... Sendrea, G. (2011a). Catching more offenders with EvoFIT facial composites: lab research and police field trials. *Global Journal of Human Social Science*, *11*, 46–58.

Frowd, C.D., Hancock, P.J.B., & Carson, D. (2004). EvoFIT: A holistic, evolutionary facial imaging technique for creating composites. *ACM Transactions on Applied Psychology (TAP)*, *1*, 1–21.

Frowd, C.D., Jones, S., Forarella, C., Skelton, F.C., Fields, S., Williams, A., ... Hancock, P.J.B. (2013a). Configural and featural information in facial-composite images. *Science & Justice*. doi:10.1016/j.scijus.2013.11.001.

Frowd, C.D., McQuiston-Surrett, D., Anandaciva, S., Ireland, C.E., & Hancock, P.J.B. (2007d). An evaluation of US systems for facial composite production. *Ergonomics*, *50*, 1987–1998. doi:10.1080/00140130701523611

Frowd, C.D., McQuiston-Surrett, D., Kirkland, I., & Hancock, P.J.B. (2005c). The process of facial composite production. In A. Czerederecka, T. Jaskiewicz-Obydzinska, R. Roesch, and J. Wojcikiewicz (Eds.), *Forensic Psychology and Law* (pp. 140–152). Krakow: Institute of Forensic Research Publishers.

Frowd, C.D., Nelson, L., Skelton, F.C., Noyce, R., Atkins, R., Heard, P., ... Hancock, P.J.B. (2012a). Interviewing techniques for Darwinian facial composite systems. *Applied Cognitive Psychology*, *26*, 576–584. doi:10.1002/acp.2829

Frowd, C.D., Park, J., McIntyre, A., Bruce, V., Pitchford, M., Fields, S., Kenirons, M., & Hancock, P.J.B. (2008b). Effecting an improvement to the fitness function. How to evolve a more identifiable face. In A. Stoica, T. Arslan, D. Howard, T. Higuchi, & A. El-Rayis (Eds.), *2008 ECSIS Symposium on Bio-inspired, Learning, and Intelligent Systems for Security* (pp. 3–10). NJ: CPS (Edinburgh).

Frowd, C.D., Pitchford, M., Bruce, V., Jackson, S., Hepton, G., Greenall, M., McIntyre, A., & Hancock, P.J.B. (2010b). The psychology of face construction: giving evolution a helping hand. *Applied Cognitive Psychology, 25,* 195–203. doi:10.1002/acp.1662

Frowd, C.D., Pitchford, M., Skelton, F., Petkovic, A., Prosser, C., & Coates, B. (2012b). Catching even more offenders with EvoFIT facial composites. In A. Stoica, D. Zarzhitsky, G. Howells, C. Frowd, K. McDonald-Maier, A. Erdogan, and T. Arslan (Eds.), IEEE *Proceedings of 2012 Third International Conference on Emerging Security Technologies* (pp. 20–26). doi:10.1109/EST.2012.26

Frowd, C.D., Skelton, F.C., Atherton, C., Pitchford, M., Bruce, V., Atkins, R., ... Hancock, P.J.B. (2012c). Understanding the multi-frame caricature advantage for recognising facial composites. *Visual Cognition*, *20*, 1215–1241. doi:10.1080/13506285.2012.743936

Frowd, C.D., Skelton F., Atherton, C., Pitchford, M., Hepton, G., Holden, L., McIntyre, A., & Hancock, P.J.B. (2012d). Recovering faces from memory: the distracting influence of external facial features. *Journal of Experimental Psychology: Applied, 18,* 224–238. doi:10.1037/a0027393

Frowd, C.D., Skelton, F., Butt, N., Hassan, A., & Fields, S. (2011b). Familiarity effects in the construction of facial-composite images using modern software systems. *Ergonomics*, *54*, 1147–1158. doi:10.1080/00140139.2011.623328

Frowd, C.D., Skelton F., Hepton, G., Holden, L., Minahil, S., Pitchford, M., ... Hancock, P.J.B. (2013b). Whole-face procedures for recovering facial images from memory. *Science & Justice*, *53*, 89–97. doi:10.1016/j.scijus.2012.12.004

Frowd, C.D., White, D., Kemp, R.I., Jenkins, R., Nawaz, K., & Herold, K. (2014). Constructing faces from memory: the impact of image likeness and prototypical representations. *Journal of Forensic Practice, 16*, 243–256.

Gawrylowicz, J., Gabbert, F., Carson, D., Lindsay, W.R. & Hancock, P.J.B. (2012). Holistic versus featural facial composite systems for people with mild intellectual disabilities. *Applied Cognitive Psychology, 26*, 716–720. doi:10.1002/acp.2850

Gibson, S.J., Solomon, C.J., Maylin, M.I.S., & Clark, C. (2009). New methodology in facial composite construction: from theory to practice. *International Journal of Electronic Security and Digital Forensics, 2*, 156–168. doi:10.1504/IJESDF.2009.024900

Glendinning, A. (2010). Face of man wanted over south Manchester rapes. *Manchester Evening News,* 13 October 2010. Retrieved from http://www.manchestereveningnews.co.uk/news/local-news/face-of-man-wanted-over-south-900960. Direct YouTube Link: http://www.youtube.com/watch?v=sotAHdZW3uw

Goldberg, D.E. (1989). *Genetic Algorithms in Search, Optimization, and Machine Learning*. Boston, MA: Addison-Wesley.

Hancock, P.J.B., Bruce, V., & Burton, A.M. (1997). Testing principal component representations for faces. In J.A. Bullinaria, D.W. Glasspool, & G. Houghton (Eds.), *Proceedings of 4th Neural Computation and Psychology Workshop* (pp. 84–97). London: Springer-Verlag.

Hasel, L., & Wells, G.L. (2007). Catching the bad guy: Morphing composite faces helps. *Law and Human Behavior, 31*, 193–207. doi:10.1007/s10979-006-9007-2

Laughery, K., & Fowler, R. (1980). Sketch artist and identikit procedures for generating facial images. *Journal of Applied Psychology, 65,* 307–316.

Liu, C.H., Chai, X., Shan, S., Honma, M., & Osada, Y. (2009). Synthesized views can improve face recognition. *Applied Cognitive Psychology, 23*, 987–998. doi:10.1002/acp.1521

Liu, C.H., & Chaudhuri, A. (2002). The effect of linear perspective on face recognition. *Perception, 31*, 19–20. doi:10.1068/v020084

MacLin, M.K. (2002). The effects of exemplar and prototype descriptors on verbal overshadowing. *Applied Cognitive Psychology, 16*, 929–936. doi:10.1002/acp.923

McQuiston-Surrett, D., Topp, L.D., & Malpass, R.S. (2006). Use of facial composite systems in U.S. law enforcement agencies. *Psychology, Crime and Law, 12*, 505–517. doi:10.1080/10683160500254904

Meissner, C.A., & Brigham, J.C. (2001). A meta-analysis of the verbal overshadowing effect in face identification. *Applied Cognitive Psychology, 15,* 603–616. doi:10.1002/acp.728

Narain, J. (2011). The changing face of crime: Powerful new Evo-fit technology helps catch rapist. *Daily Mail,* 27 July 2011. Retrieved from http://www.dailymail.co.uk/news/article-2019031/Evo-fit-New-facial-identification-technology-helps-catch-rapist-Asim-Javed.html#ixzz2fVb8YPwE

Ness, H. (2003). *Improving facial composites produced by eyewitnesses* (Unpublished PhD thesis). University of Stirling.

Shapiro, P.N., & Penrod, S.D. (1986). Meta-analysis of facial identification rates. *Psychological Bulletin, 100,* 139–156.

Sirovich, L., & Kirby, M. (1987). Low-dimensional procedure for the characterization of human faces. *Journal of the Optical Society of America, 4,* 519–524.

Solomon, C., Gibson, S., & Maylin, M. (2012). Generation of facial composites for criminal investigations. In C. Wilkinson, & C. Rynn (Eds.), *Craniofacial Identification* (pp. 67–77). Cambridge: Cambridge University Press.

Solomon, C., Gibson, S., & Mist, J.M. (2013). Interactive evolutionary generation of facial composites for locating suspects in criminal investigations.
Applied Soft Computing, 7, 3298–3306. doi:10.1016/j.asoc.2013.02.010

Tanaka, J.W., & Farah, M.J. (1993). Parts and wholes in face recognition.
*Quarterly Journal of Experimental Psychology: Human Experimental
Psychology*, 46A, 225–245.

Tanaka, J.W., & Sengco, J.A. (1997). Features and their configuration in face
recognition. *Memory & Cognition*, 25, 583–592.

Tredoux, C.G., Nunez, D.T., Oxtoby, O., & Prag, B. (2006). An evaluation of ID:
an eigenface based construction system. *South African Computer Journal*,
37, 1–9.

Tulving, E., & Thompson, D.M. (1973). Encoding specificity and retrieval processes in episodic memory. *Psychological Review*, 80, 352–373.

Valentine, T., Davis, J.P., Thorner, K., Solomon, C., & Gibson, S. (2010). Evolving
and combining facial composites: Between-witness and within-witness
morphs compared. *Journal of Experimental Psychology: Applied*, 16, 72–86.
doi:10.1037/a0018801

Wells, G.L., Charman, S.D., & Olson, E.A. (2005). Building face composites can
harm lineup identification performance. *Journal of Experimental Psychology:
Applied*, 11, 147– 156. doi:10.1037/1076-898X.11.3.147

4

Searching for Suspects: Mugshot Files and Showups (Street Identifications)

VICTORIA Z. LAWSON AND JENNIFER E. DYSART

In the immediate aftermath of a crime, law enforcement may not have evidence to suggest a particular suspect; thus, eyewitnesses may be used for the process of finding suspects. While the creation of facial composites may form part of this process (see Chapter 3), the eyewitness may also be asked to search photographs of prior offenders (i.e., a mugshot search) or they may be presented with potential suspects singly in a showup either live (termed a "street identification" in the UK) or in a single photograph. While a vast amount of research has been conducted on how decisions are made in lineups and what factors influence lineup identification decisions, there is comparatively little research on either mugshots or showups as standalone procedures.

MUGSHOTS

Mugshot searches are commonly used by law enforcement agencies in the US (Police Executive Research Forum [PERF], 2013) and the UK (Davis, Valentine, Memon, & Roberts, 2015). Indeed, 28.8% of agencies

Forensic Facial Identification: Theory and Practice of Identification from Eyewitnesses, Composites and CCTV, First Edition. Edited by Tim Valentine and Josh P. Davis.
© 2015 John Wiley & Sons, Ltd. Published 2015 by John Wiley & Sons, Ltd.

Case study: Mugshot identification

On June 23, 1984, a 25-year-old woman was leaving a convenience store in New York when she was accosted by an unknown assailant. After threatening her with a box cutter, he drove off with her and raped her first in a park and then later a second time in an abandoned building. To prevent her from identifying him, he slashed her face with the box cutter, leaving her blind in one eye. While recovering in the hospital, she looked through over 200 mugshots and eventually picked out Alan Newton's photograph. Police then placed Newton in a live lineup where he was identified a second time, and then again in court. Although he had an alibi, Newton was convicted at trial. It was not until 2006 that Newton was exonerated and freed due to DNA evidence showing that he had not been the victim's attacker. Because he had the misfortune of having his photograph included in a mugshot search, Newton wrongfully served over 21 years in prison (for more details see Innocence Project, ND; *Newton v. City of New York*, 2009; Williams, 2006).

Case study: Showup identification

On March 12, 1981, a white nurse was physically assaulted and raped by a black man after her car broke down on a side road in Louisiana. After the attack, the victim escaped and found a police officer, who took her to a nearby hospital. When the officer returned to the scene of the crime, he encountered Clyde Charles, a black man whom he had seen hitchhiking in the area an hour before the rape and who was wearing clothing similar to that described by the victim. The officer arrested him and brought him to the hospital to be viewed by the victim. Despite the fact that he did not match her initial description, the victim positively identified him as her attacker. Charles was convicted and sentenced to life in prison. Charles sought DNA testing, which eventually proved conclusively that he was not the nurse's assailant. He was released in December 1999 after spending 18 years in prison for a crime he did not commit (for more details, see Flynn, 2003; Frontline, ND; Innocence Project, ND; *State v. Charles*, 1987).

recently surveyed in the US reported using mugshot searches (PERF, 2013), while mugshot searches were used to try to identify suspects in 11.2% of robberies in several districts surveyed in England (35.6% of incidents in which an identification procedure was conducted; Davis *et al.*, 2015). However, there is relatively little research on the factors affecting the effectiveness of mugshot searches and the accuracy of mugshot selections, and most research on mugshots focuses on their use as one of multiple procedures (see, for instance, Deffenbacher, Bornstein, & Penrod, 2006). This dearth of research on the mugshot procedure may be due to an assumption that mugshot searches are similar to photo lineups; however, they are quite different procedures (McAllister, 2007). They are used for different purposes – finding a suspect versus identifying a suspect – and may be accompanied by substantially different expectations. In a mugshot search, there may be no great expectation that the perpetrator will be present at all, while in a photo lineup, an eyewitness generally knows that there is a police suspect and that the suspect is included in the array. Additionally, eyewitnesses may view hundreds of photographs in any given mugshot search, while a much smaller number (generally 6–12) is included in a photo lineup. This section on mugshot searching will review the scientific research on the procedural issues related to mugshot viewing, including the number of photographs viewed, and how they are presented and sorted. The effects of mugshot viewing on subsequent identification accuracy will be discussed at the end of the chapter along with showups, as the research relating to multiple identification procedures is relevant to both procedures. Finally, we will also address the utilization of mugshot searches (and showups) as investigative techniques in criminal cases.

Procedural Issues with Mugshots

Number of mugshots viewed Intuitively, the number of mugshots included in a mugshot search would be expected to have an impact on the likelihood of a successful search, and indeed this appears to be the case. Research has demonstrated that the number of photographs that eyewitnesses view prior to viewing the target mugshot influences the likelihood that they will correctly select the target's photograph (Laughery, Alexander, & Lane, 1971; Lindsay, Nosworthy, Martin, & Martynuck, 1994). In one of the earliest studies to examine the effect of the number of mugshots displayed, Laughery *et al.* (1971) presented participants with 150 mugshots in which the target was placed either in position 40 or position 140, finding that participants were more likely to make an accurate decision when the target was in the earlier position. Lindsay *et al.* (1994) staged a theft and then presented participants with 727 mugshots in which the perpetrator was shown after 100, 300, 500, or 700 photographs. Participants were significantly more likely to choose the perpetrator's photograph when it was viewed after 100 photographs than when it was viewed after 500 or 700 photographs.

Eyewitnesses may be influenced not only by the size of the mugshot books, but additionally by how many mugshots are shown at one time. Stewart and McAllister (2001) compared eyewitness performance when mugshots were presented one at a time to when 12 photographs were included on each page. While no significant difference was found in correct identification rates, the percentage of innocent suspects who were falsely identified was higher when photographs were presented singly than when they were presented in a group. Another study (Thompson, Zamojski, & Colangelo, 2010) similarly found the false identification rate to be higher when three photographs were presented on a page as compared to six or 12, but found no significant difference in the correct identification rate. McAllister, Michel, Tarcza, Fitzmorris, and Nguyen (2008) also found a lower false identification rate when 12 photographs versus one photograph were included on each page. These false identification rates from mugshot searching stand in contrast to lineup research showing that presenting lineup members one at a time reduces false identifications (Steblay, Dysart, & Wells, 2011; but see Chapter 6), thus further highlighting how mugshot and lineup research do not fully correspond.

Use of computerized mugshots Technology allows for the use of computerized mugshot searching, and a recent national survey of US law enforcement practices suggests that it is now more common than showing books/albums to witnesses, with 53.3% of agencies using computerized searches (PERF, 2013). This technique may be superior to using physical photographs because it allows for more efficient pruning of the mugshots shown to eyewitnesses (e.g., by allowing input of descriptors, restricting the pool to non-incarcerated offenders; Ellis, Shepherd, Shepherd, Flin, & Davies, 1989; McAllister, Bearden, Kohlmaier, & Warner, 1997). Another potential advantage of using computerized mugshot searches is that they permit the inclusion of video clips in addition to static photographs (McAllister et al., 1997). McAllister and colleagues (McAllister et al., 1997; McAllister, Blair, Cerone, & Laurent, 2000; McAllister, Stewart, & Loveland, 2003) conducted a series of experiments that compared the effectiveness of static photographs to the use of computerized mug books. Across three studies, they found that computerized mug books that included dynamic cues (e.g., voice, movement) decreased the false alarm rate. The effect on correct identifications was less clear, with two studies finding similar correct identification rates with static and dynamic (i.e., video) mug books

(McAllister *et al.*, 1997, 2000) and one finding a lower correct identification rate with dynamic mug books (McAllister *et al.*, 2003). It should also be noted that the use of dynamic mugshot searching requires a video to be taken of suspects upon arrest, a practice that consumes additional resources and is not commonly done in the US.

Mug book pruning and sorting One of the advantages of using computerized mugshots is the increased ease with which specific mugshots can be chosen for a search. In fact, the 2013 PERF survey of law enforcement agencies found that 41.5% of agencies sort mugshot searches by age, 56.7% sort by race, and 61.4% sort by gender. Not surprisingly, researchers have examined the effects of pruning or sorting mugshots based on the perpetrator's description (Laughery, Fessler, Lenorovitz, & Yoblick, 1974; Levi, Jungman, Ginton, Aperman, & Noble, 1995; Lindsay *et al.*, 1994; McAllister *et al.*, 2003). However, there is some evidence that increasing the homogeneity of the photographs to be searched may in fact harm eyewitness performance. Lindsay *et al.* (1994) compared the use of a set of mugshots that had been selected based on similarity to the target with a set of mugshots that had been randomly selected. The results showed that increasing the similarity of the photographs increased the false alarm rate: when the photographs in the mugshot search were more similar to the target, they were more likely to be mistakenly selected from the mug book. Lindsay *et al.* also found that correct identifications of the perpetrator from a subsequent lineup were considerably lower when highly similar mugshots were used in the search task. Laughery *et al.* (1974) manipulated the extent to which the mugshots were similar to the target person and the manner in which they were determined to be similar to the target face: the number of times they were mistakenly identified in a prior study, the extent to which they matched nine basic descriptors, and direct similarity ratings. They found that regardless of how the mugshots were selected, an increase in the similarity of the mugshots resulted in reduced selection accuracy.

SHOWUPS

The use of a showup procedure, where one suspect is presented to a witness, may also be part of the initial stages of an investigation. Here a person may become a suspect simply because he is found in the vicinity of the crime and matches the description provided by the eyewitness. In the UK, it is estimated that showup identifications result in the charging or cautioning of more than 20,000 suspects each year

(Valentine, Davis, Memon, & Roberts, 2012). Further, a recent survey of robberies occurring in several districts in England found that showups were conducted in 22.7% of cases – a full 72% of those crimes in which an identification procedure was conducted (Davis *et al.*, 2015). In the US, archival analyses suggest that showups comprise between 30% and 77% of the identification procedures used in various jurisdictions (Behrman & Davey, 2001; Gonzalez, Ellsworth, & Pembroke, 1993; McQuiston & Malpass, 2001). Although there are exceptions, showups are generally conducted soon after the crime, before law enforcement has enough information to arrest a potential suspect. Thus, showups theoretically serve dual purposes: to quickly exonerate the innocent and to quickly remove a criminal from the streets. Given these facts, it is somewhat surprising that approximately 77% of US agencies who responded to the PERF (2013) survey have no written policy on the use of showups.

A major concern with the showup procedure is its inherent suggestiveness: because only one person is presented to the eyewitness, it is obvious who the police suspect is. Further, the fact that the suspect may be in police custody during a showup may add to the suggestiveness of the procedure. Despite the inherent suggestiveness, however, the US Supreme Court has ruled that showups are not prohibited (e.g., *Simmons v. United States*, 1968; *Stovall v. Denno*, 1967). While they are also not prohibited in England and Wales, current codes of practice limit the circumstances under which showups can be used (Police and Criminal Evidence Act [PACE], 1984, Codes of Practice, 2011, Code D). If enough information exists to arrest a suspect, a lineup must be conducted instead; further, when multiple eyewitnesses exist, once one eyewitness has identified a suspect in a showup, any identification procedures with other eyewitnesses must take the form of a lineup.

Comparing Showups to Lineups

As with mugshots, it is not clear to what extent the research on lineups applies to showups. In addition to the issue of greater suggestiveness in the showup, the decision process may be quite different in the two procedures. A traditional simultaneous lineup allows for the use of relative judgments, wherein a witness can compare the lineup members to each other (Wells, 1984); such a process is not possible in showups, where there are no fillers for comparison. Instead, eyewitnesses must compare the suspect to their own memory of the perpetrator, an absolute judgment strategy thought to be similar to that used in a sequential lineup (where lineup members are presented one at a time; Lindsay & Wells, 1985). However, even in a sequential lineup, the knowledge that more than one person will be viewed could be expected to influence the manner in which an eyewitness approaches the procedure. Additionally, the visual behaviour of eyewitnesses presented with a face as part of a showup and as part of a sequential lineup has been found to differ, with more attention paid to internal features in a showup (Flowe, 2011).

Given the increased suggestiveness of showups, it is generally believed that showups are associated with reduced accuracy (Kassin, Tubb, Hosch, & Memon, 2001); however, the results of individual studies have been mixed in terms of whether the showup or the lineup results in greater identification accuracy. Some studies do report that showups result in lower rates of accuracy (Lindsay, Pozzulo, Craig, Lee, & Corber, 1997; Wagenaar & Veefkind, 1992; Yarmey, Yarmey, & Yarmey, 1994, 1996). By contrast, other studies report no or inconsistent differences between the two (Dekle, Beal, Elliott, & Hunnycutt, 1996; Gonzalez *et al.*, 1993; Valentine *et al.*, 2012), and some studies report that under certain circumstances, showups may actually lead to greater overall accuracy (Beal, Schmitt, & Dekle, 1995; Dekle, 1997; Flowe, 2011).

A meta-analysis examining the showup procedure conducted by Steblay, Dysart, Fulero, and Lindsay (2003) synthesized the research findings comparing showups to lineups, and found that showups result in a significantly greater percentage of correct identification decisions overall (collapsed over target-present and target-absent conditions) at 69% correct, compared with lineups at 51% correct. It is likely that this result is due at least in part to higher rates of choosing in lineups (54%) compared with showups (27%). In target-present conditions, rates of choosing were 71% in lineups and 46% in showups, while in target-absent conditions, rates of choosing were 43% in lineups and 15% in showups.

Although the percentage of incorrect identifications was smaller in showups, 100% of these decisions represent the false identification of an innocent suspect. In a lineup, some protection is afforded for an innocent suspect in the form of the other lineup members (i.e., fillers). Identification of one of these individuals is a known error, and thus could be considered less harmful from a legal standpoint. Steblay *et al.* (2003) found that when filler identifications were taken into account, showups and lineups had similar false identification rates (15% vs. 16%, respectively). Further, in studies that designated an innocent suspect, the false identification of this suspect was higher in showups (23%) than in lineups (10%). It should be noted here, however, that the majority of studies in the meta-analysis (and studies on showups in general) have not attempted to replicate the suggestive circumstances that are likely to accompany a showup in actual police practice (e.g., live procedure with suspect in handcuffs).

It is not clear to what extent the rates of choosing found in the meta-analysis reflect those found in real cases. One early archival showup study (Gonzalez *et al.*, 1993, experiment 3), reported similar choosing rates to the 2003 meta-analysis (22%). However, Behrman and Davey's (2001) archival study found that 76% of eyewitnesses viewing showups made an identification, compared with 48% of those viewing lineups. In fact, live showups produced the highest rate of identification of all procedures examined in their study. But as with all archival studies, it must be understood that researchers can only report information that was recorded by law enforcement and included in the case file. Thus, it is unknown how many "negative" (rejection) showups were conducted but not recorded. The data from the PERF (2013) survey support this conclusion, as nearly 31% of agencies do not report negative (non-identification) results from showups. Furthermore, the base rate of guilt in archival studies is unknown; however, it is of note that Behrman and Davey found similarly high choosing rates whether no additional incriminating evidence or substantial incriminating evidence against the suspect existed.

Procedural Issues with Showups

Mode of presentation One factor that may account for differences in choosing rates in the meta-analysis (Steblay *et al.*, 2003) and the archival study (Behrman & Davey, 2001) is the mode of showup presentation, which may affect both accuracy and choosing rates. Most studies included in the meta-analysis used photographic showups (Steblay *et al.*, 2003). However, the use of photographic showups is prohibited in England and Wales (Valentine *et al.*, 2012), and although photographic showups are used in the US, the majority of showups in the US are presented live (Behrman & Davey, 2001; Gonzalez *et al.*, 1993).

Although the findings have not been entirely consistent, rates of choosing in studies using live showups have generally been higher than those found in the meta-analysis (Gonzalez *et al.*, 1993; Smith, Leach, & Cutler, 2013; Steblay *et al.*, 2003; Valentine *et al.*, 2012; Yarmey *et al.*, 1996). Smith *et al.* (2013) found considerably higher choosing rates in their study using live showups; even when other potentially biasing conditions were not present, choosing rates were 69% in target-present conditions and 67% in target-absent conditions, an alarmingly high false identification rate. Yarmey *et al.* (1996) found choosing rates ranging from 53–77% in target-present conditions and 10–49% in target-absent conditions when an innocent suspect of similar appearance to the target was used.

Across four experiments, Valentine *et al.* (2012) found rates of choosing from live showups that ranged from 46–80% in target-present conditions and 4–36% in target-absent conditions; however, the low end of the choosing rates in target-absent conditions may have been anomalous: choosing rates were similarly low across all types of procedure in these experiments. Valentine *et al.* (2012) also compared live and video showups with inconsistent results. In one experiment they found that overall choosing rates were higher with video (79.2%) than live showups (51.1%). This difference seemed to result from an increase in choosing in target-present conditions; as a result, accuracy was higher in video than live showup conditions even though it did not differ in target-absent conditions. However, in a second experiment using only target-present conditions, choosing rates were somewhat lower with video (65.5%) than live showups (79.6%), although this difference was not significant. Given that video lineups are now the identification method of choice in the UK (Horry, Memon, Wright, & Milne, 2012), Valentine *et al.* also compared live and video showups to video lineups to rule out the potential confounding influence of presentation method, but found inconsistent results.

Instructions to witnesses The decision options provided to the eyewitness may also affect accuracy. Weber and Perfect (2012) investigated whether the inclusion of an implicit or explicit "don't know" option would increase showup accuracy. Presumably, allowing eyewitnesses to say they did not know whether the suspect was the perpetrator would discourage uncertain eyewitnesses from making definite identification decisions and reduce the number of identifications – both correct and false – that were the result of guessing. Weber and Perfect compared three different response options: forced report, explicit free report, and spontaneous free report. Eyewitnesses in this study were extremely unlikely to spontaneously say that they did not know whether the suspect was the perpetrator – in fact only 2% did so – and, in the absence of an explicit "don't know" response option, were quite likely to make an identification decision. By contrast, 19% of eyewitnesses said they did not know when provided with the explicit "don't know" option, resulting in significantly increased accuracy but without reducing the number of correct decisions.

Clothing bias Although presenting the suspect in the same or similar clothing to that worn by the perpetrator has been shown to affect identification decisions in other types of identification procedures (Lindsay, Lea, Nosworthy, *et al.*, 1991; Lindsay *et al.*, 1994; Lindsay, Wallbridge, & Drennan, 1987), clothing bias is of particular concern with showups (e.g., Dysart, Lindsay, & Dupuis, 2006). Showups generally occur soon after the crime, when the police first find someone matching the physical and/or clothing description that the witness has given. Witness descriptions are frequently vague and a large percentage of the description information provided by eyewitnesses may be about clothing (see, for instance, Meissner, Sporer, & Schooler, 2007; van Koppen & Lochun, 1997). Additionally, eyewitnesses may rely more heavily on clothing cues in making their identification decision when the crime and the identification procedure are temporally near to one another, as the probability of the perpetrator having changed his or her clothes is greatly reduced.

Several studies have looked at clothing bias with showups. Yarmey *et al.* (1996) examined identification rates from live showups using similar or different clothing between target viewing and suspect presentation. Similar to findings with lineups and mugshots (Lindsay *et al.*, 1987, 1994), clothing was not found to have an effect on the rate of correct identifications in target-present conditions. For innocent suspects deemed similar to the target, witnesses were less accurate (i.e., more likely to make a false identification) when the innocent suspects were wearing clothing similar to that worn by the target. When the innocent suspect was dissimilar to the target in appearance, rejection rates were high regardless of clothing.

Dysart *et al.* (2006) further investigated the effects of clothing bias on the accuracy of eyewitness identifications in showups. The researchers presented innocent suspects who were either high or low in similarity to the target to employees in various shopping mall stores. In addition to varying whether the same or different clothing was worn at initial viewing and identification, the researchers varied the distinctiveness of the clothing and whether distinct clothing was identical or merely similar to the clothing worn by the target. As in the earlier studies on clothing bias (Lindsay *et al.*, 1987, 1994; Yarmey *et al.*, 1996), the rates of correct identification of the target were unaffected by the clothing worn at the time of the crime and during the identification procedure. There was also no impact of clothing on false identifications when the clothing that had been worn by the target was considered common (a button-up dress shirt). When the target had worn distinct clothing (a Harley-Davidson t-shirt), however, significant effects of clothing were found. The rate of false identifications increased significantly for both the high and low similarity innocent suspects when they wore either identical or similar (distinct) clothing to the clothing that had been worn by the target. The clothing worn at the time of initial viewing may also be important: Valentine *et al.* (2012) found that an innocent bystander (a confederate who had been present at the time of their staged event) was more likely to be subsequently misidentified when he had been wearing distinctive clothing at the time of the incident than when he had been wearing plain clothing. Contrary to what might be expected, accuracy was not affected by whether he was also wearing the distinctive or plain clothing at the time of the showup; Lawson and Dysart (2014) argued that distinctiveness was situationally dependent, given that even quite average clothing might be seen as distinctive in certain contexts (e.g., jeans at the opera). Thus, they investigated whether the extent to which clothing was uniquely identifiable, as opposed to "distinctive", determined whether a clothing effect was found. Confederates in their study wore a generic black hooded sweatshirt, made more uniquely identifiable by two colour patches placed on the chest area. In contrast to the prior studies, they found that presenting the suspect in the same uniquely identifiable clothing worn by the perpetrator increased choosing rates in both target-present and target-absent conditions – increasing both correct and false identification rates.

Presence of stolen property Smith *et al.* (2013) argued that a suspect may be detained and presented in a showup not only because he (or his clothing) resembles the eyewitness' description, but also (at least in the case of crimes involving theft) because he may be observed in the possession of items resembling those stolen during the crime. The presence of a stolen item would presumably increase suggestiveness, but Smith *et al.* suggested that it could also increase accuracy by serving as a contextual cue. According to the encoding specificity principle (Tulving & Thomson, 1973), the more the context at the time of retrieval matches the context at the time of encoding, the better memory will be; applied to an identification scenario, the more the context at the time of identification matches the context at the time of the initial viewing of the perpetrator (i.e., during the crime), the more accurate the eyewitness will be. With this in mind, Smith *et al.* (2013) examined the effect of the presence of stolen property on target-present and target-absent live showups. While participants were completing preliminary measures, a confederate entered the room and took a backpack from a filing cabinet. Upon her return, the experimenter received a phone call that included the information that her backpack was seen in another study room, whereupon she and the participant went to the study room where the (innocent or guilty) suspect was seated. The backpack was either visible beside him or hidden from view. Consistent with their predictions, Smith *et al.* found that the presence of stolen property increased the likelihood that participants would make a correct decision. When target-present and target-absent conditions were examined separately, they found that the presence of the backpack at the time of the showup increased the correct identification rate but did not result in an increase in the false identification rate. It should be noted, however, that in real cases, police who find stolen property in the possession of a suspect may be more likely to believe that the suspect is guilty, and thus may provide additional suggestive cues to an eyewitness.

Witness Factors Affecting Showup Accuracy

Ethnicity The cross-ethnicity effect or own-ethnicity bias refers to the finding that people are more likely to correctly identify – and less likely to falsely identify – people from their own ethnic group than people from other ethnic groups (Brigham, Bennett, Meissner, & Mitchell, 2007). First studied by Malpass and Kravitz (1969), the existence of the cross-ethnicity effect has been confirmed by decades of subsequent research with facial recognition and lineup paradigms (Meissner & Brigham, 2001). However, all of these studies involved showing multiple faces to each person; thus the extent to which they generalize to a procedure wherein only one person is viewed is not clear. The one study to compare same-ethnicity to cross-ethnicity showup accuracy – which used white, black, and Hispanic confederates and participants – found no significant difference between same-ethnicity (61.7%) and cross-ethnicity (54.9%) identification accuracy, and choosing rates were almost identical (Lawson & Dysart, 2014). Although the study was conducted in a densely populated urban area where people would be expected to have a fair amount of contact with other ethnicities, the researchers did find a cross-ethnicity effect in a subsequent lineup task. Further research on whether the cross-ethnicity effect influences showup decisions is strongly recommended.

Eyewitness age The showup meta-analysis (Steblay *et al.*, 2003) suggested age of the eyewitness as a potential moderator of showup identification accuracy, and several studies have examined the showup performance of children (Beal *et al.*, 1995; Dekle *et al.*, 1996, Lindsay *et al.*, 1997). Research has shown that, with the exception of the very young, children and adults are equally able to identify the perpetrator if he or she is actually present in a lineup, but children are more likely to falsely identify an innocent suspect (Pozzulo & Lindsay, 1998). Given that any choice from a target-absent showup represents a false identification, this finding suggests that use of the showup could be particularly problematic with children. However, research examining the use of the showup with children has produced mixed results. Two studies using kindergarten-age children (Beal *et al.*, 1995; Dekle *et al.*, 1996) found that the rate of correct identifications was higher for showups than for lineups. Kindergarten-age children were also more likely to choose from target-absent lineups than showups; however, when filler identifications were taken in account, the false identification rate was higher for the showups than the lineups. One of these studies compared the children to adults (Dekle *et al.*, 1996) and found that children were more likely than adults to correctly identify the perpetrator from target-present showups, but also more likely to make false identifications from target-absent showups.

A third study (Lindsay *et al.*, 1997) compared the lineup and showup identification accuracies of groups of younger and older child eyewitnesses to those of adults using both simultaneous (all photos presented at once) and sequential (photos presented one-at-a-time) lineups. Use of sequential lineups allowed them to examine whether any differences between showups and lineups were due to the number of photographs viewed in total or to the number of photographs viewed at one time. In their first experiment, a group of adults was compared with two groups of older children: children aged 8–10 years, and children aged 11–15 years. The adults were more likely to make a correct decision than either group of children, whose overall accuracy did not differ from each other. The correct identification rate in target-present trials was similar for all three age groups and in all three types of procedure; however, for both of the child groups the false identification rate in target-absent trials was considerably higher for the showup than for either lineup type. For adults, the false identification rate was similar for all three procedures.

For the comparison with the youngest group of children (3–6 years, experiment 2), only target-present conditions were used. The correct identification rate was uniformly high for both children and adults for the showups and the simultaneous lineups. For sequential lineups, the correct identification rate remained high for children, but dropped significantly for adults. However, a greater percentage of children identified more than one person in the sequential lineups, which would not be considered a reliable identification in a real case. When these participants were treated as non-identifiers, the correct identification rate was comparable for the children and adults.

Intoxicated eyewitnesses Many crimes – including many violent crimes – are committed when the criminal, victim and/or other witnesses are intoxicated in both the UK (Budd, Sharp, & Mayhew, 2005) and the US (Greenfield, 1998; Rand, Sabol, Sinclair, & Snyder, 2010). Given that showups often occur within one hour of the crime

(PERF, 2013), there is an increased likelihood that a showup will be conducted when the eyewitness is still intoxicated. Dysart, Lindsay, McDonald, and Wicke (2002) examined the effect of alcohol intoxication on showup identification accuracy. They had two female confederates recruit bar patrons to participate in a psychology study. After bringing those who agreed to participate to the room where the study was to be conducted, the recruiters left; participants were later presented with a photographic showup and asked whether the person in the photograph was the person who had recruited them. Dysart et al. found that intoxication had no effect on correct identifications. However, those who had higher blood alcohol levels were more likely to make a false identification than those with low blood alcohol levels; thus, intoxication may increase the likelihood of misidentification.

THE USE OF MUGSHOTS AND SHOWUPS AS THE FIRST OF MULTIPLE PROCEDURES

This chapter ends with a note of caution on *both* mugshot and showup procedures due to the fact that: (a) there is, generally speaking, very little reason *a priori* to believe the suspect is guilty with mugshots and showups, and all identification procedures put innocent suspects at risk; and (b) these procedures are likely to be the first of multiple identification attempts made by the witness (e.g., Deffenbacher et al., 2006; Valentine et al., 2012). Indeed, given that mugshot searches are typically used to find suspects, it is unlikely that a mugshot search would be a standalone identification procedure. The inherent suggestiveness of a showup may also cause law enforcement to question its reliability. In both cases, police or prosecutors may seek to confirm a mugshot or showup identification with an ostensibly more reliable lineup identification. Indeed, if a showup identification is disputed in England and Wales, law enforcement is *required* to follow it with a lineup (Davis et al., 2015; Valentine et al., 2012) and a follow-up video lineup is almost invariably conducted (Davis et al., 2015). These policies presume that the decisions made in multiple identification procedures are independent of one another. In fact, research has shown that they are not: selecting – or possibly simply viewing – a person in one procedure can have significant effects on the decisions made in a subsequent procedure (e.g., Deffenbacher et al., 2006; Dysart, Lindsay, Hammond, & Dupuis, 2001; Godfrey & Clark, 2010; Goodsell, Neuschatz, & Gronlund, 2009; Haw, Dickinson, & Meissner, 2007; Lawson & Dysart, 2014; Valentine et al., 2012).

Viewing a suspect in a series of mugshots (e.g., Brown, Deffenbacher, and Sturgill, 1977; Deffenbacher *et al.*, 2006; Memon, Hope, Bartlett, & Bull, 2002) or in a showup (Behrman & Vayder, 1994; Haw *et al.*, 2007; Lawson & Dysart, 2014) has been shown to decrease witness accuracy in a subsequent lineup. An archival analysis examining multiple identification procedures found that 45% of witnesses who did not identify a suspect in an earlier procedure changed their decision and identified him in a subsequent procedure (Behrman & Davey, 2001). If the suspect is in fact identified from the first procedure, the risk is even greater: identification of an individual from a mugshot has been found to substantially increase the probability that witnesses will make a positive identification of the same person from a subsequent lineup (Behrman & Davey, 2001; Brigham & Cairns, 1988; Deffenbacher *et al.*, 2006; Dysart *et al.*, 2001; Goodsell *et al.*, 2009; Gorenstein & Ellsworth, 1980), as well as from a showup (Behrman & Vayder, 1994; Godfrey & Clark, 2010; Haw *et al.*, 2007; Lawson & Dysart, 2014; Valentine *et al.*, 2012). This effect was examined in a mugshot meta-analysis by Deffenbacher *et al.* (2006) and it was confirmed that commitment to a previously identified innocent suspect is more likely than not to result in a repeated identification of that suspect. Regarding showups, most research conducted to date has shown a commitment effect (Behrman & Vayder, 1994; Godfrey & Clark, 2010; Haw *et al.*, 2007; Lawson & Dysart, 2014); furthermore, across the three studies conducted by Valentine *et al.* (2012), almost all witnesses who chose the innocent suspect in the showup also chose from a subsequent video lineup, with 81% choosing the same innocent suspect. Hence, caution should be used when interpreting a second positive identification in a police investigation. It could be that the identification was accurate both times, or it could merely be commitment to an incorrect individual.

Deffenbacher *et al.* (2006) also examined other potential effects of viewing mugshots, including whether viewing mugshots would result in reduced accuracy at a subsequent lineup (known as interference), or if merely being exposed to a person's photograph would increase the likelihood of that person being selected from a subsequent lineup task (known as source confusion or unconscious transference). The results of the meta-analysis did not support an interference hypothesis, but unconscious transference was found. That is, if a witness views a person but does not select or identify him, the witness may be more likely to identify this person in a later procedure than if they had not seen the person before (but see Goodsell *et al.*, 2009; Valentine *et al.*, 2012).

Based on scientific research, the presumption that one procedure is independent of the next is erroneous. Indeed, the greatest danger of mugshot searches and the showup procedure may be the high likelihood of their being used in concert with other procedures and consequent increased risk of misidentification, and their use should be employed in a limited manner and with caution.

CURRENT STATE OF THE RESEARCH AND FUTURE DIRECTIONS

Research is only gradually accumulating on mugshots and showups. What has been found so far indicates that these procedures are not directly analogous to photo or live lineups, and that it cannot be assumed that the extensive body of research on lineups necessarily translates to mugshots or to showups. The research on mugshots conducted to date is somewhat equivocal in terms of what practices should be followed when conducting mugshot searches, and there is little theory regarding the decision-making processes involved in a mugshot search. Although there are some data regarding the number of mugshots to be shown, the boundaries are not clear – the optimal number of mugshots to be shown at one time or in total is at present unknown. Additionally, although their practical utility is clear, the effect of the use of computerized mug books on eyewitness accuracy has not yet been fully elucidated. One of the major advantages of a computerized mug book is the increased ease of pruning and sorting; however, such a process might also have disadvantages, given that increasing homogeneity might in fact harm eyewitnesses' ability to accurately identify perpetrators (Laughery et al., 1974; Lindsay et al., 1994). The ability to include dynamic cues is also a benefit to computerized mug books; however, the effect of such cues is somewhat uncertain. Given that mugshot searches are unlikely to be standalone procedures, however, the research regarding the effect of mugshot searches on subsequent identifications is particularly important. Here, the findings are less equivocal: a suspect who is selected, or possibly even simply viewed, in a mugshot is at greater risk of being selected in a subsequent procedure, regardless of his guilt or innocence (Deffenbacher et al., 2006).

Given the increasing use of technology and the greater efficiency of computerized mug books, future research on how to optimize the pruning and sorting process is warranted. Additionally, given the practical difficulty of widespread collection of dynamic cues alongside static photographs, research on the extent to which some of the same information that might be captured by dynamic mugshots could be effectively captured using photographs (e.g., multiple poses including "motion" shots) is warranted. At this point, however, it is not clear whether the potential benefits of mugshot use for finding suspects outweigh the dangers resulting from the use of multiple identification procedures; thus, research on potential alternatives to mugshot searching that offer greater protection to innocent suspects would be particularly beneficial.

There is a somewhat greater amount of research on the showup, although as yet there is still little theory to guide future research and to tie the existing research together. While some have posited that the decision processes used in a showup might be analogous to those used in a sequential lineup (see Chapter 6), what research exists suggests that while both encourage an absolute judgment, people may approach them quite differently (e.g., Flowe, 2011). Further, the research to date on factors that have been found to influence lineup accuracy (e.g., ethnicity, eyewitness age) is equivocal in terms of whether these factors have a comparable influence on the showup. Regarding suggestiveness, the laboratory research conducted to date indicates that not all suggestive factors may function the same way. For example, while it seems clear that clothing bias increases false identifications (e.g., Dysart *et al.*, 2006; Lawson & Dysart, 2014; Yarmey *et al.*, 1996), other potentially suggestive factors may facilitate accuracy by functioning as contextual cues (e.g., Smith *et al.*, 2013). If so, it is not clear which variables might be expected to facilitate accuracy and which might harm accuracy, nor is there theory to suggest why such differences exist. Further, it is not clear to what extent laboratory research has been able to capture the suggestiveness of the showup as it exists in the field. As with mugshots, however, it is quite clear that presentation of a suspect in a showup increases the likelihood of identification in a subsequent procedure (e.g., Godfrey & Clark, 2010; Lawson & Dysart, 2014; Valentine *et al.*, 2012). Thus, if a suspect has been presented in a showup, and particularly if he has been selected, a subsequent procedure should not be conducted with the same eyewitness as it may be tainted by the initial showup.

Given the nature of the procedure, finding ways to experimentally induce these same levels of suggestiveness so that their effect can be determined is an important next step in research on the showup. Given that showup use is likely to continue despite its suggestiveness, research aimed at determining the types of suggestiveness that are likely to be particularly dangerous for innocent suspects and how this suggestiveness might be mitigated is needed. Additionally, research aimed at determining under what circumstances showups are similar to lineups, and when they might be expected to function differently, might be helpful in terms of developing a better theory regarding the factors affecting showup accuracy, and which of the factors that have been investigated in lineups are particularly important to replicate with the showup. Finally, as with mugshots, research on alternative methods of finding suspects that might offer more protection to innocent suspects is warranted. In particular, research is needed on ways in which suspects might be shown to eyewitnesses in the field shortly after the crime that avoid the suggestiveness of showing a single person or single photograph.

REFERENCES

Beal, C.R., Schmitt, K.L., & Dekle, D.J. (1995). Eyewitness identification of children: Effects of absolute judgments, nonverbal response options, and event encoding. *Law and Human Behavior, 19*, 197–216. doi:10.1007/BF01499325

Behrman, B.W., & Davey, S.L. (2001). Eyewitness identification in actual criminal cases: An archival analysis. *Law and Human Behavior, 25*, 475–491. doi:10.1023/A:1012840831846

Behrman, B.W., & Vayder, L.T. (1994). The biasing influence of a police showup: Does the observation of a single suspect taint later identification? *Perceptual and Motor Skills, 79*, 1239–1248. doi:10.2466/pms.1994.79.3.1239

Brigham, J.C., Bennett, L.B., Meissner, C.A., & Mitchell, T.L. (2007). The influence of race on eyewitness memory. In R.C.L. Lindsay, D.F. Ross, J.D. Read, & M.P. Toglia (Eds.), *The Handbook of Eyewitness Psychology, Vol. II: Memory for People* (pp. 257–281). Mahwah, NJ: Lawrence Erlbaum Associates.

Brigham, J.C., & Cairns, D.L. (1988). The effect of mugshot inspections on eyewitness identification accuracy. *Journal of Applied Social Psychology, 18*, 1394–1410.

Brown, E., Deffenbacher, K., & Sturgill, W. (1977). Memory for faces and circumstances of encounter. *Journal of Applied Psychology, 62*, 311–318.

Budd, T., Sharp, C., & Mayhew, P. (2005). *Offending in England and Wales: First Results from the 2003 Crime and Justice Survey.* London: Home Office Research Development and Statistics Directorate. HRC 275. Retrieved from http://www.homeoffice.gov.uk/rds/pdfs05/hors275.pdf

Davis, J.P., Valentine, T., Memon, A., & Roberts, A.J. (2015). Identification on the street: A field comparison of eyewitness identification methods. *Psychology, Crime and Law, 1*, 9–27. Retrieved from http://dx.doi.org/10.1080/1068316X.2014.915322

Deffenbacher, K.A., Bornstein, B.H., & Penrod, S.D. (2006). Mugshot exposure effects: Retroactive interference, mugshot commitment, source confusion, and unconscious transference. *Law and Human Behavior, 30*, 287–307. doi:10.1007/s10979-006-9008-1

Dekle, D.J. (1997). Testing delays resulting in increased identification accuracy in line-ups and show-ups. *Journal of Offender Rehabilitation, 25*, 35–49. doi:10.1300/J076v25n03_03

Dekle, D.J., Beal, C.R., Elliott, R., & Hunnycutt, D. (1996). Children as witnesses: A comparison of lineup versus showup identification methods. *Applied Cognitive Psychology, 10*, 1–12. doi:10.1002/(SICI)1099-0720(199602)10:1<1::AID-ACP354>3.0.CO;2-Y

Dysart, J.E., Lindsay, R.C.L., & Dupuis, P.R. (2006). Show-ups: The critical issue of clothing bias. *Applied Cognitive Psychology, 20*, 1009–1023. doi:10.1002/acp.1241

Dysart, J.E., Lindsay, R.C.L., Hammond, R., & Dupuis, P. (2001). Mug-shot exposure prior to lineup identification: Interference, transference, and commitment effects. *Journal of Applied Psychology, 86*, 1280–1284. doi:10.1037//0021-9010.86.6.1280

Dysart, J.E., Lindsay, R.C.L., MacDonald, T.K., & Wicke, C. (2002). The intoxicated witness: Effects of alcohol on identification accuracy from showups. *Journal of Applied Psychology, 87*, 170–175. doi:10.1037//0021-9010.87.1.170

Ellis, H.D., Shepherd, J.W., Shepherd, J., Flin, R.H., & Davies, G.M. (1989). Identification from a computer-driven retrieval system compared with a traditional mug-shot album search: a new tool for police investigations. *Ergonomics, 32*, 167–177. doi:10.1080/00140138908966077

Flowe, H. (2011). An exploration of visual behavior in eyewitness identification tasks. *Applied Cognitive Psychology, 25*, 244–254. doi:10.1002/acp.1670

Flynn, S. (2003). DNA gothic. *The New York Times*, 27th April 2003. Retrieved from http://www.nytimes.com

Frontline (ND). Clyde Charles. Retrieved from www.pbs.org/wgbh/pages/frontline/shows/burden/profiles/charles.html

Godfrey, R.D., & Clark, S.D. (2010). Repeated eyewitness identification procedures: Memory, decision making, and probative value. *Law and Human Behavior, 34*, 241–258. doi:10.1007/s10979-009-9187-7

Gonzalez, R., Ellsworth, P.C., & Pembroke, M. (1993). Response biases in lineups and showups. *Journal of Personality and Social Psychology, 64*, 525–537. doi:10.1037/0022-3514.64.4.525

Goodsell, C.A., Neuschatz, J.S., & Gronlund, S.D. (2009). Effects of mugshot commitment on lineup performance in young and older adults. *Applied Cognitive Psychology, 23*, 788–803. doi:10.1002/acp.1512

Gorenstein, G.W., & Ellsworth, P.C. (1980). Effect of choosing an incorrect photograph on a later identification by an eyewitness. *Journal of Applied Psychology, 65*, 616–622. doi:10.1037//0021-9010.65.5.616

Greenfield, L.A. (1998). *Alcohol and Crime: An Analysis of National Data on the Prevalence of Alcohol Involvement in Crime*. Washington, DC: US Department of Justice, Bureau of Justice Statistics.

Haw, R.M., Dickinson, J.J., & Meissner, C.A. (2007). The phenomenology of carryover effects between show-up and line-up identification. *Memory, 15*, 117–127. doi:10.1080/09658210601171672

Horry, R., Memon, A., Wright, D.B., & Milne, R. (2012). Predictors of eyewitness identification decisions from video lineups in England: A field study. *Law and Human Behavior, 36*, 257–265. doi:10.1037/h0093959

Innocence Project (ND). *Know the Cases*. Retrieved from www.innocenceproject.org

Kassin, S.M., Tubb, V.A., Hosch, H.M., & Memon, A. (2001). On the "general acceptance" of eyewitness testimony research. *American Psychologist, 56*, 405–416. doi:10.1037/0003-066X.56.5.405

Laughery, K.R., Alexander, J.F., & Lane, A.B. (1971). Recognition of human faces: Effects of target exposure time, target position, pose position, and type of photograph. *Journal of Applied Psychology, 55*, 477–483.

Laughery, K.R., Fessler, P.K., Lenorovitz, D.R., & Yoblick, D.A. (1974). Time delay and similarity effects in facial recognition. *Journal of Applied Psychology, 59*, 490–496.

Lawson, V.Z., & Dysart, J.E. (2014). The showup identification procedure: An exploration of systematic biases. *Legal and Criminological Psychology, 19*, 54–68. doi:10.1111/j.2044-8333.2012.02057.x

Levi, A.M., Jungman, N., Ginton, A., Aperman, A., Noble, G. (1995). Using similarity judgments to conduct a mugshot album search. *Law and Human Behavior, 19*, 649–661. doi:10.1007/BF01499379

Lindsay, R.C.L., Lea, J.A., Nosworthy, G.J., Fulford, J.A., Hector, J., LeVan, V., & Seabrook, C. (1991). Biased lineups: Sequential presentation reduces the problem. *Journal of Applied Psychology, 76*, 796–802.

Lindsay, R.C.L., Nosworthy, G.J., Martin, R., & Martynuck, C. (1994). Using mug shots to find suspects. *Journal of Applied Psychology, 79*, 121–130. doi:10.1037/0021-9010.79.1.121

Lindsay, R.C.L., Pozzulo, J.D., Craig, W., Lee, K., & Corber, S. (1997). Simultaneous lineups, sequential lineups, and showups: Eyewitness identification decisions of adults and children. *Law and Human Behavior, 21*, 391–404. doi:10.1023/A:1024807202926

Lindsay, R.C.L., Wallbridge, H., & Drennan, D. (1987). Do the clothes make the man? An exploration of the effect of lineup attire on eyewitness identification accuracy. *Canadian Journal of Behavioural Science, 19*, 463–478.

Lindsay, R.C.L., & Wells, G.L. (1985). Improving eyewitness identifications from lineups: Simultaneous versus sequential lineup presentation. *Journal of Applied Psychology, 70*, 556–564.

Malpass, R.S., & Kravitz, J. (1969). Recognition of own and other race. *Journal of Personality and Social Psychology, 13*, 330–334.

McAllister, H.A. (2007). Mug books: More than just large photospreads. In R.C.L. Lindsay, D.F. Ross, J.D. Read, & M.P. Toglia (Eds.), *The Handbook of Eyewitness Psychology, Vol. II: Memory for People* (pp. 35–58). Mahwah, NJ: Lawrence Erlbaum Associates.

McAllister, H.A., Bearden, J.N., Kohlmaier, J.R., & Warner, M.D. (1997). Computerized mug books: Does adding multimedia help? *Journal of Applied Psychology, 82*, 688–698. doi:10.1037/0021-9010.82.5.688

McAllister, H.A., Blair, M.J., Cerone, L.G., & Laurent, M.J. (2000). Multimedia mug books: How multi should the media be? *Applied Cognitive Psychology, 14*, 277–291. doi:10.1002/(SICI)1099-0720(200005/06)14:3<277::AID-ACP653> 3.0.CO;2-G

McAllister, H.A., Michel, L.L.M., Tarcza, E.V., Fitzmorris, J.M., & Nguyen, K.H.T. (2008). Presentation procedures in lineups and mug books: A direct comparison. *Applied Cognitive Psychology, 22*, 193–206. doi:10.1002/acp.1370

McAllister, H.A., Stewart, H.A., & Loveland, J. (2003). Effects of mug book size and computerized pruning on the usefulness of dynamic mug book procedures. *Psychology, Crime and Law, 9*, 265–277. doi:10.1080/1068316031000081363

McQuiston, D., & Malpass, R.S. (2001). Eyewitness identifications in criminal cases: An archival study. Paper presented at the biennial meeting of the Society for Applied Research in Memory and Cognition, Kingston, Ontario, Canada.

Meissner, C.A., & Brigham, J.C. (2001). Thirty years of investigating the own-race bias in memory for faces. *Psychology, Public Policy, and Law, 7*, 3–35. doi:10.1037//1076-8971.7.1.3

Meissner, C.A., Sporer, S.L., & Schooler, J.W. (2007). Person descriptions as eyewitness evidence. In R.C.L. Lindsay, D.F. Ross, J.D. Read, & M.P. Toglia (Eds.), *The Handbook of Eyewitness Psychology, Vol. II: Memory for People* (pp. 3–34). Mahwah, NJ: Lawrence Erlbaum Associates.

Memon, A., Hope, L., Bartlett, J., & Bull, R. (2002). Eyewitness recognition errors: The effects of mugshot viewing and choosing in young and old adults. *Memory and Cognition, 30*, 1219–1227.

Newton v. City of New York (2009). 640 F.Supp.2d 426 (S.D. N.Y. 2009)

Police and Criminal Evidence Act (1984) Codes of Practice, Code D (2011). Retrieved from http://www.homeoffice.gov.uk/publications/police/operational-policing/pace-codes/pace-code-d-2011

Police Executive Research Forum (2013). *A National Survey of Eyewitness Identification Procedures in Law Enforcement Agencies.* Report submitted to the National Institute of Justice, Washington, DC.

Pozzulo, J.D., & Lindsay, R.C.L. (1998). Identification accuracy of children versus adults: A meta-analysis. *Law and Human Behavior, 22,* 549–570. doi:10.1023/A:1025739514042

Rand, M.R., Sabol, W.J., Sinclair, M., & Snyder, H.N. (2010). *Alcohol and Crime: Data from 2002 to 2008.* Washington, DC: Bureau of Justice Statistics. Retrieved from http://www.bjs.gov/index.cfm?ty=pbdetail&iid=2313

Simmons v. United States (1968). 390 U.S. 385 (1968).

Smith, A.M., Leach, A.M., & Cutler, B.L. (2013). Facilitating accuracy in showup identification procedures: The effects of the presence of stolen property. *Applied Cognitive Psychology, 27,* 216–221. doi:10.1002/acp.2898

State v. Charles (1987). 511 So. 2d 1164, USA.

Steblay, N., Dysart, J., Fulero, S., & Lindsay, R.C.L. (2003). Eyewitness accuracy rates in police showup and lineup presentations: A meta-analytic comparison. *Law and Human Behavior, 27,* 523–540. doi:10.1023/A:1025438223608

Steblay, N.K., Dysart, J.E., & Wells, G.L. (2011). Seventy-two tests of the sequential lineup superiority effect: A meta-analysis and policy discussion. *Psychology, Public Policy, and Law, 17,* 99–139. doi:10.1037/a0021650

Stewart, H.A., & McAllister, H.A. (2001). One-at-a-time versus grouped presentation of mug book pictures: Some surprising results. *Journal of Applied Psychology, 86,* 1300–1305. doi:10.1037//0021-9010.86.6.1300

Stovall v. Denno (1967). 388 U.S. 293 (1967).

Thompson, W.B., Zamojski, E., & Colangelo, K. (2010). Mugshot group size affects eyewitness mugshot selections. *Applied Psychology in Criminal Justice, 6,* 1–16.

Tulving, E., & Thomson, D.M. (1973). Encoding specificity and retrieval processes in episodic memory. *Psychological Review, 80,* 352–373.

Valentine, T., Davis, J.P., Memon, A., & Roberts, A. (2012). Live showups and their influence on a subsequent video line-up. *Applied Cognitive Psychology, 26,* 1-23. doi:10.1002/acp.1796

van Koppen, P.J., & Lochun, S.K. (1997). Portraying perpetrators: The validity of offender descriptions by witnesses. *Law and Human Behavior, 21,* 661–684. doi:10.1023/A:1024812831576

Wagenaar, W.A., & Veefkind, N. (1992). Comparison of one-person and many-person lineups: A warning against unsafe practices. In F. Losel, D. Bender, & T. Bliesner (Eds.), *Psychology and Law: International Perspectives* (pp. 275–285). Berlin: Walter De Gruyter.

Weber, N., & Perfect, T.J. (2012). Improving eyewitness identification accuracy by screening out those who say they don't know. *Law and Human Behavior, 36,* 28–36. doi:10.1037/h0093976

Wells, G.L. (1984). The psychology of lineup identification. *Journal of Applied Social Psychology, 14,* 89–103.

Williams, T. (2006). Freed by DNA, and expressing compassion for rape victim. *The New York Times,* July 7, 2006. Retrieved from http://www.nytimes.com

Yarmey, A.D., Yarmey, A.L., & Yarmey, M.J. (1994). Face and voice identifications in showups and lineups. *Applied Cognitive Psychology*, *8*, 453–464. doi:10.1002/acp.2350080504

Yarmey, A.D., Yarmey, M.J., & Yarmey, A.L. (1996). Accuracy of eyewitness identifications in lineups and showups. *Law and Human Behavior*, *20*, 459–477. doi:10.1007/BF01498981

5

Craniofacial Analysis and Identification

CAROLINE WILKINSON

INTRODUCTION

Craniofacial anthropology is a branch of biological anthropology that deals specifically with the human head. It involves any biological analysis and interpretation of the skull and the face and can be applied to identification of the living and the dead, including facial biometrics, facial depiction, craniofacial superimposition, facial image analysis, osteology and anatomy.

Craniofacial anthropology may be employed for identification of the dead and there are a number of scenarios where this may be of value to a forensic investigation. Craniofacial anthropology can be utilized for single unidentified human remains, multiple victims of disasters and mass graves. There are two methods available for craniofacial analysis of the dead; facial depiction and craniofacial superimposition. These methods are appropriate for entirely different scenarios, even though they may rely on similar anthropological standards and knowledge.

Forensic Facial Identification: Theory and Practice of Identification from Eyewitnesses, Composites and CCTV, First Edition. Edited by Tim Valentine and Josh P. Davis.
© 2015 John Wiley & Sons, Ltd. Published 2015 by John Wiley & Sons, Ltd.

Case study: The Jigsaw murder

On March 2, 2009, a left leg was found in a lay-by on the A507 in Hertfordshire, England, wrapped in blue plastic bags, and then, on March 29, a left forearm, dismembered at the elbow and wrist, was found on a grass verge in Wheathampstead, Hertfordshire. Two days later a head was unearthed by a farmer in a field in Asfordby, Leicestershire. The flesh had been removed and the eyes, ears, tongue and neck had been cut off. Then, on April 7, a right leg was found in a holdall near the A10 Puckeridge bypass in Hertfordshire, and on April 11 a torso, right arm and upper left arm were discovered in a ditch by a walker near Standon, Hertfordshire, inside a green suitcase of the same brand as the holdall. The body parts were from the same individual.

Detective Superintendent Michael Hanlon from the Bedfordshire and Hertfordshire Major Crime Unit led the investigation. The forensic anthropologist, Prof Sue Black from the University of Dundee, stated that the body had been dismembered by someone with a good understanding of human anatomy, as the remains had not been sawn up but "jointed" using a finely bladed knife. She said that certain body parts would have been "exceptionally difficult" to cut, and that the skill displayed was unlikely to have been acquired without practice. Police suspected that the murderer might have butchery, game-keeping, surgical or mortuary experience (Christian, 2010).

The remains suggested a middle-aged white man, who was overweight, suffered from eczema, had bleached skin pigmentation on his legs and a fungal infection on his toenails (*Daily Telegraph*, 2009). The police released a picture of the suitcase in which the torso was found, but decided to keep details of the dismemberment from the public to avoid panic. The head was scanned using computerized tomography (CT) and the Digital Imaging and Communications in Medicine (DICOM) data were sent to Prof. Caroline Wilkinson at the University of Dundee, so that a computerized facial depiction could be produced to aid the investigation. The facial depiction was produced using the Manchester method (Wilkinson, 2004) and a black and white frontal image was created for release to the public. Details of the hair, facial hair and weight of the victim were included in the depiction. It was unknown as to whether the victim was bald, balding or with a full head of hair, so a number of alternative images were produced showing different styles (Figure 5.1).

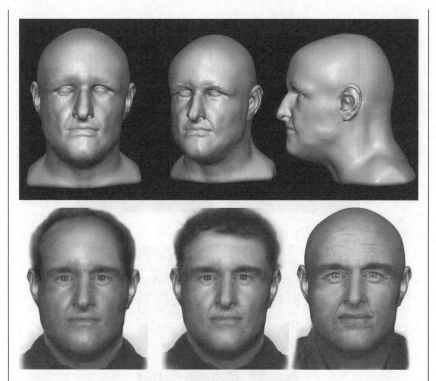

Figure 5.1 Facial depiction of the Jigsaw murder victim (top) with alternative hairstyle images (below).

Before the depiction was released to the public the police found a suspect for the identity of the victim and requested a craniofacial superimposition from Prof Caroline Wilkinson to establish whether this was a likely identification before taking the investigation forward. Since the skull had been CT scanned, this 3D model could be superimposed with an ante-mortem image of the suspected victim, Mr Jeffery Howe, provided by the police. Prof. Wilkinson utilized SensAble Technologie's Freeform Modelling Plus software and Phantom haptic device to carry out the superimposition (Figure 5.2). The ante-mortem image was in frontal view and a small part of two of the mandibular incisors could be seen on the image. These teeth were used to align and scale the skull and the image. Since Mr Howe was partially bald, the shape of the cranium could be used to match the skull to the face, along with the position of the orbits in relation to the eyes, the nasal aperture in relation to the nose, and the teeth in relation to the lips. The craniofacial superimposition gave support

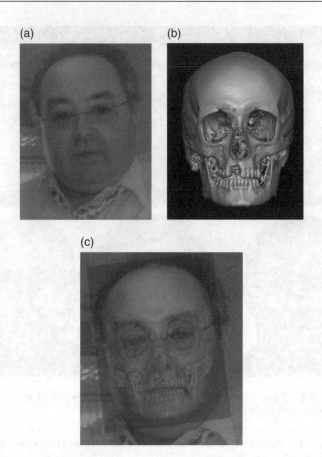

Figure 5.2 Craniofacial superimposition (C) of the image of Jeffery Howe (A) and the skull model (B).

to the assertion that the unknown remains were Mr Howe, and the police went on to ascertain a positive identification using DNA and dental record assessment (BBC News, 2010).

It transpired that Mr Howe, 49, a kitchen salesman, had allowed a work colleague, Stephen Marshall and his girlfriend, Sarah Bush, to move into his flat in Southgate, North London, in November 2008. Marshall then murdered Mr Howe for his flat and money by stabbing him to death and cutting him up before his body parts were scattered across the two counties. Blood stains were found in the bedroom and bathroom. Marshall and Bush allegedly used Mr Howe's bank account to pay bills, write cheques and shop online. His Saab car, mobile phone and furniture were sold off and they told anyone who needed to know that Mr Howe had simply "packed and gone". Eventually Marshall pleaded guilty to the charge of murder and he was sentenced to life imprisonment. Bush was also convicted of perverting the course of justice in relation to disposal of the body and lying to police. After sentencing, Marshall admitted that he had dismembered numerous bodies in the past when working for a notorious gangster family (Levy, 2010).

Facial Depiction

The majority of identification methods require a suspected identity with which to compare data, such as DNA, fingerprints or dental records (De Greef & Willems, 2005), and where there are no suspects it is impossible, from a practical point of view, to compare data with records for an entire population. Without suspects, comparison methods are impotent. In these circumstances the police may approach the public in an attempt to garner names from which identification may then be possible using comparison methods. The forensic authorities will present information to the public in order to promote recognition and this may include a biological profile (such as age, sex, ancestry and stature), personal information (such as clothing or jewellery) and circumstantial evidence (such as crime scene, cause of death and location). In addition, the police may wish to present the facial appearance of the unidentified body as an additional clue, especially where there are few other clues and where other methods have been unsuccessful (İşcan & Helmer, 1993).

The visual recognition of a decedent is commonplace in forensic investigation and is often employed for identity confirmation. However, it is acknowledged that misidentification from cadaver recognition is also frequent, especially in mass disaster scenarios where emotional, taphonomic (decomposition) and environmental factors become important (Black & Hackman, 2009). Faces of the dead may be extremely difficult to recognize due to decomposition or external damage, and even immediate post-mortem changes may be significant enough to confuse the viewer. Following major natural disasters, such as the Indian Ocean tsunami of 2004 and Hurricane Katrina of 2005, or terrorist events, such as the Bali bombing of 2002 or the London bombing of 2005, the emotional circumstances may lead to false identification by a family member, even where facial preservation appears sufficient for recognition (Hill, 2006). Ten percent of victims of the tsunami and 50% of victims of the Bali bombing were incorrectly identified by facial recognition (Lain, Griffiths, & Hilton, 2003). In the M/S Estonia shipwreck in the Baltic Sea, visual identification by next-of-kin was tentatively used in 48% of cases, but proved to be unreliable (Speers, 1977), with one member of the crew even falsely identifying another crew member based on ante-mortem (AM) and post-mortem (PM) photographs (Soomer, Ranta, & Penttilä, 2001). After the Zeebrugge ferry disaster, off the coast of The Netherlands, bodies recovered immediately were mostly identified visually by next-of-kin (Hodgkinson, 1995). However, one small group of relatives made premature misidentifications, whilst others had to make repeated visits, even when the corpse showed minimal physical damage, allowing subtle changes in the face to block acceptance of reality (Hodgkinson, 1995; Hodgkinson, Joseph, Yule, & Williams, 1993).

The depiction of faces of the dead can be a useful tool for promoting recognition leading to identification. Post-mortem facial depiction (otherwise known as reconstruction or approximation) is described as the interpretation of human remains in order to suggest the living appearance of an individual (Wilkinson, 2006). The aim of post-mortem facial prediction is to recreate an *in vivo* countenance of an individual that sufficiently resembles the decedent to allow recognition (Prag & Neave, 1997). In a forensic investigation, the publicity campaign promoting a facial depiction may lead to recognition by a member of the public and eventually identification. Since human remains may be presented in a variety of post-mortem states, different techniques of facial analysis and depiction may be appropriate for different cases (Wilkinson, 2008).

Traditionally, post-mortem facial depiction has been carried out by forensic anthropologists (Gerasimov, 1971; Helmer, Rohricht, Petersen, & Moer, 1989), anatomists (Wilkinson, 2004), artists (Prag & Neave, 1997; Taylor, 2000) and sculptors (America's Most Wanted, 2008; Paterson, 2008), or through collaborations between scientists and artists (Gatliff & Snow, 1979; Kollmann, 1898). There are many different techniques, which incorporate anatomical principles (Gerasimov, 1955), artistic skills (Taylor, 2000) and anthropological standards (Wilkinson, 2010), and may utilize photo-editing software (Stratomeier, Spee, Wittwer-Backofen, & Bakker, 2004), computer modelling (Wilkinson, 2003), automated systems (Kähler, Haber, & Seidel, 2003), sketching (Taylor, 2000) and sculpture (Prag & Neave, 1997).

Different approaches in this field have created a great deal of variability with regard to the reliability of facial depiction. However, facial depiction has without question been a valuable tool in forensic investigation, and many individuals have been successfully identified as a direct result of a publicity campaign employing a facial depiction (Algemeen, 2009; Joffe, 2008; Van den Eerenbeemt, 2001). In the UK practitioners report success rates of 70%.[1] In the US, they are between 50% (Caldwell, 1981) and 75% (Haglund & Reay, 1991). To what degree the facial depictions were directly responsible for recognition and thus identification is unclear from these success rates, and is often also unclear to practitioners who may not be provided with feedback as to the final outcome from the forensic authorities.

Craniofacial Superimposition

The majority of forensic cases include suspects in relation to identity. In single forensic cases there may be a missing persons list, in mass disasters there may be a closed list (such as a passenger list for a transport system) or an open list (reported missing by families and/or employers), and for mass graves there may be whole missing populations (De Greef & Willems, 2005). In these circumstances there may be ante-mortem data available relating to the suspects and this might include biological profiles (age, gender, stature, ethnic group), personal information (body modifications, identifying marks, clothing, jewellery, hairstyle etc.), photographs (ID cards, passport images, family albums or snapshots), hair samples (collected from a hairbrush, etc.), dental records, clinical images and/or medical records (Black & Hackman, 2009). However, much of this ante-mortem data may not be available (where the individual does not have a history of dental or medical treatment) or the available data may not be useful (where multiple members of the same family are missing, such as in a mass grave or mass disaster, and DNA analysis cannot separate family members). This may be a significant factor in areas/countries with high levels of poverty, low socio-economic status and poor medical/dental practice.

Where ante-mortem images are present, craniofacial superimposition may be effective as it does not require expensive or invasive techniques and is cost and time efficient. Craniofacial superimposition is the process where ante-mortem images are aligned and matched to the skull in order to assess the relationship between the hard and soft tissues of the face. This analysis may allow positive identification, especially where multiple ante-mortem images are available and this has been accepted in international courts, including the UK (Glaister & Brash, 1937; Simpson, 1943), the US (Ubelaker, Bubniak, & O'Donnell, 1992), South Africa (Gordon & Drennan, 1948; Prinsloo, 1953) and Brazil (Helmer, 1987).

---

[1] Reported success rate from the University of Manchester, 1982–2005. Number of forensic cases = 23, number of successful cases = 16, success rate = 70%.

Traditionally, craniofacial superimposition has been carried out by forensic anthropologists or anatomists (Gordon & Drennan, 1948; Helmer, 1987; Maat, 1989) and the techniques incorporate similar anatomical principles (Gerasimov, 1955) and anthropological standards (Wilkinson, 2010) as utilized in facial depiction. Numerous computerized systems have been developed for skull-to-face alignment (Al-Amad, McCullough, Graham, Clement, & Hill, 2006; Aung, Ngim, & Lee, 1995; Bajnoczky & Kiralyfalvi, 1995; Delfino, Colonna, Vacca, Potente, & Introna, 1986; Ibáñez, Cordon, Damas, & Santamaria, 2008; Shahrom *et al.*, 1996; Ubelaker *et al.*, 1992).

HISTORICAL CONTEXT

Facial Depiction

The earliest examples of scientific facial reconstructions were produced by the German anatomists, His (1895) and Welcker (1867), who authenticated the remains of Johann Sebastian Bach and Dante by reconstructing the soft tissues onto a plaster cast of the skull using facial tissue measurements recorded from a number of cadavers. These scientists employed sculptors to produce the three-dimensional facial reconstructions. Kollman and Buchly (1898) also reconstructed the face of a Neolithic woman using the facial tissue measurements taken from hundreds of women from the area. Other early attempts at facial reconstruction were performed on prehistoric skulls and ancient archaeological specimens (Wilkinson, 2004).

Probably the most significant pioneer in early facial reconstruction work was the Russian anthropologist, Mikhail Gerasimov (1971), who developed a technique that relied upon anatomical knowledge and sculptural skills. He was a stickler for anatomical accuracy and against the general consensus of contemporary anatomists and anthropologists; Gerasimov suggested that details of facial features could be determined from analysis of the skeletal morphology. A great deal of craniofacial research was produced in Russia, led by Lebedinskaya, Balueva and Veselovskaya (1993), following Gerasimov's death in 1979.

Although there were early attempts at facial reconstruction in the US (Taylor, 2000), it was not really taken up until 1946 when the anthropologist Wilton Krogman took a serious look at the procedure and, with the aid of sculptors, carried out studies into the accuracy of the technique (Moss, Linney, Grindrod, Arridge, & Clifton, 1987). What has become known as the American three-dimensional method was developed from the work of Krogman by the forensic artist, Betty Pat

Gatliff, and the physical anthropologist, Clyde Snow (Snow, Gatliff, & McWilliams, 1970), who carried out an accuracy study and were involved in numerous forensic investigations. Many other anthropologists worked with artists to produce 2D facial reconstructions (Taylor, 2000), several police artists developed 2D facial depiction methods (Caldwell, 1981; Taylor, 2000), and anthropologists published facial standards for use in facial reconstruction (George, 1993; Krogman & İşcan, 1986).

There have been some attempts at facial reconstruction within Europe over the last 50 years, most notably by Helmer (1984) in Germany, and Neave (Prag & Neave, 1997) in Britain. Neave developed a technique, known as the Manchester method, which incorporated both anatomical and anthropometrical standards. This method has been taken up globally by practitioners and has been further developed over the last 20 years (Cesarani, Martina, Grilletto, Boano, Roveri, Capussotto, Giuliano, Celia, & Gandini, 2004; Wilkinson, 2004) to include a dedicated period of training and the study of facial anatomy, expression, anthropometry, anthropology, and the relationship between the soft and hard tissues of the face.

There have been numerous computerized systems developed for facial depiction. Some of these systems involve automation (Evenhouse, Rasmussen, & Sadler, 1992; Evison, 1996; Evison & Bruegge, 2010; Quatrehomme *et al.*, 1997), whilst others involve digital sculpture/ animation (Kähler *et al.*, 2003; Mahoney & Wilkinson, 2012; Subke & Wittke, 2005; Wilkinson, 2003).

Craniofacial Superimposition

In the past, skulls of famous people were authenticated by comparison with portraits and sculptures. The anatomist Welcker (1883) compared the skull of Raphael with a self-portrait and the skull of Kant with his death mask, to authenticate the skulls using outline drawings of the skull. Other such authentication work includes the identification of the remains of the composer, Haydn, by Tandler, and the remains of Lord Darnley and George Buchanan by Pearson (Keith, 1928).

The first documented use of craniofacial superimposition for identification in a medico-legal investigation was in 1935 (Glaister & Brash, 1937), involving a Lancastrian GP and the mysterious disappearance of his wife. Dr Buck Ruxton claimed that his wife had left him for another man, but two weeks later two dismembered bodies were found in Glasgow. Police recovered two human heads and over 70 body parts wrapped in newspaper. The newspaper was from a special edition that was distributed only in the area where the Ruxtons lived. Dr Ruxton had killed his wife and her maid and removed the eyes, noses, lips, skin and teeth to avoid identification of the bodies. The police suspected that the maid and the wife were the victims, and a craniofacial super-imposition was carried out using ante-mortem images of the two women and photographs of the skulls (Glaister & Brash, 1953). The method used in this case was photographic, employing enlargement, measurable objects, anatomical landmarks and craniophore orienta-tion (Yoshino, 2012). Known objects in the photographs (e.g., a tiara and a picket fence) were used to enlarge the faces to life size in order to identify Mary Rogers and Isabella Ruxton.

There have been other significant forensic cases where craniofacial superimposition has been utilized for identification of human remains, including those of Josef Mengele (Helmer, 1987; Teixeira, 1985) and the identification of the victims of the serial killers Fred and Rosemary West in the UK (Whittaker, Richards, & Jones, 1998). Other significant cases are the Dobkin case (Simpson, 1943), the Worlkersdorfer case (Gordon & Drennan, 1948) and the Howick Falls murder case (Prinsloo, 1953). Detailed reviews of the techniques can be found in the literature (Auslebrook, Iscan, Slabbert, & Becker, 1995; Brocklebank & Holmgren, 1989; Brown, 1983; Cai & Lan, 1993; Glassman, 2001; Lan, 1992; Sekharan, 1993; Taylor & Brown, 1998; Yoshino, 2012), and many case studies have also been published (Basauri, 1967; Bastiaan, Dalitz, & Woodward, 1986; Bilge, Kedici, Alakoç, Ulkuer, & Ilkyaz, 2003; Brown, 1982; Fenton, Heard, & Sauer, 2008; Gejvall, 1974; Ghosh & Sinha, 2005; McKenna, Jablonski, & Fearnhead, 1984; Reddy, 1973; Sekharan, 1971; Sen, 1962; Shahrom et al., 1996; Sivaram & Wadhera, 1975; Solla & Işcan, 2001; Ubelaker et al., 1992; Webster, Murray, Brinkhous, & Hudson, 1986; Yoshino & Seta, 1989).

Craniofacial superimposition development has passed through three technological phases: photographic, video and computer-assisted (Auslebrook et al., 1995; Yoshino, 2012). The photographic technique was pioneered in the 1930s (Glaister & Brash, 1937; Gordon & Drennan, 1948; Simpson, 1943), the video technique was developed in the 1970s (Helmer & Grüner, 1977; Iten, 1987; Koelmeyer, 1982) and the computer-assisted technique was introduced in the 1980s (Aung et al., 1995; Austin, 1999; Bastiaan et al., 1986; Delfino et al., 1986).

It is professionally agreed that craniofacial superimposition is of greater value for exclusion than positive identification (Kau et al., 2006a; Yoshino, 2012), as a facial image of a different person may appear con-sistent with the skull in question. Therefore, forensic practitioners must be well trained in anatomy and anthropology for the effective utilization of craniofacial superimposition, and multiple ante-mortem images of the suspect should be analysed (Yoshino, 2012). When evaluating anatomical consistency, special attention is paid to the cranial outline, the soft tissue thickness at various anthropometric landmarks on the skull, and feature relationships between the skull and the face (Yoshino, Imaizumi, Miyasaka, & Seta, 1995).

UNDERLYING ASSUMPTIONS AND PRINCIPLES

Anatomical and Anthropological Standards

Post-mortem facial depiction and craniofacial superimposition both rely on the same anthropological and anatomical standards and principles. It is well established that the craniofacial complex is a functional matrix and the relationship between the bone and soft tissues is reciprocal and responsive (Kau *et al.*, 2006b; Rynn, Balueva, & Veselovskaya, 2012). Therefore the principles of craniofacial analysis and identification are based on the theory that the shape of the adult skull is related to the internal and external soft tissues of the face and head, as much as the face and head are related to the skull.

Early anatomical dissection research (Angel, 1978; Wolff, 1933; Whitnall, 1979) revealed the relationship between the morphology of the eye and the orbital bones and described anatomical standards. These studies showed that the palpebral ligaments tether the eyelids to the orbital bone, medially at the endocanthion and laterally at the malar tubercle (Figure 5.3). Whitnall (1921; Wilkinson, 2004) found the malar

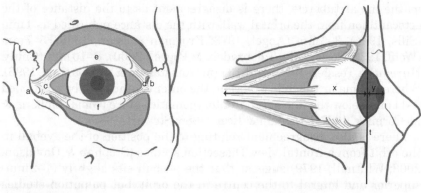

a Lacrimal crest
b Whitnall's tubercle
c Medial canthal tendon
d Lateral canthal tendon
e Superior tarsal plate
f Inferior tarsal plate

x Depth of orbit
y Eyeball prominence past iris plane
t Tangent touching mid supraorbital to
   mid infraorbital points

Figure 5.3 Features of the eye (created by Caroline Erolin, University of Dundee).

tubercle to be definable, visually or by palpation, on 95% of skulls, regardless of ancestry. Whitnall also showed that the curves of the eyelid margins are not symmetrical and the upper lid is more pronounced than the lower, its height being greatest nearer the medial angle, whereas that of the lower lid is nearer the lateral angle. He also suggested that the lateral canthal angle is more acute than the medial and lies in close contact with the globe, whereas the medial canthus extends towards the nose 5–7 mm away from the globe, being separated by the caruncula and the plica semilunaris. Merkel (Wolff, 1933) further described the radius of the upper curve as 16.5 mm and that of the lower as 22 mm.

Whilst Whitnall (1921) described the position of the two canthi as being "almost precisely determined, the inner by the naso-lacrymal duct (lacrimal fossa) and the outer by the slightly but definitely indicated malar tubercle", there is some debate as to where exactly the endocanthion and ectocanthion sit in relation to those two anatomical features (Figure 5.3). There is agreement that the medial canthus is positioned approximately 2–5 mm lateral to the anterior lacrimal crest (Angel, 1978; Krogman & İşcan, 1986; Yoshino & Seta, 1989), but where exactly on the anterior lacrimal crest this measurement is taken from is unclear. Different studies suggest the top (Balueva & Veselovskaya, 2004) middle (Angel, 1978) and base (Fedosyutkin & Nainys, 1993) as the point, whilst other studies suggest that the point can be found 4–5 mm (Angel, 1978) or 10 mm (Stewart, 1983) below the dacryon.

Although it is established that the ectocanthion is at the same height as the malar tubercle, there is disagreement as to the distance of the ectocanthion from the orbital wall, with the distance published as 1 mm (Sills, 1994), 3–5 mm (Angel, 1978; Krogman & İşcan, 1986), 5–7 mm (Wolff, 1933; Rosenstein, Talebzadeh, & Pogrel, 2000), 8–10 mm (Couly, Hureau, & Tessier, 1976) and 13 mm (Anastassov & van Damme, 1996). Where the malar tubercle is absent, the outer canthus can be positioned 8–11 mm below the line of the frontozygomatic suture (Gioia, Linberg, & McCormick, 1987; Krogman & İşcan, 1986; Stewart, 1983).

There is also disagreement relating to the position of the eyeball in the orbit from a frontal view. Dissection studies (Stephan & Davidson, 2008; Whitnall, 1979) suggest that the eyeball sits slightly (1–2 mm) superior and lateral to the centre in the orbit, but palpation studies (Balueva & Veselovskaya, 2004) suggest that the eyeball sits 2 mm closer to the medial wall than the lateral wall, and death mask studies (Krogman & İşcan, 1986) suggest the eyeball sits centrally in the orbit.

Palpation studies and studies analysing skulls in relation to ante-mortem images (Rynn *et al.*, 2012) suggest that the shape of the eyelid fold echoes the shape of the supraorbital border. The inferior edge of the eyebrow overlies the supraorbital rim, simulating its form, and more developed brow ridges bulge above the eyebrow, lowering and straightening it medially, resulting in a more angular eyebrow shape. When the brow ridge is absent and the supraorbital border is rounded, the eyebrow will be higher and more smoothly curved (Fedosyutkin & Nainys, 1993). An epicanthic or Mongoloid fold is related to open orbits, with less developed margins, a relatively thick anterior lacrimal crest coupled with a flat nasal bridge, and projecting zygomatic bones; epicanthic because the fold curves downwards, covering the ectocanthion (Rynn *et al.*, 2012; Whitnall, 1979).

The eyeball is positioned in a lateral view with the iris touching a tangent across the mid-supraorbital to mid-infraorbital bone (Wolff, 1933; Whitnall, 1921; Figure 5.3). Whilst there has been disagreement in the past between practitioners regarding eyeball placement (Stephan & Davidson, 2008), current research results (Stephan, 2002; Wilkinson & Mautner, 2003) are in agreement with Whitnall and Wolff (summarized in Bron, 1997). Measuring clinical MRI data of living subjects, one study (Wilkinson & Mautner, 2003) found eyeball protrusion to be related to orbital depth, and stated that the iris will be positioned on a straight vertical line touching mid-supraorbital and mid-infraorbital borders. This is in agreement with developmental studies that suggest a brachycephalic cranium has the shorter anterior cranial fossa, hence characteristically shallower orbital cavities, and so a tendency towards more protrusive eyeballs (Rynn *et al.*, 2012). Gerasimov (1955) found the morphology of the orbital border was also indicative of eyeball protrusion, with deep-set eyes being linked to well-developed, rugged, more "closed" orbits, with overhanging supraorbital borders, and more "open" orbits linked to more protrusive eyes.

There have been many studies assessing the relationship between the configuration of the nasal tissue with the bones surrounding the nasal aperture (George, 1993; Gerasimov, 1955; Glanville, 1969; Macho, 1986; McClintock Robison, Rinchuse, & Zullo, 1986; Prokopec & Ubelaker, 2002; Schultz, 2005; Stephan, Henneberg, & Simpson, 2003; Tandler, 1909; Virchow, 1912). From an anatomical viewpoint it is predictable that the soft nose will be wider than the bony aperture, as a narrower soft nose would have no supporting structure. Anatomically, it also makes sense that the soft nose will not be very much wider than the bony aperture, as this would create an inefficient air passage due to a necessary change in the direction of air movement entering the nostrils. Gerasimov (1955) suggested that the bony nasal aperture at its widest point will be three-fifths of the overall width of the soft nose (Figure 5.4), and this has been confirmed in a CT study of living subjects regardless

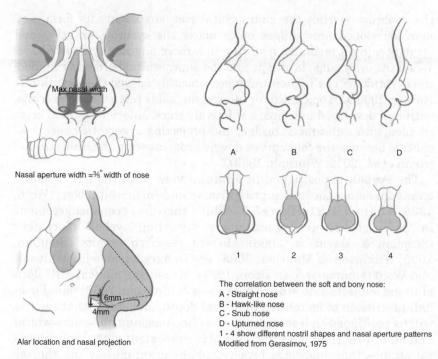

Max nasal width

Nasal aperture width =⅗˝ width of nose

6mm
4mm

Alar location and nasal projection

A - Straight nose
B - Hawk-like nose
C - Snub nose
D - Upturned nose

The correlation between the soft and bony nose:
1 - 4 show different nostril shapes and nasal aperture patterns
Modified from Gerasimov, 1975

Figure 5.4 Features of the nose (created by Caroline Erolin, University of Dundee).

of ethnic group (Rynn, 2006). Gerasimov (1955) also suggested that the nasal base angle (angle between the upper lip and the columella) is determined by the direction of the nasal spine (Figure 5.4). He stated that the axis of the nasal spine serves as a base for the soft nose and determination of nasal spine direction follows the point of the spine, as if it were an arrowhead. He also suggested that the end of the soft nose could be predicted as the point where a line following the projection of the last part of the nasal bones (at the rhinion) crosses a line following the direction of the nasal spine, and confirmed these standards with a blind study of 50 cadaver heads. This standard has been widely debated in the literature; Ullrich (Ullrich & Stephan, 2011), a former student of Gerasimov, claimed unique knowledge of his nasal standards and stated that Gerasimov did not follow the direction of the nasal spine, but rather the general direction of the floor of the anterior part of the nasal aperture (maxillary bone) laterally adjacent to the anterior nasal spine and vomer bone. However, this is strongly disputed by the academic group who worked for many years alongside Gerasimov and Lebedinskaya, and continue their work at the Russian Academy of Sciences in Moscow

(Balueva, & Veselovskaya, 2012; Rynn *et al.*, 2012), who confirm that the nasal spine was indeed the feature used by Gerasimov to determine nasal base angle.

Gerasimov (1955) also suggested that the height of the upper border of the alae is in line with the crista conchalis and the profile of the nose is a non-scaled mirror of the nasal aperture in profile (Figure 5.4). These standards have been confirmed using CT data of living subjects (Rynn, 2006). This study additionally confirmed previous papers suggesting that deviation of the nasal tip from the midline is associated with opposing nasal septum deviation (Gray, 1965; Seltzer, 1944), and that nasal tip bifurcation is associated with a bifid nasal spine (Cerkes, 2011). Rynn (2006) also produced guidelines for nasal shape prediction, utilizing three cranial measurements that can be used to predict six soft nose measurements, and tested these guidelines in a blind study (Rynn, Wilkinson, & Peters, 2010) using a sample of six skulls, where the predicted noses were compared with ante-mortem images of the faces, and showed a high level of accuracy. A recent dissection study (Davy-Jow, Decker, & Ford, 2012) showed that the shape of the nasal aperture when viewed from a posterior–anterior aspect is mirrored in the shape of the nasal tip.

Orthodontic and anatomical literature suggests that the form of the mouth is related to the occlusion of the teeth (Denis & Speidel, 1987; Holdaway, 1983; Koch, Gonzalez, & Witt, 1979; Roos, 1977; Rudee, 1964; Talass, Tollaae, & Baker, 1987; Waldman, 1982), the dental pattern (Subtelny, 1959) and the facial profile (Gerasimov, 1955). Where the upper teeth are more prominent than the lower teeth, the upper lip will be more prominent than the lower lip and vice versa, and different occlusion patterns will suggest different lip patterns (Gerasimov, 1955; Figure 5.5). There are some anatomical standards relating mouth shape to dental pattern, such as placement of the fissure at the mid-line of the maxillary incisor crowns (Angel, 1978) and the mouth corners on radiating lines from the first premolar-canine junction (Krogman & İşcan, 1986; Figure 5), with intercanine distance as 75% of overall mouth width (Stephan & Henneberg, 2003), or with the distance between the first premolars equal to mouth width (Balueva & Veselovskaya, 2004). There is a standard for skulls without teeth where the mouth corners are positioned directly below the infraorbital foramina (Stephan & Murphy, 2008). There is also a positive correlation between upper lip thickness and maxillary enamel height, and between lower lip thickness and mandibular enamel height, and sets of regression formulae can be utilized for white European and Indian populations (Wilkinson, Motwani, & Chiang, 2003). However, the exact shape of the vermillion line has not been

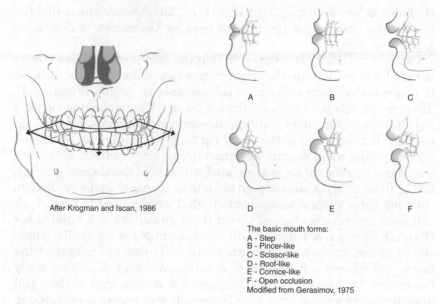

After Krogman and Iscan, 1986

The basic mouth forms:
A - Step
B - Pincer-like
C - Scissor-like
D - Roof-like
E - Cornice-like
F - Open occlusion
Modified from Gerasimov, 1975

Figure 5.5   Features of the mouth (created by Caroline Erolin, University of Dundee).

related to any dental pattern, and accuracy studies suggest that lip shape is one of the most error-prone areas of reconstruction (Wilkinson *et al.*, 2006).

Although there have been some studies relating ear morphology to skeletal structure, this is an understudied facial feature. Gerasimov (1955) considered the angle of ear to be parallel to the jaw line and stated that where the mastoid processes are directed downward, the earlobe will be attached (adherent), whereas where the mastoid processes point forward, the earlobe will be free. However, recent studies disagree as to the reliability of these standards, with dissection studies (Renwick, 2012) confirming that adherent ears relate to downward pointing mastoid processes, and other studies using CT data showing no relationship (Guyomarc'h & Stephan, 2012). Renwick (2012) suggested that there may be a developmental relationship between ear lobe shape and the mastoid process, as the external ear develops around the ends of the first and second pharyngeal arches in the areas adjacent to the first pharyngeal cleft, and the mastoid portion develops from the inferior growth and union of the petrous and squamous portions of temporal bone which are said to "embrace in the area surrounding the first pharyngeal pouch and cleft" (Dahm, Shepherd, & Clark, 1993).

Tissue Depth Data

Both facial depiction and craniofacial superimposition utilize tissue depth data in order to visualize the relationship between the skeletal structure and the soft tissue features of the face. There is a long history of facial tissue depth research dating from the 19th century (His, 1895; Kollman & Buchly, 1898; Welcker, 1883) when anatomists recorded the depth of soft tissue over the bone at anatomical points in order to describe the face topographically. Traditionally measurements were taken using needle penetration or dissection methods from the faces of cadavers, but since post-mortem faces are affected by bloating and shrinkage, these tissue measurements were not representative of living faces.

There are a large number of published facial tissue depth data-sets recorded from cadaveric white European (Berger, 1965; Czekanowski, 1907; Leopold, 1968), Chinese (Birkner, 1905), Papuan (Fischer, 1903), Namibian (Von Eggeling, 1909), Japanese (Suzuki, 1948), white US (Rhine, Moore, & Westin, 1982), black US (Rhine & Campbell, 1980) and southwest Indian populations (Rhine, 1983). Research has shown significant visible and anthropometrical differences (Galdames *et al.*, 2008b; Simpson & Henneberg, 2002) between deceased and living faces. Even so, some contemporary researchers continue to carry out soft tissue research using cadavers (Codinha, 2009; Domaracki & Stephan, 2006; Galdames, Rojas, & Munoz, 2007b; Salazar *et al.*, 2010; Tedeschi-Oliveira, Melani, De Almeida, & De Paiva, 2009), despite the development of accessible clinical imaging for use with living subjects.

Throughout the 20th century, clinical imaging methods were utilized to measure living subjects, starting with planar X-rays (Auslebrook, Becker, & Iscan, 1996; Bankowski, 1958; George, 1987; Leopold, 1968; Weining, 1958) and eventually advanced 3D imaging, such as computerized tomography (CT; Galdames, Alarcón, & López, 2007a; Phillips & Smuts, 1996), magnetic resonance imaging (Sahni *et al.*, 2002; Vander Pluym *et al.*, 2007) and ultrasound (Auslebrook *et al.*, 1996; Galdames *et al.*, 2007a; Helmer, 1984; Lebedinskaya, Balueva, & Veselovskaya, 1993; Manhein *et al.*, 2000). Problems associated with these clinical imaging methods include feature distortion caused by gravity due to the necessary supine position (MRI and CT), distortion caused by pressure (ultrasound), radiation risk (CT and X-rays), magnification (X-rays), image artefacts due to metal or the distance between scans (CT), lack of bone definition (MRI) and resolution. More recent advances in the 21st century have included the use of low dose cone-beam computerized tomography (Fourie, Damstra, Gerrits, & Ren, 2010;

Hwang *et al.*, 2012) and holographic topometry (Prieels, Hirsch, & Hering, 2009) for facial tissue research.

There are many sets of data available from different *in vivo* ethnic groups across the world for use in craniofacial analysis. There are data for adults from a variety of ethnic groups in Germany (Helmer, 1984; Prieels *et al.*, 2009), Belgium (De Greef *et al.*, 2006; De Greef, Vandermeulen, Claes, Suetens, & Willems, 2009), the former Soviet Union (Lebedinskaya *et al.*, 1993), Slovakia (Panenková, Beňuš, Masniková, Obertová, & Grunt, 2012), Japan (Alcalde *et al.*, 2000; Utsuno *et al.*, 2010), South Korea (Hwang *et al.*, 2012), the Netherlands (Fourie *et al.*, 2010), the US (Vander Pluym *et al.*, 2007), Egypt (El-Mehallawi & Soliman, 2001), Chile (Galdames *et al.*, 2007b; Salazar *et al.*, 2010), Turkey (Kurkcuoglu, Pelin, Ozener, Zagyapan, & Sahinoglu, 2011; Sipahioğlu, Ulubay, & Diren, 2011), India (Sahni *et al.*, 2002) and South Africa (Cavanagh & Steyn, 2011). There are data-sets for children from the US (Dumont, 1986), the UK (Wilkinson, 2002), Japan (Inada *et al.*, 2008; Utsuno *et al.*, 2005) and the Philippines (Barone, Jimenez, Lasky, & Braddock, 2001).

Collations of these data-sets can be found in some publications (Wilkinson, 2004; Wilkinson & Rynn, 2012) and at some websites (www. craniofacialidentification.com; www.craniofacial-id.com). Some research studies (Stephan & Simpson, 2008a, 2008b) have suggested that the data-sets should be combined rather than concentrating on small ethnic group differences, whereas other studies recommend the use of the most appropriate data-set in relation to age, sex, and geographical and ethnic origin (Galdames, Alarcon, & Matamala, 2008a; Wilkinson, 2004).

ACCURACY OF ANALYSIS

Facial Depiction

Whilst facial depiction has been successfully employed in forensic investigations, the level of reliability of the techniques is widely debated. When the remains are eventually identified, the depiction can be compared to ante-mortem photographs of the individual to establish the degree of similarity (Haglund & Reay, 1991; Suzuki, 1973). However, this is not an impartial assessment, since only successful cases can be assessed and blind studies must be utilized to rigorously analyse reliability and accuracy.

The problem with laboratory accuracy tests is that it is practically and ethically difficult to recreate a forensic scenario based on familiar face recognition, because access to skulls of known identity in combination with access to relatives of the deceased is almost impossible to achieve. Therefore these blind studies often rely on unfamiliar face recognition and evaluation. Since unfamiliar and familiar face recognition are known to use different parts of the brain and different cognitive processes (Bruce & Young, 1986) there is an inherent flaw in these studies. Psychological research has shown that although we are very good at familiar face recognition even with poor quality images, we are very poor at unfamiliar face recognition even with high quality images. Kemp, Towell, and Pike (1997) recorded extremely high error rates in the verification of identity from photo-ID cards, and Bruce et al. (1999) recorded a 30% error rate for face matching from images, with error rates increasing further when the images depicted different views or expressions. In contrast, familiar face recognition rates are closer to 90% (Burton, Bruce, & Hancock, 1999; see Chapter 9 for further examples).

Nonetheless, facial depiction accuracy studies have utilized unfamiliar face recognition as the only viable option for establishing the similarity between the depiction and the target, and a number of different assessment methods have been developed, including face pool identification and morphometric comparison. Face pool assessment (Snow et al., 1970; Stephan & Henneberg, 2001) involves the comparison of the depiction with a pool of face photographs or 3D face scans that includes the target alongside a number of other faces of similar age, sex and ethnic group. Volunteers are then asked to choose the face from the pool that most resembles the depiction in order to determine the recognition level. There have been a number of face pool studies and the results are variable. The first such study by Snow et al. (1970) depicted two adult white American faces and recorded an average recognition level of 47% from a pool of seven ante-mortem images. Other studies have produced recognition rates ranging from 8% for a white Australian man from a pool of 10 facial photographs (Stephan & Henneberg, 2001), 23% for a Brazilian woman from a pool of 10 facial photographs (Fernandes et al., 2012), 44% for five white British girls from a pool of 10 facial photographs (Wilkinson & Whittaker, 2002), to 71% for two adult white Americans from a pool of five face-scan images (Wilkinson et al., 2006). One face pool study using an automated system recorded a recognition rate of 81% for 18 Belgian male depictions from a pool of 12 face scan images (Claes, Vandermeulen, DeGreef, Willems, & Suetens, 2006), but this study did not actually use any skulls and employed a method that reverse engineered each skull from a face model using average tissue depth data and then used that same tissue depth data to predict the face, so this result must be treated with caution.

It may be possible to assess accuracy using morphometric comparison between the reconstruction and the target face. With the development of CT imaging and computerized facial reconstruction, it is possible to compare the surfaces of the reconstruction and the target face using 3D reverse modelling software (e.g., Geomagic). Two studies have employed this technique (Lee, Wilkinson, & Hwang, 2011; Wilkinson et al., 2006) and the results suggested that approximately 65% of the facial surface had less than 2 mm error. The study suggested that the nose, eyes, jaw line, forehead and chin can be reconstructed reliably (<2 mm error), with the mouth and ears showing the most errors. The Belgian study (Claes et al., 2006) recorded an average error of 1.14 mm between the facial depictions and the face scans, but since average tissue depth data was utilized to reverse engineer the skull and the same tissue depth data used to create the depiction, this is not a surprising result.

One study (Lee, 2012) looked at the cross-race effect on craniofacial practitioners by asking practitioners from the UK, South Africa and China to depict faces from skulls of mongoloid (Chinese), negroid (South African) or caucasoid (European or Indian) origins. The researcher then recorded the recognition rates for these depictions using assessors from Korea, UK and South Africa. The results suggested that practitioners are better at depicting faces from their own ethnicity than from a different ethnicity, but that training and exposure to other ethnicity depiction will reduce the cross-ethnicity effect significantly (see Chapter 7 for a discussion of the cross-ethnicity effect in face recognition).

In conclusion, the laboratory studies suggest that it is not possible to produce an exact portrait, and there are many non-anatomical details of the face that cannot be determined from the skull, but it should be possible to estimate the majority of facial feature morphology from skeletal detail with enough accuracy to allow recognition.

Craniofacial Superimposition

It is vitally important to practitioners and law enforcement agencies to establish the level of accuracy of these craniofacial techniques, especially in the case of craniofacial superimposition where this may be utilized in court for positive identification. The credibility of craniofacial superimposition was first established in a study using a database of 52 skulls from the Smithsonian collection (Ubelaker et al., 1992). An unknown skull was shown to match an ante-mortem facial photograph, while the four most similar skulls from the collection showed distinct differences to the facial photograph. Another blind study (Austin-Smith & Maples, 1994) used three skulls and compared them with 97 lateral view and

98 frontal view photographs of subjects (including the targets): a total of 585 superimpositions. False matches were recorded for 9.6% of the lateral view, and 8.5% of the frontal view superimpositions and all three targets were correctly matched. The incidence of false matches was reduced to 0.6% when both frontal and lateral view photographs of the same individual were used, suggesting that multiple photographs are optimal to prove or disprove identity by craniofacial superimposition (Austin, 1999; Austin-Smith & Maples, 1994). A further study (Yoshino *et al.*, 1995) found that the outline from trichion to gonion in the lateral or oblique view was the optimal portion for personal identification. Tillotson (2011) studied the use of craniofacial super-imposition for disaster victim identification using a missing person's database of face images. She utilized 20 skulls (10 male and 10 female) and a database of 40 facial images (20 female and 20 male): a total of 400 superimpositions. This study recorded a false match rate of 11%, with only 45% of the skulls being correctly matched to the target. Tillotson (2011) confirmed that frontal passport-style images alone are not optimal, and multiple views or an oblique view are preferable for identification purposes.

FURTHER RESEARCH

There are many areas relating to craniofacial analysis that require a further research focus. We do not currently know a great deal in relation to how these depictions are presented to the public. Police expectations of successful identification are often greater than the possible predictions and realistic photographic representations of the unidentified person that may be requested. Many experts prefer to only depict facial details that can be ascertained with some degree of accuracy, and facial models may then be presented in a neutral base colour without hair (Prag & Neave, 1997; Wilkinson, 2004). However, some previous research has shown that faces are more difficult to recognize without any texture. Bruce *et al.* (1993) found that laser scans of faces were recognized by colleagues significantly less accurately than photographs, especially for women's faces. Consequently, some experts will estimate eye and skin textures and plausible hairstyles (Gerasimov, 1971; Taylor, 2000), but it is also likely that incorrect textures will reduce the chance of recognition. It has been demonstrated that exterior cues (such as hairstyle) can be extremely powerful (Andrews, Davies-Thompson, Kingstone, & Young, 2010; Sinha & Poggio, 1996; see case study), and there is evidence that recognition deficits are accompanied by fairly typical changes in appearance, including alterations to moustache shape and hair, or omitting a characteristic head-piece for pictures of well-known celebrity faces. In these forensic scenarios it is unclear how accurate facial textures need to be to prompt recognition, especially when the face has some inevitable errors in shape. Recent research (Frowd *et al.*, 2012) revealed that altering the appearance of a facial composite, by reducing the likeness of hair, promoted a large negative effect on the ability to correctly recognize the face. A single change to hair (style, length and shade) promoted worse performance relative to veridical, with two such changes applied to the same image promoting even worse performance. However, such hair changes promoted only small decrements in recognition when applied to photographs of faces, indicating that hair is important when the face is not a precise representation.

Further research to establish relationships between facial features and skeletal structure is always welcomed, and features for which there is a paucity of standards for prediction are ears, lips and creases. Ideally this research should involve clinical images of living subjects, but human dissection studies would also be of benefit where post-mortem distortion and embalming effects can be limited.

Finally, further research into the accuracy and reliability of crani-ofacial superimposition is necessary in order to establish optimal conditions for utilization in a medico-legal scenario. This technique could be of vital importance in future disaster victim identification situations, and may be an effective tool for identification in the correct circumstances.

REFERENCES

Al-Amad, S., McCullough, M., Graham, J., Clement, J., & Hill, A. (2006). Craniofacial identification by computer-mediated superimposition. *Journal of Forensic Odonto-Stomatology, 24*, 47–52.

Alcalde, R.E., Jinno, T., Orsini, M.G., Sasaki, A., Sugiyama, R.M., & Matsumura, T. (2000). Soft tissue cephalometric norms in Japanese adults. *American Journal of Orthodontics and Dentofacial Orthopedics, 118*, 84–89. doi:10.1155/2013/806203

Algemeen (2009). Vader maasmeisje overleden in gevangenis. *Algemeen*, 12 May 2009. Retrieved from http://www.nu.nl/algemeen/1962980/vader-maasmeisje-overleden-in-gevangenis.html

America's Most Wanted (2008). *Notorious AMW Fugitive John List Dead at 82.* Retrieved from http://www.amw.com/features/feature_story_detail.cfm?id=2613

Anastassov, G.E., & van Damme, P.A. (1996). Evaluation of the anatomical position of the lateral canthal ligament: clinical implications and guidelines. *Journal of Craniofacial Surgery, 7*, 429–436.

Andrews, T.J., Davies-Thompson, J., Kingstone, A., & Young, A.W. (2010). Internal and external features of the face are represented holistically in face-selective regions of visual cortex. *Journal of Neuroscience, 30*, 3544–3552. doi:10.1523/JNEUROSCI.4863-09.2010

Angel, J. (1978). *Restoration of head and face for identification.* Paper presented at the Proceedings of Meetings of American Academy of Forensic Science, St Louis, USA.

Aung, S., Ngim, R., & Lee, S. (1995). Evaluation of the laser scanner as a surface measuring tool and its accuracy compared with direct facial anthropometric measurements. *British Journal of Plastic Surgery, 48*, 551–558. doi:org/10.1016/0007-1226 (95)90043-8

Auslebrook, W.A., Becker, P.J., & İşcan, M.Y. (1996). Facial soft tissue thicknesses in the adult male Zulu. *Forensic Science International, 79*, 83–102. doi:org/10.1016/0379-0738(96)01893-2

Auslebrook, W.A., İşcan, M., Slabbert, J., & Becker, P. (1995). Superimposition and reconstruction in forensic facial identification: A survey. *Forensic Science International, 75*, 101–120. doi:10.1016/0379-0738(95)01770-4

Austin, D. (1999). Video superimposition at the CA Pound Laboratory 1987 to 1992. *Journal of Forensic Sciences, 44*, 695–699. doi:10.1520/JFS14537J

Austin-Smith, D., & Maples, W.R. (1994). The reliability of skull/photograph superimposition in individual identification. *Journal of Forensic Sciences, 39*, 446.

Bajnoczky, I., & Kiralyfalvi, L. (1995). A new approach to computer-aided comparison of skull and photograph. *International Journal of Legal Medicine, 108*, 157–161. doi:10.1007/BF01844829

Balueva, T.S., & Veselovskaya, E.V. (2004). New developments in facial reconstruction. *Archaeology, Ethnology and Anthropology of Eurasia, 1*, 143–152.

Balueva, T.S., & Veselovskaya, E.V. (2012). Personal communication. International Meeting for Craniofacial Reconstruction at the University of Dundee; July 2012.

Bankowski, I.M. (1958). *Die Bedeutung der Unterkieferform und--stellung für die photographische Schädelidentifizierung.* Frankfurt.

Barone, C.M., Jimenez, D.F., Lasky, A.L., & Braddock, S.R. (2001). Establishment of normative data for orbital and nasal soft-tissue measurements among Filipino children. *Journal of Craniofacial Surgery, 12*, 427–432.

Basauri, C. (1967). A body identified by forensic odontology and superimposed photographs. *International Criminal Police Review, 204*, 37–43.

Bastiaan, R.J., Dalitz, G.D., & Woodward, C. (1986). Video superimposition of skulls and photographic portraits – a new aid to identification. *Journal of Forensic Sciences, 31*, 1373–1379.

BBC News. (2010). Man admits dismembering salesman. 12 January 2010. Retrieved from http://news.bbc.co.uk/1/hi/england/8454031.stm

Berger, D. (1965). *Untersuchungen über die Weichteildickenmasse des Gesichts.* Frankfurt/Main: Diss.

Bilge, Y., Kedici, P.S., Alakoç, Y.D., Ulkuer, K.U., & İlkyaz, Y.Y. (2003). The identification of a dismembered human body: a multidisciplinary approach. *Forensic Science International, 137*, 141–146. doi:org/10.1016/S0379-0738(03)00334-7

Birkner, F. (1905). Beiträge zur Rassenanatomie der Chinesen. *Archiv für Anthropologie, IV*, 1–40.

Black, S., & Hackman, L. (2009). *Disaster Victim Identification.* Chichester: John Wiley & Sons, Ltd.

Brocklebank, L., & Holmgren, C. (1989). Development of equipment for the standardization of skull photographs in personal identifications by photographic superimposition. *Journal of Forensic Sciences, 34*, 1214–1221.

Bron, A.J. (1997). *Wolff's Anatomy of the Eye and Orbit*. London: Chapman & Hall.

Brown, K.A. (1982). The identification of Linda Agostini: The significance of dental evidence in the Albury Pyjama Girl case. *American Journal of Forensic Medicine and Pathology, 3*, 131–142.

Brown, K.A. (1983). Developments in cranio-facial superimposition for identification. *Journal of Forensic Odonto-Stomatology, 1*, 57.

Bruce, V., Burton, A.M., Hanna, E., Healey, P., Mason, O., Coombes, A., Fright, R., & Linney, A. (1993). Sex discrimination: How do we tell the difference between male and female faces? *Perception, 22*, 131–152.

Bruce, V., Henderson, Z., Greenwood, K., Hancock, P.J.B., Burton, A.M., & Miller, P. (1999). Verification of face identities from images captured on video. *Journal of Experimental Psychology: Applied, 5*, 339–360. doi:10.1037/1076-898x.5.4.339

Bruce, V., & Young, A. (1986). Understanding face recognition. *British Journal of Psychology, 77*, 305–327.

Burton, A.M., Bruce, V., & Hancock, P.J.B. (1999). From pixels to people: A model of familiar face recognition. *Cognitive Science, 23*, 1–31. doi:org/10.1016/S0364-0213(99)80050-0

Cai, D., & Lan, Y. (1993). Standards for skull-to-photo superimposition. In M.Y. İşcan, & R.P. Helmer (Eds.), *From the Bare Bone to the Full Face* (pp. 171–198). New York: Wiley-Liss.

Caldwell, M.C. (1981). *The relationship of the details of the human face to the skull and its application in forensic anthropology*. (Master's thesis.) Arizona State University.

Cavanagh, D., & Steyn, M. (2011). Facial reconstruction: Soft tissue thickness values for South African black females. *Forensic Science International, 206*, 215. e211–215. e217. doi:10.1016/j.forsciint.2011.01.009

Cerkes, N. (2011). The crooked nose principles of treatment. *Aesthetic Surgery Journal, 31*, 241–257.

Cesarani, F., Martina, M.C., Grilletto, R., Boano, R., Roveri, A.M.D., Capussotto, V., Gandini, G. (2004). Facial reconstruction of a wrapped Egyptian mummy using MDCT. *American Journal of Roentgenology, 183* (3), 755–758.

Christian, P. (2010). Cops recall snaring jigsaw killer. *East Herts Herald*. Retrieved from http://www.herald24.co.uk/news/cops_recall_snaring_jigsaw_killer_1_89430

Claes, P., Vandermeulen, D., DeGreef, S., Willems, G., & Suetens, P. (2006). Craniofacial reconstruction using a combined statistical model of face shape and soft tissue depths: Methodology and validation. *Forensic Science International, 159*, S147–S158.

Codinha, S. (2009). Facial soft tissue thicknesses for the Portuguese adult population. *Forensic Science International, 184*, 80. e81–80. e87. doi:10.1016/j.forsciint.2008.11.011

Couly, G., Hureau, J., & Tessier, P. (1976). The anatomy of the external palpebral ligament in man. *Journal of Maxillofacial Surgery, 4*, 195–197.

Czekanowski, J. (1907). *Untersuchungen über das verhältnis der kopfmasse zu den schädelmassen*. Braunschweig: Druck von F. Vieweg und Sohn.

Dahm, M.C., Shepherd, R.K., & Clark, G.M. (1993). The postnatal growth of the temporal bone and its implications for cochlear implantation in children. *Acta Oto-laryngologica (Stockholm), 505,* 207–212.

Daily Telegraph (2009). Timeline of police investigation to identify dismembered man Jeffrey Howe. *Daily Telegraph,* 24 April 2009. Retrieved from http://www.telegraph.co.uk/news/uknews/law-and-order/5210130/Timeline-of-police-investigation-to-identify-dismembered-man-Jeffrey-Howe.html

Davy-Jow, S.L., Decker, S.J., & Ford, J.M. (2012). A simple method of nose tip shape validation for facial approximation. *Forensic Science International, 214,* 208. e201–208. e203. doi:10.1016/j.forsciint.2011.07.039

De Greef, S., Claes, P., Vandermeulen, D., Mollemans, W., Suetens, P., & Willems, G. (2006). Large-scale in-vivo Caucasian facial soft tissue thickness database for craniofacial reconstruction. *Forensic Science International, 159,* S126. doi:10.1016/j.forsciint.2006.02.034

De Greef, S., Vandermeulen, D., Claes, P., Suetens, P., & Willems, G. (2009). The influence of sex, age and body mass index on facial soft tissue depths. *Forensic Science, Medicine, and Pathology, 5,* 60–65.

De Greef, S., & Willems, G. (2005). Three-dimensional cranio-facial reconstruction in forensic identification: Latest progress and new tendencies in the 21st century. *Journal of Forensic Sciences, 50,* 12. doi:10.1007/s12024-009-9085-9

Delfino, P.V., Colonna, M., Vacca, E., Potente, F., & Introna, Jr., F. (1986). Computer-aided skull/face superimposition. *American Journal of Forensic Medicine and Pathology, 7,* 201–212.

Denis, K.L., & Speidel, T.M. (1987). Comparison of three methods of profile change prediction in the adult orthodontic patient. *American Journal of Orthodontics and Dentofacial Orthopedics, 92,* 396–402.

Domaracki, M., & Stephan, C.N. (2006). Facial soft tissue thicknesses in Australian adult cadavers. *Journal of Forensic Sciences, 51,* 5–10. doi:10.1111/j.1556-4029.2005.00009.x

Dumont, E.R. (1986). Mid-facial tissue depths of white children: an aid in facial feature reconstruction. *Journal of Forensic Sciences, 31,* 1463–1469. doi:10.1520/JFS11925J

El-Mehallawi, I.H., & Soliman, E.M. (2001). Ultrasonic assessment of facial soft tissue thicknesses in adult Egyptians. *Forensic Science International, 117,* 99–107. doi:10.1016/S0379-0738(00)00453-9

Evenhouse, R., Rasmussen, M., & Sadler, L. (1992). Computer-aided forensic facial reconstruction. *Journal of Biocommunication, 19,* 22–28.

Evison, M.P. (1996). Computerised 3D facial reconstruction. *Assemblage: The Sheffield Graduate Journal of Archaeology, 1,* 59.

Evison, M.P., & Bruegge, R.W.V. (2010). *Computer-aided Forensic Facial Comparison.* Boca Raton, FL: CRC Press.

Fedosyutkin, B.A., & Nainys, J.V. (1993). The relationship of skull morphology to facial features. In M.Y. İşcan, & R.P. Helmer (Eds.), *Forensic Analysis of the Skull* (pp. 199–213). New York: Wiley-Liss.

Fenton, T.W., Heard, A.N., & Sauer, N.J. (2008). Skull-photo superimposition and border deaths: Identification through exclusion and the failure to exclude. *Journal of Forensic Sciences, 53,* 34–40. doi:10.1111/j.1556-4029.2007.00624.x

Fernandes, C.M.S., da Costa Serra, M., Da Silva, J.V.L., Yoshito Noritomi, P., de Sena Pereira, F.D.A., & Melani, R.F.H. (2012). Tests of one Brazilian facial reconstruction method using three soft tissue depth sets and familiar assessors. *Forensic Science International*, *214*, 211-e1.

Fischer, E. (1903). Anatomische untersuchungen an den kopfweichteilenzweier Papua. *Korrespondenzblatt der deutschen Gesellschaft für Authropologie, Ethnologie und Urgeschichte 36*, 118–122.

Fourie, Z., Damstra, J., Gerrits, P.O., & Ren, Y. (2010). Accuracy and reliability of facial soft tissue depth measurements using cone beam computer tomography. *Forensic Science International, 199*, 9–14. doi:10.1016/j.forsciint.2010.02.018

Frowd, C.D., Skelton F., Atherton, C., Pitchford, M., Hepton, G., Holden, L., McIntyre, A., & Hancock, P.J.B. (2012). Recovering faces from memory: The distracting influence of external facial features. *Journal of Experimental Psychology: Applied, 18*, 224–238. doi:10.1037/a0027393

Galdames, I.C.S., Alarcón, P.G.E., & López, R.M.G. (2007a). Evaluación ultrasonográfica del tejido blando facial en adultos chilenos. *International Journal of Morphology, 25*, 643–648. doi:10.4067/S0717-95022007000300029

Galdames, I.C.S., Alarcón, G.E.S., & Matamala, D.A.Z. (2008a). Best parameters for sexual dimorphism in the facial thickness tissue with ultrasonic assessment. *Saúde, Ética & Justiça, 13*, 60–64.

Galdames, I.C.S., López, M.C., Matamala, D.A.Z., Rojas, F.J.P., Muñoz, S.R.T., Suazo, G., ... Torres, M. (2008b). Comparisons in soft-tissue thicknesses on the human face in fresh and embalmed corpses using needle puncture method. *International Journal of Morphology, 26*, 165–169. doi:10.4067/S0717-95022008000100027

Galdames, I.C.S., Rojas, P.F.J., & Muñoz, R.S.R. (2007b). Grosores Tisulares Faciales en Cadáveres de Españoles y su Aplicación en la Identificación Médicolegal. *International Journal of Morphology, 25*, 109–116. doi:10.4067/S0717-95022007000100015

Gatliff, B.P., & Snow, C.C. (1979). From skull to visage. *Journal of Biocommunication, 6*, 27–30.

Gejvall, N. (1974). Superimposition plus SEM-comparison of hair cuticle for identification purpose. *International Journal of Skeletal Research, 1*, 99–103.

George, R.M. (1987). The lateral craniographic method of facial reconstruction. *Journal of Forensic Sciences, 32*, 1305–1330.

George, R.M. (1993). Anatomical and artistic guidelines for forensic facial reconstruction. In M.Y. İşcan, & R.P. Helmer (Eds.), *Forensic Analysis of the Skull* (pp. 215–227). New York: Wiley-Liss.

Gerasimov, M. (1955). *The Reconstruction of the Face from the Basic Structure of the Skull*. Moscow: Nauka.

Gerasimov, M.M. (1971). *The Face Finder*. New York: Lippincott.

Ghosh, A., & Sinha, P. (2005). An unusual case of cranial image recognition. *Forensic Science International, 148*, 93–100. doi:10.1016/j.forsciint.2004.04.070

Gioia, V.M., Linberg, J.V., & McCormick, S.A. (1987). The anatomy of the lateral canthal tendon. *Archives of Ophthalmology, 105*, 529–532.

Glaister, J., & Brash, J.C. (1937). *Medico-Legal Aspects of the Ruxton Case (Vol. 33)*. Edinburgh: E. & S. Livingstone.

Glaister, J., & Brash, J.C. (1953). The Ruxton Case. *Medical Jurisprudence and Toxicology*, 90–101.

Glanville, E.V. (1969). Nasal shape, prognathism and adaptation in man. *American Journal of Physical Anthropology, 30*, 29–37.

Glassman, D. (2001). Methods of superimposition. In K.T. Taylor (Ed.), *Forensic Art and Illustration* (pp. 477–498). Boca Raton, FL: CRC Press.

Gordon, I., & Drennan, M. (1948). Medico-legal aspects of the Wolkersdorfer case. *South African Medical Journal, 22,* 543–549.

Gray, L. (1965). The deviated nasal septum – 1: Ætiology. *Journal of Laryngology & Otology, 79,* 567–575.

Guyomarc'h, P., & Stephan, C.N. (2012). The validity of ear prediction guidelines used in facial approximation. *Journal of Forensic Sciences, 57,* 1427–1441. doi:10.1111/j.1556-4029.2012.02181.x

Haglund, W.D., & Reay, D.T. (1991). Use of facial approximation techniques in identification of Green River serial murder victims. *American Journal of Forensic Medicine and Pathology, 12,* 132–142.

Helmer, R.P. (1984). *Schädelidentifizierung Durch Elektronische Bildmischung.* Heidelberg: Kriminalistik-Verlag.

Helmer, R.P. (1987). Identification of the cadaver remains of Josef Mengele. *Journal of Forensic Sciences, 32,* 1622.

Helmer, R.P., & Grüner, O. (1977). Vereinfachte schädelidentifizierung nach dem superprojektionsverfahren mit hilfe einer video-Anlage. *International Journal of Legal Medicine, 80,* 183–187.

Helmer, R.P., Rohricht, S., Petersen, D., & Moer, F. (1989). Plastische Gesichtsrekonstruktion als Möglichkeit der Identi.zierung unbekannter Schädel (II). *Archives Kriminology, 184,* 142–160.

Hill, I. (2006). Physical appearance. In S.T. Black (Ed.), *Forensic Human Identification: An Introduction* (pp. 365–378). Boca Raton, FL: CRC Press.

His, W. (1895). *Anatomische Forschungen über Johann Sebastian Bach's Gebeine und Antlitz, nebst Bemerkungen über dessen Bilder, von Wilhelm His.* S. Hirzel.

Hodgkinson, P. (1995). Viewing the bodies following disaster: Does it help? *Bereavement Care, 14,* 2–4.

Hodgkinson, P., Joseph, S., Yule, W., & Williams, R. (1993). Viewing human remains following disaster: helpful or harmful? *Medicine, Science, and the Law, 33,* 197–122.

Holdaway, R. (1983). A soft-tissue cephalometric analysis and its use in orthodontic treatment planning. Part I. *American Journal of Orthodontics, 84,* 1–28.

Hwang, H-S., Park, M-K., Lee, W-J., Cho, J-H., Kim, B-K., & Wilkinson, C. (2012). Facial soft tissue thickness database for craniofacial reconstruction in Korean adults. *Journal of Forensic Sciences, 57,* 1442–1447. doi:10.1111/j.1556-4029.2012.02192.x

Ibáñez, O., Cordón, O., Damas, S., & Santamaría, J. (2008). Craniofacial superimposition based on genetic algorithms and fuzzy location of cephalometric landmarks. *Hybrid Artificial Intelligence Systems, LNAI, 5271,* 599–607.

Inada, E., Saitoh, I., Hayasaki, H., Yamada, C., Iwase, Y., Takemoto, Y., Matsumoto, Y., & Yamasaki, Y. (2008). Cross-sectional growth changes in skeletal and soft tissue cephalometric landmarks of children. *Cranio: The Journal of Craniomandibular Practice, 26,* 170–181.

İşcan, M.Y., & Helmer, R.P. (1993). *Forensic Analysis of the Skull: Craniofacial Analysis, Reconstruction, and Identification.* New York: Wiley-Liss.

Iten, P.X. (1987). Identification of skulls by video superimposition. *Journal of Forensic Sciences, 32,* 173–188.

Joffe, H. (2008). The power of visual material: Persuasion, emotion and identification. *Diogenes, 55,* 84–93. doi:10.1177/0392192107087919

Kau, C.N., Cronin, A., Durning, P., Zhurov, A.I., Sandham, A., & Richmond, S. (2006a). A new method for the 3D measurement of postoperative swelling following orthognathic surgery. *Orthodontics & Craniofacial Research, 9,* 31–37. doi:10.1111/j.1601-6343.2006.00341.x

Kau, C.N., Zhurov, A., Richmond, S., Cronin, A., Savio, C., & Mallorie, C. (2006b). Facial templates: a new perspective in three dimensions. *Orthodontics & Craniofacial Research, 9,* 10–17. doi:10.1111/j.1601-6343. 2006.00359.x

Kähler, K., Haber, J., & Seidel, H.P. (2003). *Reanimating the dead: reconstruction of expressive faces from skull data.* Paper presented at the ACM Transactions on Graphics (TOG). doi:10.1145/882262.882307

Keith, A. (1928). The skull of Lord Darnley. *British Medical Journal, 2* (3531), 456.

Kemp, R., Towell, N., & Pike, G. (1997). When seeing should not be believing: Photographs, credit cards and fraud. *Applied Cognitive Psychology, 11,* 211–222.

Koch, R., Gonzales, A., & Witt, E. (1979). Profile and soft tissue changes during and after orthodontic treatment. *European Journal of Orthodontics, 1,* 193–199. doi:10.1093/ejo/1.3.193

Koelmeyer, T.D. (1982). Videocamera superimposition and facial reconstruction as an aid to identification. *American Journal of Forensic Medicine and Pathology, 3,* 45–48.

Kollmann, J. (1898). Die weichteile des gesichts und die persistenz der rassen. *Anatomischer Anzeiger, 15,* 165–177.

Kollmann, J., & Buchly, W. (1898). Die persistenz der rassen und die reconstruction der physiognomie prahistorischer schadel. *Archives fur Anthropologie, 25,* 329–359.

Krogman, W.M., & İşcan, M.Y. (1986). *The Human Skeleton in Forensic Medicine.* Springfield, IL: C.C. Thomas.

Kurkcuoglu, A., Pelin, C., Ozener, B., Zagyapan, R., & Sahinoglu, Z. (2011). Facial soft tissue thickness in individuals with different occlusion patterns in adult Turkish subjects. *HOMO – Journal of Comparative Human Biology, 62,* 288–297. doi:10.1016/j.jchb.2011.06.001

Lain, R., Griffiths, C., & Hilton, J. (2003). Forensic dental and medical response to the Bali bombing: A personal perspective. *Medical Journal of Australia, 179,* 362–365.

Lan, Y. (1992). Development and current status of skull-image superimposition-methodology and instrumentation. *Forensic Science Review, 4,* 125–136.

Lebedinskaya, G., Balueva, T., & Veselovskaya, E. (1993). Principles of facial reconstruction. In M.Y. İşcan, & R.P. Helmer (Eds.), *Forensic Analysis of the Skull* (pp. 183–198). New York: Wiley-Liss.

Lee, W.J. (2012) *Cross-race effect on forensic facial reconstruction and recognition of reconstructed faces* (PhD thesis). University of Dundee.

Lee, W.J., Wilkinson, C.M., & Hwang, H.S. (2012). An accuracy assessment of forensic computerized facial reconstruction employing cone-beam computed tomography from live subjects. *Journal of Forensic Sciences, 57,* 318–327. doi:10.1111/j.1556-4029.2011.01971.x

Leopold, D. (1968). *Identifikation Durch Schädel Untersuchung Unter Besonderer Berücksichtigung der Superprojektion.* Leipzig: Habilitationsschrift.

Levy, A. (2010). Jigsaw killers admission that he disposed of four other bodies could bring crime family to justice. *Daily Mail* 2 Feb 2010. Retrieved from http://www.dailymail.co.uk/news/article-1247710/Jigsaw-killer-Stephen-Marshall-spend-36-years-jail-Jeffrey-Howes-murder.html

Maat, G. (1989). The positioning and magnification of faces and skulls for photographic superimposition. *Forensic Science International, 41*, 225–235. doi:10.1016/0379-0738(89)90215-6

Macho, G. (1986). An appraisal of plastic reconstruction of the external nose. *Journal of Forensic Sciences, 31*, 1391–1403. doi:10.1520/JFS11917J

Mahoney, G., & Wilkinson, C. (2012). Computer-generated facial depiction. In C.M. Wilkinson, & C. Rynn (Eds.), *Craniofacial Identification* (pp. 222–237). Cambridge: Cambridge University Press.

Manhein, M.H., Barsley, R.E., Listi, G.A., Musselman, R., Barrow, N.E., & Ubelaker, D.H. (2000). In vivo facial tissue depth measurements for children and adults. *Journal of Forensic Sciences, 45*, 48–60. doi:10.1520/JFS14640J

McClintock Robison, J., Rinchuse, D.J., & Zullo, T.G. (1986). Relationship of skeletal pattern and nasal form. *American Journal of Orthodontics, 89*, 499–506. doi:10.1016/0002-9416(86)90008-4

McKenna, J., Jablonski, N.G., & Fearnhead, R. (1984). A method of matching skulls with photographic portraits using landmarks and measurements of the dentition. *Journal of Forensic Sciences, 29*, 787–797. doi:10.1520/JFS11737J

Moss, J., Linney, A., Grindrod, S., Arridge, S., & Clifton, J. (1987). Three-dimensional visualization of the face and skull using computerized tomography and laser scanning techniques. *European Journal of Orthodontics, 9*, 247–253. doi:10.1093/ejo/9.4.247

Panenková, P., Beňuš, R., Masnicová, S., Obertová, Z., & Grunt, J. (2012). Facial soft tissue thicknesses of the mid-face for Slovak population. *Forensic Science International, 220*, 293. e291–293. e296. doi:10.1016/j.forsciint.2012.02.015

Paterson, K. (2008). Skulls and faces: Investigations and the pursuit of justice for women in Juarez. *Newspaper Tree – El Paso's Online Newspaper.* Retrieved from http://newspapertree.com/features/2645-skulls-and-faces-investigations-and-the-pursuit-of-justice-for-women-in-juarez

Phillips, V.M., & Smuts, N.A. (1996). Facial reconstruction; utilisation of computerised tomography to measure facial tissue thickness in a mixed population. *Forensic Science International, 83*, 51–59. doi:10.1016/0379-0738(96)02010-5

Prag, J., & Neave, R.A.H. (1997). *Making Faces: Using Forensic and Archaeological Evidence.* London: British Museum Press.

Prieels, F., Hirsch, S., & Hering, P. (2009). Holographic topometry for a dense visualization of soft tissue for facial reconstruction. *Forensic Science, Medicine, and Pathology, 5*, 11–16. doi:10.1007/s12024-009-9078-8

Prinsloo, I. (1953). The identification of skeletal remains in Regina versus K and another: The Howick Falls murder case. *Journal of Forensic Medicine, 1*, 11–17.

Prokopec, M., & Ubelaker, D.H. (2002). Reconstructing the shape of the nose according to the skull. *Forensic Science Communications, 4*, 1.

Quatrehomme, G., Cotin, S., Subsol, G., Delingette, H., Garidel, Y., Grévin, G., … Ollier, A. (1997). A fully three-dimensional method for facial reconstruction based on deformable models. *Journal of Forensic Sciences, 42*, 649–652. doi:10.1520/JFS14175J

Reddy, K. (1973). Identification of dismembered parts: The medicolegal aspects of the Nagaraju case. *Forensic Science, 2*, 351–374.

Renwick, N. (2012). *Ear estimation from the mastoid portion of the temporal bone.* BSc Hons Forensic Anthropology, University of Dundee, Dundee.

Rhine, J.S. (1983). *Tissue thickness for South-Western Indians* (PhD thesis). University of New Mexico.

Rhine, J.S., & Campbell, H.R. (1980). Thickness of facial tissues in American Blacks. *Journal of Forensic Sciences, 25,* 847–858.

Rhine, J.S., Moore, C.E., & Westin, J.T. (Eds.). (1982). *Facial Reproduction: Tables of Facial Tissue Thickness of American Caucasoids in Forensic Anthropology.* University of New Mexico.

Roos, N. (1977). Soft-tissue profile changes in Class II treatment. *American Journal of Orthodontics, 72,* 165–175.

Rosenstein, T., Talebzadeh, N., & Pogrel, M.A. (2000). Anatomy of the lateral canthal tendon. *Oral Surgery, Oral Medicine, Oral Pathology, Oral Radiology, and Endodontology, 89,* 24–28. doi:10.1016/S1079-2104(00)80009-8

Rudee, D.A. (1964). Proportional profile changes concurrent with orthodontic therapy. *American Journal of Orthodontics, 50,* 421–434. doi:10.1016/0002-9416(64)90205-2

Rynn, C. (2006). *Craniofacial approximation and reconstruction: Tissue depth patterning and the prediction of the nose* (PhD thesis). University of Dundee.

Rynn, C., Balueva, T., & Veselovskaya, E. (2012). Relationships between the skull and face. In C.M. Wilkinson, & C. Rynn (Eds.), *Craniofacial Identification* (pp. 193–202). Cambridge: Cambridge University Press.

Rynn, C., Wilkinson, C.M., & Peters, H.L. (2010). Prediction of nasal morphology from the skull. *Forensic Science, Medicine, and Pathology, 6,* 20–34. doi:10.1007/s12024-009-9124-6

Sahni, D., Jit, I., Gupta, M., Singh, P., Suri, S., & Kaur, H. (2002). Preliminary study on facial soft tissue thickness by magnetic resonance imaging in Northwest Indians. *Forensic Science Communications, 4,* 1–7.

Salazar, C.B., Matamala, D.Z., Cantín, M., Galdames, I.S., Barriga, S., Zavando, M., Cantín, L., & Suazo, G. (2010). Facial tissue thickness in Chilean cadavers with medico-legal purposes. *International Journal of Odontostomatmol, 4,* 215–222.

Schultz, A.H. (2005). Relation of the external nose to the bony nose and nasal cartilages in whites and negroes. *American Journal of Physical Anthropology, 1,* 329–338. doi:10.1002/ajpa.1330010304

Sekharan, P.C. (1971). Revised superimposition technique for identification of the individual from the skull and photograph. *Journal of Criminal Law, Criminology & Police Science, 62,* 107–113.

Sekharan, P.C. (1993). Positioning the skull for superimposition. In M.Y. İşcan, & R.P. Helmer (Eds.), *Forensic Analysis of the Skull* (pp. 105–118). New York: Wiley-Liss.

Seltzer, A.P. (1944). The nasal septum: plastic repair of the deviated septum associated with a deflected tip. *Archives of Otolaryngology – Head & Neck Surgery, 40,* 433–444. doi:10.1001/archotol.1944.00680020563001.

Sen, N. (1962). Identification by superimposed photographs. *International Criminal Police Review, 162,* 284–286.

Shahrom, A., Vanezis, P., Chapman, R., Gonzales, A., Blenkinsop, C., & Rossi, M. (1996). Techniques in facial identification: Computer-aided facial reconstruction using a laser scanner and video superimposition. *International Journal of Legal Medicine, 108,* 194–200. doi:10.1007/BF01369791

Sills, J.D. (1994). Computer photographic skull reconstruction (methods used in facial restoration). In L.G. Farkas (Ed.), *Anthropometry of the Head and Face*. New York: Raven Press.

Simpson, E., & Henneberg, M. (2002). Variation in soft tissue thicknesses on the human face and their relationship to craniometric dimensions. *American Journal of Physical Anthropology, 118*, 121–133. doi:10.1002/ajpa.10073

Simpson, K. (1943). Rex vs. Dobkin: The Baptist Church Cellar Murder. *Medico-Legal Review, II*, 132–145.

Sinha, P., & Poggio, T. (1996) I think I know that face. *Nature, 384*, 404. doi:10.1038/384404a0

Sipahioğlu, S., Ulubay, H., & Diren, H.B. (2011). Midline facial soft tissue thickness database of Turkish population: MRI study. *Forensic Science International, 219*, 282. e1–8. doi:10.1016/j.forsciint.2011.11.017

Sivaram, S., & Wadhera, C. (1975). Identity from skeleton – a case study. *Forensic Science, 5*, 166.

Snow, C.C., Gatliff, B.P., & McWilliams, K.R. (1970). Reconstruction of facial features from the skull: an evaluation of its usefulness in forensic anthropology. *American Journal of Physical Anthropology, 33*, 221–227. doi:10.1002/ajpa.1330330207

Solla, H.E., & Işcan, M.Y. (2001). Skeletal remains of Dr. Eugenio Antonio Berríos Sagredo. *Forensic Science International, 116*, 201–211. doi:10.1016/S0379-0738(00)00364-9

Soomer, H., Ranta, H., & Penttilä, A. (2001). Identification of victims from the M/S Estonia. *International Journal of Legal Medicine, 114*, 259–262.

Speers, W.F. (1977). Rapid positive identification of fatal air disaster victims. *South African Medical Journal, 52*, 150–152.

Stephan, C.N. (2002). Facial approximation: Globe projection guideline falsified by exophthalmometry literature. *Journal of Forensic Sciences, 47*, 730–735. doi:10.1520/JFS15457J

Stephan, C.N., & Davidson, P.L. (2008). The placement of the human eyeball and canthi in craniofacial identification. *Journal of Forensic Sciences, 53*, 612–619. doi:10.1111/j.1556-4029.2008.00718.x

Stephan, C.N., & Henneberg, M. (2001). Building faces from dry skulls: are they recognized above chance rates? *Journal of Forensic Sciences, 46*, 432–440.

Stephan, C.N, & Henneberg, M. (2003). Predicting mouth width from inter-canine width – a 75% rule. *Journal of Forensic Sciences, 48*, 725–727. doi:10.1520/JFS2002189

Stephan, C.N., Henneberg, M., & Simpson, W. (2003). Predicting nose projection and pronasale position in facial approximation: A test of published methods and proposal of new guidelines. *American Journal of Physical Anthropology, 122*, 240–250. doi:10.1002/ajpa.10300

Stephan, C.N, & Murphy, S. (2008). Mouth width prediction in craniofacial identification: cadaver tests of four recent methods, including two techniques for edentulous skulls. *Journal of Forensic Odonto-Stomatology, 27*, 2–7.

Stephan, C.N., & Simpson, E.K. (2008a). Facial soft tissue depths in craniofacial identification (Part I): An analytical review of the published adult data. *Journal of Forensic Sciences, 53*, 1257–1272. doi:10.1111/j.1556-4029.2008.00852.x

Stephan, C.N., & Simpson, E.K. (2008b). Facial soft tissue depths in craniofacial identification (Part II): An analytical review of the published sub-adult data. *JournalofForensicSciences,53*,1273–1279.doi:10.1111/j.1556-4029.2008.00853.x

Stewart, T. (1983). The points of attachment of the palpebral ligaments: their use in facial reconstructions on the skull. *Journal of Forensic Sciences, 28*, 858–863. doi:10.1520/JFS11591J

Stratomeier, H., Spee, J., Wittwer-Backofen, U., & Bakker, R. (2004). *Methods of forensic facial reconstruction* (Master's thesis). Academy of Visual Arts, Maastricht.

Subke, J., & Wittke, M. (2005). *CAD enhanced soft-tissue reconstruction in forensics with phantom-three-dimensional touch – an electronic modelling tool with haptic feedback*. Paper presented at the Second International Conference on Reconstruction of Soft Facial Parts (RSFP), Remagen, Germany.

Subtelny, J. (1959). A longitudinal study of soft tissue facial structures and their profile characteristics, defined in relation to underlying skeletal structures. *American Journal of Orthodontics, 45*, 481–507.

Suzuki, K. (1948). On the thickness of the soft parts of the Japanese face. *Journal of the Anthropology Society of the Nippon, 60*, 7–11.

Suzuki, T. (1973). Reconstitution of a skull. *International Criminal Police Review, 264*, 76–80.

Talass, M.F., Tollaae, L., & Baker, R.C. (1987). Soft-tissue profile changes resulting from retraction of maxillary incisors. *American Journal of Orthodontics and Dentofacial Orthopedics, 91*, 385–394. doi:10.1016/0889-5406(87)90391-X

Tandler, J. (1909). Über den Schädel Haydns. *Mitteilungen der Anthropologie Gesellschaft Wien, 39*, 260–280.

Taylor, J., & Brown, K. (1998). Superimposition techniques. In J.G. Clement, & D.L. Ranson (Eds.), *Craniofacial Identification in Forensic Medicine* (pp. 151–164). London: Hodder Arnold.

Taylor, K.T. (2000). *Forensic Art and Illustration*. Boca Raton, FL: CRC Press.

Tedeschi-Oliveira, S.V., Melani, R.F.H., De Almeida, N.H., & De Paiva, L.A.S. (2009). Facial soft tissue thickness of Brazilian adults. *Forensic Science International, 193*, 127. e121–127. e127. doi:10.1016/j.forsciint.2009.09.002

Teixeira, W.R.G. (1985). The Mengele report. *American Journal of Forensic Medicine and Pathology, 6*, 279–283.

Tillotson, A. (2011) *Disaster victim identification using craniofacial analysis* (PhD thesis). University of Dundee.

Ubelaker, D.H., Bubniak, E., & O'Donnell, G. (1992). Computer-assisted photographic superimposition. *Journal of Forensic Sciences, 37*, 750–762. doi:10.1520/JFS11986J

Ullrich, H., & Stephan, C.N. (2011). On Gerasimov's plastic facial reconstruction technique: New insights to facilitate repeatability. *Journal of Forensic Sciences, 56*, 470–474. doi:10.1111/j.1556-4029.2010.01672.x

Utsuno, H., Kageyama, T., Deguchi, T., Yoshino, M., Miyazawa, H., & Inoue, K. (2005). Facial soft tissue thickness in Japanese female children. *Forensic Science International, 152*, 101–107. doi:10.1016/j.forsciint.2004.07.010

Utsuno, H., Kageyama, T., Uchida, K., Yoshino, M., Oohigashi, S., Miyazawa, H., & Inoue, K. (2010). Pilot study of facial soft tissue thickness differences among three skeletal classes in Japanese females. *Forensic Science International, 195*, 165. e161–165. e165. doi:10.1016/j.forsciint.2009.10.013

Van den Eerenbeemt, M. (2001). Van Nulde'krijgt gezicht. *De Volkskrant*, 16 October 2001.

Vander Pluym, J., Shan, W., Taher, Z., Beaulieu, C., Plewes, C., Peterson, A., Beattie, O., & Bamforth, J. (2007). Use of magnetic resonance imaging to measure facial soft tissue depth. *The Cleft Palate-Craniofacial Journal, 44*, 52–57. doi:10.1597/04-191

Virchow, H. (1912). Die anthropologische untersuchung der nase. *Zeitschrift für Ethnologie, 44*, 289–337.

Von Eggeling, H. (1909). Anatomische untersuchungen an den kopfen von vier Hereros, einem Herero- und einem Hottentottenkind. L. Schultze, Forschungsreise im westlichen und zentralen sudafrka, ausgefuhrt 1903–1905. *Denkschriften der Medizinisch-naturwissenschaftlichen Gesellschaft zu Jena, 15*, 323–448.

Waldman, B.H. (1982). Change in lip contour with maxillary incisor retraction. *The Angle Orthodontist, 52*, 129–134. doi:10.1043/0003-3219(1982)052<0129% 3ACILCWM>2.0.CO%3B2

Webster, W., Murray, W., Brinkhous, W., & Hudson, P. (1986). Identification of human remains using photographic reconstruction. In J.R. Kathleen (Ed.), *Forensic Osteology: Advances in the Identification of Human Remains* (pp. 256–289). Springfield: Charles C Thomas.

Weining, W. (1958). *Rontgenologische untersuchungen zur bestimmung der weichteildickenmaße des gesichts.* BSc, Frankfurt/M.

Welcker, H. (1867). On the skull of Dante. *Anthropological Review*, 56–71.

Welcker, H. (1883). *Schiller's Schadel und Todtenmaske, nebst Mittheilungen uber Schadel und Todtenmaske Kant's.* Braunschweig: Viehweg F. and Son.

Whitnall, S.E. (1921). *The Anatomy of the Human Orbit.* London: Oxford Medical Publications.

Whitnall, S.E. (1979). *Anatomy of the Human Orbit and Accessory Organs of Vision.* Huntington, NY: Krieger.

Whittaker, D., Richards, B., & Jones, M. (1998). Orthodontic reconstruction in a victim of murder. *Journal of Orthodontics, 25*, 11–14. doi:10.1093/ortho/25.1.11

Wilkinson, C.M. (2002). In vivo facial tissue depth measurements for white British children. *Journal of Forensic Sciences, 47*, 459–465. doi:10.1520/ JFS15286J

Wilkinson, C.M. (2003). *Virtual sculpture as a method of computerized facial reconstruction.* Proceedings of the 1st International Conference on Reconstruction of Soft Facial Parts, Potsdam, Germany.

Wilkinson, C.M. (2004). *Forensic Facial Reconstruction.* Cambridge: Cambridge University Press.

Wilkinson, C.M. (2006). Facial anthropology and reconstruction. In T.J.K. Thompson, & S.J. Black (Eds.), *Forensic Human Identification* (pp. 231–256). Boca Raton, FL: CRC Press.

Wilkinson, C.M. (2008). The facial reconstruction of ancient Egyptians. In R. David (Ed.), *Egyptian Mummies and Modern Science* (pp. 162–180). Cambridge: Cambridge University Press.

Wilkinson, C.M. (2010). Facial reconstruction – anatomical art or artistic anatomy? *Journal of Anatomy, 216*, 235–250. doi:10.1111/j.1469-7580.2009.01182.x

Wilkinson, C.M., & Mautner, S.A. (2003). Measurement of eyeball protrusion and its application in facial reconstruction. *Journal of Forensic Sciences, 48*, 12–16. doi:10.1520/JFS2002053

Wilkinson, C.M., Motwani, M., & Chiang, E. (2003). The relationship between the soft tissues and the skeletal detail of the mouth. *Journal of Forensic Sciences, 48*, 728–732. doi:10.1520/JFS2002412

Wilkinson, C.M., & Rynn, C. (2012). *Craniofacial Identification.* Cambridge: Cambridge University Press.

Wilkinson, C.M., Rynn, C., Peters, H., Taister, M., Kau, C.H., & Richmond, S. (2006). A blind accuracy assessment of computer-modeled forensic facial reconstruction using computed tomography data from live subjects. *Forensic Science, Medicine, and Pathology, 2*, 179–187. doi:10.1007/s12024-006-0007-9

Wilkinson, C.M., & Whittaker, D.K. (2002). Juvenile forensic facial reconstruction – a detailed accuracy study. In *Proceedings of the 10th Meeting of the International Association of Craniofacial Identification, Bari, Italy* (pp. 98–110).

Wolff E. (1933). *The Anatomy of the Eye and Orbit*. London: H.K. Lewis & Co.

Yoshino, M. (2012). Craniofacial superimposition. In C.M. Wilkinson, & C. Rynn (Eds.), *Craniofacial Identification* (pp. 238–253). Cambridge: Cambridge University Press.

Yoshino, M., Imaizumi, K., Miyasaka, S., & Seta, S. (1995). Evaluation of anatomical consistency in craniofacial superimposition images. *Forensic Science International, 74*, 125–134. doi:10.1016/0379-0738(95)01742-2

Yoshino, M., & Seta, S. (1989). Personal identification of the human skull: Superimposition and radiographic techniques. *Forensic Science Review, 1*, 23–42.

Part 3

Identification by Eyewitnesses

6

Lineup Composition and Lineup Fairness

STEVEN E. CLARK, MOLLY B. MORELAND, AND RYAN A. RUSH

The US Supreme Court has described the identification lineup as a "critical stage" in the prosecution's case (*US v. Wade*, 1967). This chapter examines a critical aspect of that critical stage – the composition and construction of the lineup. How should the lineup members be selected? How many lineup members should there be? Should the lineup be presented live, on video, or through static photographs? How does the composition of the lineup interact with other lineup variables? These are the central questions addressed in this chapter.

These decisions would make little difference were it not for the fact that witnesses make mistakes. They fail to correctly identify the guilty and they falsely identify the innocent. False identifications of the innocent have had a profound impact on the criminal justice system. There is a consensus among social scientists and legal scholars that false identification errors are the primary cause of false convictions in the US (Garrett, 2011; Gross, Jacoby, Matheson, Montgomery & Patil, 2005; Gross & Shaffer, 2013). Much attention has been given to false convictions in the US in recent years, and although the problem of false

Forensic Facial Identification: Theory and Practice of Identification from Eyewitnesses, Composites and CCTV, First Edition. Edited by Tim Valentine and Josh P. Davis.
© 2015 John Wiley & Sons, Ltd. Published 2015 by John Wiley & Sons, Ltd.

Case study: The strange case of Adolf Beck

Adolf Beck was convicted in London in 1896, and again in 1904, for a string of crimes defrauding women of their money, jewels, and other treasured possessions. The criminal investigations and trials were bizarre in several ways, and his convictions were based on a host of errors – physical impossibilities, false forensic evidence, a disregarded alibi, and mistaken identification. The convictions spurred an inquiry and a detailed report (Collins, Walpole & Edge, 1904). Notably, several victims identified Beck from different live lineups or parades.

How could so many witnesses have been wrong? Law enforcement officials who testified at the Inquiry described the procedure for composing the lineup:

> When a prisoner is brought to a police station on a charge of stealing property we try to get men somewhat similar as near as possible, and to get them from the street or from shops, or anyone who will come in, and the person who is detained is then asked by the officer on duty if he is satisfied with the men he is placed with. (Minutes of Evidence, p. 83, Sgt. John Watts)
>
> We arranged them, and I asked Mr. Beck if he was satisfied. He said, "Perfectly, I am innocent". (Inquiry Minutes of Evidence, p. 85, Ins. George Waldock)
>
> There were some 16 or 17 persons selected from those whom we could get round the Court. Some were older and some were younger, and some were as much like him as we were able to get. (Inquiry Minutes of Evidence, p. 91, Ins. Alfred Ward)

Mr. Beck may have been perfectly satisfied with the lineups. However, the imperfections of those lineups are perhaps best revealed by the women who identified him.

> I went to Rochester Row Police-court ... and picked the prisoner out ... without the slightest difficulty. There was no one there a bit like him. (Inquiry Appendix, p. 257, Marion Taylor)
>
> I recognised him among the other men; they were not the least like him. There was one other man, oldish, with grey hair, and well dressed. (Inquiry Appendix, p. 259, Alice Sinclair)
>
> None of the men among whom the prisoner was placed was like the prisoner as far as I saw. There was another man with a grey moustache, but he was too tall and had a ruddy face. (Inquiry Appendix, p. 263, Daisy Grant)

When I came out I said I had identified him at once. I looked at the other men before identifying the prisoner. There was no other oldish, short man with grey hair there; no one like it. I knew there was a man in custody who answered the description of an oldish man, with grey hair, and well-dressed. (Inquiry Appendix, p. 261, Juliette Kluth)

For all of the police efforts in putting together the various lineups, it appears that the identification of Beck was relatively effortless for the witnesses. To identify Beck, one needed only to exclude implausible lineup members who were too young, too tall, too ruddy, or lacking a moustache.

convictions may be more acute in the US than in European countries (Killias, 2013), the problem is neither new nor specific to the US, as false convictions have been well-documented in many countries (Huff & Killias, 2010; Jolicoeur, 2010) for many years (Borchard, 1932; Munsterberg, 1908; Watson, 1924). These false convictions have had an important role in changing the criminal justice process in many countries.

This chapter is divided into three main sections. The first section describes the evolution of law and guidelines regulating eyewitness identification procedures generally, and lineup composition specifically, focusing primarily on the US and the UK. The second section describes conceptual development and research related to the evaluation of identification lineups, first in terms of fairness and bias and then in terms of accuracy and the probative value of identification evidence. The third section discusses the implications of that research.

MISTAKEN IDENTIFICATION, FALSE CONVICTIONS, AND THE REGULATION OF EYEWITNESS IDENTIFICATION PROCEDURES

The evolution of legal guidelines may originate with Adolf Beck, who was convicted of fraud in London not once, but twice, His convictions spurred an extensive inquiry, and thus it is a well-documented textbook case of police and judicial errors (see box). Most relevant to this chapter, Beck was misidentified by several of the victims. The case was also a catalyst for the development of guidelines for eyewitness identification and appellate procedures, not only in England and Wales

(Davies & Griffiths, 2008), but also in the US (Wall, 1965) and Canada (Bellemare & Finlayson, 2004).

In the US, the Supreme Court decided three cases involving eyewitness identification, *US v. Wade*, *Gilbert v. California*, and *Stovall v. Denno*, all on the same day (June 12, 1967). These cases are known as the *Wade Trilogy*. In these decisions, the Court recognized the potential for error in eyewitness identification evidence, and recognized that such errors could arise as a result of suggestive procedures. However, the Court did not rule that identifications based on suggestive procedures should always be excluded at trial, recognizing also that reliable identification evidence may be obtained despite suggestive procedures. Thus, they determined that the admissibility of identification evidence should be based on the "totality of the circumstances" (*Stovall*), or an "independent test" of the reliability (*Wade*). Two subsequent cases, *Neil v. Biggers* (1972) and *Manson v. Brathwaite* (1977) articulated the two-pronged test for the admissibility of eyewitness identification evidence. The first prong asks whether the identification procedure was suggestive. If the answer is no, then the evidence is admissible. If the procedure is determined to have been suggestive, the second prong is to determine whether other circumstances indicate that the identification is reliable, despite the suggestive procedure.

Similar issues were considered in England around the same time. Two exonerations in 1974, of Laszlo Virag and Luke Dougherty, led the Home Secretary to appoint a committee to review the cases, the law, and the identification procedures, and to make recommendations for reform. The committee, chaired by the Right Honourable Lord Devlin, filed its extensive report, which has become known as the *Devlin Report*, in 1976. Two months after publication of the Devlin Report, the Court of Appeal, in *R. v. Turnbull and Others* (1976) made a ruling similar to those of the US Supreme Court, distinguishing between good quality identifications and poor quality identifications: "Where the quality of the identification is good, the jury can safely be left to assess the value of the evidence, but where the quality is poor, the case should be withdrawn from the jury unless there is other evidence capable of supporting the identification" (p. 225). In Turnbull, many of the factors that distinguished good from poor quality identifications were the same as those that distinguished reliable from unreliable identifications in *Wade*, *Biggers*, and *Manson*.

Both the US (*Biggers*, *Manson*) and UK (*Turnbull*) decisions have generated considerable criticism (Clark, 2011; Davies & Griffiths, 2008; Wells & Quinlivan, 2009). We will not review those criticisms here, except to make one point. The *Turnbull*, *Manson*, *Biggers*, and *Wade*

Trilogy focus on how trial courts should deal with identification evidence that is of questionable reliability. Another approach is to develop guidelines and procedures to increase the reliability of identification evidence. Such guidelines were developed in Scotland (Scottish Home and Health Department, 1982), and in England and Wales in the Police and Criminal Evidence (PACE) Act of 1984. In the US, some state and local law enforcement jurisdictions had developed guidelines for eye-witness identification procedures, but a unified set of guidelines at a national level was not developed until 1999 (referred to here as the US Justice Department Guidelines), based in large part on a scientific review paper commissioned by the American Psychology and Law Society (Wells *et al.*, 1998). These guidelines have since been adopted by many state and local law enforcement jurisdictions (National Institute of Justice, 1999).

EVALUATION OF LINEUP FAIRNESS AND IDENTIFICATION ACCURACY

Here we discuss legal and conceptual definitions of lineup fairness, as well as methods of empirically evaluating lineup fairness. We then evaluate various methods for constructing lineups and how the various methods affect identification accuracy.

Evaluation of Lineup Fairness

The specific issue of lineup composition was addressed by the US Supreme Court in *Foster v. California* (1969), reversing the conviction of Walter Foster, noting that Foster was, "a tall man – close to six feet in height," whereas the other lineup members "were short – five feet, five or six inches". But six years later the Court of Appeals in *US v. Reid* (1975) affirmed Daniel Reid's conviction on six of seven counts related to the shooting of an FBI agent, noting, "There is no requirement ... in line-ups that the accused must be surrounded by persons nearly identical in appearance". The inconsistency of these two rulings provides little guidance regarding the proper composi-tion of identification lineups. The US Justice Department guidelines instruct that the suspect should not "unduly stand out". We will return to the "stand out" standard later. For now, we return to England and Wales.

Home Office Circular No. 9/1969 (which is reproduced as Appendix A in the Devlin Report) stated that: "The object of an identification parade is to make sure that the ability of the witness to recognize the suspect has been fairly and adequately tested". And further, "Identification parades should be fair, and should be seen to be fair". Seven years later Devlin (1976) made an important distinction between the identification of the suspect, judgments of resemblance, and the recognition of distinctive features. These points about memory and fairness and the distinctions drawn by Devlin have important implications for the evaluation of lineup composition. To synthesize and summarize the key points in one sentence: A *fair* test of the witness' *memory* of the perpetrator requires a lineup of individuals who *resemble* that perpetrator on all relevant *features*.

Fairness is not an easy concept to operationalize; however, it has a clear statistical definition that is easily applied to eyewitness identification. In the same way that a fair die should, when rolled, turn up any given face with a probability of 1/6, a fair lineup is defined as one in which an innocent person should be identified at a rate no greater than chance (Malpass, Tredoux, & McQuiston-Surrett, 2007).

The remainder of our one-sentence summary describes the conditions by which such a lineup may be achieved. An important point that we (and the 1969 Circular) highlighted is that the purpose of the lineup is to test the witness' memory. The implication of this is that a person who is not a witness (and thus has no memory of the perpetrator) should not be able to identify the suspect from the lineup at a rate above chance.

This reasoning provides the basis for an empirical test of lineup fairness first introduced by Doob and Kirshenbaum (1973). At its core, the procedure is simple: Present the lineup to a group of non-witnesses whose task is to pick out the person they believe to be the suspect. If the proportion of non-witnesses who pick the suspect is above chance, the lineup is determined to be biased against the suspect.[1] To illustrate, if a six-person lineup were shown to 120 non-witnesses, one should expect no more than 20 to pick out the suspect.

One commonly used variation of this procedure is to provide participants with a brief description of the perpetrator along with the visual record of the lineup. This procedure assesses the possibility that a witness could identify the suspect by relying on nothing more than the description he or she gave to the police. Such circumstances were illustrated in the statements of Juliette Kluth in the Beck case.

---

[1] Other measures of lineup quality have also been devised, based on the functional (Wells, Leippe, & Ostrom, 1979) or effective size (Malpass, 1981) of the lineup. See Tredoux (1998, 1999) for a sophisticated review of measures of lineup fairness.

Evaluation of Identification Accuracy

In assessing eyewitness identification accuracy, there are two possible states of the world that must be considered: the person suspected by the police may be guilty or may be innocent. In criminal cases the determination of guilt and innocence can be quite difficult, and as a result, much of the research on eyewitness identification has used a *staged crime* procedure. Because the crime is staged, and the "perpetrator" is an actor, guilt is known to a certainty. Researchers often examine guilt and innocence within a single experiment by showing guilty-suspect lineups to some witnesses and innocent-suspect lineups to other witnesses.

If the suspect is guilty, the correct response is to identify him as the perpetrator, a response that we will appropriately call a *correct identification*. If the suspect is innocent, the correct response is to respond that the suspect is not the perpetrator, a response that is sometimes called a *correct rejection*. Overall accuracy, considering both guilty-suspect and innocent-suspect conditions, has, in some of the experiments we will review, been computed as the proportion or percentage of correct responses, by averaging correct identification and correct rejection rates.

Another means of assessing overall accuracy is to focus on suspect identifications by comparing the correct identification rate for guilty suspects to the *false identification* rate for innocent suspects. Such analyses have important legal relevance because suspect identifications, whether they are correct or false, are taken as direct evidence of guilt. A suspect identification has probative value to the extent that the probability of a correct identification is high and the probability of a false identification is low. Most often in the eyewitness research literature, probative value has been expressed as a diagnosticity ratio, that is, the ratio of correct to false identification rates (C/F). However, there is a fundamental problem with the C/F ratio (Clark, 2012; Kaye, 1986; Wixted & Mickes, 2012). Specifically, the ratio is extremely sensitive to small values in the denominator, which produces extremely large C/F ratios if witnesses simply refuse to make *any* identification (and C and F become very small). As a result, researchers have recently begun using other measures of accuracy, most notably d' (Clark, 2012; Palmer & Brewer, 2012) and receiver operating characteristic (ROC) curves (Gronlund, Carlson, Neuschatz, Goodsell, Wetmore, Wooten, & Graham, 2013; Mickes, Flowe, & Wixted, 2012). ROC curves require data that are often not available in eyewitness identification experiments, but d' can be easily calculated from correct and false identification rates using programs that are available on-line (for example, see http://memory.psych.mun.ca/ models/dprime/) (although see Palmer & Brewer, 2012, for an alternative method for calculating d').[2]

With these preliminary considerations, we now turn our attention to the central questions regarding the composition of lineups.

How Should Lineup Members be Selected?

There is widespread agreement that a lineup should contain some number of individuals who are known to be innocent. These known-innocent individuals are referred to as *foils*, *distractors* or *fillers*, and they serve an important purpose in that they reveal known identification errors and provide a statistical basis for evaluating an identification of the suspect (see Wells & Turtle, 1986). Specifically, if the lineup consists of a single suspect and five foils, one can assume – if the lineup is fair – that the probability that the witness would identify the suspect by chance alone would be one in six.

We have described a fair lineup as one in which the suspect does not unduly stand out, requiring the witness to distinguish, based on his or her memory, between the perpetrator and innocent individuals (foils) who resemble the perpetrator. If the foils do not resemble the perpetrator, correct identifications of guilty suspects and false identifications of innocent suspects both increase (Clark, 2012; Fitzgerald, Price, Oriet, & Charman, 2013). Increasing foil similarity thus has both benefits and costs; false identifications are avoided, but correct identifications are lost. Analyses by both Clark (2012) and Fitzgerald *et al.* (2013) suggest that the benefits outweigh the costs, such that increasing the similarity of the foils increases overall accuracy.

---

[2]The theory and mathematics that underlie the calculation of d' are somewhat complicated, and many books have been devoted to the subject. In eyewitness identification experiments, d' will be zero when witnesses cannot discriminate between suspects who are guilty and suspects who are innocent, as would be the case if the correct and false identification rates were equal. For many eyewitness identification studies, d' varies between a low of 0.50 and a high of about 3.0. For example, for a typical experiment with a correct identification rate of 0.50 and a false identification rate of 0.10, d' would be 1.28. To illustrate the problem with C/F ratios, and how d' addresses the problem, note that in the present example, if the witness simply becomes less willing to make an identification, such that the correct and false identification rates both decrease from 0.5 and 0.1 to 0.27 and 0.03, d' changes only very slightly, to 1.27. However, the C/F ratios increase from 0.50/0.10 = 5.0 to 0.27/0.03 = 9.0. The example illustrates that a shift in the witness' willingness to make an identification is incorrectly represented by the C/F ratio as an increase in accuracy, rather than a decrease in the witness' willingness to make any identification.

In real criminal investigations and in laboratory simulations, resemblance to the perpetrator can be achieved in two ways: by selecting foils who are similar in appearance to the suspect, or by selecting foils who are consistent with the witness' description of the perpetrator. Arguably the most intuitive strategy, if one's goal is to prevent the suspect from standing out, is to select foils who resemble the suspect. This is the procedure that is prescribed in the PACE guidelines (PACE Code D, 2011), and it is the procedure that has historically been followed by law enforcement jurisdictions in the US (Wogalter, Malpass, & McQuiston-Surrett, 2004). However, this intuitively reasonable strategy has two potential problems. First, as noted by Luus and Wells (1991) there is no clear standard for how similar is similar enough. At some point, the foils may be so similar to the suspect that even a good witness, with a reasonably clear memory of the perpetrator, will have difficulty identifying him from a lineup of too-similar, look-alike foils. Second, the strategy may backfire by creating conditions in which an innocent suspect is the person in the lineup who is most likely to be identified. The mechanism that underlies this *backfire effect* has been described in detail elsewhere (Clark & Tunnicliff, 2001; Navon, 1992), and is illustrated through a simple example and a single question. Consider a case in which an innocent person becomes a suspect in part because the police judge his appearance to be consistent with the witness' description of the perpetrator. He is placed in a lineup with five foils who are selected based on their similarity to that innocent suspect. Question: How many people are in the lineup because they were judged to be consistent with the witness' description of the perpetrator? The answer is only one, and that one person is the innocent suspect. The five foils were selected to be in the lineup not because they were judged to be consistent with the witness' description of the perpetrator, but rather because they were judged to look similar to someone who was judged to be consistent with the witness' description. These conditions conspire to make the innocent suspect the person in the lineup who is most likely to be identified.

As a solution to these problems, Luus and Wells (1991) and Navon (1992) recommended that lineup foils be selected based on their match to the witness' description of the perpetrator, rather than their visual match to the suspect. This recommendation is the basis of the "unduly stand out" rule in the US guidelines. It is also consistent with the distinctions drawn by Devlin as well as the logic of empirical lineup fairness assessments. The witness cannot rely solely on his or her prior description of the perpetrator, and a non-witness should not be able to deduce the identity of the suspect, if *all* lineup members match the witness' description of the perpetrator.

The first experiment that directly compared suspect-matched foil selection to description-matched foil selection showed a huge advantage for description-matched lineups over suspect-matched lineups, with a correct identification rate that was much higher for description-matched lineups than for suspect-matched lineups. False identification rates did not differ across the two methods (Wells, Rydell, & Seelau, 1993). Based largely on the results of this experiment, the APLS Scientific Review Paper explicitly recommended that foils be selected based on their match to the witness' description of the perpetrator, rather than their match to the appearance of the suspect. This recommendation was incorporated into the US Justice Department guidelines as well as the guidelines of several US states that have followed the Justice Department Guidelines.

However, subsequent experiments have not replicated the Wells *et al.* (1993) results. Rather, studies that have directly compared suspect-matched and description-matched foil selection, taken together, do show higher correct identification rates, but also show higher false identification rates for description-matched lineups than for suspect-matched lineups (Clark, Rush, & Moreland, 2013). Overall accuracy, considering both correct and false identification rates, appears to be equal or slightly worse for description-matched lineups than for suspect-matched lineups. Moreover, description-matched lineups may be less fair than suspect-matched lineups, with fairness measured by the probability of a suspect identification conditional upon any identification from an innocent-suspect lineup. These results are surprising. Not only did description-matched foil selection not reduce the bias in the lineup, it appears on the whole to have made it worse.

There are other problems that may arise from description-based foil selection, noted by Lindsay, Martin and Webber (1994), and more recently by Fitzgerald *et al.* (2013). Witness descriptions are often vague, lacking in detail, or simply incorrect, providing little guidance for selecting foils. In addition, the suspect may not match the witness' description of the perpetrator for any of several reasons – because the witness' description was inaccurate, or because the perpetrator changed his appearance, or because the suspect is not the perpetrator. For such cases, the US guidelines recommend that foils be selected based on their match to the suspect, rather than the witness' description. The solution may not be as simple as it sounds, however, as it requires law enforcement to evaluate the extent to which the suspect, at the time of the lineup, matches the witness' description of the perpetrator.

Description-matching: necessary but not sufficient? The empirical results suggest that the selection of foils based only on their match to the witness' description of the perpetrator is not sufficient for creating fair, unbiased lineups. However, the explicit equating of lineup members in terms of their match to a witness' description of the perpetrator may be a necessary procedure. Again, this necessity can be illustrated with an example (borrowed from Clark *et al.*, 2013). Consider a case in which a witness provides a detailed description of the perpetrator, noting amongst other things that the person had unusually large ears. An innocent person becomes a suspect because the police notice that he too has unusually large ears, and he is placed in a lineup along with several individuals who are very similar in appearance – except for the unusually large ears. The example illustrates an important point: foils can be selected that are indeed very similar to the suspect, and yet the lineup may be biased, and the suspect may stand out, based on a single unique feature. This point returns us to Devlin's (1976) distinction between identifying the suspect versus recognizing a particular distinctive feature. The two cases can be disentangled if all lineup members are consistent regarding that distinctive feature.

A proposed general rule The foregoing analysis suggests a general rule: The selection of foils should be based, at least in part, on the same criteria that led to the suspect's inclusion in the lineup. If the suspect became a suspect because a police officer made a judgment that he matched the witness' description of the suspect, then the foils should also be evaluated based on their fit to the witness' description. In a similar fashion, if the suspect became a suspect because of his similarity to a composite drawing, then the foils should also be evaluated based on their similarity to that composite drawing. Of course, one must be cautious when proposing broad and sensible-sounding rules. They must be evaluated in terms of their practical implementation and with empirical data.[3]

How many lineup members? This question has clear answers in procedural guidelines that are based on very little empirical research. The US Justice Department Guidelines state that lineups should have a minimum of six individuals, one suspect plus at least five foils, and

---

[3]The creation of rules does not remove the need to rely on human judgments which may be influenced by a host of external factors. For example, Charman, Gregory, and Carlucci (2009) showed that judgments of similarity between lineup members and a composite photograph of the perpetrator vary with beliefs regarding guilt. We are not suggesting equating lineup members through similarity ratings, of course, but rather checking to ensure that if the composite has feature X, and the suspect has feature X, that all of the foils have feature X. However, even this check for feature equivalence may be influenced by various aspects of human judgment.

many US states and local law enforcement jurisdictions within the US have adopted that standard. The PACE Guidelines instruct that video and live lineups should include only one suspect, but allow lineups to include two suspects if they are "of roughly similar appearance". The Guidelines require a minimum of eight foils for a lineup with one suspect (for a total of nine), and a minimum of 12 foils for a lineup with two suspects (for a total of 14). But why? Why not four? Why not 40? There is little research to guide the guidelines on this issue.

Cutler, Penrod, and Martens (1987) and Cutler, Penrod, O'Rourke, and Martens (1986) compared 6-person and 12-person lineups, and reported no significant differences in accuracy (measured as proportion correct, collapsed across guilty-suspect and innocent-suspect lineups). Nosworthy and Lindsay (1990) compared lineup sizes of 4, 8, 12, 16 and 20. Correct identification rates varied from 0.33 to 0.48 and false identification rates varied from 0.00 to 0.07, but with no consistent (monotonic) pattern. Given such weak and inconsistent results, it is not surprising that researchers would conclude that lineup size does not matter – as long as there are at least three plausible foils in the lineup (Brewer & Palmer, 2010). However, Nosworthy and Lindsay (1990) noted an important limitation of their study that may have contributed to the inconsistent results. In their study, larger lineups included all of the foils in the smaller lineups, and added unique foils that were not included in the smaller lineups. Thus, there is a confounding of the number of lineup members with the actual lineup members.

This is a difficult problem to solve. Obviously, a larger lineup cannot contain the exact same lineup members as a smaller lineup. However, the lineup members can be equated through counterbalancing or random sampling from the same population of lineup members. An experiment by Meissner, Tredoux, Parker, and MacLin (2005) incorporated the random sampling solution in a study that compared lineups with 1, 2, 4, 6, 8, 10 or 12 members. They used a lineup recognition task in which participants viewed 8 faces followed by 16 lineup test trials. Correct and (estimated) false identification rates both decreased with increasing lineup size. Accuracy decreased as lineup size increased.

There are some important limitations of this study, given its departure from the staged-event procedure used in most eyewitness identification experiments. One specific limitation is that lineup size was varied between participants. Participants in the 1-person lineup condition were presented with a total of 16 faces at test, whereas participants in the 12-person lineup condition were presented with a total of 192 faces at test. To the extent that the test faces may have produced memory interference, this interference would have increased with lineup size. The lack of data, the inconsistency of data, and the limitations of the studies leaves this most fundamental issue about lineup construction unresolved and in need of additional research.

A study by Brewer, Caon, Todd, and Weber (2006) addressed the limitations of these previous studies (with random sampling of foils and a between-subjects manipulation of lineup size). They examined identification performance for guilty-suspect and innocent-suspect lineups, with 3, 7 or 11 foils, for two different staged crimes, one using a video of a shoplifter and the other using a video of a car thief. Based on their analyses they reported no significant effects of lineup size. However, a closer analysis shows that identification performance did in fact vary as a function of lineup size. Correct identification rates decreased as the number of foils increased, for both the shoplifter and car thief videos, although neither was statistically significant (χ^2 (2)$=4.08$, $p=0.13$, $r=0.20$ for the shoplifter and χ^2 (2)$=3.19$, $p=0.20$, $r=0.18$ for the car thief). However, the decreases were statistically significant when the effect sizes are meta-analytically aggregated across the shoplifter and car thief videos ($z=2.68$, $p=0.007$). The decreases were largest comparing 4-person lineups to 8-person lineups, with very small differences comparing 8-person to 12-person lineups. The analysis by Brewer $et\ al.$ did not designate an innocent suspect, but false identification rates can be estimated by dividing the total identification rate for innocent-suspect lineups by the lineup size. This analysis shows that false identification rates also decreased as a function of lineup size (0.07, 0.04, and 0.03 for lineup sizes of 4, 8 and 12, for the shoplifter video, and 0.13, 0.09, and 0.06 for the car thief video). Calculation of d' from the correct and estimated false identification rates revealed a consistent pattern for the shoplifter and car thief videos: a decrease in d' comparing 4-person to 8-person lineups (from 1.24 to 0.93 for the shoplifter and from 2.04 to 1.74 for the car thief), and a slight increase in d' comparing 8-person lineups to 12-person lineups (from 0.93 to 1.04 for the shoplifter and from 1.74 to 1.87 for the car thief). These results suggest that correct and false identification rates both decrease as foils are added to the lineup, and that the decreases may combine to produce a non-monotonic discriminability function.

Lineup Format: Photos, Videos, or Live Lineups?

In many (but not all) US states, lineups are composed of head-and-shoulders photographs, rather than live human beings. In the UK, lineups have historically been conducted as live "parades", but since 2008 are conducted through video and are only rarely conducted live (Valentine, Hughes, & Munro, 2009). The American preference for photo lineups is likely driven by several practical and legal considerations, many of which were reviewed by Brooks (1983) and by Cutler, Berman, and Fisher (1994).

First, it is much simpler to conduct a photo lineup than a live lineup. A photo lineup is portable; it can slipped into a police officer's notebook and taken to the witness, rather than having to arrange for the witness to come to the lineup. Photographs can be digitally altered to create consistency in background and size, or to replicate or remove distinctive features (Zarkadi, Wade, & Stewart, 2009). The photographs can be, and now often are, selected from enormous on-line databases that contain tens or even hundreds of thousands of photographs. Collecting live bodies is much more difficult. This is not simply a convenience issue; to the extent that the composition of live lineups is limited by the availability of people to participate in the role of foils, the fairness of live lineups may be severely compromised. The availability problem appears to have been a core problem in the many false identifications of Adolf Beck.

In addition, as with any event conducted live, some aspects may be difficult to control. For example, lineup participants may not follow directions, or may subvert the process. To illustrate, in a Wisconsin murder case, the suspect Ralph Armstrong, on the advice of his attorney, refused to participate in the live lineup, and as a result police dragged him in front of the witness. Certainly Armstrong would have stood out in such a lineup as the only person who was dragged by police officers.[4]

The unique circumstances of the suspect within the lineup may also be apparent in more subtle ways. Typically, the foils know that they are not the subject of the lineup, and thus they know that there are no consequences for them if they are identified. However, the consequences for the suspect, guilty or innocent, are serious, and the anxiety produced by the situation may be apparent. Weigold and Wentura (2004) explored this "suspect effect" experimentally. College students were lineup members and mock witnesses. A person was more likely to be identified from a lineup if the person knew that he or she was the "suspect" and given an incentive to not be identified.

The legal consideration in the use of live lineups is that in the US a suspect who participates in a live lineup is entitled to presence of counsel, whereas no such right exists for a suspect in a photographic lineup. This is useful to the defence in that it provides an opportunity to voice

---

[4]Armstrong stood out in other ways as well. Many of the lineup foils were police officers who wore wigs in order to match Armstrong's shoulder length hair. Armstrong was convicted in 1980 and exonerated in 2009. The first author of this chapter participated in Armstrong's post-conviction appeal.

concerns and possibly replace foils that are deemed unsuitable, and it is useful to the prosecution in that such concerns are expressed and dealt with at the lineup rather than at trial.

Despite the practical problems associated with the composition and conduct of live lineups, there is reason to think that live lineups should result in greater accuracy than photo lineups. Live lineups present the witness with more information, and more *kinds* of information, than a photo lineup; they present the witness with more information about body size and shape, more views of each lineup member's face, and importantly dynamic information about movement.

As a result of revisions in the PACE guidelines in 2003 and 2008, lineups in the UK are now almost always conducted through video, and are rarely conducted as live parades (Valentine *et al.*, 2009). Presumably, video lineups incorporate the advantages of live lineups (i.e., the presentation of more information, including dynamic information), but do not suffer from the practical limitations of live lineups.

We turn our attention now to relevant data, from both laboratory and field studies. The distinction between laboratory and field studies is important because experimental studies can control away the practical limitations inherent in the conduct of live lineups, or equate those limitations across live, photo, and video conditions. For example, through appropriate experimental control, live, video, and photo lineups may all have the same foils; this is a level of control that may be easy to achieve in the lab, but difficult to achieve in the police station. To the extent that experimental studies control away such practical limitations, they may overestimate the accuracy of live identification procedures conducted in actual criminal investigations.

It is also important to note that conditions labelled as "photo", "video" or "live" are not levels of a single independent variable, but rather denote constellations of variables. Photo lineups are inherently static, video lineups are inherently dynamic, and live lineups can go either way, depending on whether lineup members move, or stand still. Photo and live lineups can be presented simultaneously or sequentially, but video lineups are inherently sequential. There are other procedural variations as well. For example, in the UK witnesses are required to withhold their decisions until they view the entire lineup twice through, whereas in the US, in both experimental paradigms and real-world applications, witnesses who are presented with a sequential lineup make their responses immediately, even if they have not yet seen the rest of the lineup. These variations require that comparisons across lineup formats be considered and interpreted carefully.

More versus less information With these caveats, comparisons among lineup formats can be analysed in terms of the amount of information that is conveyed. For example, a series of studies conducted by Cutler and colleagues compared static head-and-shoulders photo lineups with videotaped lineups that provided whole-body, dynamic, and voice information for each lineup member. These studies were reviewed by Cutler *et al.* (1994), who concluded that the additional information produced a "trivial effect on identification accuracy" (p. 179), such that, "there is no reason to believe that live lineups, videotaped lineups, or photo arrays produce substantial differences in identification performance" (p. 181).

We re-examined those studies, plus three additional studies. The correct identification rates were taken directly from the original studies. The false identification rates were either taken directly from the original studies or in some cases were estimated by dividing the total identification rate for innocent-suspect lineups by the number of lineup members. The correct and false identification rates were used to calculate d'. We also calculated the total proportion of correct responses, $p(c)$, as the average of the correct identification rates and correct rejection rates. For one study, by Kerstholt, Koster, and van Amelsvoort (2004), only $p(c)$ was reported for the relevant comparison.

The results are shown in Table 6.1. Averaging across seven comparisons, correct identification rates were slightly (but not significantly) higher, $t(6) = 0.608, p = 0.283,$[5] and false identification rates were lower, $t(6) = 2.833,$ $p = 0.015,$ for lineups that provided more information compared with lineups that provided less information. Overall accuracy, measured by d', was slightly higher for lineups that presented more information than for lineups that presented less information $(t(6) = 1.81, p = 0.060)$. We also calculated Pearson's r as a general measure of effect size. The average $r = 0.049$ was small, but showed a statistically significant advantage for lineups with more information over lineups with less information $(t(6) = 2.20, p = 0.034)$. Overall accuracy measured by the proportion of correct responses was also higher for lineups that presented more information than for lineups that presented less information $(t(7) = 3.123, p = 0.009)$. A word of caution is necessary regarding the use of proportion correct as a measure of identification accuracy. The term "accuracy" is attached to fundamentally different responses depending on the guilt or innocence of the suspect, and previous analyses have shown that correct identifications and correct rejections are uncorrelated (Clark, Howell, & Davey, 2008). More

---

[5]All p values are one-tailed for these directional tests of the hypothesis that lineups that provide more information lead to higher levels of accuracy than lineups that provide less information.

Table 6.1 Comparison of Lineup Formats with Less Versus More Information, Correct and False Identifications, d' and Proportion Correct

Study	Less information				More information			
	Correct ID	False ID	d'	pc	Correct ID	False ID	d'	pc
Cutler et al. (1987)	0.620	0.082	1.697	0.430	0.670	0.076	1.872	0.490
Cutler & Penrod (1988)	0.720	0.055	2.181	0.690	0.820	0.043	2.633	0.780
O'Rourke et al. (1989)	0.440	0.100	1.131	0.420	0.380	0.060	1.250	0.450
Valentine et al. (2007) (w)	0.607	0.037	2.058	0.637	0.708	0.014	2.748	0.792
Valentine et al. (2007) (i)	0.310	0.019	1.573	0.568	0.417	0.004	2.419	0.690
Darling et al. (2008) (sm)	0.538	0.036	1.898	0.680	0.444	0.034	1.678	0.619
Darling et al. (2008) (dm)	0.478	0.048	1.614	0.549	0.417	0.045	1.428	0.641
Kerstholt et al. (2004)				0.416				0.592
Mean	0.530	0.054	1.736	0.549	0.551	0.039	2.012	0.632

Note: pc denotes proportion correct; (w) denotes existing UK procedure in which witnesses withhold their decisions until they view the entire lineup twice through; (i) denotes research and US sequential procedure in which witnesses make immediate decisions; (sm) denotes suspect-matched foil selection; (dm) denotes description-matched foil selection.

importantly, proportion correct, like the ratio of correct to false identifications, may increase due to a conservative criterion shift. Note in Table 6.1 for example, for the Darling *et al.* (2008) study (with description-matched lineups), the proportion correct increased, whereas d' decreased, with more lineup information.

The results in Table 6.1 suggest that eyewitness identification accuracy increases with more information in the lineup. It is not clear what additional information produces the increase in identification accuracy in the studies that compared more versus less information (see Cutler *et al.*, 1986). In addition, more research is needed to establish the generality and identify possible moderators of the "more information" effect. Results from Cutler *et al.* (1987) showed that the increase in accuracy was moderated by the similarity of the lineup foils as well as by the retention interval.

Video versus live lineups Many of the practical limitations of live lineups can be minimized through the use of video lineups while maintaining the additional information available in live lineups. In the UK, video lineups are constructed through the PROMAT (Promat Envision International) and VIPER (Video Identification Parade Electronic Recording) systems, which maintain very large databases of video recordings in the same way that US image software maintains large databases of mugshots. Thus, these video lineups may have the advantage of presenting dynamic information without the live lineup disadvantages (i.e., shortage of suitable foils, non-cooperation of lineup members, etc.). Also, the PACE guidelines provide a legal safeguard by allowing presence of counsel at video lineups.

The key empirical question is whether video lineups show the same level of accuracy as live lineups. There are, to our knowledge, only two[6] published studies that have made this comparison, for both guilty-suspect and innocent-suspect conditions. Cutler, Fisher, and Chicvara (1989) showed slightly higher overall accuracy for live lineups ($d' = 2.39$, $p(c) = 0.73$) than for videotaped lineups ($d' = 1.93, p(c) = 0.67$). Correct identification rates were slightly lower for live lineups (0.65) than for video lineups (0.69), and false identification rates were much lower for live lineups (0.022) than for video lineups (0.076). More recently, Kerstholt *et al.*

---

[6]A third study, by Cutler and Fisher (1990) used a two-perpetrator staged crime; the guilty-suspect lineup was based on one perpetrator and the innocent-suspect lineup was based on the other perpetrator. The results showed slightly higher overall accuracy for video lineups ($d' = 1.17, p(c) = 0.56$) than live lineups ($d' = 1.04, p(c) = 0.54$). However, it is impossible to interpret overall accuracy across guilty- and innocent-suspect conditions, as the results are based on different perpetrators.

(2004) also compared live and video lineups. Their results, reported as $p(c)$, collapsed over guilty- and innocent-suspect lineups, also showed a very small advantage for live lineups (0.63) over videotaped lineups (0.59). The two studies are consistent in showing a slight advantage for live lineups over video lineups, which seems sensible to the extent that live lineups may provide more information than video lineups. With only two studies (and the caveats associated with proportion correct as a measure of accuracy), it is difficult to draw firm conclusions.

As noted earlier, experimental studies can avoid the practical problems that are associated with the conduct of live lineups. In particular, experimental studies control away the problem of restricted foil selection that can occur for live lineups. Thus, it is important to compare live and video lineups as they are conducted in actual cases. Of course, in actual cases one cannot evaluate lineup procedures in terms of correct and false identification rates because the guilt of the suspect cannot be determined. However, there are other useful comparisons that can be made.

Valentine and Heaton (1999) used a mock-witness procedure to evaluate the fairness of video and live lineups in England. Mock witnesses were provided with a witness' description of the perpetrator and were asked to identify the best match to that description from a series of nine-person video lineups or the photographs corresponding to a series of nine-person live lineups. They evaluated lineup fairness with several dependent measures; we focus on one measure, the average proportions of mock-witnesses who identified the suspect. These proportions were 0.25 averaged across the 25 live lineups and 0.15 averaged across the 16 video lineups. Statistically, 9 of the 25 live lineups (36%) and 4 of the 16 video lineups (25%) showed suspect ID choice rates that were significantly higher than expected by the fair lineup baseline of 1/9 (11%). These results suggest that the video lineups were fairer overall, and more likely to be fair, relative to the live lineups.

Lineup Composition and Lineup Presentation

In this section we examine how lineup composition interacts with other aspects of lineup procedure.

Lineup instructions The US and PACE guidelines recommend that witnesses be instructed prior to the presentation of the lineup that the perpetrator may, *or may not*, be in the lineup. These unbiased instructions have the effect of reducing both correct and false identification rates, with no change in accuracy (Clark, 2012). These results are consistent with the hypothesis that the "not present" instruction induces witnesses to raise their decision criterion for making an identification. One might reasonably expect the effects of lineup instructions to vary with lineup composition. Specifically, if the instructions are biased by suggesting or explicitly stating that the perpetrator is in the lineup, the increase in the overall identification rate should fall proportionally more on suspect identifications rather than foil identifications. An important question is whether the double-dose of biased instructions and biased lineup composition might reduce accuracy by increasing false identifications of innocent suspects proportionally more than correct identifications of guilty suspects. There is only one published study that examines the 2×2 interaction of lineup instructions and lineup composition for both guilty-suspect and innocent-suspect lineups (Leippe, Eisenstadt & Rauch, 2009). Somewhat surprisingly, the lowest performance was not produced in the double-biased condition, but rather in the condition that combined biased instructions with less biased lineups.

Lineup administrator influence How does lineup composition interact with various forms of lineup administrator influence? By lineup administrator influence we mean suggestive behaviours by the lineup administrator that would *push* the witness toward making an identification rather than a non-identification response, or that would *steer* the witness specifically toward the suspect. Here again, the interactions appear complex. First it is important to note that lineup administrators can influence witnesses even when they are blind as to the position of the suspect in the lineup. Clark, Marshall, and Rosenthal (2009) showed that if the suggestiveness is diffuse and non-specific (with seemingly innocuous phrases such as "take your time"), the increase in identifications may fall upon lineup members who are less similar to the perpetrator. However, if the suggestiveness is more pointed ("Is there anyone in the lineup who looks most like the perpetrator?"), the increase in identifications is – perhaps not surprisingly – focused on lineup members who are more similar to the suspect (Clark *et al.*, 2009; Clark & Tunnicliff, 2001). Clark, Brower, Rosenthal, Hicks, and Moreland (2013) examined pushing and steering when lineup administrators were not blind. Their results suggested that it may be easier to steer the witness towards a suspect who is guilty than a suspect who is innocent, although both guilty and innocent suspect identification rates increased. It is interesting to note that Scottish procedures explicitly include such similarity questions. For witnesses who are "unable" to make an identification, police may ask, "Is there anyone … who resembles the person?" Results from Clark and colleagues suggest that such similarity questions will increase the identification rate for guilty and innocent suspects to the extent that those suspects look more similar to the perpetrator than do the foils.

Simultaneous and sequential presentation Here we take up the issue of whether (or how) lineup composition affects identification outcomes differentially for simultaneous and sequential lineups. In a simultaneous lineup, all lineup members are presented at the same time, whereas in a sequential lineup the lineup members are presented one at a time. Our review is motivated by four considerations:

1. Some researchers have argued that sequential presentation is pro-cedurally superior to simultaneous presentation (Steblay, Dysart, & Wells, 2011).
2. As a result, many jurisdictions in the US present lineups sequen-tially either as a best-practice recommendation or by law.
3. Some researchers have suggested that sequential presentation can ameliorate or even eliminate the negative effects of biased lineups (Levi, 1999; Lindsay *et al.*, 1991).
4. Sequential lineup presentation is a necessary component of video lineups that are conducted in the UK. Each of these points is consid-ered in turn.

Based on their meta-analysis, Steblay *et al.* (2011) declared sequential lineups to be superior to simultaneous lineups because they reduce the false identification rate with only a small reduction in the correct iden-tification rate. More recent meta-analyses by Clark (2012) and by Palmer and Brewer (2012) suggest that the sequential superiority effect reported by Steblay *et al.* was a product of their use of the C/F ratio as a measure of accuracy and their exclusion of key studies. In addition, two studies that have used ROC analysis suggest that sequen-tial lineups may produce *lower* accuracy than simultaneous lineups (Gronlund *et al.*, 2013; Mickes *et al.*, 2013).

Despite the controversy, many US state and local jurisdictions now present lineups sequentially. Even if sequential lineups do not pro-vide more accurate identification evidence in general, they may have one specific benefit in that they reduce the negative effects of biased lineups (Levi, 1999; Lindsay *et al.*, 1991). However, results from two studies, by Carlson, Gronlund, and Clark (2008), and by Gronlund *et al.* (2009), and a recent meta-analysis by Fitzgerald *et al.* (2013), challenge this view. In their meta-analysis, Fitzgerald *et al.* used measurements of lineup fairness from each study to assign lineups to categories of low similarity, moderate similarity, and high similarity foils. Thus, their comparisons were not simply lower versus higher similarity, but rather low-to-moderate, moderate-to-high, and low-to-high. In addition, they conducted separate analyses for simultaneous and sequential lineups. The results, from their Table 1, are shown

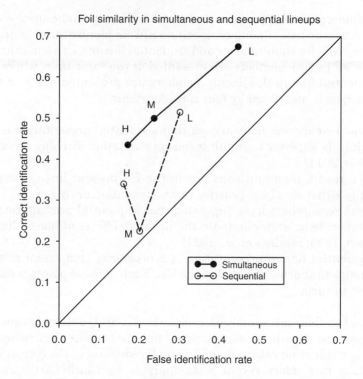

Figure 6.1 Foil similarity for high (H), moderate (M), and low similarity (L) foils, in simultaneous and sequential lineups, from Fitzgerald *et al.* (2013).

here in Figure 6.1, which plots the correct identification rates on the *x*-axis and the false identification rates on the *y*-axis, in much the same way as they would be plotted in an ROC analysis (see Chapter 11 for a discussion of ROC analysis).

Two results are clear from the figure. First, consistent with recent analyses, sequential lineups produced lower levels of accuracy than simultaneous lineups. Second, the similarity effects were monotonic for simultaneous lineups, but not for sequential lineups. For simultaneous lineups, correct and false identification rates both increased as foil similarity decreased. Sequential lineups, however, showed the lowest level of accuracy when the foils were of moderate similarity. The relatively lower accuracy of sequential lineups raises a question as to whether the sequential presentation of video lineups lowers identification accuracy.

As noted earlier, the procedure for sequential presentation of video lineups in the UK differs from the procedure for sequential presentation used in research and US jurisdictions. In the research and US protocols the witness makes a yes (that's him) or no (that's not him) decision for each lineup member at the time that lineup member is presented. In the research protocol the sequential lineup may terminate upon a yes response, or the remaining lineup members may be presented to the witness. In those jurisdictions that have implemented sequential lineups, witnesses are presented with the entire lineup, even after a yes response, and witnesses may request to see the lineup more than once. That is, they may take a "second lap" through the lineup. By contrast, in the UK, all lineup members are presented *twice* before the witness is permitted to make any response. The core of the difference is that in the UK, witness decisions must be *withheld*, whereas in the research protocol and in the US, the witness' identification decisions must be *immediate*, at the time that the lineup member is presented.

Valentine, Darling, and Memon (2007) examined identification performance in video and photo lineups, with a direct comparison between the withheld decision procedure and the immediate decision procedure. The results are shown in Table 6.1. For both video and photo lineups, overall accuracy, measured by d', was higher for the withheld decision procedure than for the immediate decision procedure. These results suggest that, to the extent that sequential presentation may reduce accuracy, that reduction may be minimized (or reversed) through the use of the withheld decision procedure.

IMPLICATIONS FOR LAW ENFORCEMENT POLICY AND FUTURE RESEARCH

Changes in eyewitness identification procedures often involve trade-offs (Clark, 2012). Increases in foil similarity reduce the false identification rate, but also reduce the correct identification rate. Selection of foils based on their match to the witness' description, rather than the suspect, increases the correct identification rate, but also increases the false identification rate. Although there are few empirical studies, there is some evidence that increasing the number of foils reduces both correct and false identification rates. Such trade-offs complicate policy decisions (Clark, 2012); to the extent that policy-makers base policy choices on overall accuracy or expected utility, they must consider these trade-offs carefully, and consider real-world base rates (the proportion of lineups in which the suspect is guilty) as well as the objective and subjective utilities associated with eyewitness identification outcomes.

Regarding the question as to whether foils should be selected based on their similarity to the suspect or their match to the witness' description, there is no clear "winner". Description-matched foil selection has been shown to reduce overall accuracy; however, suspect-matched foil selection may sometimes produce lineups that look good in that the suspect does not stand out, and yet fail to equate lineup members on a key, diagnostic feature. We cautiously suggest that this is a false choice and that the best procedure may be one that selects foils based on their similarity to the suspect, and also checks that all of the features described by the witness match all of the foils to the same extent that they match the suspect. Our caution arises primarily from the lack of data. Although it may sound good to match both ways, the point raised by Luus and Wells (1991) still holds: there may be a point at which increasing foil similarity serves primarily to reduce the correct identification rate with little benefit in terms of a reduced false identification rate.

In contrast to the general trade-off pattern reported by Clark (2012), Clark *et al.* (2013), and Fitzgerald *et al.* (2013), our analysis of lineup information showed a reduction in the false identification rate *and* an increase in the correct identification rate for lineups that provided witnesses with more information (voice information, movement, whole-body information) relative to lineups that provided witnesses with less information (no voice information, no movement, head-and-shoulders photographs only). We make this observation also with caution, noting that such no-cost patterns have been claimed for both sequential lineups and unbiased instructions, only to be contradicted subsequently by new data (Clark, 2012).

Although there has been considerable progress in our understanding of the relationship between eyewitness identification procedures and identification accuracy, there are fundamental questions that remain unanswered. Additional research is needed to examine how eyewitness identification outcomes vary across photo, live, and video lineups and vary with the number of lineup foils. In both cases, researchers have concluded – perhaps prematurely – that the number of foils and the format of the lineup have little or no effect on accuracy. More research is needed regarding these two fundamental aspects of lineup composition and construction.

It is also important to understand how lineup composition interacts with other lineup variables. Foil similarity may produce different patterns of results for simultaneous and sequential lineups. There is relatively little research that examines how lineup composition interacts with lineup instructions (Clark, 2005; Steblay, 1997) or various forms of lineup administrator influences (Clark *et al.*, 2009, 2013; Greathouse & Kovera, 2008).

REFERENCES

Bellemare, D.A., & Finlayson, R. (2004). *Report on the Prevention of Miscarriages of Justice. Department of Justice, Canada.* Retrieved from www.justice.gc.ca

Borchard, E.M. (1932). *Convicting the Innocent: Errors of Criminal Justice.* New Haven, CT: Yale University Press.

Brewer, N., Caon, A., Todd, C., & Weber, N. (2006). Eyewitness identification accuracy and response latency. *Law and Human Behavior, 30,* 31–50. doi:10.1007/s10979-006-9002-7

Brewer, N., & Palmer, M.A. (2010). Eyewitness identification tests. *Legal and Criminological Psychology, 15,* 77–96. doi:10.1348/135532509X414765

Brooks, N. (1983). *Pretrial Eyewitness Identification Procedures.* Ottawa: Law Reform Commission of Canada.

Carlson, C.A., Gronlund, S.D., & Clark, S.E. (2008). Lineup composition, suspect position, and the sequential lineup advantage. *Journal of Experimental Psychology: Applied, 14*(2), 118–128. doi:10.1037/1076-898X.14.2.118

Charman, S.D., Gregory, A.H., & Carlucci, M. (2009). Exploring the diagnostic utility of facial composites: Beliefs of guilt can bias perceived similarity between composite and suspect. *Journal of Experimental Psychology: Applied, 15,* 76–90. doi:10.1037/a0014682

Clark, S.E. (2005). A re-examination of the effects of biased lineup instructions in eyewitness identification. *Law and Human Behavior, 29,* 395–424. doi:10.1007/s10979-005-5690-7

Clark, S.E. (2011). Blackstone and the balance of eyewitness identification evidence. *Albany Law Review, 75,* 101–152.

Clark, S.E. (2012). Costs and benefits of eyewitness identification reform: Psychological science and public policy. *Perspectives on Psychological Science, 7,* 238–259. doi:10.1177/1745691612439584

Clark, S.E., Brower, G.L., Rosenthal, R., Hicks, J.M., & Moreland, M.B. (2013). Lineup administrator influences on eyewitness identification and eyewitness confidence. *Journal of Applied Research in Memory and Cognition, 2,* 158–165. doi:10.1016/j.jarmac.2013.06.003

Clark, S.E., Howell, R.T., & Davey, S.L. (2008). Regularities in eyewitness identification. *Law and Human Behavior, 32,* 187–218. doi:10.1007/s10979-006-9082-4

Clark, S.E., Marshall, T., & Rosenthal, R. (2009). Lineup administrator influence on eyewitness identification decisions. *Journal of Experimental Psychology: Applied, 15,* 63–75. doi:10.1037/a0015185

Clark, S.E., Rush, R.A., & Moreland M.B. (2013). Constructing the lineup: Law, reform, theory, and data. In B.L. Cutler (Ed.), *Reform of Eyewitness Identification Procedures* (pp. 87–112). Washington DC: APA.

Clark, S.E., & Tunnicliff, J.T. (2001). Selecting lineup fillers in eyewitness identification experiments: Experimental control and real-world simulation. *Law and Human Behavior, 25,* 199–216. doi:10.1023/A:1010753809988

Collins, R.H., Walpole, S., & Edge, J. (1904). *Committee of Inquiry into the Case of Mr. Adolf Beck: Report from the Committee Together with Minutes of Evidence, Appendix and Facsimiles of Various Documents.* London: Wyman & Sons, Ltd.

Cutler, B.L., Berman, G.L., & Fisher, R.P. (1994). Conceptual, practical, and empirical issues associated with eyewitness identification test media. In D.F. Ross, J.D. Read, & M.P. Toglia (Eds.), *Adult Eyewitness Testimony: Current Trends and Developments* (pp. 163–181). New York: Cambridge University Press.

Cutler, B.L., & Fisher, R.P. (1990). Live lineups, videotaped lineups, and phtotoarrays. *Forensic Reports, 3*, 439–448.

Cutler, B.L., Fisher, R.P., & Chicvara, C.L. (1989). Eyewitness identification from live versus videotaped lineups. *Forensic Reports, 2*, 93–106.

Cutler, B.L., & Penrod, S.D. (1988). Improving the reliability of eyewitness identification: Lineup construction and presentation. *Journal of Applied Psychology, 73*, 281–290. doi:10.1037/0021-9010.73.2.281

Cutler, B.L, Penrod, S.D., & Martens, T.K. (1987). Improving the reliability of eyewitness identifications: Putting context into context. *Journal of Applied Psychology, 72*, 629–637. doi:10.1037/0021-9010.72.4.629

Cutler, B.L., Penrod, S.D., O'Rourke, T.E., & Martens, T.K. (1986). Unconfounding the effects of contextual cues on eyewitness identification accuracy. *Social Behavior: An International Journal of Applied Social Psychology, 2*, 113–134.

Darling, S., Valentine, T., & Memon, A. (2008). Selection of lineup foils in operational contexts. *Applied Cognitive Psychology, 22*, 159–169. doi:10.1002/acp.1366

Davies, G., & Griffiths, L. (2008). Eyewitness identification and the English Courts: A century of trial and error. *Psychiatry, Psychology and Law, 15*, 435–449. doi:10.1080/13218710802101605

Devlin, P.A. (1976). *Report to the Secretary of State for the Home Department of the Departmental Committee on Evidence of Identification in Criminal Cases.* London: Her Majesty's Stationery Office.

Doob, A.N., & Kirshenbaum, H.M. (1973). Bias in police lineups – partial remembering. *Journal of Police Science and Administration, 1*, 287–293.

Fitzgerald, R.J., Price, H.L., Oriet, C., & Charman, S.D. (2013). The effect of foil-suspect similarity on eyewitness identification decisions: A meta-analysis. *Psychology, Public Policy & Law, 19*, 151–164. doi:10.1037/a0030618

Foster v. California (1969). 394 U.S. 440.

Garrett, B.L. (2011). *Convicting the Innocent: Where Criminal Prosecutions Go Wrong.* Cambridge, MA: Harvard University Press.

Gilbert v. California (1967). 388 U.S. 263.

Greathouse, S.M., & Kovera, M.B. (2008). Instruction bias and lineup presentation moderate the effects of administrator knowledge on eyewitness identification. *Law and Human Behavior, 33*, 70–82. doi:10.1007/s10979-008-9136-x

Gronlund, S.D., Carlson, C.A., Dailey, S.B., & Goodsell, C.A. (2009). Robustness of the sequential lineup advantage. *Journal of Experimental Psychology: Applied, 15*, 140–152. doi:10.1037/a0015082

Gronlund, S.D., Carlson, C.A., Neuschatz, J.S., Goodsell, C.A., Wetmore, S.A., Wooten, A., & Graham, M. (2013). Showups versus lineups: An evaluation using ROC analysis. *Journal of Applied Research in Memory and Cognition, 1*, 221–228. doi:10.1016/j.jarmac.2012.09.003

Gross, S.R., Jacoby, K., Matheson, D.J., Montgomery, N., & Patil, S. (2005). Exonerations in the United States 1989 through 2003. *Journal of Criminal Law and Criminology, 95*, 523–560.

Gross, S.R., & Shaffer, M. (2013). *Exonerations in the United States, 1989–2012.* University of Michigan Public Law Working Paper, No. 277. Retrieved from papers.ssrn.com

Home Office (1969). Identification parades. Home Office Circular 9/1969. In P.A. Devlin (1976), *Report to the Secretary of State for the Home Department of the Departmental Committee on Evidence of Identification in Criminal Cases* (pp. 158–161). London: Her Majesty's Stationery Office.

Huff, C.R., & Killias, M. (2010). *Wrongful Conviction: International Perspectives on Miscarriages of Justice*. Philadelphia: Temple University Press.

Jolicoeur, M. (2010). International Perspectives on Wrongful Convictions: Workshop Report. Washington, DC: US Department of Justice.

Kaye, D.H. (1986). Quantifying probative value. *Boston University Law Journal, 66*, 761–766.

Kerstholt, J.H., Koster, E.R., & van Amelsvoort, A.G. (2004). Eyewitnesses: A comparison of live, video, and photo line-ups. *Journal of Police and Criminal Psychology, 19*, 15–22.

Killias, M. (2013). Errors occur everywhere – but not at the same frequency: The role of procedural systems in wrongful convictions. In C.R. Huff & M. Killias (Eds.), *Wrongful Convictions and Miscarriages of Justice: Causes and Remedies in North American and European Criminal Justice Systems* (pp. 61–76). New York: Routledge.

Leippe, M.R., Eisenstadt, D., & Rauch, S.M. (2009). Cueing confidence in eye-witness identifications: Influence of biased lineup instructions and pre-identification memory feedback under varying lineup conditions. *Law and Human Behavior, 33*, 194–212. doi:10.1007/s10979-008-9135-y

Levi, A.M. (1999). An honourable discharge for line-up fairness measurement. *Applied Cognitive Psychology, 13*, S121–S124. doi:10.1002/(SICI)1099-0720 (199911)13:1+<S121::AID-ACP680>3.0.CO;2-R

Lindsay, R.C.L., Lea, J.A., Nosworthy, G.J., Fulford, J.A., Hector, J., LeVan, V., & Seebrook, C. (1991). Biased lineups: Sequential presentation reduces the problem. *Journal of Applied Psychology, 76*, 796–802. doi:10.1037/ 0021-9010.76.6.796

Lindsay, R.C.L., Martin, R., & Webber, L. (1994). Default values in eyewitness descriptions: A problem for the match-to-description lineup foil selection strategy. *Law and Human Behavior, 18*, 527–541. doi:10.1007/BF01499172

Luus, C.A.E., & Wells, G.L. (1991). Eyewitness identification and the selection of distracters for lineups. *Law and Human Behavior, 15*, 43–57. doi:10.1007/ BF01044829

Malpass, R.S. (1981). Effective size and defendant bias in eyewitness identification lineups. *Law and Human Behavior, 5*, 299–309. doi:10.1007/BF01044945

Malpass, R.S., Tredoux, C., & McQuiston-Surrett, D. (2007). Lineup construction and measuring lineup fairness. In R. Lindsay, D. Ross, D. Read, & M. Toglia (Eds.), *Handbook of Eyewitness Psychology, Vol. 2* (pp. 155–178). Mahwah: Lawrence Erlbaum.

Manson v. Brathwaite (1977). 432 U.S. 98.

Meissner, C.A., Tredoux, C.G., Parker, J.F., & MacLin, O.H. (2005). Eyewitness decisions in simultaneous and sequential lineups: A dual-process signal detection theory analysis. *Memory and Cognition, 33*, 783–792. doi:10.3758/ BF03193074

Mickes, L., Flowe, H.D., & Wixted, J.T. (2012). Receiver operating characteristic analysis of eyewitness memory: comparing the diagnostic accuracy of simultaneous vs. sequential lineups. *Journal of Experimental Psychology: Applied, 18,* 361–376. doi:10.1037/a0030609

Munsterberg, H. (1908). *On the Witness Stand*. New York: Clark, Boardman.

Navon, D. (1992). Selection of lineup fillers by similarity to the suspect is likely to misfire. *Law and Human Behavior 16*, 575–593. doi:10.1007/BF01044624

Neil v. Biggers (1972). 409 U.S. 188.

National Institute of Justice (1999). *Eyewitness Evidence: A Guide for Law Enforcement*. Washington, DC: US Department of Justice.

Nosworthy, G.J., & Lindsay, R.C. (1990). Does nominal lineup size matter? *Journal of Applied Psychology, 75*, 358–361. doi:10.1037/0021-9010.75.3.358

O'Rourke, T., Penrod, S., Cutler, B., & Stuve, T. (1989). The external validity of eyewitness identification research: Generalizing across subject populations. *Law and Human Behavior, 13*, 385–395. doi:10.1007/BF01056410

Palmer, M.A., & Brewer, N. (2012). Sequential lineup presentation promotes less biased criterion setting but does not improve discriminability. *Law and Human Behavior, 36*, 247–255. doi:10.1037/h0093923

Police and Criminal Evidence Act (PACE) (1984) Code D. 2011. Retrieved from https://www.gov.uk.government/publications/pace-code-d-2011

R v. Turnbull and Others (1976). 63 Cr. App. R 224.

Scottish Home and Health Department (1982). *Guidelines on the Conduct of Identification Parades*.

Steblay, N.M. (1997). Social influence in eyewitness recall: A meta-analytic review of lineup instruction effects. *Law and Human Behavior, 21*, 283–297. doi:10.1023/A:1024890732059

Steblay, N.K., Dysart, J.E., & Wells, G.L. (2011). Seventy-two tests of the sequential lineup superiority effect: A meta-analysis and policy discussion. *Psychology, Public Policy, and Law, 17*, 99–139. doi:10.1037/a0021650

Stovall v. Denno (1967). 388 U.S. 293.

Tredoux, C.G. (1998). Statistical inference on measures of lineup fairness. *Law and Human Behavior, 22*, 217–237. doi:10.1023/A:1025746220886

Tredoux, C.G. (1999). Statistical considerations when determining measures of lineup size and lineup bias. *Applied Cognitive Psychology, 13*, S9–S26. doi:10.1002/(SICI)1099-0720(199911)13:1+<S9::AID-ACP634>3.0.CO;2-1

US v. Reid (1975). 517 F.2d 953.

US v. Wade (1967). *388 U.S. 218.*

Valentine, T., Darling, S., & Memon, A. (2007). Do strict rules and moving images increase the reliability of sequential identification procedures? *Applied Cognitive Psychology, 21*, 933–949. doi:10.1002/acp.1306

Valentine, T., & Heaton, P. (1999). An evaluation of the fairness of police line-ups and video identifications. *Applied Cognitive Psychology, 13*, S59–S72. doi:10.1002/(SICI)1099-0720(199911)13:1+<S59::AID-ACP679>3.0.CO;2-Y

Valentine, T., Hughes, C., & Munro, R. (2009). Recent developments in eyewitness identification procedures in the United Kingdom. In R. Bull, T. Valentine, & T. Williamson (Eds.), *The Handbook of Psychology of Investigative Interviewing* (pp. 221–240). Chichester: John Wiley & Sons, Ltd.

Wall, P.M. (1965). *Eye-witness Identification in Criminal Cases*. Springfield, IL: Thomas.

Watson, E.R. (1924). *The Trial of Adolf Beck*. Glasgow: Hodge.

Weigold, A., & Wentura, D. (2004). Who's the one in trouble? Experimental evidence for 'psychic state' bias in lineups. *European Journal of Social Psychology, 34*, 121–133. doi:10.1002/ejsp.193

Wells, G.L., Leippe, M.R., & Ostrom, T.M. (1979). Guidelines for empirically assessing the fairness of a lineup. *Law and Human Behavior, 3*, 285–293. doi:10.1007/BF01039807

Wells, G.L., & Quinlivan D.S. (2009). Suggestive eyewitness identification procedures and the Supreme Court's reliability test in light of eyewitness science: 30 years later. *Law and Human Behavior, 33*, 1–24. doi:10.1007/s10979-008-9130-3

Wells, G.L., Rydell, S.M., & Seelau, E.P. (1993). The selection of distractors for eyewitness lineups. *Journal of Applied Psychology, 78*, 835–844. doi:10.1037/0021-9010.78.5.835

Wells, G.L., Small, M., Penrod, S., Malpass, R.S., Fulero, S.M., & Brimacombe, C.A.E. (1998). Eyewitness identification procedures: Recommendations for lineups and photospreads. *Law and Human Behavior, 22*, 603–647. doi:10.1023/A:1025750605807

Wells, G.L., & Turtle, J.W. (1986). Eyewitness identification: The importance of lineup models. *Psychological Bulletin, 99*, 320–329. doi:10.1037/0033-2909.99.3.320

Wixted, J.T., & Mickes, L. (2012). The field of eyewitness memory should abandon probative value and embrace receiver operating characteristic analysis. *Perspectives on Psychological Science, 7*, 275–278. doi:10.1177/1745691612442906

Wogalter, M.S., Malpass, R.S., & McQuiston, D.E. (2004). A national survey of U.S. police on preparation and conduct of identification lineups. *Psychology, Crime, & Law, 10*, 69–82. doi:10.1080/10683160410001641873

Zarkadi, T., Wade, K.A., & Stewart, N. (2009). Creating fair lineups for suspects with distinctive features. *Psychological Science, 20*, 1448–1453. doi:10.1111/j.1467-9280.2009.02463.x

7

Estimator Variables and Memory for Faces

HANNAH RYDER, HARRIET M. J. SMITH, AND HEATHER D. FLOWE

The objective of psychological research is often to improve the human condition through the application of basic behavioural principles that are discovered in the laboratory to the real world. Legal psychology is no exception, and psychologists working in this domain have long been interested in how we can improve the accuracy of eyewitness identification. In 1976, the Devlin Report reviewed the outcomes of two particular UK cases involving eyewitnesses. The report also identified numerous other cases in which eyewitnesses had been mistaken, concluding that "... in cases which depend wholly or mainly on eye-witness evidence of identification, there is a special risk of wrong conviction" (p. 149). Similar miscarriages of justice have been reported in the US. The Innocence Project (ND) has assisted in over 300 such cases – mistaken eyewitnesses were a factor in almost 75%. In order to prevent such errors, psychologists and legal professionals worldwide have worked closely together to improve the validity of eyewitness testimony (Wells *et al.*, 1998).

Forensic Facial Identification: Theory and Practice of Identification from Eyewitnesses, Composites and CCTV, First Edition. Edited by Tim Valentine and Josh P. Davis.
© 2015 John Wiley & Sons, Ltd. Published 2015 by John Wiley & Sons, Ltd.

Case study: Eyewitness evidence against William Beck

In March 1982, William Beck was convicted of armed robbery against two postal workers in Livingston and the theft of a postal van in Glasgow. The case against him was based primarily on eyewitness identification evidence. However, not only did this evidence consist of the bare minimum necessary for conviction, but of 12 witnesses, five made positive identifications, only two of which were of Beck. He served six years in prison and still maintains his innocence. In 2011, his case was taken up by the University of Bristol's Innocence Project. Professor Tim Valentine, an eyewitness memory expert, provided expert advice. Having reviewed the case, he highlighted various issues relating to the evidence against Beck, emphasizing the "low probative value of eyewitness identification" (Valentine, 2010, p. 25).

This case helps to demonstrate the impact of estimator variables that may affect eyewitness identification accuracy, including exposure duration, quality of view and the use of disguises. The robbery in question occurred during daylight, and one witness who made a positive identification stated he was 18–20 feet (between 5 and 6 metres) from the perpetrator, which by the "rule of fifteen [metres]" (Wagenaar & Van de Schrier, 1996) should have been optimal viewing conditions. However, both of the witnesses who made the positive identification had limited exposure to the witness due to the speed of the robbery and the quick escape of the perpetrators. The judge stated that it is "easy to make a mistake if you only get a fleeting glimpse" (*William Beck v. Her Majesty's Advocate*, 2006, para. 50). Moreover, despite stating they had "a good look at the driver" (para. 50), the witnesses' opportunities to view the perpetrator would have been hindered due to a balaclava worn (which was removed when driving off). One of the witnesses who identified Beck mentioned he was intent on getting the registration number of the escape car, so would have averted his attention away from the perpetrator's face. Finally, the stress caused from witnessing a crime could have limited the witnesses' ability to remember the perpetrators' faces.

Case study: Peter Jarvis rapes an elderly woman at knifepoint

The Peter Jarvis case also demonstrates the potential impact of estimator variables on eyewitness identification accuracy (BBC News, 2006). In September 2004, a 63-year-old woman was violently and repeatedly raped in her own home. Arguably, the attack lasted long enough to assume that the victim had the opportunity to encode the perpetrator's face. She was able to give a detailed description to the police. However, when shown a video lineup, the victim could not identify Jarvis – the suspect. As the case was supported by other strong evidence, Professor Tim Valentine was called upon to offer advice. The case involved some estimator variables: delay, stress, age of the witness, and a possible own-age bias. The victim did not report the crime immediately because she was afraid that her attacker might return. Indeed, an important factor was that the lineup was held a long time after the date of the offence. Jarvis was not arrested until June 2005, over 9 months after the crime had occurred. Professor Valentine advised that the victim's failure to identify the suspect was, therefore, unsurprising, and it was concluded that her inability to positively identify Jarvis should not undermine other evidence against him. Jarvis was convicted in 2006 and jailed for life.

Variations in the accuracy of witness identification are related to a host of factors. Wells (1978) differentiated such influences into *system* and *estimator* variables. Whilst system variables can be *controlled* by the criminal justice system in an attempt to prevent witness mistakes (see Chapter 6), estimator variables are *uncontrollable* factors that are associated with the likelihood of remembering the perpetrator. Estimator variables are properties inherent to the eyewitness, the perpetrator and the encoding conditions. Researchers measure key aspects of the participant (e.g., age, stress), of the to-be-remembered person (e.g., ethnicity, whether s/he was holding a weapon), and of the viewing conditions (e.g., for how long the faces were seen, the length of time between seeing a face and the identification procedure) to *estimate* the degree to which they are associated with eyewitness accuracy. It is essential to have a good understanding of the effects of estimator variables on the accuracy of eyewitness identification, derived from theoretical models of memory and carefully controlled empirical observations. This will help judgements reached in court and the deliberation of juries to be based on sound science rather than naïve intuition. However, it is necessary to mention that the estimation of eyewitness accuracy is dependent upon the validity of the witness reports of the witnessing conditions. Lampinen, Neuschatz, and Cling (2012) stated: "A witness who says they saw a perpetrator for 10 minutes may have seen the perpetrator for only 6 minutes" (p. 51). The US guidelines

(*State v. Henderson*, 2011) fortunately are aware of this, and point to witness' overestimations of short durations, particularly when stressed. This interaction between estimator variables (duration and stress) is also necessary to consider.

This chapter will review research on estimator variables that have the largest and most reliable effects on identification accuracy. Studies conducted in both the laboratory and the field will be reviewed, as will the results of archival studies of criminal cases. Laboratory studies allow for precise control of the variables of interest, but at the expense of external validity, which may mean that the results are less generalizable to a real-world context. Data from quasi-experimental field studies will also be examined, such as one undertaken by Valentine and Mesout (2009), in which passers-by were used as participants in realistic settings. In this study participants visited a tourist attraction designed to induce levels of state-anxiety to measure its effect on subsequent identification accuracy. Field studies can be controlled (as in this example of a quasi-experimental field study), or can involve collecting data from real crimes – in which case no control over extraneous variables is possible. Archival investigations involve analysing data from existing case records, and allow researchers to examine the external validity of theories of eyewitness memory, as they represent situations found in actual criminal cases. However, when analysing archival cases, the ground truth is not known. Ground truth refers to whether the suspect was in fact the perpetrator. Therefore, in field and archival studies conducted with actual eyewitnesses, researchers do not know whether a given lineup was target-present or target-absent as the guilt or innocence of the suspect in the lineup is not definitively known.

We will also differentiate between findings from *face recognition* paradigms and *eyewitness identification* paradigms. In face recognition paradigms, participants view a number of faces in the initial encoding stage of the experiment. During the test phase, half of the test faces are "old" faces (i.e., they were presented during the encoding stage), referred to as "targets", while the other half that have not been seen before are "new" faces, or "lures". Identifying a target face is known as a "hit" or a correct positive identification, whereas incorrectly picking a lure face is known as a "false alarm" or an incorrect identification. In an eyewitness identification paradigm, participants are shown, say, a video of a crime re-enactment that displays a perpetrator, and then they are shown either a target-present or a target-absent lineup. In a target-present lineup, the perpetrator is present among filler faces in the lineup, whereas in a target-absent lineup, the perpetrator is absent (i.e., the lineup members are all fillers, or an innocent suspect is presented among fillers in the lineup). Selecting the perpetrator in a target-present lineup is a correct identification, whereas selecting a filler (or an innocent suspect) is an incorrect identification. While there is no evidence that we are aware of that indicates that the underlying memory mechanisms differ across paradigms for the variables reviewed here (also see Lane & Meissner, 2008), we will distinguish results by type of paradigm.

We will also make reference to major judicial rulings that affect the presentation of estimator variable research in the courtroom. When eyewitness evidence is presented in court, judges issue warnings to better equip juries to use their own judgment to critically evaluate the probable accuracy of identification evidence. In the UK, the judge is required to give the Turnbull warning (*R v. Turnbull*, 1977), which outlines a number of variables believed to affect identification accuracy. In the US, a recent high profile case heard by the New Jersey Supreme Court has impacted on how judges instruct juries in New Jersey (*State v. Henderson*, 2011). This case is likely to have a reverberating effect on other jurisdictions in the US; hence, we will focus attention on it in this chapter. Where possible, we will indicate whether the balance of psychological research supports the content of these warnings, or whether there is evidence to suggest that the guidelines require revision.

PERPETRATOR AND WITNESS CHARACTERISTICS

Perpetrator Characteristics

Perpetrator distinctiveness and attractiveness Research suggests that memory traces for faces are stronger for relatively more distinctive faces (Dewhurst, Hay, & Wickham 2005). Using a modification of the face recognition paradigm, Carlson (2011) showed that distinctive faces are better remembered. Participants viewed pictures of a number of different faces before being tested on lineups. Hit rates were higher and false alarm rates were lower when target faces were more distinctive. Valentine's (1991) face space model can account for these findings. According to the model, faces are arranged around a central prototypical face on a multidimensional psychological similarity space, with increased distance from the centre reflecting increased distinctiveness. Typical faces are located closely together within the densely populated central area of the face space. As such, typical faces are more easily confused with one another, which may account for why participants are more likely to make a false alarm decision for typical compared with distinctive faces.

Attractive perpetrators are also more likely to be remembered, although results across studies are not consistent (Fleishman, Buckley, Klosinsky, Smith, & Tuck, 1976; Wickham & Morris, 2003). Some studies have reported higher false alarm rates for attractive perpetrators, but no differences in correct identification rates (Wickham & Morris, 2003). Arguably, attractive faces are rated as being more typical than less attractive faces (Langlois & Roggman, 1990). If attractive faces are typical, the face space model (Valentine, 1991) would predict that more attractive individuals are harder to remember than less attractive but more distinctive faces. However, perpetrators on both ends of the attractiveness spectrum are more accurately remembered (Fleishman *et al.*, 1976). The relationship between distinctiveness and attractiveness has been proposed as an explanation for why attractive faces are sometimes better remembered than average faces (Narby, Cutler, & Penrod, 1996). Faces eliciting extreme values on the attractiveness scale (i.e., very attractive and very unattractive faces) may be processed as exemplars of distinctive faces (although see Wickham & Morris, 2003). That is, there may be a U-shaped function between attractiveness and typicality, meaning that both very attractive and very unattractive faces are more distinctive.

Perpetrator disguise If the perpetrator was disguised during the crime, encoding of the perpetrator's face will be limited. The presence of a disguise may provide the witness with insufficient information at encoding to facilitate accurate lineup identification (Brewer, Weber, & Semmler, 2005). The encoding specificity principle, which specifies that memory performance is best when the cues available at test match the cues available at encoding (Tulving & Thompson, 1973), provides a suitable account for the relationship between disguise and performance. If the perpetrator is disguised during the crime, but not at test, there will be a mismatch between the learning and testing conditions and memory performance will suffer. This theory suggests that if the perpetrator was disguised during the crime, it is important for the police to ask all lineup members to wear the same disguise as the perpetrator at test. Research has considered this issue for masked perpetrators. Results showed that participants who viewed targets masked with a nylon stocking at encoding, but unmasked targets at test, performed worse than participants who viewed targets who were masked at both encoding and test (Davies & Flin, 1984).

Even subtle, everyday disguises, such as sunglasses (Hockley, Hemsworth, & Consoli, 1999) and hats (Cutler, Penrod, & Martens, 1987), have an effect. The effect of being unable to encode hair prevents witnesses from using helpful cues to distinguish between individuals.

Even if the perpetrator's hair is visible at encoding, a change of hairstyle before test roughly halves correct identification rates (Pozzulo & Marciniak, 2006). In person descriptions, hair is referred to more consistently than other features (Shepherd & Ellis, 1996). However, recent research comparing the disruptive effect of hats and sunglasses shows that correct identification rates are most affected if the perpetrator wore sunglasses at encoding rather than a hat (Mansour *et al.*, 2012). This may be because sunglasses occlude key facial features, and thereby prevent the participant from holistically processing the face. Holistic processing supports accurate face recognition (Tanaka & Farah, 1993; Tanaka, Kiefer & Bukach, 2004; see Chapter 3 for a discussion of holistic processing).

Both Turnbull (*R v. Turnbull*, 1977) and Henderson (*State v. Henderson*, 2011) refer to the potentially disruptive influence of disguise on witness identification performance.

Witness characteristics

Age The association between witness age and remembering faces has been extensively investigated. Research suggests that children and older adults demonstrate poorer encoding in comparison with younger adults, and that their memory traces are weaker (Ceci, Ross & Toglia, 1987; Hasher & Zacks, 1979). Compared with other individual difference factors, age has a large effect size (Shapiro & Penrod, 1986). Evidence suggests that both children (Pozzulo & Lindsay, 1998) and older adults (Searcy, Bartlett, & Memon, 1999) demonstrate poorer performance compared with younger adults on target-absent lineups. An effect of age is less consistently detected in target-present lineups (Pozzulo & Lindsay, 1998; Wells & Olson, 2003).

Child witnesses Researchers have debated the reliability of child witness memory. Early face recognition studies suggested that 4-year-olds demonstrate correct identification rates of only 35–40%, whilst 14-year-olds perform at adult-like rates of 70–80% (Chance & Goldstein, 1984). In contrast, Pozzulo and Lindsay's (1998) meta-analysis indicated that whilst children over five years of age perform similarly to adults on target-present lineups, children are markedly less accurate than adults at correctly rejecting target-absent lineups. Correct rejection rates are thought to reach adult levels at some point in mid-adolescence (Pozzulo & Lindsay, 1998).

Pozzulo and Lindsay (1998) concluded that inconsistencies in results between early and later studies could be accounted for by methodological differences. Early studies (Chance & Goldstein, 1984) used a face recognition paradigm, whereas later studies tested performance using eyewitness designs (e.g., Beal, Schmitt & Dekle, 1995) to investigate children's identification abilities. Conclusions about child witnesses therefore depend on the type of test. Face recognition studies involve viewing numerous faces at study, and therefore have a higher memory load. At test, further faces are presented and participants indicate which are "old" and which are "new". Eyewitness studies require a lower memory load at study, usually only requiring encoding and storage of a single perpetrator's face.

The balance of evidence suggests that the likelihood of false identifications is greater in children than young adults, although rates of correct identification are probably more similar. Greater false identification rates by children may be due to a number of different factors, such as a desire to give a positive response (Zajac & Karageorge, 2009), or because children assume that the perpetrator will be in the lineup (Gross & Hayne, 1996). Recent eyewitness studies showed that including a black silhouette of a mystery man with a white question mark reduces false identifications in children as young as 5 years (Havard & Memon, 2013; Karageorge & Zajac, 2011; Zajac & Karageorge, 2009). Children were told to select the mystery man if they could not recognize the perpetrator in the lineup. Although the option to select the "mystery man" reduced false identifications, it did not reduce correct identifications.

Older witnesses Searcy *et al.* (1999) analysed the results from ten studies testing older witnesses. Data showed that although correct identification rates for older and younger adults were almost the same, false alarm rates for older adults were twice those of younger adults, with greater age differences for target-absent lineups in comparison with target-present lineups.

Impairments in target-present lineup performance may not manifest until a later developmental stage, when gradual memory deficits associated with ageing are more marked (e.g., Salthouse & Babcock, 1991; Mitchell, Johnson, & Mather, 2003; Balota, Dolan, & Duchek, 2000). The literature commonly categorizes older adults as being over the age of 60 (Wilcock, Bull, & Vrij, 2007). Savaskan *et al.* (2007) included two older adult categories in a face recognition study: 60–80 years, and those over 80. Younger (20–40) and older adults (60–80) performed similarly in terms of correct identification rates, but the over-80s produced significantly lower correct identification rates. Both categories of older adults produced higher false alarm rates than younger adults. As few studies have included a category of participants over the age of 80, further research is needed to establish the reliability of this effect.

The judgement in *State v. Henderson* (2011) took the view that witnesses are most accurate in young adulthood (aged 18–19), with a consistent decline in accuracy after this age. By age 60–72, witness performance is said to be half as accurate as young adults. However, the psychological evidence outlined above suggests that the US courts may have overestimated the influence of age on eyewitness identification accuracy. US courts also fail to differentiate between performance on target-present and target-absent lineups. The Turnbull guidelines (*R v. Turnbull*, 1977) do not refer to age at all.

Witness intoxication Few studies have addressed the effect of witness intoxication on identification accuracy. Alcohol is believed to influence performance at lineup by impairing encoding and reducing memory storage capacity (Cutler & Penrod, 1995). Researchers have also drawn from the alcohol myopia framework (Steele & Josephs, 1990; Steele & Southwick, 1985), arguing that alcohol leads to an encoding deficit by narrowing attention to the most salient features. If this is the case, performance on target-present lineups would not be affected. However, in a target-absent lineup, the witness is likely to find it difficult to reject faces that are similar to the offender's. Support has been found for this proposition in three studies that found that alcohol impaired the accuracy of target-absent lineups (Dysart, Lindsay, MacDonald, & Wicke, 2002; Read, Yuille, & Tollestrup, 1992; Yuille & Tollestrup, 1990).

In Dysart *et al.*'s (2002) study, two female confederates approached people in a bar and asked them to volunteer for a study. Volunteers completed a filler task in a separate room with a male experimenter. Blood alcohol levels (BALs) were recorded before participants tried to identify one of the females from a single photograph (i.e., a showup test). A higher BAL was associated with elevated rates of false identification. Because participants were still intoxicated at test, the results could have arisen due to alcohol-related memory retrieval problems at testing rather than the effects of alcohol at encoding. Yuille and Tollestrup (1990) found that sober participants, who had witnessed a staged crime when intoxicated, exhibited a similar pattern of increased false identifications on target-absent lineups, but the difference was not significant.

Witness intoxication deserves more extensive research than it has received, especially as alcohol is thought to be involved in around half of violent crimes (British Crime Survey, 2005/2006; Palmer, Flowe, Takarangi, & Humphries, 2013). Research in the US has also found that police often encounter witnesses who were drinking at the time of the crime (US Department of Justice, 1996). The Henderson ruling

(*State v. Henderson*, 2011) acknowledges the influence of alcohol on false identification rates, although British guidelines (*R v. Turnbull*, 1977) do not.

Interactions between Witness and Perpetrator Characteristics

Own-ethnicity bias The own-ethnicity bias has received the most research attention of all estimator variables, and has been the subject of an exhaustive meta-analysis of 5000 participants over a 30-year period (Meissner & Brigham, 2001). Laboratory studies show the own-ethnicity bias to be robust, and the effect has been found across a range of ethnic groups, such as in Hispanic participants (e.g., MacLin, MacLin, & Malpass, 2001), East Asian participants (e.g., Goldstein & Chance, 1980), and Middle Eastern participants (e.g., Megreya, White, & Burton, 2011). Unlike the effects of age and alcohol, ethnicity appears to affect both hit rates and false alarm rates, making own-ethnicity perpetrators 1.40 times more likely to be remembered, but other-ethnicity perpetrators 1.56 times more likely to be misidentified (Meissner & Brigham, 2001). An own-ethnicity bias is evident in both face recognition and eyewitness paradigms.

Both expertise (Valentine, 1991; Valentine & Endo, 1992) and in-group/out-group accounts (Sporer, 2001) have been offered as theoretical explanations for the bias. Expertise may lead to the use of different processing styles, and varying depths of processing. There is some evidence that own-ethnicity faces are encoded at a deeper level than other-ethnicity faces (MacLin, Van Sickler, MacLin, & Li, 2004). Viewing own-ethnicity faces also appears to prompt the use of more holistic processing, thus facilitating subsequent identification and more accurate discrimination between similar-looking faces (Tanaka *et al.*, 2004). Another view posits that differences in the perceptual encoding of other- versus same-ethnicity faces contribute to the effect (Megreya *et al.*, 2011).

Laboratory studies have found some evidence that the magnitude of the own-ethnicity bias increases in line with children's age as they gain more experience and expertise in processing own-ethnicity faces. Although results have not been wholly consistent (e.g., Goodman *et al.*, 2007; Pezdek, Blandon-Gitlin, & Moore, 2003), some evidence supports the contact hypothesis, which proposes that contact with people of other ethnicities mitigates the bias. Contact increases levels of familiarity, and therefore expertise, with other-ethnicity faces. White participants, both adults (Meissner & Brigham, 2001) and children (Bennett & Brigham, 2005), are more likely to exhibit an own-ethnicity bias than black participants. This may be because most studies are conducted in countries where the majority of inhabitants are white, and therefore encounter minority inhabitants less frequently than the black minority encounter whites (Brigham, Bennett, Meissner, & Mitchell, 2007).

Other studies have not found evidence in support of the contact hypothesis. To illustrate, responses to the Social Experience Questionnaire, which measures the amount of social contact people have with other- and same-ethnicity persons, did not correlate with correct recognition rates, although there was a small negative correlation with false alarm rates (Jackiw, Arbuthnott, Pfeifer, Marcon, & Meissner, 2008). Over the period of 30 years covered by Meissner and Brigham's (2001) meta-analysis, the own-ethnicity bias appears to manifest in higher false alarm rates for other-ethnicity compared with same-ethnicity faces, whilst the effect on correct identification rates has decreased in size over time. This may be because of increases in inter-ethnicity contact over this period. Through media exposure to other-ethnicity faces, people may have experienced "unconscious" contact (and therefore expertise) that would not be detected in the Social Experience Questionnaire. However, the wealth of evidence suggests that although contact may play a limited role in the own-ethnicity bias, quality of contact better predicts the effect (Chiroro & Valentine, 1995; Meissner & Brigham, 2001; Valentine, Chiroro, & Dixon, 1995). Attitudes moderate the extent to which people engage with individuals of a different ethnicity, and prejudiced people report less engagement with people outside their own ethnic group (Brigham & Meissner, 2000).

Analysis of police lineup data by Horry, Memon, Wright, and Milne (2012) indicated that in England, white witnesses are less likely than black witnesses to view cross-ethnic lineups. Cross-ethnic lineups comprised 16.88% of those viewed by white witnesses, but 82.17% of those viewed by black witnesses. As has been shown, experimental studies suggest that white participants are more likely to exhibit an own-ethnicity bias than black witnesses (Bennett & Brigham, 2005; Meissner & Brigham, 2001). Therefore, the own-ethnicity bias may only be an issue in a minority of cases involving eyewitness identification in England.

No mention of a possible own-ethnicity bias is made in Turnbull (*R v. Turnbull*, 1977), but US guidance (*State v. Henderson*, 2011) is based on the findings of Meissner and Brigham's (2001) meta-analysis. Guidance does not refer to possible moderating factors referred to above, such as age and contact.

Own-age bias Wright and Stroud (2002) showed that younger adults, aged 18 to 25 years, and older adults, aged 35 to 55 years, were more accurate at identifying the perpetrator from a crime video if the perpetrator was a similar age to the eyewitness, an effect known as the own-age bias. Literature about ethnicity and face recognition may be extended to account for a possible own-age bias. For example, the bias could be explained by theories of expertise, in that increased exposure to own-age faces leads to greater expertise in processing (Valentine, 1991; Valentine & Endo, 1992). Alternatively, an in-group/out-group model of face processing (Sporer, 2001) would suggest that whilst own-age faces are processed automatically and configurally, thus facilitating discrimination, other-age faces may simply be categorized as out-group. This hypothesis predicts that out-group faces are processed more featurally rather than in a holistic manner (Rhodes, Brake, Taylor, & Tan, 1989). Holistic rather than featural processing facilitates accurate face identification (Tanaka & Farah, 1993; Tanaka et al., 2004).

Young witnesses, however, seem to show a more marked own-age bias on target-absent lineups (Havard & Memon, 2009; Memon, Bartlett, Rose, & Gray, 2003a). Although the own-age bias has been found in adults older than 55 years (Anastasi & Rhodes, 2006; Perfect & Harris, 2003; Perfect & Moon, 2005), other studies have not found the bias in this age group (Fulton & Bartlett, 1991; Memon et al., 2003a; Wiese, Schweinberger, & Hansen, 2008; Wilcock et al., 2007). Meissner, Brigham, and Butz (2005) surmised that the own-age bias may diminish with advanced age because memory encoding is generally impaired, thereby reducing the encoding advantage for own-age faces.

An own-age bias may generalize to real-world forensic contexts, resulting in a reduction in suspect identifications when the age difference between the witness and suspect is large. Horry et al. (2012) analysed decisions from 1039 real video lineups in England. Results showed that as the age gap between witnesses and suspects increased, filler identifications increased and suspect identifications decreased. However, as most suspects were young, large age differences most commonly involved an older witness. Horry et al. (2012) concluded that this feature of the data-set makes it difficult to conclude whether variations in accuracy were related to an own-age bias, or arose because older witnesses may perform less accurately than younger witnesses. As has been shown, experimental studies most commonly find that older witnesses are less accurate for target-absent lineups (e.g., Searcy et al., 1999).

VIEWING CONTEXT

Retention interval The retention interval between witnessing a crime and providing testimony (e.g., culprit description, identification decision) can last many months or even years, and thus understanding its impact is crucial. Put simply, memory accuracy decreases as the length of the retention interval increases. A meta-analysis of 53 face recognition studies found retention interval length to have a large effect (Deffenbacher, Bornstein, McGorty, & Penrod, 2008). However, whilst some archival studies have also found that increased retention intervals (in the case of Horry *et al.*, 2012, approximately six months and over) are associated with increased filler identifications (Wright & McDaid, 1996), other studies have found that the length of the retention interval is weakly associated with decreased suspect identification (e.g., Horry *et al.*, 2012), and still others have not found a significant association between retention interval length and suspect identification rate (e.g., Valentine, Pickering, & Darling, 2003; Wright & McDaid, 1996).

Early research suggested memory loss followed Ebbinghaus' (1885) forgetting curve, with an initial rapid decrease in forgetting, eventually slowing to an asymptote. The longer the retention interval, the more opportunity there is for decay (weakening of the memory trace) and interference between old and new information (Baddeley, 1999), which results in forgetting. More recently, researchers have attempted to capture the complexity of the process by examining the extent to which forgetting across the retention interval may be moderated by other factors. The extent to which memory and thus identification and recognition accuracy decreases across time is associated with other estimator variables including witness age (Memon *et al.*, 2003a) and distinctiveness of the to-be-remembered face (Metzger, 2006; Wickham, Morris, & Fritz, 2000). Additionally, Deffenbacher *et al.* (2008) found that the strength of a memory is a function of initial memory strength, the amount of time that has passed since encoding, and interference caused by other information encountered during the retention interval. This meta-analysis contributed to the US guidelines (*State v. Henderson*, 2011), which highlight the decline in memory over time and the impact of memory contamination that can occur with such memory decay.

The introduction of video lineups in place of live lineups in the UK has been shown to help reduce delay (Horry *et al.*, 2012). The Turnbull guidelines (*R v. Turnbull*, 1977) warn juries to consider the amount of time that has elapsed between observation and identification.

Stress Early work found an inverted U-shaped relationship between physiological stress and memory performance, known as the Yerkes–Dodson Law (Yerkes & Dodson, 1908). Moderate arousal was associated with the highest levels of accuracy, whilst extremes of arousal (high/low) were associated with the lowest levels. In stressful circumstances, eyewitnesses who experience high levels of arousal show decreased identification accuracy compared with eyewitnesses experiencing more moderate levels of arousal (see Deffenbacher, 1983, as cited in Deffenbacher, Bornstein, Penrod, & McGorty, 2004). However, Christianson's (1992) critical review argued that this account is too simplistic, and that memory for negative emotional events exceeds that of neutral events, specifically for central details.

Similarly, Deffenbacher (1994) argued against arousal being easily measurable by a single dimension. Drawing on existing models, Deffenbacher theorized that very high levels of arousal activate the "defensive response", characterized by increased heart rate, blood pressure and muscle tone. Situations threatening personal safety lead to increased cognitive anxiety and conscious awareness of these physiological changes. This "activation mode of attention control" triggers behaviours such as the flight/fight response. Increases in the level of arousal result in continuous gradual increases in performance, followed at some point by a sudden catastrophic drop in performance. In contrast, a state free of stress, the "arousal mode", is characterized by decreased heart rate, blood pressure and muscle tone. This "orienting response" is elicited by non-threatening events, wherein the central aspects of the event will be remembered best whilst peripheral details will suffer. Deffenbacher believed this theory could explain the findings in Christianson's (1992) review. The manipulation of arousal through negative emotional content elicits an orienting response rather than a threat to the observer, and thus memory for central details improves. In an attempt to test his theory, Deffenbacher et al. (2004) reviewed 27 laboratory experiments investigating the impact of arousal on identification, finding support for the negative effect of high cognitive and somatic anxiety on identification accuracy for both adults and children. Arousal had a larger negative effect on identification from target-present lineups, with no effect on target-absent lineups, and was more pronounced in studies employing a staged crime procedure than those inducing the stress response in alternative ways.

One widely cited study examined the association between stress and remembering in soldiers who were undergoing a training exercise in a mock prisoner of war camp (POWC) (Morgan et al., 2004). The soldiers, who were also food- and sleep-deprived, were subject to a series of interrogations. Stress was operationally defined as whether the soldier was physically confronted or not during the interrogation. The interrogator was identified from a target-present lineup less often when the soldier had been physically confronted. These findings contributed to the US court's advice that "an eyewitness under high stress is less likely to make a reliable identification of the perpetrator" (State vs. Henderson, 2011, p. 43). How the findings should be interpreted, however, is not clear-cut. In particular, the soldiers were *more* likely to *correctly* reject a target-absent lineup when they had been physically confronted. Without additional theoretical detail, it is difficult to explain why stress had a positive impact on memory when the interrogator was absent from the lineup. Additionally, it is difficult to generalize these findings to real world identifications because the lineups were not composed in accordance with practice guidelines. The soldiers were presented with a multi-perpetrator lineup (i.e., the guard and the interrogator were both in the lineup in the target-present condition) and the fillers may have been familiar to the soldiers (i.e., the fillers were other survival school instructors). Additionally, due to the conditions of POWC, the soldiers would have been pre-trained to handle stressful situations (see Morgan *et al.*, 2000), and perhaps even to avoid making eye contact with the interrogator. Based on these methodological considerations, it is difficult to make generalizations from this study to other circumstances.

More recently, Reisberg and Heuer (2007) have noted that those with higher predetermined vulnerability to stress will suffer the highest negative effects of stress on their memory performance, a factor which has also been contended by Valentine and Mesout (2009) and Deffenbacher *et al.* (2004). Conducted in the London Dungeon tourist attraction, Valentine and Mesout (2009) tested the association between state anxiety and physiological arousal (increased heart rate) on the ability of visitors to identify someone that had previously blocked their path in the Horror Labyrinth. They found that higher state anxiety as opposed to lower state anxiety was highly correlated with increased heart rate, and resulted in decreased ability to report correct descriptions and identify the person they had previously encountered in the Horror Labyrinth from a target-present lineup.

In line with quasi-experimental field data such as that by Valentine and Mesout (2009), possibly as a consequence of stress, real eyewitnesses to violent and sexual offences produce the highest filler identification rates compared with eyewitnesses to other crimes such as robbery (Horry *et al.*, 2012).

Weapon-focus The weapon-focus effect refers to an effect in which the presence of a weapon negatively affects remembering by narrowing attention towards the weapon, thereby decreasing allocation of attention to the perpetrator (e.g., Loftus, Loftus, & Messo, 1987). Some researchers have theorized that people focus on weapons because they are threatening (Hope & Wright, 2007), whereas others have argued that weapons draw attention because they are unexpected (Loftus & Mackworth, 1978; Pickel, 2009).

Whilst laboratory studies find weapons to have a negative impact on eyewitness accuracy (see meta-analysis by Steblay, 1992), it is more so for the ability to recall specific features of the perpetrator (e.g., height, hair colour, facial hair) than identification accuracy (Fawcett, Russell, Peace, & Christie, 2013). Data from real crimes reveal that there is no consistent impact of weapons on photographic lineups, live showups, identifications or feature accuracy (e.g., Behrman & Davey, 2001; Mecklenberg, 2006; Pike, Brace, & Kyman, 2002; Valentine *et al.*, 2003).

However, a more recent meta-analysis by Fawcett *et al.* (2013) found weapon presence to have a negative impact on feature recall accuracy and eyewitness memory performance in both controlled laboratory and simulation studies and in real crimes, albeit a smaller effect in the latter. This effect in actual crimes was found when only including "study type" as a moderator, and disappears when other moderators are included due to their stronger ability to predict the outcome. The authors offer explanations why there have been no reports of a negative impact of weapon presence in real crimes. Firstly, the effects of weapon focus are too small in real crimes in isolation, and only appear once combined such as in a meta-analysis. Secondly, the results of their meta-analysis show factors such as retention interval, level of threat and exposure duration of the weapon all moderate the negative impact of weapon presence. As such, lower effect sizes in real studies are expected, as the general conditions inherent in real crimes (e.g., longer weapon durations and retention intervals) interact with the presence of the weapon and moderate the effect. Indeed, the effect sizes found in laboratory studies that emulate the conditions of real world crimes are comparable to the effect sizes found in archival studies. This emphasizes the need for laboratory studies to be more accurate simulations of real-world crimes. Future research should tailor their variables to mirror real crimes where possible.

Fawcett *et al.* (2013) found the largest effect sizes of weapon presence with intermediate exposure duration, and the smallest effect sizes when the weapon was present for particularly short or long durations. However, the US guidelines advise that the effect is more pronounced during shorter crimes (*State v. Henderson*, 2011). Whilst the UK guidelines (*R v. Turnbull*, 1977) consider the negative effect of hindered viewing opportunities, they do not directly refer to the impact of weapons.

Quality of view It is not surprising that optimal viewing conditions (increased illumination) and closer viewing distance will improve recognition performance (Wagenaar & Van de Schrier, 1996). Wagenaar and Van de Schrier suggested the "Rule of Fifteen" for optimal viewing conditions; that is, a maximum distance of 15 metres and minimum lighting of 15 lux is considered optimal. Lindsay, Semmler, Weber, Brewer, and Lindsay (2008) also found larger distances to decrease identification accuracy, but did not find a 15-metre viewing distance crucial for accuracy. Nevertheless, Lampinen *et al.* (2012) provided an equation for calculation of image quality and the level of detail that permits accurate perception by the witness using the length of the image (as larger images will be more visually detailed) and distance from the target. However, archival studies have found that there was not a significant effect of unobstructed view or better lighting on suspect identification rates (Valentine *et al.*, 2003).

The Turnbull guidelines (*R v. Turnbull*, 1977) highlight the importance of the lighting conditions and the witness' distance from the suspect. The US guidelines also recognize the unreliability of witness' self-reports of distance (*State v. Henderson*, 2011).

Exposure time Longer exposure to a face provides more opportunity to analyse, encode, and thereby remember a face (Bornstein, Deffenbacher, Penrod, & McGorty, 2012). Identification accuracy of both young adults and the elderly appears to benefit from longer exposures (Memon, Hope, & Bull, 2003b), as do witnesses to real crimes (Valentine *et al.*, 2003). Witnesses exposed to the perpetrator for over a minute were more likely to identify the suspect than those who had less than a minute of exposure (Valentine *et al.*, 2003).

Shapiro and Penrod's (1986) meta-analysis showed that increased hit rates were associated with increased exposure duration, but so were increased false alarms. Read (1995) explained how longer exposures could bias participants' decisions due to the belief they had seen the face for longer, and therefore *should* be able to recognize the perpetrator. He also found longer interactions between eyewitness and perpetrator to result in higher hit rates, but also more false alarms.

The relationship between exposure time and remembering can be influenced by other variables, including similarity between learning and testing conditions (Read, Vokey & Hammersley, 1990), ethnicity (see MacLin *et al.*, 2001), and some apparent, although not significant, effects of participant age (Memon *et al.*, 2003b). Although exposure time is an important consideration, other moderating factors should be considered when assessing accuracy. Both the UK (*R v. Turnbull*, 1977) and the US (*State v. Henderson*, 2011) guidelines prompt consideration of exposure time. However, the Henderson guidelines offer more guidance, suggesting that a "brief or fleeting contact is less likely to produce an accurate identification" (p. 44), and consider the unreliability of witness' reports of exposure. Whilst it is advisable to consider other

moderating factors, it seems reasonable to suggest that longer exposures may help to improve the accuracy of the witness' memory.

SUMMARY AND CONCLUSION

This chapter has highlighted various estimator variables that can
impact the accuracy of eyewitness memory. We have aimed to offer an
up-to-date review of the literature. A vast body of psychological research
has been undertaken since the Turnbull guidelines (*R v. Turnbull*,
1977) were drawn up. Although the principle of warning juries about
the possibility of mistaken identification is valuable, key estimator
variables, such as age and the ethnicity of the witness and culprit, are
not explicitly mentioned in the guidelines. Advice given to US juries
(*State v. Henderson*, 2011) is more exhaustive. In addition, guidance in
both the US and UK should acknowledge the possibility of interactions
between variables to better reflect the true complexity of witness
memory.

The foregoing review highlights that a confluence of factors affect
whether an eyewitness remembers a criminal perpetrator. On the one
hand, estimator variables can be used to estimate eyewitness accuracy.
Remembering can, in some instances, be predicted by an estimator
variable on its own (e.g., the effect of perpetrator disguise), but at other
times, one may need to take into account several estimator variables in
making a prediction (e.g., own-ethnicity bias and the effect of retention
interval can vary in relation to the age of the witness). The US guidelines (*State v. Henderson*, 2011) consider the potentially changeable
relationship between variables, such as the additive effect of shorter
durations and stress on the weapon-focus effect.

We have reviewed the findings of different types of studies and
emphasized differences that have emerged across different methodological approaches in an attempt to establish the robustness of findings
across laboratory and field settings. When assessing the influence of
estimator variables on eyewitness identification, it is important to
consider how well studies enable us to predict and assess the accuracy
of lineup performance in real cases. Archival studies (e.g., Horry *et al.*,
2012; Valentine *et al.*, 2003; Wright & McDaid, 1996) are particularly
valuable in achieving this aim as they allow researchers to cross-reference
the findings of experimental and field studies with data from real cases.
We think the meta-analysis by Fawcett *et al.* (2013) is particularly exem-
plary in this regard. It summarizes the state of the research in both the
laboratory and in field settings, and also provides for a full discussion
with respect to how to translate laboratory findings to real world

witnesses. We believe that such an approach has great potential to advance the field.

REFERENCES

Anastasi, J.S., & Rhodes, M.G. (2006). Evidence for an own-age bias in face recognition. *North American Journal of Psychology, 8*, 237–252.

Baddeley, A.D. (1999). *Essentials of Human Memory*. Hove: Psychology Press.

Balota, D.A., Dolan, P.O., & Duchek. J.M. (2000). Memory changes in healthy young and older adults. In E. Tulving, & F.I.M. Craik (Eds.), *The Oxford Handbook of Memory* (pp. 395–410). New York: Oxford University Press.

BBC News (2006). Knifepoint rapist jailed for life. 24 April 2006. Retrieved from http://news.bbc.co.uk/1/hi/england/dorset/4939540.stm

Beal, C.R., Schmitt, K.L., & Dekle, D.J. (1995). Eyewitness identification of children. *Law and Human Behavior, 19,* 197–216. doi:10.1007/BF01499325

Behrman, B.W., & Davey, S.L. (2001). Eyewitness identification in actual criminal cases: an archival analysis. *Law and Human Behavior, 25*, 475–491. doi:10.1023/A:1012840831846

Bennett, L.B., & Brigham. J.C. (2005). *The development of the "cross-race effect" in children's face recognition memory*. Unpublished manuscript, Florida State University.

Bornstein, B.H., Deffenbacher, K.A., Penrod, S.D., & McGorty, E.K. (2012). Effects of exposure time and cognitive operations on facial identification accuracy: A meta-analysis of two variables associated with initial memory strength. *Psychology, Crime and Law, 18*, 472–490. doi:10.1080/10683 16X.2010.508458

Brewer, N., Weber, N., & Semmler, C. (2005). Eyewitness identification. In N. Brewer, & K.D. Williams (Eds.), *Psychology and Law: An Empirical Perspective* (pp. 177–221). New York: Guilford Press.

Brigham, J.C., Bennett, L.B., Meissner, C.A., & Mitchell, T.L. (2007). The influence of race on eyewitness memory. In M.P. Toglia, J.D. Read, D.F. Ross, & R.C.L. Lindsay (Eds.), *The Handbook of Eyewitness Psychology, Volume I: Memory for Events* (pp. 309–338). Mahwah, NJ: Lawrence Erlbaum Associates.

Brigham, J.C., & Meissner, C. (2000). Representation and memory for same- and other-race faces. In J.C. Brigham (Ed.), *What Do We Know About the "Own-race Bias" in Face Recognition?* Symposium conducted at the biennial meeting of the American Psychology-Law Society. New Orleans, LA.

British Crime Survey (2005/2006). Retrieved from http://discover.ukdataservice. ac.uk/catalogue/?sn=5543&type=Data%20catalogue

Carlson, C.A. (2011). Influence of a perpetrator's distinctive facial feature on eyewitness identification from simultaneous versus sequential lineups. *Applied Psychology in Criminal Justice, 7*, 77–92.

Ceci, S.J., Ross, D.F., & Toglia, M.P. (1987). Suggestibility of children's memory: psycholegal implications. *Journal of Experimental Psychology: General, 116*, 38–49. doi:10.1037/0096-3445.116.1.38

Chance, J.E., & Goldstein, A.G. (1984). Face-recognition memory: Implications for children's eyewitness testimony. *Journal of Social Issues, 40*, 69–85. doi:10.1111/j.1540-4560.1984.tb01094.x

Chiroro, P., & Valentine, T. (1995). An investigation of the contact hypothesis of the own-race bias in face recognition. *Quarterly Journal of Experimental Psychology, 48*, 879–894. doi:10.1080/14640749508401421

Christianson, S. (1992). Emotional stress and eyewitness memory: A critical review. *Psychological Bulletin, 112*, 284–309. doi:10.1037/0033-2909.112.2.284

Cutler, B.L., & Penrod, S.D. (1995). *Mistaken Identification: The Eyewitness, Psychology and the Law.* Cambridge: Cambridge University Press.

Cutler, B.L., Penrod, S.D., & Martens, T.K. (1987). The reliability of eyewitness identification: The role of system and estimator variables. *Law and Human Behavior, 11*, 233–258. doi:10.1007/BF01044644

Davies, G.M., & Flin, R. (1984). The man behind the mask – disguise and face recognition. *Human Learning: Journal of Practical Research & Applications, 3*, 83–95.

Deffenbacher, K.A. (1994). Effects of arousal on everyday memory. *Human Performance, 7*, 141–161. doi:10.1207/s15327043hup0702_3

Deffenbacher, K.A., Bornstein, B.H., McGorty, E.K., & Penrod, S.D. (2008). Forgetting the once-seen face: Estimating the strength of an eyewitness's memory representation. *Journal of Experimental Psychology: Applied, 14*, 139–150. doi:10.1037/1076-898X.14.2.139

Deffenbacher, K.A., Bornstein, B.H. Penrod, S.D., & McGorty, E.K. (2004). A meta-analytic review of the effects of high stress on eyewitness memory. *Law and Human Behavior, 28*, 687–706. doi:10.1007/s10979-004-0565-x

Devlin, Lord. (1976). *Report to the Secretary of State for the Home Department of the Departmental Committee on Evidence of Identification in Criminal Cases.* Her Majesty's Stationery Office, London

Dewhurst, S.A., Hay, D.C., & Wickham, L.H.V. (2005). Distinctiveness, typicality, and recollective experience in face recognition: A principal components analysis. *Psychonomic Bulletin and Review, 12*, 1032–1037. doi:10.3758/BF03206439

Dysart, J.E., Lindsay, R.C.L., MacDonald, T.K., & Wicke, C. (2002). The intoxicated witness: Effects of alcohol on identification accuracy from showups. *Journal of Applied Psychology, 87*, 170–175. doi:10.1037/0021-9010.87.1.170

Ebbinghaus, H. (1885). *Memory: A Contribution to Experimental Psychology.* New York: Dover Publications. (Transl. by H.A. Ruger, & C.E. Bussenuss, 1964, with a new introduction by Erhest R. Hilgard.)

Fawcett, J.M., Russell, E.J., Peace, K.A., & Christie, J. (2013). Of guns and geese: a meta-analytic review of the 'weapon focus' literature. *Psychology, Crime & Law, 19*, 35–66. doi:10.1080/1068316X.2011.599325

Fleishman, J.J., Buckley, M.L., Klosinsky, M.J., Smith, N., & Tuck, B. (1976). Judged attractiveness in recognition memory of women's faces. *Perceptual and Motor Skills, 43*, 709–710. doi:10.2466/pms.1976.43.3.709

Fulton, A., & Bartlett, J.C. (1991). Young and old faces in young and old heads: The factor of age in face recognition. *Psychology and Aging, 6*, 623–630. doi:10.1037/0882-7974.6.4.623

Goldstein, A.G., & Chance, J.E. (1980). Memory for faces and schema theory. *Journal of Psychology: Interdisciplinary and Applied, 105*, 47–59. doi:10.1080/00223980.1980.9915131

Goodman, G.S., Sayfan, L., Lee, J.S., Sandhei, M., Walle-Olsen, A., Magnussen, S., Pezdek, K., & Arredondo, P. (2007). The development of memory for own and other-race faces. *Journal of Experimental Child Psychology, 98*, 233–242. doi:10.1016 /j.jecp.2007.08.004

Gross, J., & Hayne, H. (1996). Eyewitness identification by 5- to 6-year old children. *Law and Human Behavior, 20,* 359–373. doi:10.1007/BF01499028

Hasher, L., & Zacks, R.T. (1979). Automatic and effortful processes in memory. *Journal of Experimental Psychology: General, 108,* 356–388. doi:10.1037/0096-3445.108.3.356

Havard, C., & Memon, A. (2009). The influence of face age on identification from a video line-up: A comparison between older and younger adults. *Memory, 17,* 847–859. doi:10.1080/09658210903277318

Havard, C., & Memon, A. (2013). The mystery man can help reduce false identification for child witnesses: Evidence from video line-ups. *Applied Cognitive Psychology, 27,* 50–59. doi:10.1002/acp.2870

Hockley, W.E., Hemsworth, D.H., & Consoli, A. (1999). Shades of the mirror effect: Recognition of faces with and without sunglasses. *Memory and Cognition, 27,* 128–138. doi:10.3758/BF03201219

Hope, L., & Wright, D. (2007). Beyond unusual? Examining the role of attention in the weapon focus effect. *Applied Cognitive Psychology, 21,* 951–961. doi:10.1002/acp.1307

Horry, R., Memon, A., Wright, D.B., & Milne, R. (2012). Predictors of eyewitness identification decisions from video lineups in England: A field study. *Law and Human Behavior, 36,* 257–265. doi:10.1037/h0093959

Innocence Project (ND). *Eyewitness Misidentification.* Retrieved from http://www.innocenceproject.org/understand/Eyewitness-Misidentification.php

Jackiw, L.B., Arbuthnott, K.D., Pfeifer, J.E., Marcon, J.L., & Meissner, C.A. (2008). Examining the cross-race effect in lineup identification using Caucasian and First Nations samples. *Canadian Journal of Behavioural Science, 40,* 52–57. doi:10.1037/0008-400x.40.1.52

Karageorge, A., & Zajac, R. (2011). Exploring the effects of age and delay on children's person identifications: Verbal descriptions, lineup performance, and the influence of wildcards. *British Journal of Psychology, 102,* 161–183. doi:10.1348/000712610X507902

Lampinen, J.M.M., Neuschatz, J.S.S., & Cling, A.D.D. (2012). *The Psychology of Eyewitness Identification.* Hove: Psychology Press.

Lane, S.M., & Meissner, C.A. (2008). A 'middle road' approach to bridging the basic-applied divide in eyewitness identification research. *Applied Cognitive Psychology, 22(6),* 779–787. doi:10.1002/acp.1482

Langlois, J.H., & Roggman, L.A. (1990). Attractive faces are only average. *Psychological Science, 1,* 115–121. doi:10.1111/j.1467-9280.1990.tb00079.x

Lindsay, R.C.L., Semmler, C., Weber, N., Brewer, N., & Lindsay, M.R. (2008). How variations in distance affect eyewitness reports and identification accuracy. *Law and Human Behavior, 32,* 526–535. doi:10.1007/s10979-008-9128-x

Loftus, E.F., Loftus, G.R., &. Messo, J. (1987). Some facts about weapon focus. *Law and Human Behavior, 11,* 55–62. doi:10.1007/BF01044839

Loftus, G.R., & Mackworth, N.H. (1978). Cognitive determinants of fixation location during picture viewing. *Journal of Experimental Psychology: Human Perception and Performance, 4,* 565–572. doi:10.1037/0096-1523.4.4.565

MacLin, O.H., MacLin, M.K., & Malpass, R.S. (2001). Race, arousal, attention, exposure and delay: An examination of factors moderating face recognition. *Psychology, Public Policy, and Law, 7,* 134–152. doi:10.1037/1076-8971.7.1.134

MacLin, O.H., Van Sickler, B.R., MacLin, M.K., & Li, A. (2004). A re-examination of the cross-race effect: The role of race, inversion, and basketball trivia. *North American Journal of Psychology, 6,* 189–204.

Mansour, J.K., Beaudry, J.L., Bertrand, M.I., Kalmet, N., Melsom, E.I., & Lindsay, R.C.L. (2012). Impact of disguise on identification decisions and confidence with simultaneous and sequential lineups. *Law and Human Behavior, 36,* 513–526. doi:10.1037/h0093937

Mecklenburg, S.H. (2006). *Report to the Legislature of the State of Illinois: The Illinois Pilot Program on Double-blind, Sequential Lineup Procedures.* Springfield, IL: Illinois State Police.

Megreya, A.M., White, D., & Burton, A.M. (2011). The other-race effect does not rely on memory: Evidence from a matching task. *Quarterly Journal of Experimental Psychology, 64,* 1473–1483. doi:10.1080/17470218.575228

Meissner, C.A., & Brigham, J.C. (2001). Thirty years of investigating the own race bias in memory for faces: A meta-analytic review. *Psychology, Public Policy, and Law, 7,* 3–35. doi:10.1037/1076-8971.7.1.3

Meissner, C.A., Brigham, J.C., & Butz, D.A. (2005). Memory for own-and other-race faces: A dual-process approach. *Applied Cognitive Psychology, 19,* 545–567. doi:10.1002/acp.1097

Memon, A., Bartlett J., Rose, R., & Gray, C. (2003a). The aging eyewitness: Effects of age on face, delay, and source-memory ability. *Journals of Gerontology Series B: Psychological Sciences and Social Sciences, 58,* 338–345. doi:10.1093/geronb/58.6.P338

Memon, A., Hope, L., & Bull, R. (2003b). Exposure duration: Effects on eyewitness accuracy and confidence. *British Journal of Psychology, 94,* 339–354. doi:10.1348/000712603767876262

Metzger, M.M. (2006). Face distinctiveness and delayed testing: Differential effects on performance and confidence. *Journal of General Psychology, 133,* 209–216. doi:10.3200/GENP.133.2.209-216

Mitchell, K.J., Johnson, M.K., & Mather, M. (2003). Source monitoring and suggestibility to misinformation: Adult age-related differences. *Applied Cognitive Psychology, 17,* 107–119. doi:10.1002/acp.857

Morgan, C., Hazlett, G., Doran, A., Garrett, S., Hoyt, G., Thomas, P., Baraniski, M., & Southwich, S.M. (2004). Accuracy of eyewitness memory for persons encountered during exposure to highly intense stress. *International Journal of Law and Psychiatry, 27,* 265–279.

Morgan III, C.A., Wang, S., Mason, J., Hazlett, G., Fox, P., Southwick, S.M., Charney, D.S., & Greenfield, G. (2000). Hormone profiles in humans experiencing military survival training. *Biological Psychiatry, 47,* 891–901.

Narby, D.J., Cutler, B.L., & Penrod, S.D. (1996). The effects of witness, target, and situational factors on eyewitness identifications. In S.L. Sporer, R.S. Malpass, & G. Guenter (Eds.), *Psychological Issues in Eyewitness Identification* (pp. 23–52). Hillsdale: Lawrence Erlbaum Associates.

Palmer, F.T., Flowe, H.D., Takarangi, M.K.T., & Humphries, J.E. (2013). Intoxicated witnesses and suspects: An archival analysis of their involvement in criminal case processing. *Law and Human Behavior, 13,* 54–59. doi:10.1037/lhb0000010

Perfect, T.J., & Harris, L.J. (2003). Adult age differences in unconscious transference: source confusion or identity blending? *Memory and Cognition, 31,* 570–580. doi:10.3758/BF03196098

Perfect, T.J., & Moon, H. (2005). The own age effect in face recognition. In J. Duncan, & P. McLeod (Eds.), *Measuring the Mind: Speed, Control, and Age* (pp. 317–340). Oxford: Oxford University Press.

Pezdek, K., Blandon-Gitlin, I., & Moore, C. (2003). Children's face recognition memory: more evidence for the cross-race effect. *Journal of Applied Psychology, 88*, 760–763. doi:10.1037/0021-9010.88.4.760

Pickel, K.L. (2009). The weapon focus effect on memory for female versus male perpetrators. *Memory, 17*, 664–678. doi:10.1080/09658210903029412

Pike, G., Brace N., & Kyman, S. (2002). *The visual identification of suspects: Procedures and practices (Briefing Note 2/02)*. London: Policing and Reducing Crime Unit Home Office Research Development and Statistics Directorate. Retrieved from http://webarchive.nationalarchives.gov.uk/20110218135832/http://rds.homeoffice.gov.uk/rds/pdfs2/brf202.pdf

Pozzulo, J.D., & Lindsay, R.C.L. (1998). Identification accuracy of children versus adults: A meta-analysis. *Law and Human Behavior, 22*, 549–570. doi:10.1023/A:1025739514042

Pozzulo, J.D., & Marciniak, S. (2006). Comparing identification procedures when the perpetrator has changed appearance. *Psychology, Crime and Law, 12*, 429–438. doi:10.1080/10683160500050690

R v. Turnbull (1977). Queen's Bench 224.

Read, J.D. (1995). The availability heuristic in person identification: The sometimes misleading consequences of enhanced contextual information. *Applied Cognitive Psychology, 9*, 91–121. doi:10.1002/acp.2350090202

Read, J.D., Vokey, J.R., & Hammersley, R. (1990). Changing photos of faces: Effects of exposure duration and photo similarity on recognition and the accuracy-confidence relationship. *Journal of Experimental Psychology: Learning, Memory and Cognition, 16*, 870–882. doi:10.1037/0278-7393.16.5.870

Read, J.D., Yuille, J.C., & Tollestrup, P. (1992). Recollections of a robbery. *Law and Human Behavior, 16*, 425–446. doi:10.1007/BF02352268

Reisberg, D., & Heuer, F. (2007). The influence of emotion on memory in forensic settings In M.P. Toglia, J.D. Read, D.F. Ross, & R.C.L. Lindsay (Eds.), *The Handbook of Eyewitness Psychology, Vol. I: Memory for Events* (pp. 81–116). Mahwah, NJ: Lawrence Erlbaum Associates.

Rhodes, G., Brake, S., Taylor, K., & Tan, S. (1989). Expertise and configural coding in face recognition. *British Journal of Psychology, 80*, 313–331. doi:10.1111/j.2044-8295.1989.tb02323.x

Salthouse, T.A., & Babcock, R.L. (1991). Decomposing adult age differences in working memory. *Developmental Psychology, 27*, 763–776. doi:10.1037/0012-1649.27.5.763

Savaskan, E., Müller, S.E., Böhringer, A., Philippsen, C., Müller-Spahn, F., & Schächinger, H. (2007). Age determines memory for face identity and expression. *Psychogeriatrics, 7*, 49–57. doi:10.1111/j.1479-8301.2007.00179.x

Searcy, J.H., Bartlett, J.C., & Memon, A. (1999). Age differences in accuracy and choosing in eyewitness identification and face recognition. *Memory and Cognition, 27*, 538–552. doi:10.3758/BF03211547

Shapiro, P.N., & Penrod, S. (1986). Meta-analysis of facial identification studies. *Psychological Bulletin, 100*, 139–156. doi:10.1037/0033-2909.100.2.139

Shepherd, J.W., & Ellis, H.D. (1996). Face recall – methods and problems. In S.L. Sporer, R.S. Malpass, and G. Guenter (Eds.), *Psychological Issues in Eyewitness Identification* (pp. 87–115). Hillsdale: Lawrence Erlbaum Associates.

Sporer, S.L. (2001). Recognizing faces of other ethnic groups: An integration of theories. *Psychology, Public Policy, and Law, 7*, 36–97. doi:10.1037/1076-8971.7.1.36

State v. Henderson (2011). N.J. 2011. 27 A.3d 872, 879.

Steblay, N.M. (1992). A meta-analytic review of the weapon focus effect. *Law and Human Behavior, 16,* 413–424. doi:10.1007/BF02352267

Steele, C.M., & Josephs, R.A. (1990). Alcohol myopia: Its prized and dangerous effects. *American Psychologist, 45,* 921–933. doi:10.1037/0003-066X.45.8.921

Steele, C.M., & Southwick, L. (1985). Alcohol and social behavior: I. The psychology of drunken excess. *Journal of Personality and Social Psychology, 48,* 18–34. doi:10.1037/0022-3514.48.1.18

Tanaka, J.W., & Farah, M.J. (1993). Parts and wholes in face recognition. *Quarterly Journal of Experimental Psychology, 46,* 225–245. doi:10.1080/14640749308401045

Tanaka, J.W., Kiefer, M., & Bukach, C.M. (2004). A holistic account of the own race effect in face recognition: Evidence from a cross-cultural study. *Cognition, 93,* 1–9. doi:10.1016/j.cognition.2003.09.011

Tulving, E., & Thompson, D.M. (1973). Encoding specificity and retrieval processes in episodic memory. *Psychological Review, 80,* 352–373. doi:10.1037/h0020071

US Department of Justice, Federal Bureau of Investigation (1996). *Crime in the United States: Uniform Crime Reports, 1995.* Washington, DC: US Department of Justice.

Valentine, T. (1991). A unified account of the effects of distinctiveness, inversion, and race in face recognition. *Quarterly Journal of Experimental Psychology, 43,* 161–204. doi:10.1080/14640749108400966

Valentine, T. (2010). Report on the eyewitness evidence in the case of William Beck. Retrieved from http://justiceforwulliebeck.webs.com/documents/Tim%20Valentine's%20Report%20to%20SCCRC%20dated%2012th%20April%202010136%20(1).pdf

Valentine, T., Chiroro, P. & Dixon, R. (1995). An account of the own-race bias and the contact hypothesis in terms of a face space model of face recognition. In T. Valentine (Ed.), *Cognitive and Computational Aspects of Face Recognition: Explorations in Face Space* (pp. 69–112). London: Routledge.

Valentine, T. & Endo, M. (1992). Towards an exemplar model of face processing: The effects of race and distinctiveness. *Quarterly Journal of Experimental Psychology, 44,* 671–703. doi:10.1080/14640749208401305

Valentine, T., & Mesout, J. (2009). Eyewitness identification under stress in the London Dungeon. *Applied Cognitive Psychology, 23,* 151–161. doi:10.1002/acp.1463

Valentine, T., Pickering, A., & Darling, S. (2003). Characteristics of eyewitness identification that predict the outcome of real lineups. *Applied Cognitive Psychology, 17,* 969–993. doi:10.1002/acp.939

Wagenaar, W.A., & Van der Schrier, J. (1996). Face recognition as a function of distance and illumination: A practical tool for use in the courtroom. *Psychology, Crime & Law, 2,* 321–332.

Wells, G.L. (1978). Applied eyewitness-testimony research: System variables and estimator variables. *Journal of Personality and Social Psychology, 36,* 1546–1557. doi:10.1037/0022-3514.36.12.1546

Wells, G.L., & Olson, E.A. (2003). Eyewitness testimony. *Annual Review of Psychology, 54,* 277–295. doi:10.1146/annurev.psych.54.101601.145028

Wells, G.L., Small, M., Penrod, S.D., Malpass, R.S., Fulero, S.M., & Brimacombe, C.A.E. (1998). Eyewitness identification procedures: recommendations for lineups and photospreads. *Law and Human Behavior, 22,* 603–607.

Wickham, L.H.V., & Morris, P.E. (2003). Attractiveness, distinctiveness, and recognition of faces: Attractive faces can be typical or distinctive but are not better recognized. *American Journal of Psychology, 116,* 455–468.

Wickham, L.H.V., Morris, P.E., & Fritz, C.O. (2000). Facial distinctiveness: Its measurement, distribution and influence on immediate and delayed recognition. *British Journal of Psychology, 91,* 99–123. doi:10.1348/000712600161709

Wiese, H., Schweinberger, S.R., & Hansen, K. (2008). The age of the beholder: ERP evidence of an own age bias in face memory. *Neuropsychologia, 46,* 2973–2985. doi:10.1016/j.neuropsychologia.2008.06.007

Wilcock, R.A., Bull, R., & Vrij, A. (2007). Are old witnesses always poorer witnesses? Identification accuracy, context reinstatement, own age bias. *Psychology, Crime and Law, 13,* 305–316. doi:10.1080/10683160600822212

William Beck v. Her Majesty's Advocate (2006). HCJAC 35.

Wright, D.B., & McDaid, A.T. (1996). Comparing system and estimator variables using data from real line-ups. *Applied Cognitive Psychology, 10,* 75–84. doi:10.1002/(SICI)1099-0720(199602)10:1<75::AID-ACP364>3.0.CO;2-E

Wright, D.B., & Stroud, J.N. (2002). Age differences in lineup identification accuracy: People are better with their own age. *Law and Human Behavior, 26,* 641–654. doi:10.1023/A:1020981501383

Yerkes, R.M., & Dodson, J.D. (1908). The relation of strength of stimulus to rapidity of habit-formation. *Journal of Comparative Neurology and Psychology, 18,* 459–482. doi:10.1002/cne.920180503

Yuille, J.C., & Tollestrup, P.A. (1990). Some effects of alcohol on eyewitness memory. *Journal of Applied Psychology, 75,* 268–273. doi:10.1037/0021-9010.75.3.268

Zajac, R., & Karageorge, A. (2009). The wildcard: A simple technique for improving children's lineup performance. *Applied Cognitive Psychology, 23,* 358–368. doi:10.1002/acp.1511

8

Confidence and Accuracy of Eyewitness Identification

JAMES D. SAUER AND NEIL BREWER[1]

The demonstrated fallibility of eyewitness identification evidence has motivated researchers to search for indices of identification decision accuracy. These are generally characteristics of the identification decision that are likely to be informative about the nature of the decision process and, importantly, considered to speak to the quality of the witness' memory for the event and the culprit. For example, potential indices include the witness' confidence in the accuracy of their identification decision, and the speed with which the identification response is made. Confidence is the most researched index of identification accuracy and the focus of this chapter. Although research demonstrates that (a) confidence can provide useful diagnostic information about identification accuracy, (b) confidence influences perceptions of both witness credibility and the likely reliability of the identification evidence, and (c) consideration of witness confidence should accompany any evaluation of likely identification accuracy, formal mechanisms for measuring and

[1]Supported by Australian Research Council Grant DP1093210 and Flinders FRG Grant.

Case study: In-court expressions of confidence

In 1982, Robert Clark was convicted of rape, kidnapping and armed robbery; 23 years later he was exonerated. The victim's mistaken identification of Clark as the perpetrator was one of the primary contributing factors to Clark's wrongful conviction (Innocence Project, 2013). In court, the victim testified "I will never forget the face, the skin color and his voice" (Benjamin N. Cardozo School of Law Yeshiva University, 2013). This testimony implies a high degree of certainty. However, a more thorough consideration of the identification evidence suggests that this level of certainty was misleading. Several days after the attack, the victim was shown a mug book of potential suspects and identified someone other than Clark. Almost a month after the attack, the victim viewed a photo lineup containing Clark's picture, and identified Clark as someone "...looking very much like the person that committed the crimes" (Benjamin N. Cardozo School of Law Yeshiva Univeristy, 2013). Two days later the victim identified Clark from a live lineup in which Clark was the only lineup member whose photograph had also appeared in the previous photo lineup. As indicated by her testimony, by the time the witness reached court there was little doubt in her mind that Clark was her attacker.

A number of important points can be drawn from these case facts to illustrate that in-court expressions of confidence are not reliable predictors of identification accuracy. First, the level of confidence expressed in court appears inflated compared with the level of confidence that may be inferred from the statement that accompanied the victim's initial identification of Clark. Second, the level of confidence expressed in court was inconsistent with the victim's initial identification of someone other than Clark. The exact mechanisms for the apparent confidence inflation in this case are unclear, although we can speculate about the effects of pre-court preparation, and the implicit feedback associated with (a) seeing Clark's face (and only Clark's face) in two separate lineups, and (b) knowing that the case against Clark was proceeding to court. What is clear, however, is that the level of confidence expressed in court was not consistent with the victim's prior identification behaviour, the victim's prior expressions of confidence, or the accuracy of the victim's identification decision. The level of certainty expressed in court was not informative about the quality of the witness' memory at the time of the identification, or the extent to which the identified lineup member matched the witness' memory of the culprit. Thus, it can only have undermined attempts to evaluate the reliability of the identification evidence.

interpreting identification confidence are non-existent in identification test protocols across the world.

The initial sections of this chapter discuss perceptions of the confidence–accuracy (CA) relationship held by lay-persons and decision-makers in the criminal justice system, and then review theoretical and empirical investigations of the CA relationship. Here we also highlight areas of convergence and divergence between these legal, theoretical, and empirical perspectives. Given that much of this has been covered in depth elsewhere (e.g., Brewer, 2006; Brewer & Weber, 2008; Brewer, Weber, & Semmler, 2005), a significant part of this chapter is then spent addressing a largely ignored but extremely important issue relating to eyewitness identification confidence: how current identification test practices fail to exploit the applied value of confidence as an index of identification accuracy. Finally, we discuss how theories of recognition memory and confidence processing highlight new – and important – opportunities for using confidence in the criminal justice system.

PERCEPTIONS OF EYEWITNESS CONFIDENCE IN LEGAL SETTINGS

Three lines of evidence converge to demonstrate the influence that eyewitness confidence can exert on decision-making in legal settings. First, survey research has illustrated that police, lawyers and jurors clearly believe that confidence is reliably linked to accuracy (Deffenbacher & Loftus, 1982; Potter & Brewer, 1999). Second, mock-juror research – where jury-eligible samples make decisions in some form of trial simulation – has consistently shown that experimental manipulations of witness confidence affect mock-jurors' perceptions of witness credibility and defendant guilt (Bradfield & Wells, 2000; Brewer & Burke, 2002; Cutler, Penrod & Dexter, 1990; Cutler, Penrod & Stuve, 1988; Lindsay, Wells & Rumpel, 1981). Finally, the United States Supreme Court has ruled that courts must consider confidence when evaluating the reliability of identification evidence (*Neil v. Biggers*, 1972).[2] Importantly, although these lines of evidence demonstrate that legal decision-makers *believe* that witness confidence can predict identification accuracy, they say nothing about whether witness confidence *actually* predicts identification

---

[2]Note that recent judgments (e.g., *State v Henderson*, 2011; *Oregon v. Lawson*, 2012) discuss the CA relationship, but the emphasis of their recommendations is primarily on recording confidence immediately after the decision to combat the inflationary effects of feedback on confidence, and not because confidence recorded at that point can provide a pointer to the reliability of the identification.

accuracy. Nor do they speak to decision-makers' awareness of issues that may undermine the CA relationship. Finally, as we argue later in this chapter, beliefs about the influence that confidence can exert in legal settings, together with failures to appreciate the limits of the CA relationship, may have (a) inadvertently obstructed the development of protocols necessary for ensuring a meaningful CA relationship in forensic settings, and (b) led to practices that (intentionally or not) obscure a vital function of eyewitness confidence.

THEORETICAL PERSPECTIVES ON THE CA RELATIONSHIP

There are solid theoretical grounds for expecting a positive relationship between confidence and accuracy for recognition decisions. Current theories of confidence processing for recognition decisions can be broadly classified into two categories: decisional and post-decisional locus models. These theories were intended to describe the mechanisms underlying decision-making and confidence processing for simple decision-making tasks. However, the mechanisms described can be extended to provide a compelling rationale for predicting a positive CA relationship for more complex decision-making tasks, such as when a witness views a lineup and must decide which, if any, of the lineup members is the culprit (at least in cases where the witness identifies a lineup member as the culprit). We first present these accounts as they relate to basic memory tasks and then extend them to account for the CA relationship for eyewitness identification decisions. An understanding of the basic processes linking response and confidence for recognition decisions is particularly important as it motivates our later discussions of (a) the importance of considering confidence when evaluating identification evidence (and, consequently, the importance of appropriately assessing witness confidence), and (b) novel uses of confidence in legal settings.

Decisional locus (or single-process) models, such as those developed within the signal detection theory (SDT) framework (e.g., Green & Swets, 1966; Macmillan & Creelman, 1991), argue that recognition decisions and confidence emerge simultaneously, and are based on the same information. According to SDT-based models, when attempting to judge whether or not a presented stimulus has been previously seen, that stimulus is compared with a representation of a previously viewed item stored in memory. This comparison generates a value that lies somewhere along a familiarity continuum, with previously viewed stimuli generating values (generally) towards the higher end of the continuum and previously unseen stimuli producing values (generally) towards the lower end of the continuum. Stimuli producing values exceeding a preset criterion are judged to be previously seen, while those resulting in values below the criterion are deemed to be previously unseen. Confidence is thought to index the strength of this familiarity value, or the distance by which the obtained familiarity value exceeds the preset criterion. Thus, a comparison of a presented stimulus and the memorial representation of a previously viewed stimulus generates a value which, when compared to a preset criterion, simultaneously establishes the decision and decision confidence. This shared evidential basis for the decision and confidence supports a positive CA relationship.

The extension of this SDT theoretical framework to a lineup context (see also Horry, Palmer, & Brewer, 2012; Palmer & Brewer, 2012; Palmer, Brewer, & Weber, 2010) provides a clear basis for expecting a positive relationship between witness confidence and identification accuracy when the witness identifies a lineup member as the culprit. When viewing a lineup, let us assume that an initial inspection of the lineup members reveals one lineup member that the witness believes might be the perpetrator. The witness can then compare this individual to their memory of the offender. The extent to which this lineup member matches the witness' memory of the offender will form the primary evidential basis for both the decision and confidence. When the degree of match between the lineup member and witness' memory is high, confidence and accuracy are also likely to be high.[3] As this degree of match decreases, so too do confidence and likely accuracy.

Post-decisional locus models assume that confidence is determined after a decision is reached. However, these models also propose a direct relationship between the evidence upon which the decision and confidence are based and, therefore, predict a positive relationship between confidence and accuracy. In the context of a recognition decision, post-decisional models generally assume that a comparison of a presented stimulus with a memorial representation of a previously seen stimulus will provide evidence favouring either of two response alternatives: this stimulus is the same as one seen before or this stimulus is not the same as one seen before. Evidence favouring each of these two alternatives is stored in independent accumulators. Each accumulator has a preset criterion and a response is made when the evidence in one of the accumulators exceeds the criterion (Van Zandt, 2000). These models

---

[3]Note that it is possible that the presence of two or more lineup members who closely match the witness' memory of the offender might reduce confidence in the accuracy of the eventual decision, despite a high degree of match between the selected lineup member and the witness' memory of the offender. Ongoing research in our laboratory addresses this issue, but does not yet permit reliable conclusions.

tend to employ Vickers' (1979) balance of evidence hypothesis to account for confidence. According to the balance of evidence hypothesis, confidence indexes the difference between the amounts of evidence in the competing accumulators when the response is made. If the difference between the amounts of evidence in the two stores is large, confidence (and likely accuracy) will be high; if the difference is small, confidence (and likely accuracy) will be low.

Again, this logic can be extended to predict a meaningful CA relationship when a witness identifies a lineup member. Once more let us assume that an initial inspection of the lineup reveals one lineup member that the witness believes might be the perpetrator. The witness compares this individual to their memory of the culprit, and this comparison generates some evidence suggesting that the individual is the culprit (i.e., some degree of match between the individual and the witness' memory of the culprit) and some evidence that the individual is not the culprit (i.e., some degree of mismatch between the individual and the witness' memory of the culprit). As the degree of match between the lineup member and the witness' memory of the offender increases, so does the discrepancy between the accumulated evidence favouring the two response alternatives (i.e., this lineup member is the culprit versus this lineup member is not the culprit). As this discrepancy increases, so does the likely accuracy of the decision and the witness' confidence in that decision.

Although the conceptualization of confidence processing offered by post-decisional locus models differs from that proposed by SDT-based models, both classes of models suggest that confidence indexes stimulus discriminability. Thus, both classes of models hold that confidence is derived from the same evidence that underlies the decision-making process and, consequently, that conditions facilitating improved memory and accurate responding (e.g., long exposure durations, focused attention, short retention intervals) should also produce higher confidence. Conversely, conditions that hinder accurate responding should produce lower levels of confidence.

RESEARCH ON THE CONFIDENCE–ACCURACY RELATIONSHIP FOR EYEWITNESS IDENTIFICATION DECISIONS

Despite sound theoretical support for a positive CA relationship, research initially converged on the view that eyewitness confidence is a poor predictor of identification accuracy. Meta-analyses of correlational investigations of the CA relationship typically reported average correlation coefficients ranging from around zero to 0.3 or 0.4 (e.g., Bothwell, Deffenbacher, & Brigham, 1987; Cutler, Penrod, & Martens, 1987; Sporer, Penrod, Read, & Cutler, 1995). Although stronger correlations were reported for participants who chose someone from the lineup (cf. those who reject the lineup; Sporer *et al.*, 1995), the correlational research suggested a moderate relationship at best.

However, there are good reasons to believe that this research inadequately assessed the relationship between confidence and accuracy. These arguments are covered in detail elsewhere (e.g., Brewer *et al.*, 2005; Brewer & Wells, 2006; Juslin, Olsson, & Winman, 1996) so are only briefly reviewed here. Researchers have argued that the point-biserial correlation may be an inappropriate statistical index of the relationship (Juslin *et al.*, 1996). When assessing the CA relationship, the point-biserial correlation compares a continuous variable (e.g., confidence as typically assessed on 0%, 10%, 20%, ... 100% scale) with a binary outcome variable (accuracy). Correlation therefore indexes the distance between the distributions of confidence ratings for correct and incorrect decisions (Brewer *et al.*, 2005), comparing confidence with an unrealistic standard of discrimination (Juslin *et al.*, 1996). Others have argued that the typical homogeneity of encoding and testing conditions across participants in eyewitness identification research may artificially constrain variation in memory quality (and, consequently, in confidence and accuracy), undermining CA correlations. These researchers have demonstrated that conditions producing variations in memory quality produce stronger CA correlations (Lindsay, Nilsen & Read, 2000; Lindsay, Read & Sharma, 1998). Further, research using an alternative method of analysis – calibration – has repeatedly demonstrated (a) positive and generally monotonic relationships between eyewitness confidence and identification accuracy when witnesses identify a lineup member as the culprit, and (b) that these relationships often exist alongside typically weak CA correlations (Brewer, Keast, & Rishworth, 2002; Brewer & Wells, 2006; Juslin *et al.*, 1996; Olsson, 2000; Olsson, Juslin, & Winman, 1998; Palmer, Brewer, Weber, & Nagesh, 2013; Sauer, Brewer, Zweck, & Weber, 2010; Sauerland & Sporer, 2009). Thus, low to moderate CA correlations may exist in association with meaningful CA relationships, and a consideration of the CA relationship should not rely on correlational analyses.

CA Calibration

The calibration approach involves plotting the proportion of accurate decisions at each level of confidence (see Figure 8.1 for a schematic representation). In a typical eyewitness identification experiment, a

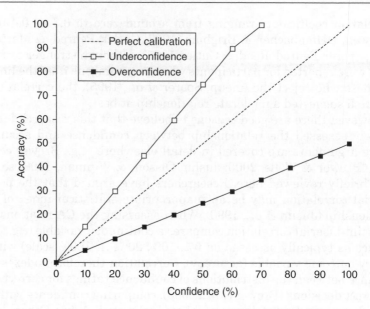

Figure 8.1 Schematic representation of confidence–accuracy (CA) calibration displaying perfect calibration, overconfidence and underconfidence.

witness will be shown a crime stimulus and then, after a delay, asked to view a lineup and make an identification decision (i.e., either identify a lineup member as the culprit or reject the lineup as a whole). After making this decision, the eyewitness will be asked to rate their confidence (typically on a 0–100% scale) in the accuracy of the decision. Researchers can then, across participants, determine the accuracy rates of decisions made at each level of confidence. Confidence and accuracy are perfectly calibrated when, as indicated by the dotted line in Figure 8.1, 100% of decisions made with 100% confidence are correct, 80% of decisions made with 80% confidence are correct, 50% of decisions made with 50% confidence are correct, and so on. The calibration approach provides useful information about the CA relationship in a number of ways. For example, by plotting variations in accuracy as a function of confidence, a visual inspection of the calibration curve provides an indication of the linearity of the relationship. Also, by comparing the obtained curve with the ideal, the "realism" of confidence judgements can be assessed for over- or underconfidence. As indicated in Figure 8.1, functions that fall below the ideal indicate overconfidence, while those above the ideal indicate underconfidence.

Calibration research is common in a variety of human judgment and decision-making domains, but the approach has been used much more sparingly when examining the relationship between eyewitness confidence and identification accuracy. Nevertheless, there is now sufficient research using the calibration approach to support a number of general conclusions about the CA relationship for eyewitness identification. First, when a witness identifies a lineup member as the culprit, there is a generally linear, positive relationship between confidence and accuracy. Second, calibration curves tend to display overconfidence in the upper half of the confidence scale. That is, although accuracy increases systematically with confidence, mean accuracy at each level of confidence tends to be lower than the level of confidence expressed. The degree of overconfidence varies as a function of experimental conditions related to task difficulty (e.g., delay between viewing the crime and viewing the lineup; Sauer *et al.*, 2010), target-absent base rate (Brewer & Wells, 2006), participants' metacognitive appraisals of their own memory ability (e.g., Brewer *et al.*, 2002) and age (Keast, Brewer, & Wells, 2007).

The extant CA calibration literature is generally encouraging regarding the predictive value of eyewitness confidence when a witness identifies a lineup member as the culprit (especially when confidence is very high). However, research also clearly demonstrates a number of robust phenomena that limit this conclusion. For example, even very high levels of confidence do not guarantee that an identification is correct (Brewer & Wells, 2009). For young children calibration is poor, although we do not yet have a firm explanation for this (Keast *et al.*, 2007). Also, the systematic CA relationship described above holds for witnesses who identified a lineup member as the culprit, but not for witnesses who rejected the lineup (see Brewer, 2006; Brewer *et al.*, 2005).

CA Calibration for Lineup Rejections

Lineup rejections are common in both lab and field settings (e.g., Behrman & Davey, 2001; Pike, Brace, & Kynan, 2002; Valentine, Pickering, & Darling, 2003), and can provide useful information about the likely guilt of a suspect (Clark, Howell, & Davey, 2008; Wells & Lindsay, 1980; Wells & Olson, 2002). Consequently, we will devote some discussion here to the perplexing, and under-researched, issue of why confidence is meaningfully related to accuracy for identifications but not for lineup rejections. Again, the theoretical mechanisms underlying confidence processing are informative. Confidence and accuracy should be meaningfully related when they share an evidential basis: when both are based on the degree of match between a presented stimulus (i.e., a lineup member) and the witness' memorial image of a previously viewed stimulus (i.e., the culprit). Weber and Brewer (2004, 2006) proposed the *information asymmetry hypothesis* to account for the superior CA calibration observed for positive (i.e., I have seen this face before) compared with negative (i.e., I have not seen this face before) face recognition decisions, arguing that the comparison process underlying positive and negative decisions differs. Specifically, a positive decision allows confidence to be based on an assessment of the degree of match between a single test face and a specific face in memory. In contrast, a negative decision indicates that the test face does not match any relevant face in memory. Thus, a negative decision does not provide a one-to-one comparison upon which confidence can be based.

This reasoning may also help to explain the consistent discrepancy between CA relationships observed for identifications and rejections from lineups. When a witness identifies a lineup member, a comparison of this individual with the witness' memory of the perpetrator provides a common basis for both the decision and the confidence. Confidence and accuracy are related because both index the quality of the witness' memory and the degree of match between an individual lineup member and the witness' memory of the culprit. In contrast, confidence ratings for lineup rejections refer to the rejection of the lineup as a whole, rather than the rejection of individual lineup members, and the basis for rejection confidence is not obvious.

Empirical support for the information asymmetry hypothesis has been mixed. While Weber and Brewer's (2006) initial investigation using an old–new face recognition paradigm provided little support, recent research using an eyewitness identification paradigm has produced results consistent with the hypothesis. Sauerland, Sagana, and Sporer (2012) used "showups" (a type of identification procedure in which a witness is presented with a single suspect and asked to either identify or reject the stimulus) to ensure that, regardless of whether the witness identified or rejected the suspect, the decision and confidence would be based on a comparison of the degree of match between a single test stimulus and the witness' memory of the culprit. These conditions produced a monotonic positive relationship between confidence and accuracy for rejections. Recent data from two projects in which one of the authors (JS) has been involved provide additional tentative support. Using face recognition and identification paradigms, and various confidence protocols that required participants to provide confidence ratings for individual rejected faces (cf. rejected lineups as wholes), this research suggests that rejection confidence can be meaningfully related to accuracy when confidence indexes a comparison of the degree of match between a single lineup member with the memorial image of a previously seen stimulus (e.g., Lindsay *et al.*, 2013).

The available evidence is certainly not sufficient to support a general conclusion that confidence is meaningfully related to rejection accuracy, even when rejection confidence is based on comparisons of single test stimuli with single items in memory. However, these early findings highlight two issues for future research. First, alternative protocols for collecting confidence may provide information that can assist in evaluating the accuracy of lineup rejections. If alternative methods of collecting confidence can increase the diagnostic value of confidence for lineup rejections, then the exculpatory value of lineup rejections will also be improved, and the risks of wrongful prosecution and the mismanagement of investigative resources may be reduced. Second, this research more generally demonstrates that protocols for collecting confidence ratings should be informed by an understanding of the theoretical basis for the CA relationship. Specifically, when protocols for collecting confidence are designed to permit an assessment of the degree of match between lineup members and the witness' memory for the culprit, the predictive value of confidence is likely to increase. The importance of designing confidence protocols that allow confidence to reflect an assessment of match becomes even clearer when we consider non-memorial factors that can influence confidence ratings, and weaken the CA association.

The Malleability of Confidence

Confidence is vulnerable to a variety of non-memorial (e.g., social and environmental) influences that reduce the correspondence between the evidential bases for confidence and accuracy, and undermine the CA relationship. For example, post-identification feedback is a powerful source of non-memorial influence, with research consistently demonstrating that post-identification feedback affects confidence for recognition decisions and undermines the CA relationship (Bradfield, Wells, & Olson, 2002; Luus & Wells, 1994; Semmler & Brewer, 2006; Semmler, Brewer, & Wells, 2004; Wells & Bradfield, 1998, 1999). After making an identification decision, a witness may receive feedback from various sources. The lineup administrator may indicate that the witness has picked the suspect (or someone other than the suspect), and this may be communicated through explicit, verbal means or inferred by the witness from the administrator's non-verbal behaviour (e.g., body language or facial expression). Alternatively, following discussions with a co-witness, a witness may learn that the co-witness provided the same (or a different) response. Confirming feedback generally inflates witness confidence, while disconfirming feedback generally reduces confidence. Importantly, these feedback effects on confidence do not depend on the witness' decision type (i.e., identification or rejection), the nature of the feedback (e.g., confirmation that the witness selected the suspect or simply confirmation that another witness made the same decision), the source of the feedback (e.g., administrator, co-witness, or even computer-based feedback), or whether the feedback is verbal or non-verbal (Garrioch & Brimacombe, 2001).

Research investigating feedback effects on confidence has demonstrated that these effects are robust. However, research also suggests that these effects are likely to be strongest when the witness' memory of the event is weak, and the relative paucity of internal cues for confidence may increase witness reliance on external cues (Bradfield *et al.*, 2002; Wells & Bradfield, 1998, 1999). For example, conditions that encourage accurate responding tend to reduce the influence of feedback on confidence (Brewer *et al.*, 2005). Further, feedback effects tend to be less pronounced when the witness is able to make their decision quickly (Semmler & Brewer, 2006; Semmler *et al.*, 2004). Presumably this is because quick decisions tend to indicate a strong memorial basis for the decision (i.e., a clear match between a lineup member and the witness' memory of the offender, or the clear absence of any match between lineup members and the witness' memory). Nonetheless, the fluency of a quick recognition decision and the quality of the underlying memorial information may provide salient internal cues for confidence, reducing reliance on external cues. Witnesses' expectations about the likely accuracy of their decisions also appear to moderate feedback effects on confidence. Confidence inflation effects tend to be reduced when the feedback agrees with a witness' prior expectations regarding the accuracy of their decision (Semmler & Brewer, 2006). Again this suggests that when internal cues to the accuracy of the decision are accessible, external cues to confidence are less influential. The effects of feedback on confidence can also be reduced by explicitly increasing the accessibility or salience of internal cues to confidence (e.g., by having witnesses think about their confidence before feedback is provided; Wells & Bradfield, 1999) or by undermining the perceived credibility of the feedback source (e.g., by creating suspicion that the feedback provider may have attempted to mislead the witness: Neuschatz *et al.*, 2007; or that the feedback provider was mistaken: Quinlivan, Wells & Neuschatz, 2010). Together, these results converge to suggest that witnesses will attempt to draw inferences from both internal and external cues when assessing confidence, especially when (a) internal cues are weak or inaccessible and (b) external cues are seen as valid sources of information. However, if confidence is to offer useful information about the reliability of an identification decision, it must index the witness' memory. Thus, the influence of external cues must be minimized.

The established effects of post-identification feedback on confidence have clear implications for practice. First, as recommended by the National Institute of Justice Guidelines for the Collection of Eyewitness Evidence (Technical Working Group for Eyewitness Evidence, 1999), confidence should be assessed immediately following the decision, and before a witness interacts with lineup administrators, investigating officers, or other witnesses. This objective is, of course, most easily realized if lineup administration and recording of witness responses occurs on a computer. Our concern in this chapter is not with the actual method of lineup administration; however, arguments have been made elsewhere for computerized lineup administration and the advantages this has for recording confidence judgments (see, for example, Brewer, 2011). Confidence is an influential index of witness credibility and identification reliability. Thus, feedback effects that inflate confidence (but, by their nature, cannot improve accuracy) distort the CA relationship and can make a witness and their identification appear more compelling than they should. Second, the confidence rating recorded immediately after the decision is made should be the "confidence evidence" tendered in court. Unsurprisingly, preparing witnesses for cross-examination, and having witnesses answer the same question repeatedly, increases confidence (Shaw, 1996; Shaw & McClure, 1996; Wells, Ferguson, & Lindsay, 1981). Thus, in-court expressions of confidence are likely to bias evaluations of identification credibility (see case study). One approach to combat the confidence-inflating effects of post-identification feedback and pre-trial preparation would be to present confidence as measured at the time of the identification alongside any in-court assessment of identification confidence. When their attention is drawn to confidence inflation, jurors are able to adjust their perceptions of witness and identification credibility (Bradfield & McQuiston, 2004). However, research also demonstrates that jurors do not appropriately adjust perceptions of witness credibility in light of apparent confidence inflation when the witness offers a plausible justification for their increased confidence (e.g., by attributing their lower initial confidence to nervousness at the time of the identification, and/ or explaining that they have since recalled additional, confirming information; Jones, Williams, & Brewer, 2008). Thus, from the perspective of preserving the informational value of confidence ratings, it would be reasonable to argue that only confidence recorded immediately following the decision should be tendered as evidence in court, even though any such recommendation would probably attract considerable opposition from within the legal system.

In sum, the literature supports the following conclusions about the CA relationship for eyewitness identifications. Eyewitness confidence and identification accuracy are meaningfully related when (a) an adult witness positively identifies a lineup member as the culprit and (b) confidence is assessed immediately after the decision is made, and prior to any interaction with the lineup administrator or other witnesses (Brewer, 2006; Brewer *et al.*, 2005; Brewer & Wells, 2009).

APPLIED FACTORS THAT LIMIT THE EFFECTIVE USE OF CONFIDENCE

A major factor limiting the effectiveness of confidence as an index of accuracy for identification decisions may be the absence of established protocols for collecting witness confidence ratings in a way that maximizes their informativeness. The National Institute of Justice Guidelines for the Collection of Eyewitness Evidence (US) recommends that records of the witness' decision include "the witness' own words regarding how sure he/she is" (Technical Working Group for Eyewitness Evidence, 1999, p.38). Similarly, in other Western legal systems (e.g., the UK and Canada) administrators are told to record anything the witness says regarding their identification (Police and Criminal Evidence Act Code D, 2011; Sherrin, 2007). Thus, if the witness volunteers an assessment of confidence it will be recorded, but administrators are not instructed to probe for confidence. This means that there is no guarantee that confidence will be assessed. Moreover, the way in which any obtained confidence rating is expressed may limit its usefulness. We discuss each of these issues in turn.

Why is it necessary to explicitly assess witness confidence? The obvious answer is identifications are prone to error, and confidence may help discriminate between identifications that are more or less likely to be reliable. However, in a broader sense, confidence is valuable because (when measured appropriately) it provides additional information about the quality of the witness' memory and the extent to which the identified lineup member matches the witness' memory of the culprit. A positive identification of the suspect may be extremely attractive to police and prosecutors, but in no way guarantees the suspect is the culprit. It is reasonable to assume that a suspect identification indicates that, of the presented lineup members, the suspect provides the best match with a witness' memory of the culprit. However, procedural and social factors can affect a witness' decision criterion, making them more or less likely to pick someone from the lineup, without affecting the degree of match between individual lineup members and the witness' memorial image of the culprit. Thus, although a suspect identification probably indicates that the suspect provides the best available match, it is much less informative about the quality of this match in an absolute sense. Confidence can provide additional information here. Furthermore, research in laboratory and field settings, together with inferences drawn from the limited available evidence concerning confidence in identifications in actual criminal cases, clearly demonstrates that identifications are made with varying degrees of confidence (e.g., Brewer & Wells, 2006; Sauer *et al.*, 2010). Given the theoretical relationship between confidence and memory quality, variations in confidence can be viewed as indicating qualitatively different degrees of recognition. Thus, it would be foolish not to consider confidence (i.e., to effectively treat all identifications as equally certain) when evaluating identification evidence. Confidence should be viewed as a further source of information about the witness' memory, rather than simply as a potential index of accuracy.

However, if confidence is to provide this useful information, methods for assessing confidence must (a) attenuate non-memorial influences on confidence, thereby allowing it to index the witness' memory quality, and (b) record confidence in a way that permits meaningful interpretation. How, then, should witness confidence be measured? As already indicated, confidence must be assessed immediately following the identification. Preferably this process would be run blind for the lineup administrator (and possibly automated), to avoid the influence of any explicit or implicit verbal or non-verbal feedback.

A second issue to be considered is the type of scale used to measure confidence. When guidelines discuss recording confidence ratings, they typically state or imply that confidence should be recorded in the witness' own words. However, such assessments are likely to be of limited value as spontaneous utterances are likely to be ambiguous. Consider a witness who says "I'm not certain, but I think it is number four". This statement could apply equally to a witness who would have responded with 90% or 40% given a numerical confidence scale and, thus, this expression of confidence offers little discrimination regarding the quality of the witness' memory, or the likely reliability of the identification. Furthermore, in conversation, meaning is added to such utterances through tone of voice, and accompanying non-verbal behaviours. This contextual information may be difficult to preserve in a written record, further reducing the informativeness of the confidence rating. The motivation for current practice – assessing confidence in the witness' own words – may share a foundation with concerns expressed by researchers over a witness' ability to translate internal confidence states into numerical scales (Soll & Klayman, 2004, Windschitl & Wells, 1996). Researchers have argued that although conceptualizing certainty numerically may be natural for statistically-trained individuals, this may not be true for the general population, and that verbal scales (e.g., using anchor points such as *likely, very likely, extremely likely, certain*) may better approximate internal confidence states. Despite these concerns, and encouraged by the similar CA calibration patterns reported for identification decisions regardless of whether numerical and verbal scales were used (Weber, Brewer & Margitich, 2008), we recommend assessing confidence on a standardized numerical scale (e.g., 0–100%, 1–10, etc.). There is sufficient evidence to demonstrate that adult participants can effectively use numerical scales to discriminate between decisions for which they have higher and lower confidence, and decisions that are more or less likely to be accurate (e.g., Brewer & Wells, 2006; Juslin *et al.*, 1996; Sauer *et al.*, 2010; Sauerland & Sporer, 2009; Weber & Brewer, 2003, 2004). An interval scale also offers an internal hierarchy of responses and provides a less ambiguous metric for those interpreting the reported level of confidence. In contrast, a confidence response such as "rather likely" or "quite likely" (which may come from a witness' own words or from responses on a verbal confidence scale) is more difficult to interpret. For example, these responses could conceivably indicate levels of confidence falling toward the middle or the upper end of the confidence continuum. Admittedly, fine-grained numerical confidence scales may not be appropriate for all eyewitnesses (e.g., young children, people with learning difficulties). Keast *et al.* (2007) found that children in the 11–13 age range appeared just as capable as adults at interpreting such confidence scales, although, despite that, their confidence judgments were not diagnostic of identification accuracy (Keast *et al.*, 2007). However, such scales are unlikely to be suitable for younger children.

When research clearly indicates that (a) confidence is highly influential and (b) confidence can be informative under certain conditions, and some courts even require that confidence be recorded (e.g., *State v. Henderson*, 2011) and considered when evaluating identification evidence (e.g., *Neil v. Biggers*, 1972), why would criminal justice systems be reluctant to establish systematic protocols for eliciting, recording and maximizing the informational value of witness confidence ratings? We can only speculate here. Perhaps practitioners believe, contrary to the scientific literature, that recognition memory is an "all or nothing" process. The witness both recognizes (and identifies) the suspect or they do not, and confidence ratings are irrelevant because they offer no additional information regarding the validity of recognition. Or perhaps practitioners may believe, again contrary to empirical evidence, that a witness would not identify a lineup member if they were uncertain. Alternatively, if practitioners acknowledge that some identifications are made with less than complete certainty, perhaps they believe that uncertain identifications are of no value. Specifically, prosecutors may feel that an identification made with, for example, 70% confidence will be easily undermined by the defence. They may be right. However, it is certainly true that not to consider confidence – and instead present all identifications as implying certainty, despite all evidence to the contrary – undermines the informational value of the evidence. If such beliefs contribute to the desire to avoid collecting explicit confidence ratings, they systematically undermine efforts to appropriately evaluate identification evidence and increase the risk of miscarriages of justice.

If legal decision-makers are concerned that assessing confidence may undermine prosecutorial efforts, the answer may be to correct faulty perceptions of identification evidence within the legal system rather than avoid the issue and risk misrepresenting the diagnostic value of identification evidence. As Brewer and Wells (2009) note, rather than treating an identification as a clear-cut indication of guilt, it is more useful to view the identification as an indication that a suspect is worth further investigation or, if there is sufficient corroborating evidence, that the suspect should be charged. Similarly, in court, although jurors view identification evidence (particularly when provided by confident witnesses) as a compelling indication of defendant guilt, they should be encouraged to view the identification as one piece of probabilistic evidence that must be considered alongside the other evidence when assessing the defendant's guilt. During investigations and at trial, confidence can enrich this source of information to help guide the decision-making process regarding the likely guilt of the accused.

A NOVEL USE FOR EYEWITNESS CONFIDENCE: CONFIDENCE AS AN INDEX OF RECOGNITION

In line with the re-conceptualization of identification evidence suggested above, we now discuss a radical departure from traditional identification practice. Although this approach involves a drastic change in the way identification evidence is collected and interpreted, we argue that it provides a more informative index of recognition, and represents a more valid approach to testing witness memory. As discussed previously, various theories of confidence processing for recognition memory hold that confidence indexes the degree of match between a presented item and an image in memory. This suggests an interesting possibility for assessing witness recognition. Specifically, avoiding explicit, categorical identification responses (and thereby attenuating non-memorial influences on witnesses' decision criteria) and instead simply asking the witness to rate their confidence (on a scale from 0–100%) that each lineup member is the culprit (henceforth, *ecphoric confidence ratings*) may provide a more sensitive and informative index of recognition, and a more direct assessment of the degree of match between individual lineup members and the witness' memory of the culprit (Brewer, Weber, Wootton, & Lindsay, 2012; Sauer, Brewer, & Weber, 2008, 2012a; Sauer, Weber, & Brewer, 2012b).

Early investigations of the diagnostic value of ecphoric confidence ratings have provided a number of encouraging findings. First, basic face recognition research revealed a generally linear, positive relationship between ecphoric confidence ratings and the likelihood that a face has been previously seen (Sauer *et al.*, 2012b). Second, after the application of classification algorithms to determine when a confidence rating or pattern of confidence ratings could be treated as a positive identification of the suspect (described in detail in Sauer *et al.*, 2008), ecphoric confidence ratings consistently produced higher classification accuracy than categorical recognition decisions in face recognition tasks, and from simultaneous and sequential lineups (Brewer *et al.*, 2012; Sauer *et al.*, 2008, 2012a, 2012b). That is, confidence ratings were more effective than participants' decisions at indicating whether or not participants had seen a presented face or lineup member before. Finally, analyses of classification performance using SDT-based measures of discrimination (i.e., the sensitivity of the index of recognition) and response bias (i.e., the general tendency to return an increased or decreased number of positive classifications) demonstrated that the improved classification accuracy associated with the use of ecphoric confidence ratings (cf. categorical decisions) was attributable to improvements in discrimination rather than any change in bias (Sauer *et al.*, 2012b). Compared with participants' recognition decisions, ecphoric confidence ratings provided a more sensitive index of recognition.

Collapsing confidence ratings into categorical classifications in order to compare classification performance using ecphoric ratings with performance based on categorical recognition decisions permits a valuable demonstration of the diagnostic value of the confidence procedure. However, it also reduces the richness of the recognition information provided. Brewer *et al.*'s (2012) analyses included an additional and more informative treatment of the data. Specifically, for each lineup, the researchers determined whether there was a single highest, maximum confidence value. If there was a maximum confidence value, the researchers examined variations in the likely guilt of the suspect as a function of the discrepancy between the maximum and next-highest values. Across three experiments, this *profile analysis* produced striking results. First, consistent with models that conceptualize the strength of, or confidence in, recognition as an index of the relative similarity of decision alternatives to a previously viewed item (e.g., Valentine, 1991), the likely guilt of the suspect increased almost monotonically as a function of the discrepancy between the maximum and next-highest confidence ratings. Second, when this discrepancy was large (e.g., ≥80%) the likely guilt of the suspect was very high (e.g., 80–100%) and, until the discrepancy fell to 30–50%, confidence ratings were a better predictor of suspect guilt than were categorical identification decisions.

These findings have two important implications. First, as Brewer *et al.* (2012) noted, they extend demonstrations of group-level differences in classification accuracy to show that patterns of confidence ratings can offer reliable diagnostic information about suspect guilt for individual witnesses. Second, the monotonic positive relationship between the discrepancy measure and the likely guilt of the suspect hints at the plausibility of avoiding categorical classifications entirely, in favour of a probabilistic treatment of identification evidence. Traditional identification testing approaches basically assign a witness' recognition memory "output" to categories such as "It's number 6" or "He's not there" or "I'm not sure". The legal system may benefit, however, from maximizing the amount of information available from the witness' memory, and considering what this information says about the *likely* guilt of the suspect/defendant.

Although the boundary conditions for the confidence procedure described above clearly require further investigation, this procedure has the potential to address a number of the problems that have plagued traditional identification practices. First, avoiding explicit, categorical decisions attenuates the various non-memorial influences on criterion placement that compromise the extent to which the eventual decision reflects the degree of match between a lineup member, or members, and the witness' memory of the culprit (i.e., the construct of interest), and contribute to mistaken identifications. Second, this approach provides legal decision-makers with a richer source of information upon which to base assessments of likely guilt. As mentioned previously, a single decision provides little information about the extent to which the identified lineup member matches the witness' memory of the culprit. Further, this decision provides no information about the extent to which the identified lineup member is favoured over the alternatives and, if the suspect is not identified, the eventual decision provides no information about the degree of match between the suspect and the witness' memory of the culprit (other than that the degree of match did not exceed the criterion for identification in the case of a lineup rejection, or that the suspect was not the best match in the case of a foil identification). In contrast, in all cases, the confidence procedure provides investigators with useful information about (a) the extent to which the suspect matches the witness' memory of the culprit and (b) the similarity of the suspect to the witness' memory, relative to other lineup members.

As Brewer and Wells (2011) recently argued, although a procedure that does not involve a witness actually picking or rejecting a suspect is likely to encounter strong resistance from the police and courts, "...any procedure that reduces the likelihood that culprits go free and innocent people are convicted warrants serious attention from a research perspective and from the perspective of giving away psychological science" (p. 26). We believe that some variant of the confidence procedure outlined above may well offer an opportunity to abandon the problematic conceptualization of identification evidence as some absolute indication of guilt, in favour of a more scientific consideration of identification evidence as yet another piece of probabilistic evidence – evidence that must be considered alongside the available corroborating evidence when evaluating the likely guilt of a suspect/defendant.

REFERENCES

Behrman, B.W., & Davey, S.L. (2001). Eyewitness identification in actual criminal cases: An archival analysis. *Law and Human Behavior, 25*, 475–491. doi:10.1023/A:1012840831846

Benjamin, N. Cardozo School of Law Yeshiva University. (2013). *Summary of Robert Clark Case*. Retrieved from http://www.gainnocenceproject.org/images/Clark_PressSummary_WEB1.pdf

Bothwell, R.K., Deffenbacher, K.A., & Brigham, J.C. (1987). Correlations of eyewitness accuracy and confidence: Optimality hypothesis revisited. *Journal of Applied Psychology, 72*, 691–695. doi:10.1037/0021-9010.72.4.691

Bradfield, A., & McQuiston, D.E. (2004). When does evidence of eyewitness confidence inflation affect judgments in a criminal trial? *Law and Human Behavior, 28*, 369–387. doi:10.1023/B:LAHU.0000039331.54147.ff

Bradfield, A.L., & Wells, G.L. (2000). The perceived validity of eyewitness identification testimony: A test of the five Biggers criteria. *Law and Human Behavior, 24*, 581–594. doi:10.1023/A:1005523129437

Bradfield, A.L., Wells, G.L., & Olson, E.A. (2002). The damaging effect of confirming feedback on the relation between eyewitness certainty and identification accuracy. *Journal of Applied Psychology, 87*, 112–120. doi:10.1037/0021-9010.87.1.112

Brewer, N. (2006). Uses and abuses of eyewitness identification confidence. *Legal and Criminological Psychology, 11*, 3–23. doi:10.1348/135532505X79672

Brewer, N. (2011). Practical advantages in computerized photo line-ups. *The Police Journal (Opinion section), 92*(2). Retrieved from http://journal.pasa.asn.au/

Brewer, N., & Burke, A. (2002). Effects of testimonial inconsistencies and eyewitness confidence on mock-juror judgements. *Law and Human Behavior, 26*, 353–364. doi:10.1023/A:1015380522722

Brewer, N., Keast, A., & Rishworth, A. (2002). The confidence-accuracy relationship in eyewitness identification: The effects of reflection and disconfirmation on correlation and calibration. *Journal of Experimental Psychology: Applied, 8*, 44–56. doi:10.1037/1076-898X.8.1.44

Brewer, N., & Weber, N. (2008). Eyewitness confidence and latency: Indices of memory processes not just markers of accuracy. *Applied Cognitive Psychology, 22*, 827–840. doi:10.1002/acp.1486

Brewer, N., Weber, N., & Semmler, C. (2005). Eyewitness identification. In N. Brewer, & K.D. Williams (Eds.), *Psychology and Law: An Empirical Perspective* (pp. 177–221). New York: Guilford.

Brewer, N., Weber, N., Wootton, D., & Lindsay, D.S. (2012). Identifying the bad guy in a lineup using confidence judgments under deadline pressure. *Psychological Science, 23*, 1208–1214. doi:10.1177/0956797612441217

Brewer, N., & Wells, G.L. (2006). The confidence-accuracy relationship in eyewitness identification: Effects of lineup instructions, functional size and target-absent base rates. *Journal of Experimental Psychology: Applied, 12*, 11–30. doi:10.1037/1076-898X.12.1.11

Brewer, N., & Wells, G.L. (2009). Obtaining and interpreting eyewitness identification test evidence: The influence of police-witness interactions. In T. Williamson, R. Bull, & T. Valentine (Eds.), *Handbook of Psychology of Investigative Interviewing: Current Developments and Future Directions* (pp. 205–220). Chichester: Wiley-Blackwell.

Brewer, N., & Wells, G.L. (2011). Eyewitness identification. *Current Directions in Psychological Science, 20*, 24–27. doi:10.1177/0963721410389169

Clark, S., Howell, R., & Davey, S. (2008). Regularities in eyewitness identification. *Law and Human Behavior, 32*, 187–218. doi:10.1007/s10979-006-9082-4

Cutler, B.L., Penrod, S.D., & Dexter, H.R. (1990). Juror sensitivity to eyewitness identification evidence. *Law and Human Behavior, 14*, 185–191. doi:10.1007/bf01062972

Cutler, B.L., Penrod, S.D., & Martens, T.K. (1987). The reliability of eyewitness identification: The role of system and estimator variables. *Law and Human Behavior, 11*, 233–258. doi:10.1007/bf01044644

Cutler, B.L., Penrod, S.D., & Stuve, T.E. (1988). Jury decision making in eyewitness identification cases. *Law and Human Behavior, 12*, 41–56. doi:10.1007/BF01064273

Deffenbacher, K.A., & Loftus, E.F. (1982). Do jurors share a common understanding concerning eyewitness behavior? *Law and Human Behavior, 6*, 15–30. doi:10.1007/BF01049310

Garrioch, L., & Brimacombe, C.A.E. (2001). Lineup administrators' expectations: Their impact on eyewitness confidence. *Law and Human Behavior, 25*, 299–315. doi:10.1023/a:1010750028643

Green, D.M., & Swets, J.A. (1966). *Signal Detection Theory and Psychophysics.* New York: Wiley.

Horry, R., Palmer, M.A., & Brewer, N. (2012). Backloading in the sequential lineup prevents within-lineup criterion shifts that undermine eyewitness identification performance. *Journal of Experimental Psychology. Applied, 18*, 346–360. doi:10.1037/a0029779

Innocence Project. (2013). *Robert Clark Case.* Retrieved from http://www.innocenceproject.org/Content/Robert_Clark.php

Jones, E.E., Williams, K.D., & Brewer, N. (2008). "I had a confidence epiphany!": Obstacles to combating post-identification confidence inflation. *Law and Human Behavior, 32,* 164–176. doi:10.1007/s10979-007-9101-0

Juslin, P., Olsson, N., & Winman, A. (1996). Calibration and diagnosticity of confidence in eyewitness identification: Comments on what can be inferred from the low confidence-accuracy correlation. *Journal of Experimental Psychology: Learning, Memory, and Cognition, 22,* 1304–1316. doi:10.1037/0278-7393.22.5.1304

Keast, A., Brewer, N., & Wells, G.L. (2007). Children's metacognitive judgments in an eyewitness identification task. *Journal of Experimental Child Psychology, 97,* 286–314. doi:10.1016/j.jecp.2007.01.007

Lindsay, D.S., Nilsen, E., & Read, J.D. (2000). Witnessing-condition heterogeneity and witnesses' versus investigators' confidence in the accuracy of witnesses' identification decisions. *Law and Human Behavior, 24,* 685–697. doi:10.1023/A:1005504320565

Lindsay, D.S., Read, J.D., & Sharma, K. (1998). Accuracy and confidence in person identification: The relationship is strong when witnessing conditions vary widely. *Psychological Science, 9,* 215–218. doi:10.1111/1467-9280.00041

Lindsay, R.C.L., Kalmet, N., Leung, J., Bertrand, M.I., Sauer, J.D., & Sauerland, M. (2013). Confidence and accuracy of lineup selections and rejections: Postdicting rejection accuracy with confidence. *Journal of Applied Research in Memory and Cognition, 2,* 179–184. doi:10.1016/j.jarmac.2013.06.002

Lindsay, R.C.L., Wells, G.L., & Rumpel, C.M. (1981). Can people detect eyewitness-identification accuracy within and across situations? *Journal of Applied Psychology, 66,* 79–89. doi:10.1037/0021-9010.66.1.79

Luus, C., & Wells, G.L. (1994). The malleability of eyewitness confidence: Co-witness and perseverance effects. *Journal of Applied Psychology, 79,* 714–723. doi:10.1037/0021-9010.79.5.714

Macmillan, N.A., & Creelman, C.D. (1991). *Detection Theory: A User's Guide.* New York: Cambridge University Press.

Neil v. Biggers (1972). 409 U.S. 188.

Neuschatz, J., Lawson, D., Fairless, A., Powers, R., Neuschatz, J., Goodsell, C., & Toglia, M. (2007). The mitigating effects of suspicion on post-identification feedback and on retrospective eyewitness memory. *Law and Human Behavior, 31,* 231–247. doi:10.1007/s10979-006-9047-7

Olsson, N. (2000). A comparison of correlation, calibration, and diagnosticity as measures of the confidence-accuracy relationship in witness identification. *Journal of Applied Psychology, 85,* 504–511. doi:10.1037/0021-9010.85.4.504

Olsson, N., Juslin, P., & Winman, A. (1998). Realism of confidence in earwitness versus eyewitness identification. *Journal of Experimental Psychology: Applied, 4,* 101–118. doi:10.1037/1076-898X.4.2.101

Oregon v. Lawson (2012). CC 03CR1469FE; CA A132640; SC S059234

Palmer, M.A., & Brewer, N. (2012). Sequential lineup presentation promotes less-biased criterion setting but does not improve discriminability. *Law and Human Behavior, 36,* 247–255. doi:10.1037/h0093923

Palmer, M.A., Brewer, N., & Weber, N. (2010). Postidentification feedback affects subsequent eyewitness identification performance. *Journal of Experimental Psychology: Applied, 16,* 387–398. doi:10.1037/a0021034

Palmer, M.A., Brewer, N., Weber, N., & Nagesh, A. (2013). The confidence-accuracy relationship for eyewitness identification decisions: Effects of exposure duration, retention interval, and divided attention. *Journal of Experimental Psychology: Applied, 19*, 55–71. doi:10.1037/a0031602.

Pike, G., Brace, N., & Kynan, S. (2002). *The Visual Identification of Suspects: Procedures and Practice.* (Briefing Note 2/02). London: Home Office. Retrieved from http://webarchive.nationalarchives.gov.uk/20110220105210/ http://rds.homeoffice.gov.uk/rds/pdfs2/brf202.pdf

Police and Criminal Evidence Act (PACE, 1984) Codes of Practice: Code D (2011). Retrieved from http://www.homeoffice.gov.uk/publications/police/ operational-policing/pace-codes/pace-code-d-2011?view=Binary

Potter, R., & Brewer, N. (1999). Perceptions of witness behaviour – accuracy relationships held by police, lawyers and mock-jurors. *Psychiatry, Psychology and Law, 6*, 97–103. doi:10.1080/13218719909524952

Quinlivan, D., Wells, G., & Neuschatz, J. (2010). Is manipulative intent necessary to mitigate the eyewitness post-identification feedback effect? *Law and Human Behavior, 34*, 186–197. doi:10.1007/s10979-009-9179-7

Sauer, J.D., Brewer, N., & Weber, N. (2008). Multiple confidence estimates as indices of eyewitness memory. *Journal of Experimental Psychology: General, 137*, 528–547. doi:10.1037/a0012712

Sauer, J.D., Brewer, N., & Weber, N. (2012a). Using confidence ratings to identify a target among foils. *Journal of Applied Research in Memory and Cognition, 1*, 80–88. doi:10.1016/j.jarmac.2012.03.003

Sauer, J.D., Brewer, N., Zweck, T., & Weber, N. (2010). The effect of retention interval on the confidence-accuracy relationship for eyewitness identification. *Law and Human Behavior, 34*, 337–347. doi:10.1007/s10979-009-9192-x

Sauer, J. D., Weber, N., & Brewer, N. (2012b). Using ecphoric confidence ratings to discriminate seen from unseen faces: The effects of retention interval and distinctiveness. *Psychonomic Bulletin & Review, 19*, 490–498. doi:10.3758/ s13423-012-0239-5

Sauerland, M., Sagana, A., & Sporer, S.L. (2012). Assessing nonchoosers' eyewitness identification accuracy from photographic showups by using confidence and response times. *Law and Human Behavior, 36*, 394–403. doi:10.1037/h0093926

Sauerland, M., & Sporer, S.L. (2009). Fast and confident: Postdicting eyewitness identification accuracy in a field study. *Journal of Experimental Psychology: Applied, 15*, 46–62. doi:10.1037/a0014560

Semmler, C., & Brewer, N. (2006). Postidentification feedback effects on face recognition confidence: Evidence for metacognitive influences. *Applied Cognitive Psychology, 20*, 895–916. doi:10.1002/acp.1238

Semmler, C., Brewer, N., & Wells, G.L. (2004). Effects of postidentification feedback on eyewitness identification and nonidentification confidence. *Journal of Applied Psychology, 89*, 334–346. doi:10.1037/0021-9010.89.2.334

Shaw, J.S. (1996). Increases in eyewitness confidence resulting from postevent questioning. *Journal of Experimental Psychology: Applied, 2*, 126–146. doi:10.1037/1076-898X.2.2.126

Shaw, J.S., & McClure, K.A. (1996). Repeated postevent questioning can lead to elevated levels of eyewitness confidence. *Law and Human Behavior, 20*, 629–653. doi:10.1007/BF01499235

Sherrin, C. (2007). *Comment on the Report on the Prevention of Miscarriages of Justice.* University of Western Ontario. Retrieved from http://heinonline. org/HOL/Page?handle=hein.journals/clwqrty52&div=17&g_sent= 1&collection=journals

Soll, J.B., & Klayman, J. (2004). Overconfidence in interval estimates. *Journal of Experimental Psychology: Learning, Memory, and Cognition, 30*, 299–314. doi:10.1037/0278-7393.30.2.299

Sporer, S.L., Penrod, S.D., Read, D., & Cutler, B.L. (1995). Choosing, confidence, and accuracy: A meta-analysis of the confidence-accuracy relation in eyewitness identification studies. *Psychological Bulletin, 118*, 315–327. doi:10.1037/0033-2909.118.3.315

State v. Henderson, WL (2011) 3715028.

Technical Working Group for Eyewitness Evidence (1999). *Eyewitness Evidence: A Guide for Law Enforcement.* Washington, DC: US Department of Justice.

Valentine, T. (1991). A unified account of the effects of distinctiveness, inversion, and race in face recognition. *Quarterly Journal of Experimental Psychology, 43*, 161–204. doi:10.1080/14640749108400966

Valentine, T., Pickering, A., & Darling, S. (2003). Characteristics of eyewitness identification that predict the outcome of real lineups. *Applied Cognitive Psychology, 17*, 969–993. doi:10.1002/acp.939

Van Zandt, T. (2000). ROC curves and confidence judgments in recognition memory. *Journal of Experimental Psychology: Learning, Memory, and Cognition, 26*, 582–600. doi:10.1037/0278-7393.26.3.582

Vickers, D. (1979). *Decision Processes in Visual Perception.* New York: Academic Press.

Weber, N., & Brewer, N. (2003). The effect of judgment type and confidence scale on confidence-accuracy calibration in face recognition. *Journal of Applied Psychology, 88*, 490–499. doi:10.1037/0021-9010.88.3.490

Weber, N., & Brewer, N. (2004). Confidence-accuracy calibration in absolute and relative face recognition judgements. *Journal of Experimental Psychology: Applied, 10*, 156–172. doi:10.1037/1076-898X.10.3.156

Weber, N., & Brewer, N. (2006). Positive versus negative face recognition decisions: Confidence, accuracy and response latency. *Applied Cognitive Psychology, 20*, 17–31. doi:10.1002/acp.1166

Weber, N., Brewer, N., & Margitich, S.D. (2008). The confidence-accuracy relation in eyewitness identification: effects of verbal versus numeric confidence scales. In K.H. Kiefer (Ed.), *Applied Psychology Research Trends* (pp. 103–118). Hauppauge, NY: Nova Publishers.

Wells, G.L., & Bradfield, A.L. (1998). "Good, you identified the suspect": Feedback to eyewitnesses distorts their reports of the witnessing experience. *Journal of Applied Psychology, 83*, 360–376. doi:10.1037/0021-9010.83.3.360

Wells, G.L., & Bradfield, A.L. (1999). Distortions in eyewitnesses' recollections: Can the postidentification-feedback effect be moderated? *Psychological Science, 10*, 138–144. doi:10.1111/1467-9280.00121

Wells, G.L., Ferguson, T.J., & Lindsay, R.C.L. (1981). The tractability of eyewitness confidence and its implications for triers of fact. *Journal of Applied Psychology, 66*, 688–696. doi:10.1037/0021-9010.66.6.688

Wells, G.L., & Lindsay, R.C.L. (1980). On estimating the diagnosticity of eyewitness nonidentifications. *Psychological Bulletin, 88*, 776–784. doi:10.1037/0033-2909.88.3.776

Wells, G.L., & Olson, E.A. (2002). Eyewitness identification: Information gain from incriminating and exonerating behaviors. *Journal of Experimental Psychology: Applied, 8*, 155–167. doi:10.1037/1076-898X.8.3.155

Windschitl, P.D., & Wells, G.L. (1996). Measuring psychological uncertainty: Verbal versus numeric methods. *Journal of Experimental Psychology: Applied, 2*, 343–364. doi:10.1037/1076-898X.2.4.343

Part 4

Identification from CCTV Images

9

Human Verification of Identity from Photographic Images

JOSH P. DAVIS AND TIM VALENTINE

It has long been known that human memory is fallible (e.g., Borchard, 1932; Munsterberg, 1908/1925), and that this can create legal controversies when a police investigation relies upon eyewitness testimony. Evidence from exoneration cases, as well as the vast body of empirical research reported in this volume, has shown that witnesses often make highly confident but mistaken identifications of someone they wrongly believe to be the perpetrator of a crime. On the other hand, witnesses also regularly fail to identify the true offender from an identity parade or lineup. Recognition can be adversely influenced by both system variables (see Chapter 6) and estimator variables (see Chapter 7), and for many years these identification errors were attributed purely to the fragility of human memory. However, there are many important forensic and security situations for which no memory is required, and this chapter describes the large body of relatively recent research demonstrating that there is a similar risk of identification error with these tasks.

Forensic Facial Identification: Theory and Practice of Identification from Eyewitnesses, Composites and CCTV, First Edition. Edited by Tim Valentine and Josh P. Davis.
© 2015 John Wiley & Sons, Ltd. Published 2015 by John Wiley & Sons, Ltd.

Case study: Jean Charles de Menezes (1978–2005)

On July 7, 2005, four suicide bombers detonated devices on three London underground trains and a bus, murdering 56 people and injuring many more. Two weeks later, four more explosive devices failed to explode on the underground. The four perpetrators went into hiding. One – Osman Hussain – had left a gym photograph membership card in his bag containing one of the unexploded bombs. With security forces on high alert, the police retrieved this card, and a few hours later staked out a South London block of flats – the address registered by the gym card owner. A Brazilian, Jean Charles de Menezes who lived in this building, left the communal entrance the following morning. A police surveillance officer who had seen a copy of the gym card, and a poor-quality CCTV image of Osman, watched de Menezes leave and suggested by radio he deserved "another look". For the following hour, other officers briefly viewed de Menezes as he travelled on buses to his workplace. His entirely innocent behaviour was deemed suspicious as it inadvertently replicated tactics for evading surveillance, adding to the growing belief that de Menezes was one of the bombers. de Menezes arrived at Stockwell underground station at about the same time as a firearms team. From operational command information, they were convinced de Menezes was carrying a primed explosive device, and he was shot at very close range shortly after he boarded a train.

Several official investigations were held into the wrongful killing of this innocent man – the Metropolitan Police Service were criticized for their operations, communication and surveillance procedures. On October 1, 2007, a criminal prosecution against the force was bought under the Health and Safety at Work Act (1974). The force pleaded "not guilty", but for "failing to provide for the health, safety, and welfare of Jean Charles de Menezes" it was fined £175,000, with £385,000 legal costs on November 1, 2007 (BBC News, 2007).

Evidence provided by the defence had included presenting to the jury "chimeric" composite images created by aligning the left side of Osman's face with the right side of de Menezes' face (Figure 9.1). The aim was to demonstrate that the two men were highly similar in appearance and that the original errors of misidentification were partly a consequence of this similarity. An expert witness for the prosecution argued that the images had been manipulated so that contrast and colour matched, and had also been stretched in some places to align them – reducing the salience of differences between the two faces (note that the images in Figure 9.1 have not been manipulated in this manner). There is also evidence that chimeric display will

Figure 9.1   Hussain Osman (left) and Jean Charles de Menezes (centre), presented as a chimeric facial image (right). Note that this image has not been manipulated by standardizing skin tone or stretching the images to align facial features, as was suggested by the prosecution to have occurred in the Health and Safety court case reported in this chapter (kind permission Metropolitan Police Service, London). From Strathie *et al.* (2011), reproduced with permission of John Wiley & Sons, Ltd.

increase the similarity of any two pairs of faces, regardless of manipulations (Strathie, McNeill, & White, 2012). Faces are primarily processed in a holistic or whole face manner (e.g., Tanaka & Farah, 1993; Tanaka & Sengco, 1997), and this technique increases the likelihood that a viewer will view the two halves as a Gestalt or as a single individual. Strathie *et al.* argued that employing this procedure in court should therefore be avoided as it may mislead the jury.

Other research reported in this chapter also informs as to why errors may have been made in this operation. The inquest reports do not make clear whether any of the surveillance teams attempted to simultaneously match de Menezes with Osman's gym card or CCTV image. However, unfamiliar face matching from even high-quality photographs to live actors can be error prone (Davis & Valentine, 2009), particularly with passport-sized images (Kemp, Towell, & Pike, 1997). With lower-quality images taken from a distance, which if digital may be pixelated, face-matching performance will be worse (Bindemann, Attard, Leach, & Johnston, 2013). This may have been relevant as, even though higher-quality images were available, the police were criticized for supplying the surveillance teams with poor-quality CCTV images of Osman. Of course, to avoid attracting the attention of de Menezes, the team may have kept the images concealed and made their identification decisions based on memory, further reducing the likelihood of an accurate judgement. Nevertheless, the first view of the two images may have biased all subsequent decisions anyway, particularly if the gym card and CCTV images of Osman appeared dissimilar, as is surprisingly common when viewing images of the same unfamiliar person from different sources (Jenkins, White, van Montfort, & Burton, 2011). Information that a suspect may have changed appearance can induce a liberal response bias in both matching (Davis & Valentine, 2009) and recognition tasks (Charman & Wells, 2007), and being told that two dissimilar images depict the same person may have been interpreted as an implicit instruction that de Menezes' appearance had changed, and to therefore be more "flexible" when making their identification judgements. Furthermore, there are no details of the face recognition abilities of the surveillance team which may have influenced all the tasks listed above. Individuals with average ability are likely to make more identification errors than so called super-recognizers (Davis, Lander, & Jansari, 2013).

Finally, although not central to the current chapter, all human decision-making is susceptible to error. The first police radio call of de Menezes needing "another look" appears to have initiated a *confirmation bias* for the operations team to interpret subsequent information as evidence of guilt (see Cole & Thompson, 2013). If so, evidence pointing towards de Menezes' innocence will have been ignored or misinterpreted, whereas information pointing towards his guilt will have been assimilated into a model of escalating guilt. Indeed, by the time of the shooting, operations team transcripts suggest there was confidence in the belief that de Menezes was a terrorist, and that he had been visually identified as Osman by at least one of his police pursuers.

Examples include:

1. Border control or other security checkpoints where officials are required to verify the identity of individuals from photographs on documents such as passports.
2. Closed-circuit television (CCTV) camera operators may be required to match a face on a wanted list with an individual under surveillance.
3. Police officers may simultaneously compare CCTV or other photographic images collected from the scene of the crime, with images of known suspects in order to gather evidence to secure a prosecution.
4. In some cases, the identification of victims of crime from photographic images may be as important as identifying the culprits. One such highly distressing scenario is when the police attempt to identify minors depicted in footage of pornographic events displayed on the internet. For this, officers will similarly use comparison photographs to match with the evidential images.

An important distinction is, however, made in the law, and is supported by empirical research. Viewers familiar with those depicted are, in most circumstances, highly accurate at identity verification tasks (e.g., Bruce, Henderson, Newman, & Burton, 2001; Burton, Wilson, Cowan, & Bruce, 1999b). In contrast, unfamiliar face identification is error prone, even when the task requires no memory (e.g., Bruce *et al.*, 1999; Burton, White, & McNeill, 2010; Burton *et al.*, 1999; Davis & Valentine, 2009; Henderson, Bruce, & Burton, 2001; Kemp *et al.*, 1997; Megreya & Burton, 2006, 2008). Furthermore, as with eyewitness identification, many of the variables described elsewhere in this volume will negatively influence these procedures. Of course, familiarity can vary from a fleeting encounter to knowing someone for many years, and differences in the level of familiarity will influence identification accuracy. Furthermore, there are large individual differences in the ability to learn new faces. Nevertheless, it is perhaps rather ironic that the officials tasked with determining identity in the scenarios listed above are extremely unlikely to have ever previously encountered those who are under scrutiny.

THE USE OF PHOTOGRAPHIC IMAGES IN COURT

The UK has led the world in the widespread installation of CCTV in most city and town centres. There are estimated to be between 1.85 (Thompson & Gerrard, 2011) and 5.9 million CCTV cameras (Barrett, 2013) in the UK. These numbers may be dwarfed by alternative sources of photographic evidence including mobile phone cameras, social media websites, police mugshots, as well as GPS-enabled smart video cameras carried by cyclists and other vehicles such as police cars. Some offenders, particularly those in youth gangs, upload images of their activities onto websites, as a "badge of honour". As a consequence of government support for the proliferation of CCTV, many of the principles for the use of such images in legal proceedings were first applied in the UK, and therefore the primary English legislation will be described in the following section (see chapters 10 and 12 for further details).

Photographs have been admissible in court since 1864 (*R v. Tolson*, 1864, cited in Murphy, 1999), and CCTV footage itself was first admitted in 1982 to provide information about a theft from a retail store (*R v. Fowden and White*, 1982). The use of such evidence for identification purposes in England and Wales was recently summarized in an Attorney General's Reference (2003), with an important distinction between evidence presented by witnesses who are familiar with the defendant, and evidence provided by those who did not know the defendant prior to the police investigation.

Firstly, if identifications have been made after viewing a video or photograph by individuals previously familiar with a defendant, they may give evidence as a witness for the case, even if the footage is no longer available (e.g., *R v. Caldwell and Dixon*, 1993; *R v. Grimer*, 1982; *Taylor v. The Chief Constable of Cheshire*, 1987). In these circumstances, identifications have the same status as those from eyewitnesses present at the incident, and witnesses can therefore be cross-examined in court. In many cases, witnesses will be police officers and to protect them, or indeed any witness, from accusations of collusion, the Police and Criminal Evidence Act 1984 Codes of Practice Code D (2011) additionally prescribes the procedures by which images should be distributed for eliciting reliable identifications. For instance, police intelligence may lead an investigating team to believe an officer may have encountered the suspect previously. They may wish the officer to view crime scene footage to confirm the suspect's identity. Such identifications should be spontaneous and independently acquired – witnesses should not be prompted. Therefore, witnesses are required to provide details as to how they were previously familiar with the suspect, and the circumstances by which they first viewed the images. A failure to adhere to these codes of practice has resulted in the courts rejecting improperly collected identification evidence (see, for instance, Fort, 2013).

Similar principles designed to protect against evidence contamination operate in Australia. In *Strauss v. the Police* (2013), an eyewitness who was intoxicated at the time of the crime, and who may not have had a good view of the perpetrator, was encouraged by an acquaintance a few hours later to view images from a social website (Facebook) in order to identify the eventual defendant. This identification formed a central component of the prosecution's case. The conviction was overturned on appeal. The court ruled that the identification procedure was highly suggestive and therefore unsafe, as the defendant's name had been provided to the witness by the same acquaintance prior to viewing the website images.

The remaining three circumstances in which photographic identification evidence may be admitted in court in England and Wales concerns witnesses who were not previously familiar with the defendant (Attorney General's Reference, 2003).

First, expert practitioners may apply *facial mapping* or *facial comparison* techniques to provide evidence as to whether an individual captured in photographic evidence is the defendant depicted in a confirmed photograph (e.g., *R v. Clarke*, 1995; Davis, Valentine, & Wilkinson, 2012). The generally poor reliability of these techniques is discussed in Chapter 10. When presented in court with professional gravitas, alongside circumstantial evidence, evidence from a facial comparison expert can be highly compelling.

Second, evidence may be admissible if a witness, not previously familiar with the defendant, spends "substantial time viewing and analysing photographic images from the scene" (Attorney General's Reference, 2003), thus familiarizing themselves with the accused and gaining a *special ad-hoc* expertise. For instance, in *R v. Clare and Peach* (1995) a police officer viewed black-and-white CCTV footage of a football crowd riot more than 40 times, examining stills and evaluating details in slow motion. He compared this footage with undisputed photographs of the defendants taken the same day. There is evidence that matching performance is partly diagnostic of familiarity, as increased exposure can increase accuracy at this type of face-matching task (Clutterbuck & Johnston, 2002), although not necessarily with low-quality images (Davis, 2007; Lee, Wilkinson, Memon, & Houston, 2009). However, even forensic scientists can be susceptible to "cognitive biases", or tunnel vision encouraging faulty decision-making, so that prior case information can inadvertently influence judgements (Cole & Thompson, 2013). It is possible that individuals repetitively viewing poor-quality photographic images will be vulnerable to such biases by ignoring "exculpatory" visual cues in some frames that do not match the appearance of the defendant, while placing greater weight on alternative frames as there appears to be a greater similarity of appearance between the defendant and the individual depicted.

Third, "where the photographic image is sufficiently clear, the jury can compare it with the defendant sitting in the dock" (Attorney General's Reference, 2003). The prosecution may explicitly encourage a jury to provide a verdict based on their perception that the perpetrator on video is the defendant. For instance, in *R v. Dodson and Williams* (1984), the jury were shown CCTV stills from a bank raid and invited to compare them with the two defendants. No alternative corroborating identification evidence was submitted, although the court was also presented with undisputed photographs of one of the accused, contemporaneous to the time of the crime – again, to demonstrate a similarity of appearance. Although this judgement applies to cases in which a jury is *directed* to compare the evidential images to the defendant, it is possible that regardless of instructions, an individual juror may base their verdict on the similarity of appearance between the defendant and crime scene images. Indeed, anyone involved in a police investigation or in court may make such identification judgements. Jurors will be previously unfamiliar with the defendant and may be susceptible to identity judgement errors. Unfortunately, face-matching accuracy is not improved, even after warnings of the high risk of error (Thompson, Dunkelberger, & Vescio, 2013).

These legal principles will not necessarily apply in different jurisdictions. Indeed, in Australia, evidence from police officers who claim to recognize the defendant is not normally admissible (*Smith v. The Queen*, 2001). Instead, juries are encouraged to make their own identity decisions from viewing images and directly comparing them to the defendant.

THE IDENTIFICATION OF SUSPECTS FROM CCTV

CCTV operators often view and record criminal acts as they occur (for research on the surveillance strategies of operators, see Stainer, Scott-Brown, & Tatler, 2013; Troscianko *et al.*, 2004). They may concurrently report what they observe to the police in order to direct them to the crime scene. If the suspect is apprehended, the operator acting as an eyewitness could in court theoretically provide a commentary as to what is depicted on crime scene footage. However, in most cases, criminal activity is not directly observed, and therefore images will be collected for retrospective examination in a police station. The police may "track" suspects if they move in and out of footage captured by different cameras, in order to obtain the best possible images. This is often achieved by focusing on clothing, and sometimes officers capture incidences in which a suspect discards their outer clothing or a disguise in an attempt to evade detection.

Familiar Face Recognition

The manner in which images are distributed and publicized can have an important influence on the likelihood of identification and subsequent detection. Images are regularly distributed internally by police forces and displayed on "wanted" websites. In serious cases they may be depicted in the media as part of an information gathering appeal. The aim is that they will be recognized by someone familiar. In London, if a suspect is located and shown CCTV imagery, over 70% confess in police interview (Davis *et al.*, 2013). Others may admit to being at the scene of the crime, but to having no involvement. In cases in which the suspect disputes the identification entirely, the same witnesses (police or member of the public) who identified that suspect may be asked to provide evidence of identity in court. In some cases, the defence may successfully argue that the quality of the images is inadequate for a reliable identification to be made, and/or that the witness, who is often a police officer, does not possess sufficient prior familiarity with the defendant to make an objective identification.

The identifications made in the scenarios above are by someone familiar with the suspect, and most research has found that identifications of individuals well-known to the observer are normally highly reliable, even when image quality is poor (Bruce *et al.*, 2001; Burton *et al.*, 1999). Nevertheless, familiar face recognition performance is rarely 100%, even by those with the best face recognition ability (Davis *et al.*, 2013). Readers will be aware that photographs of even the closest family members will occasionally fail to "capture their likeness". Indeed, consequential errors of familiar person identification do occur, even with high-quality images. Close family members of a missing person all mistakenly identified a man depicted in airport CCTV footage as their relative (BBC News, 2003). There may be confounding explanations. Nevertheless, this case does illustrate that recognition of even highly familiar people in high-quality photographs is not infallible.

Unfamiliar Face Matching

Despite the occasional identification difficulties we may encounter when viewing images of those we know from an unusual perspective, it might be thought that when images depict an offender in high-quality images, identity verification should be relatively easy, regardless of familiarity. However, a large body of recent research employing a variety of different facial databases and experimental designs has demonstrated that the identification of unfamiliar people is often unreliable, even when there are no memory demands and the high-quality images to match are taken at approximately the same time with no attempt to change appearance (e.g., Bindemann, Avetisyan, & Blackwell, 2010; Bruce *et al.*, 1999, 2001; Burton *et al.*, 1999, 2010; Davis & Valentine, 2009; Henderson *et al.*, 2001; Megreya & Bindemann, 2009; Megreya, Bindemann, Havard, & Burton, 2012; Megreya & Burton, 2006, 2007, 2008; Özbek & Bindemann, 2011; Strathie *et al.*, 2012). Error rates inevitably increase when the images to be matched are taken some time apart (Davis & Valentine, 2009; Megreya, Sandford, & Burton, 2013).

Two studies directly compared familiar and unfamiliar face identification using poor-quality CCTV images. Burton *et al.* (1999b; Experiment 1) displayed a series of video stills of university lecturers. In a subsequent recognition task, students familiar with the lecturers were far more accurate at recognising their lecturers than police officers who were unfamiliar with those depicted.

Similarly, Bruce *et al.* (2001; Experiment 1) employed a *face-matching* task involving no memory, in which participants were presented with a series of pairs of facial images. One image was from a poor-quality CCTV system, the other a good-quality facial photograph. Participants were asked to decide whether they depicted the same person or not. When both images were of the same individual (*match trials*), the correct identification rate (*hits*) of participants familiar with those depicted was approximately 93%. However, when targets were unfamiliar, the hit rate was only 76%. If the targets were presented with a distracter image (*mismatch trials*), accuracy at correctly identifying that different people were depicted was high (*correct rejections;* 91%), but only if the targets were familiar. When unfamiliar with those depicted, correct rejection rates were approximately 55%, not much higher than would be expected if guessing (i.e., 50%).

Pre-processing of images taken under different lighting conditions to reduce discrepancies in their illumination can reduce face-matching error rates (Liu, Chen, Han, & Shan, 2013). Furthermore, matching judgements, particularly to poor-quality images, may be improved when the whole body is available (Rice, Phillips, & O'Toole, 2013). However, unfamiliar face-matching errors from facial photographs may be common even when the images to be matched are of high quality, close-up and taken in optimum conditions. Bruce *et al.* (1999) designed a task requiring the matching of one of a series of 40 male frontal, high-quality facial video stills, with a simultaneously presented frontal, high-quality facial photograph of the target person among an array of nine distracters (Figure 9.2). Error rates in target-present trials were 30%. Two-thirds of these errors involved failures to identify any array image. In the remainder, participants selected the wrong array face, even though the correct image was available. Photographs and videos were from a standardized distance and facial angle, under standardized lighting and taken on the same day, so that the appearance of the actors would not have substantially changed. Indeed, they also posed with neutral facial expressions. Similarly high false negative error rates were found in target-absent trials (30%), in which the target was replaced by an additional distracter. Furthermore, when the single target image was depicted from a 30° angle, error rates increased to 40% in target-present trials and 38% in target-absent trials. Even a change in the facial expression of the single target from neutral to smiling significantly increased the likelihood of error, with errors of 34% in target-present and 38% in target-absent trials. These reported values also reflect average performance. In one specific target-present trial with the same pose and expression in both target and array, 80% of participants failed to correctly match the target. These findings demonstrate that minor image format differences across even high-quality images can be responsible for high error rates.

Two different experiments by Henderson *et al.* (2001) illustrate that even with reduced task demands, face-matching is still error prone. In the first (Experiment 4) participants were asked to identify which of two professional studio portrait photographs depicted a target actor shown in a close-up high-quality television broadcast still. One was a

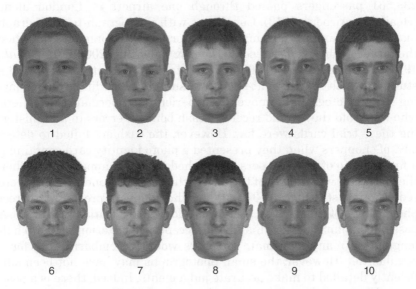

Figure 9.2 Example of a target-present simultaneous face-matching trial from Bruce *et al.* (1999). The target is number 3 in the array. Copyright © [1999] by the American Psychological Association. Reproduced with permission.

picture of the target, one a distracter of similar appearance. Overall, 24% of decisions were incorrect. However, in one trial, approximately a third of participants incorrectly responded that a still of a first actor was more similar in appearance to a second actor's photograph than the first actor's own photograph. In a follow-up experiment (Experiment 5), in which participants were presented with a single pair of images, approximately 45% of participants wrongly reported that two images of the same person were of different people. A further 27.5% incorrectly matched the images of two different actors. Decision confidence ratings were collected in both of the above studies (Bruce *et al.*, 1999; Henderson *et al.*, 2001). Confidence was often high, even when participants were incorrect. In addition, Papesh and Goldinger (2014) conducted a study designed to better replicate real security conditions in which the carriers of fraudulent identity documents will be rare. They demonstrated that the likelihood of detecting mismatched pairs of images was proportionally worse when mismatch trials were rare (one-in-ten trials) than when they were relatively common (one-in-two-trials).

Some security officials such as passport officers compare photograph identity documents to a person standing in front of them. Many millions of such decisions are made every day. Indeed, on July 31, 2011, 233,561 passengers passed through one airport in London alone (Heathrow Airport, 2013). Consistent with photograph-to-photograph matching, unfamiliar face-matching errors are still common even when the target is physically present (Davis & Valentine, 2009; Kemp *et al.*, 1997; Megreya & Burton, 2008). For instance, Kemp *et al.* conducted a study in which "participant-shoppers" submitted credit cards displaying $2 cm^2$ photographic images to experienced supermarket cashiers, who were told they would receive a cash bonus if errors in administering these trial cards were low. However, the cashiers failed to detect 64% of shoppers when they presented a photo identity card containing a facial photo of another person matched for facial appearance. When the distracter was simply of the same ethnicity and gender, errors were reduced, but still high at 34%. When the shoppers presented correct photographs of themselves, there was a low false negative rate of 7%. A possible explanation for this liberal acceptance criterion is that challenging too many legitimate shoppers would be embarrassing for a retail outlet. However, the small photographs may have not been sufficiently detailed to make accurate judgements. Indeed, there is a positive relationship between image size and unfamiliar face recognition accuracy (Loftus & Harley, 2005).

Davis and Valentine (2009) also found high simultaneous matching error rates in both match and mismatch trials across a series of three experiments employing much larger higher-quality images in which approximately 1200 participants were recruited. In these experiments, participants were required to match a target actor present in person against a good quality full-body or close-up facial moving video image displayed on a large display screen. In Experiment 1, videos were three weeks old and the error rate in match trials was 22%; in mismatch trials it was 17%. These results may partly be a consequence of the delay, as some of the eight actors had changed their hairstyle. However, in another experiment (Experiment 3), the close-up facial videos in one condition were taken 10 minutes beforehand, and yet 17% of participants failed to correctly respond that the video depicted the actor standing by the screen. Errors increased substantially to 33% with images taken a week beforehand. In a further experiment (Experiment 2), videos sometimes depicted the actors in disguise (no disguise, dark glasses, hat), and all videos were one year old to replicate a situation in which a defendant's court appearance may occur a long time after crime scene footage is captured. Some participants were informed of this delay, and providing such information biased responses, particularly when actors were in disguise, by increasing both false negative and false positive error rates. As with the photograph-to-photograph matching studies above, many highly confident participants made incorrect decisions, although overall, confidence was correlated with accuracy.

An important feature of the studies reported above was the use of relatively small databases to locate individuals who might be mistaken for one another. Each array in Bruce *et al.* (1999) was constructed by selecting faces from a database of 200 trainee police officers rated as similar in appearance to the target, whilst Henderson *et al.* (2001) "searched through several hundred actor-agency photographs" (p. 463), to locate appropriate distracters. Kemp *et al.* (2007) recruited 56 students from a university course to act as shoppers. Davis and Valentine (2009) selected eight rugby players from a student club with approximately 70 members. It therefore appears comparatively easy to construct experiments in which errors in identification matching occur. There are likely to be many more people in the population who could be the subject of similar mistaken identity decisions. Furthermore, passports are issued for 10 years, and the holder's appearance may substantially change in that time, making matching even more prone to error.

Identification errors are also more likely as a consequence of the typical positioning of CCTV cameras, often located above head height (Davies & Thasen, 2000; Thompson, Grattan, Rawding, & Buchholz, 2010). Differences in viewpoint, expression, size, and environmental lighting can reduce face matching and recognition accuracy (e.g., Bruce, 1982; Bruce *et al.*, 1999; Bruce, Valentine, & Baddeley, 1987; Hill & Bruce, 1996; Hill, Schyns, & Akamatsu, 1997). A change in the distance from which images are taken, and in the focal length of a camera lens, can influence facial appearance (Harper & Latto, 2001). From close-up, a face will appear "long and narrow" with a greater distance between the eyes, whereas from further away it will appear "rounder" with the eyes closer together.

PARALLELS BETWEEN FACE RECOGNITION AND FACE MATCHING RESEARCH

There is evidence that many of the variables that influence face recognition can be replicated in the absence of memory. Indeed, face recognition and eyewitness identification tasks correlate (e.g., Bindemann, Brown, Koyas, & Russ, 2012b; Darling, Martin, Hellman, & Memon, 2009), and there are large consistent individual differences in face recognition and face matching ability (Bindemann *et al.*, 2012b; Burton *et al.*, 2010; Davis *et al.*, 2013; Megreya & Burton, 2006; Russell, Duchaine, & Nakayama, 2009). In addition, familiar face recognition is primarily driven by the internal features of a face: eyes, nose and mouth (Bonner & Burton, 2004; Ellis, Shepherd, & Davies, 1979; Young, Hay, McWeeny, Flude, & Ellis, 1985). In contrast, unfamiliar face processing is more influenced by external features: hairstyle and face shape (Bruce *et al.*, 1999, Experiment 4; Ellis *et al.*, 1979; Young *et al.*, 1985; although see Megreya & Bindemann, 2009). This partly explains why we still easily recognize close acquaintances following substantial changes to hairstyle, but minor changes to the appearance of someone less familiar may be far more disruptive.

To explore the role of internal and external features in simultaneous face matching, Bruce *et al.* (1999) presented high-quality images in three different conditions. In the *whole-face* condition, no manipulation of images was conducted. In the *external feature* condition, a blank oval mask obscured the internal features; whereas, for the *internal feature* condition, the mask obscured the external features. Whole-face matching accuracy was highest. Accuracy was higher in the external feature condition than the internal feature condition. The authors suggest that participants may have primarily been employing a strategy based on matching hairstyle in the external feature condition, as this is the most salient feature. For this experiment, such a strategy would be successful as all images were taken on the same day – it is unlikely that hairstyle would have significantly altered. However, it would be far less effective with images collected some time apart, or with the target in disguise. Interestingly, Megreya and Bindemann (2009) suggested that face-matching performance may be influenced by cultural norms. In contrast to UK participants, those from Egypt demonstrated an advantage for matching own-nationality unfamiliar faces using internal features. The authors suggest that such a strategy develops due to the common use of the headscarf hiding the external facial features in Middle Eastern countries.

Evidence from a study that recorded eye movements found that when comparing images taken at least a day apart, an internal feature processing style is advantageous, particularly when viewing time is restricted (Fletcher, Butavicius, & Lee, 2008). Participants who naturally tended to focus more on internal features were more accurate at face matching. However, this effect was only found for images displayed for 2 seconds. Gaze direction had no influence on accuracy when images were depicted for 6 seconds, suggesting that the longer display time allowed for greater inspection. As would be expected given these results, disguises reduce face recognition and face-matching accuracy (Davis & Valentine, 2009; Henderson *et al.*, 2001), increasing the likelihood of both false positives and false negatives.

Another estimator variable that has been extensively replicated in eyewitness identification and face recognition studies is the cross-ethnicity effect. People tend to be better at recognizing individuals from their own ethnicity than those from other ethnicities (see Chapter 7). It is likely that passport officers in particular will be required to judge the identity of people from many nationalities, and similar cross-ethnicity effects have been found in face-matching tasks (Megreya, White, & Burton, 2011b; Meissner, Susa, & Ross, 2013). Furthermore, in comparison to males, females demonstrate an advantage for matching same-gender faces (Megreya, Bindemann, & Havard, 2011a), an effect also found in face recognition tasks (e.g., Wright & Sladden, 2003).

Another well-studied estimator variable that can influence face recognition is state anxiety. Participants stressed at the time of encoding a crime scene are less likely to be able to identify the culprit later (e.g., Valentine & Mesout, 2009; for a meta-analysis see Deffenbacher, Bornstein, Penrod, & McGorty, 2004). Similar effects have been found in a face-matching study (Attwood, Penton-Voak, Burton, & Munafo, 2013) in which acute state anxiety was induced in a laboratory by the administration of carbon dioxide. In this study, participants completed a face-matching test twice – once while breathing normal air, and once while breathing carbon dioxide. State-induced anxiety reduced accuracy at matching two images of the same person, whilst having no effect on matching decisions to images depicting two different people. This replicates the negative effects of stress found in eyewitness research for target-present but not target-absent lineups (Deffenbacher *et al.*, 2004).

This section has focused on parallels between face recognition and face-matching ability. However, there is at least one image manipulation technique that can improve face recognition ability, but does not appear to assist in face-matching decisions. Caricaturing facial images enhances the idiosyncratic facial features that are most salient in an individual, making familiar faces more distinctive and thus recognisable (e.g., Brennan, 1985; Lee, Byatt & Rhodes, 2000; see Chapter 7 for an explanation of distinctiveness effects in facial recognition). The same technique reduces the likelihood that a foil will be selected from an array in an unfamiliar face-matching design, but it also reduces rates of correct target identifications (McIntyre, Hancock, Kittler, & Langton, 2013).

THEORETICAL MODELS OF FACE RECOGNITION AND MATCHING

Theories of face recognition distinguish between the processing of familiar and unfamiliar faces (Bruce & Young, 1986; Burton, Bruce, & Johnston, 1990; Hancock, Bruce, & Burton, 2000). These models propose that internal, structural, view-independent mental representations are employed in the recognition of familiar faces. In contrast, unfamiliar face recognition is primarily based on feature processing derived from surface information. As such, familiar faces are easily recognized across a wide range of viewing conditions, whereas unfamiliar face recognition or matching can be adversely affected by surprisingly minor image changes. Neurological support for this dissociation comes from some prosopagnosic patients who exhibit selective impairments to either familiar or unfamiliar faces (e.g., Malone, Morris, Kay, & Levin, 1982). Different patterns of brain activity were observed when non-clinical participants viewed familiar and unfamiliar faces (e.g., Leveroni *et al.*, 2000; Rossion, Schlitz, & Crommelinck, 2003). There is also experimental evidence for this dissociation. When faces are familiar, even from relatively brief experimental exposure, face identification tasks display the *mirror effect*, in that there is a relationship between performance on individual stimuli in both target-present/match and target-absent/mismatch trials (Megreya & Burton, 2007). Faces that are easily recognized when present (hits) are easily rejected when not previously seen (correct rejections). This effect is common to many classes of stimuli (for reviews see Glanzer & Adams, 1985; Glanzer, Adams, & Kim, 1993). In contrast, the mirror effect is absent in tasks of unfamiliar face recognition (Deffenbacher, Johanson, Vetter, & O'Toole, 2000; Hancock, Burton, & Bruce, 1996; Vokey & Read, 1992) and matching (Megreya & Burton, 2007), in that there is no relationship between hit rates and correct rejection rates for the same stimuli. Perhaps counterintuitively, an unfamiliar face that appears to be easy to recognize when it has been seen previously, due to its distinctiveness, is not necessarily equally easy to correctly reject if it has not been seen before. The face-matching mirror effect is also absent when both unfamiliar and familiar faces are inverted (Megreya & Burton, 2007). Inversion is believed to disrupt the *holistic* or whole face processes that drive efficient face recognition. Megreya and Burton (2007) argued that inversion therefore bestows on a normally familiar face the processing status of an unfamiliar face.

Burton (2013; see also Burton, Jenkins, Hancock, & White, 2005; Burton & Jenkins, 2011; Burton, Jenkins, & Schweinberger, 2011; Hancock *et al.*, 2000; Megreya & Burton, 2006) explains the dissociation between processing unfamiliar and familiar faces for identity as a consequence of unfamiliar faces being processed as "simple visual patterns". This does not suggest that unfamiliar faces have the same status as purely abstract visual information, because inverted unfamiliar faces are matched and recognized less well than upright unfamiliar faces (Megreya & Burton, 2006), which would not be the case with completely random patterns. Some salient identity information must be provided by an unfamiliar upright face. Nevertheless, Burton proposes that the primary reason that unfamiliar face-matching is prone to failure is that humans effectively employ an unsophisticated image-matching strategy. The greater the variation between images being matched, the greater the likelihood of error in such a task.

Burton (2013) draws upon a recent study examining within-person variability in the appearance of photographic images by Jenkins *et al.* (2011) to illustrate this point. The authors entered the names of two different Dutch celebrities into an internet search engine. They collected the first 20 images of those celebrities that were of a pre-specified minimum quality, and asked participants to group the 40 images into "identities" without specifying the actual number of people depicted. Dutch participants, familiar with the celebrities, almost always grouped the images correctly. However, UK participants grouped images of the same unfamiliar celebrity into an average set of nine different identities. This study demonstrates that images depicting the same individual can possess characteristics that make them appear to belong to completely different people. In a later experiment, Jenkins *et al.* (2011) also found large within-person variability in likeness ratings to familiar face photographs. Some photos appear to capture an individual's identity better than others. Varying levels of image likeness may be why unfamiliar face recognition and matching ability is error-prone. A simple pattern matching strategy using superficial surface cues may not provide enough information for an accurate identity match.

Face familiarization may involve the development of a representation of the appearance of a familiar face "averaged" across many images of their face (Burton *et al.*, 2005). An *average* or *prototype* forms the basic representation of each face in memory. As we encounter that person again, different perspectives of their face are added to that internal representation, until the face becomes highly familiar. To test this proposal, Burton *et al.* morphed 16 different photographs of famous faces to form a prototype of each celebrity. Participants were presented with a name and either a single photograph or the morphed image of one of the celebrities. Name verification reaction times to the morphed images were consistently faster than to the single photographs. This supports the proposal that composite images are a better match than any single image to our internal representations. Interestingly, Jenkins and Burton (2008) found that the same technique improved the matching accuracy of an automatic face recognition system.

PRACTICAL ASPECTS OF FACE MATCHING

Research has also been conducted with the aim of improving face-matching performance using different types of training (e.g., Alenezi & Bindemann, 2013; Moore & Johnston, 2013; O'Toole *et al.*, 2007; Towler, White, & Kemp, 2014; White, Kemp, Jenkins, & Burton, 2014), by providing motivational rewards (Moore & Johnston, 2013), and by averaging responses using the wisdom-of-the-crowds technique (White, Burton, Kemp, & Jenkins, 2013). Until recently, research into training techniques was disappointing (e.g., O'Toole *et al.*, 2007). For instance, Towler *et al.* (2014) demonstrated that a component of many training courses for detecting identity fraud – analysing the external shape of faces based on pre-determined templates – does not improve face matching. Some research, however, has demonstrated that success can be achieved (e.g., Alenezi & Bindemann, 2013; White *et al.*, 2014). It should be noted that face-matching performance is improved by repeated exposure (Clutterbuck & Johnston, 2002, 2004, 2005; Megreya & Burton, 2006), although these effects tend to be stimulus-specific and do not necessarily generalize to the matching of novel faces. Indeed, matching extremely large sets of faces results in a gradual decrease in performance (Alenezi & Bindemann, 2013).

Alenezi and Bindemann (2013; Experiment 6) asked participants to make a series of 1000 face-matching decisions, with one face in profile view, the other facing the camera. Half the trials were matched. The authors found that participants increasingly made more errors in mismatch trials. Indeed, by the final set of trials, participants were responding at chance levels. In contrast, accuracy consistently increased in match trials. These results represent a response bias in that participants were increasingly likely to respond "same" regardless of trial type, suggesting that fatigue may reduce the ability to tell two different but highly similar people apart. This implies that officials, such as passport officers, tasked with the continual monitoring of facial identities may become less able to identify a holder of a fake photograph identification document – particularly as this is likely to be a rare occurrence anyway. In later experiments, Alenezi and Bindemann (2013) found that providing trial-by-trial performance feedback reduced this decline in mismatch trial performance. In particular, providing such feedback during the first few blocks of the experiment helped to *maintain* performance when no feedback was provided. It should be emphasized that feedback did not *improve* face matching when compared with baseline accuracy established at the start of the experimental trials, suggesting there is a limit to its positive effects.

Similarly, White *et al.* (2014) found that providing trial-by-trial performance feedback on a preliminary face-matching task, involving equal numbers of match and mismatch stimuli, improved *some* participants' ability on subsequent face-matching tasks with an entirely different stimulus set. No feedback was provided in the subsequent task. Nevertheless, the performance of those with the highest aptitude at face matching, as measured using a pre-trial test, was not improved by this feedback. Only those with prior low face-matching ability were assisted by this technique. They reached the same level of overall matching accuracy as the high ability group. Tests revealed that these positive effects were not a consequence of response bias, or an optimization of response strategy, but were a consequence of greater sensitivity to both match and mismatch stimuli. The authors argue that some participants have a pre-conceived belief that face matching is easy, and the feedback drew their attention to the true difficulty of the task. They also suggest that the feedback may have encouraged the lower ability participants to focus on the stable internal features of the face, as these will normally provide more reliable cues to identity. Alenezi and Bindemann (2013) suggested that introducing face-matching trial feedback on a daily basis to those tasked with matching faces in real-life situations (e.g., passport issuance officers) might reduce potential errors. The authors note that such procedures are applied in airport baggage screening to maintain the vigilance of operators (see Hofer & Schwaninger, 2005).

Offering motivational incentives can also improve face-matching performance. Moore and Johnston (2013) demonstrated that inducements of chocolate particularly improved performance on mismatch trials when the ratio of match to mismatch trials was 16:16 (Experiment 1) and 30:2 (Experiment 2). The latter condition more closely replicates the expected rarity of mismatch trials in real-life security settings, although the authors acknowledge that the number of trials was far fewer than would be experienced by most security officials.

One recent proposal for improving decisions of face matching is to use crowd-sourcing techniques, in which decisions of identity made by multiple untrained assessors are averaged and compared with the decisions made by the individual assessors (White *et al.*, 2013). Over a series of experiments, the authors found that employing this wisdom-of-the-crowds technique resulted in higher accuracy rates than the mean performance of the individual participants making up the "crowds".

In summary, it is clear that positive effects may be derived from feedback training, incentives and crowd sourcing, but further research is required to ensure these effects are long-lasting and practicable. Indeed, feedback may not assist those with the highest face-matching ability, and it may not always be possible to employ a wisdom-of-the-crowds technique in security roles when the official is alone and time to process those under scrutiny is at a premium. Therefore it might be more appropriate (and easier) for occupational selectors to pre-screen those tasked with checking proof of photographic identity, to ensure they possess high levels of face recognition and matching ability in the first place.

SELECTION OF NATURALLY GIFTED FACE PROCESSORS

There are large individual differences in face recognition and matching ability (Bindemann *et al.*, 2012b; Burton *et al.*, 2010; Davis *et al.*, 2013; Megreya & Burton, 2006; Russell *et al.*, 2009). For instance, in a study by Russell *et al.* (2009), four so-called *super-recognizers* performed more than two standard deviations above the population mean on a standardized unfamiliar face recognition test (Cambridge Face Memory Test, CFMT). Anecdotes provided by the super-recognizers suggest that they are able, years later, to remember previously unfamiliar people encountered in a fleeting glimpse. Their scores on the CFMT test were the polar opposite of sufferers of *prosopagnosia* or face blindness. The prevalence of developmental prosopagnosia – a congenital inability to recognize faces in the population – is approximately 1–2% (Kennerknecht *et al.*, 2006). If face recognition ability is normally distributed, Russell *et al.* suggests that a similar prevalence of super-recognizers may exist – perhaps these individuals would be the most suitable for some security and policing roles?

For such a purpose in London, the Metropolitan Police Service (MPS) has recently instituted a unit of over 200 officers possessing superior face recognition ability from across the city's diverse geographical districts. As part of their occupational role, these officers are provided with images of crime types matching their specialist knowledge, or in some cases, their locality within London. They have also been tasked with observing events with large crowds from CCTV operations rooms, in order to identify, track and direct other officers towards known offenders (see Taylor, 2013, for example).

In 2011, approximately 5000 images were displayed on the MPS *Caught on Camera* website, and 18 of these officers identified over 600 suspects (Davis *et al.*, 2013). One officer identified 190 suspects. The success of these officers dramatically contrasts with the performance of the remaining 31,000 officers in the service, who are also encouraged to view the website – mostly to no effect. The 18 best-performing officers were examined by Davis *et al.* (2013) who employed a battery of face recognition and visual processing tests. Some, but not all, of these officers performed far better than a control group of members of the general public ($n = 104$) on the combined scores from two unfamiliar face-recognition tests, a familiar face-recognition test, and an unfamiliar face-matching test. One officer performed more than 3 standard deviations (SD) above the control mean, and a few others were more than 2 SD above the control mean. High performance on these tests is indicative of the ability to learn and remember facial images far more efficiently than those of average ability, as well as to be able to extrapolate identity from images taken from different viewpoints. The largest effect sizes were found with a familiar face recognition test based on 12-year-old, poor-quality images of celebrities – designed to replicate an identification of a suspect not seen for many years from poor-quality CCTV. However, the officers were no better than the controls at object recognition (flowers) or source monitoring, suggesting that their extreme abilities are limited to faces alone and may not generalize to other visual recognition tasks.

The utilization of the skills of police "super-recognizers" proved successful following a series of riots in London in August 2011, as they were responsible for identifying approximately a third of the 4000 riot suspects who were identified from over 200,000 hours of footage. In contrast, a face recognition software programme identified one suspect, probably a consequence of the generally poor quality of the riot images captured from above head height and often after dark (Associated Press, 2013). Chapter 11 gives a contrasting description of the extremely high performance of automatic face recognition algorithms when images are captured in ideal conditions.

CONCLUSIONS AND POLICY RECOMMENDATIONS

The consistent story from the research described in this chapter is that unless the viewer is familiar with those depicted, or they possess exceptional face-processing abilities, errors in unfamiliar face-matching may be common, and that these errors are similar to those made when memory is involved. Depending on the circumstances, both false positive and false negative errors are of equal concern, as can be illustrated by applying these findings to the security and police roles listed at the start of this chapter. For instance, a false negative error by a CCTV operator might mean they fail to realize the person under surveillance is the same person whose photograph they are simultaneously viewing on a wanted person database. On the other hand, a false positive error may represent a scenario whereby an innocent suspect could be wrongly mistaken for the offender depicted in an image. The box describing the case of Jean Charles de Menezes illustrates the potentially disastrous consequences of a false positive error.

Some recent research suggests that providing performance feedback training or motivational incentives may improve face-matching performance. However, this research is in its infancy, and feedback may be most effective with individuals possessing lower face recognition or matching ability. Bruce (2013) astutely asks "given the evident difficulties most of us have in matching or remembering images of faces, why do we continue to place so great an emphasis, in identity documents, and legal processes, on such a flimsy thing as an image of a face?" (p. 779). Perhaps, until appropriate alternatives are developed, one of the most effective ways of reducing the potential of this error is to recruit individuals with exceptional face-processing abilities for key security roles. The research on super-recognizers demonstrates that some individuals perform very much better in face recognition and matching tasks, and this ability could be an occupational selection criterion for roles in border control, security checkpoints, CCTV operator control rooms, police officers with identification roles, and a multitude of other tasks where facial recognition ability is at a premium.

REFERENCES

Alenezi, H.M., & Bindemann, M. (2013). The effect of feedback on face-matching accuracy. *Applied Cognitive Psychology*, 27, 735–753. doi:10.1002/acp.2968

Associated Press (2013). UK cops hire 'super recognizers' to find criminals. *New York Post*, September 27. Retrieved from http://nypost.com/2013/09/27/uk-cops-hire-super-recognizers-to-find-criminals-in-a-crowd/

Attorney General's Reference (2003) No. 2 of 2002. EWCA Crim 2373.

Attwood, A.S., Penton-Voak, I.S., Burton, A.M., & Munafò, M.R. (2013). Acute anxiety impairs accuracy in identifying photographed faces. *Psychological Science*, 24, 1591–1594. doi:10.1177/0956797612474021

Barrett, D. (2013). One surveillance camera for every 11 people in Britain, says CCTV survey. *Daily Telegraph*, July 10. Retrieved from http://www.telegraph.

co.uk/technology/10172298/One-surveillance-camera-for-every-11-people-in-Britain-says-CCTV-survey.html

BBC News (2003). Tourist mistaken for missing doctor. *BBC News*, August 16. Retrieved from http://news.bbc.co.uk/1/hi/uk_news/england/merseyside/3156819.stm

BBC News (2007). Police guilty over Menezes case. BBC News, November 1. Retrieved from http://news.bbc.co.uk/1/hi/uk/7069796.stm

Bindemann, M., Attard, J., Leach, A., & Johnston, R.A. (2013). The effect of image pixelation on unfamiliar-face matching. *Applied Cognitive Psychology. 27*, 707–717. doi:10.1002/acp.2970

Bindemann, M., Avetisyan, M., & Blackwell, K. (2010). Finding needles in haystacks: Identity mismatch frequency and facial identity verification. *Journal of Experimental Psychology: Applied, 16*, 378–386. doi:10.1037/a0021893

Bindemann, M., Brown, C., Koyas, T., & Russ, A. (2012). Individual differences in face identification postdict eyewitness accuracy. *Journal of Applied Research in Memory and Cognition, 1*, 96–103. doi:10.1016/j.jarmac.2012.02.001

Bonner, L., & Burton, A.M. (2004). 7-11-year-old children show an advantage for matching and recognizing the internal features of familiar faces: Evidence against a developmental shift. *Quarterly Journal of Experimental Psychology, 57A*, 1019–1029. doi:10.1080/02724980343000657

Borchard, E.M. (1932). *Convicting the Innocent: Sixty-five Actual Errors of Criminal Justice*. Garden City, NJ: Doubleday.

Brennan, S.E. (1985). Caricature generator, the dynamic exaggeration of faces by computer. *Leonardo, 18*, 170–178. doi:10.2307/1578048

Bruce, V. (1982). Changing faces: Visual and non-visual coding processes in face recognition.*British Journal of Psychology,73*,105–116.doi:10.1111/j.2044-8295.1982.tb01795.x

Bruce, V. (2013). Comment. *Applied Cognitive Psychology. 27*, 707–717. doi:10.1002/acp.2962

Bruce, V., Henderson, Z., Greenwood, K., Hancock, P., Burton, A.M., & Miller, P. (1999). Verification of face identities from images captured on video. *Journal of Experimental Psychology: Applied, 5*, 339–360. doi:10.1037/1076-898X.5.4.339

Bruce, V., Henderson, Z., Newman, C., & Burton, A.M. (2001). Matching identities of familiar and unfamiliar faces caught on CCTV images. *Journal of Experimental Psychology: Applied, 7*, 207–218. doi:10.1037/1076-898X.7.3.207

Bruce, V., Valentine, T., & Baddeley, A. (1987). The basis of the ¾ view advantage in face recognition. *Applied Cognitive Psychology, 1*, 110–120. doi:10.1002/acp.2350010204

Bruce, V., & Young A. (1986). Understanding face recognition. *British Journal of Psychology, 77*, 305–327. doi:10.1111/j.2044-8295.1986.tb02199.x

Burton, A.M. (2013). Why has research in face recognition progressed so slowly? The importance of variability. *Quarterly Journal of Experimental Psychology, 66*, 1467–1485. doi:10.1080/17470218.2013.800125

Burton, A.M., Bruce, V., & Johnston, R.A. (1990). Understanding face recognition with an interactive activation model. *British Journal of Psychology, 81*, 361–380. doi:10.1111/j.2044-8295.1990.tb02367.x

Burton, A.M., & Jenkins, R. (2011). Unfamiliar face perception. In A.J. Calder, G. Rhodes, M.H. Johnson, & J. Haxby (Eds.), *The Oxford Handbook of Face Perception* (pp. 287–306). Oxford: Oxford University Press.

Burton, A.M., Jenkins, R., Hancock, P.J.B., & White, D. (2005). Robust representations for face recognition: The power of averages. *Cognitive Psychology*, *51*, 256–284. doi:10.1016/j.cogpsych.2005.06.003

Burton, A.M., Jenkins, R., & Schweinberger, S.R. (2011). Mental representations of familiar faces. *British Journal of Psychology*, *102*, 943–958. doi:10.1111/j.20448295.2011.02039.x

Burton, A.M., White, D., & McNeill, A. (2010). The Glasgow Face Matching Test. *Behavior Research Methods*, *42*, 286–291. doi:10.3758/BRM.42.1.286

Burton, A.M, Wilson, S., Cowan, M., & Bruce, V. (1999). Face recognition in poor quality video: Evidence from security surveillance. *Psychological Science*, *10*, 243–248. doi:10.1111/1467-9280.00144

Charman, S.D., & Wells, G.L. (2007). Eyewitness lineups: Is the appearance-change instruction a good idea? *Law and Human Behavior*, *7*, 3–22. doi:10.1007/s10979-006-9006-3

Clutterbuck, R., & Johnston, R.A. (2002). Exploring levels of face familiarity by using an indirect face-matching measure. *Perception*, *31*, 985–994. doi:10.1068/p3335

Clutterbuck, R., & Johnston, R.A. (2004). Demonstrating the acquired familiarity of faces by using a gender-decision task. *Perception*, *33*, 159–168. doi:10.1068/p5115

Clutterbuck, R., & Johnston, R.A. (2005). Demonstrating how unfamiliar faces become familiar using a face matching task. *European Journal of Cognitive Psychology*, *17*, 97–116. doi:10.1080/09541440340000439

Cole, S.A., & Thompson, W.C. (2013). Forensic science and wrongful convictions. In C.R. Huff, & M. Killias (Eds.), *Wrongful Convictions & Miscarriages of Justice* (pp. 111–135). London: Routledge.

Darling, S., Martin, D., Hellman, J.H., & Memon, A. (2009). Some witnesses are better than others. *Personality and Individual Differences*, *47*, 369–373. doi:10.1016/j.paid.2009.04.010

Davies, G., & Thasen, S. (2000). Closed-circuit television: How effective an identification aid? *British Journal of Psychology*, *91*, 411–426. doi:10.1348/000712600161907

Davis, J.P. (2007). *The forensic identification of CCTV images of unfamiliar faces* (unpublished PhD thesis). Goldsmiths, University of London.

Davis, J.P., Lander, K., & Jansari, A. (2013). I never forget a face! *The Psychologist*, *26*, 726–729.

Davis, J.P., & Valentine, T. (2009). CCTV on trial: Matching video images with the defendant in the dock. *Applied Cognitive Psychology*, *23*, 482–505. doi:10.1002/acp.1490

Davis, J.P., Valentine, T., & Wilkinson, C. (2012). Facial image comparison. In C. Wilkinson, & C. Rynn (Eds.), *Craniofacial Identification* (pp. 136–153). Cambridge: Cambridge University Press.

Deffenbacher, K.A., Bornstein, B.H., Penrod, S.D., & McGorty, E.K. (2004). A meta-analytic review of the effects of high stress on eyewitness memory. *Law and Human Behavior*, *28*, 687–706. doi:10.1007/s10979-004-0565-x10

Deffenbacher, K.A., Johanson, J., Vetter, T., & O'Toole, A.J. (2000). The face typicality-recognizability relationship: Encoding or retrieval locus? *Memory & Cognition*, *28*, 1173–1182. doi:10.1007/s10979-004-0565-x

Ellis, H.D., Shepherd, J.W., & Davies, G.M. (1979). Identification of familiar and unfamiliar faces from internal and external features: Some implications for theories of face recognition. *Perception*, *8*, 431–439. doi:10.1068/p080431

Fletcher, K.I., Butavicius, M.A., & Lee, M.D. (2008). Attention to internal face features in unfamiliar face matching. *British Journal of Psychology*, *99*, 379–394. doi:10.1348/000712607X235872

Fort, L. (2013). Burglary case blunder as police break evidence rule. *Get Reading*, July 11. Retrieved from http://www.getreading.co.uk/news/local-news/burglary-case-blunder-police-break-5066779

Glanzer, M., & Adams, J. K. (1985). The mirror effect in recognition memory. *Memory and Cognition*, *13*, 8–20. doi:10.1037/0033-295X.100.3.546

Glanzer, M., Adams, J.K., & Kim, K. (1993). The regularities of recognition memory. *Psychological Review*, *100*, 546–567. doi:10.1037/0033-295X.100.3.546

Hancock, P.J.B., Bruce, V., & Burton, A.M. (2000). Recognition of unfamiliar faces. *Trends in Cognitive Sciences*, *4-9*, 330–337. doi:10.1016/S1364-6613(00)01519-9

Hancock, P.J.B., Burton, A.M., & Bruce, V. (1996). Face processing: human perception and principal components analysis. *Memory and Cognition*, *24*, 26–40. doi:10.3758/BF03197270

Harper, B., & Latto, R. (2001). Cyclopean vision, size estimation, and presence in orthostereoscopic images. *Presence*, *10*, 312–330. doi:10.1162/105474601300343630

Heathrow Airport (2013). *Facts and Figures*. Retrieved from http://www.heathrowairport.com/about-us/company-news-and-information/company-information/facts-and-figures

Henderson, Z., Bruce, V., & Burton, A.M. (2001). Matching the faces of robbers captured on video. *Applied Cognitive Psychology*, *15*, 445–464. doi:10.1002/acp.718

Hill, H., & Bruce, V. (1996). Effects of lighting on matching facial surfaces. *Journal of Experimental Psychology: Human Perception and Performance*, *22*, 986–1004. doi:10.1037/0096-1523.22.4.986

Hill, H., Schyns, P.G., & Akamatsu, S. (1997). Information and viewpoint dependence in face recognition. *Cognition*, *62*, 201–222. doi:10.1016/s0010-0277(96)00785-8

Hofer, F., & Schwaninger, A. (2005). Using threat image projection data for assessing individual screener performance. *Safety and Security Engineering*, *82*, 417–426.

Jenkins, R., & Burton A.M. (2008). 100% accuracy in automatic face recognition. *Science*, *319*, 435. doi:10.1126/science.1149656

Jenkins, R., White, D., van Montfort, X., & Burton, A.M. (2011). Variability in photos of the same face. *Cognition*, *121*, 313–323. doi:10.1016/j.cognition.2011.08.001

Kemp, R., Towell, N., & Pike, G. (1997). When seeing should not be believing: Photographs, credit cards and fraud. *Applied Cognitive Psychology*, *11*, 211–222. doi:10.1002/(SICI)1099-0720(199706)11:3<211::AID-ACP430>3.0.CO;2-O

Kennerknecht, I., Grueter, T., Welling, B., Wentzek, S., Horst, J., Edwards, S., & Grueter, M. (2006). First report of prevalence of non-syndromic hereditary prosopagnosia (HPA). *American Journal of Medical Genetics*, *140A*, 1617–1622. doi:10.1002/ajmg.a.31343

Lee, K., Byatt, G., & Rhodes, G. (2000). Caricature effects, distinctiveness, and identification: testing the face-space framework. *Psychological Science*, *11*, 379–385. doi:10.1111/1467-9280.00274

Lee, W.J., Wilkinson, C., Memon, A., & Houston, K.A. (2009). Matching unfamiliar faces from poor quality CCTV footage: an evaluation of the effect of training on facial identification ability. *Axis*, *1*, 19–28.

Leveroni, C.L., Seidenberg, M., Mayer, A.R., Mead, L.A., Binder, J.R., & Rao, S.M. (2000). Neural systems underlying the recognition of familiar and newly learned faces. *Journal of Neuroscience, 20*, 878–886.

Liu, C.H., Chen, W., Han, H., & Shan, S. (2013). Effects of image preprocessing on face matching and recognition in human observers. *Applied Cognitive Psychology, 27*, 718–724. doi:10.1002/acp.2967

Loftus, G.R., & Harley, E.M. (2005). Why is it easier to identify someone close than far away? *Psychonomic Bulletin & Review, 12*, 43-65. doi:10.3758/BF03196348

Malone, D.R., Morris, H.H., Kay, M.C., & Levin, H.S. (1982). Prosopagnosia: a double dissociation between the recognition of familiar and unfamiliar faces. *Journal of Neurological Neurosurgical Psychiatry, 45*, 820–822. doi:10.1136/jnnp.45.9.820

Mcintyre, A.H., Hancock, P.J.B., Kittler, J., & Langton, S.R.H. (2013). Improving discrimination and face matching with caricature. *Applied Cognitive Psychology, 27*, 725–734. doi:10.1002/acp.2966

Megreya, A.M., & Bindemann, M. (2009). Revisiting the processing of internal and external features of unfamiliar faces: The headscarf effect. *Perception, 38*, 1831–1848. doi:10.1068/p6385

Megreya, A.M., Bindemann, M., & Havard, C. (2011a). Sex differences in unfamiliar face identification: Evidence from matching tasks. *Acta Psychologica, 137*, 83–89. doi:10.1016/j.actpsy.2011.03.003

Megreya, A.M., Bindemann, M., Havard, C., & Burton, A.M. (2012). Identity-lineup location influences target selection: Evidence from eye movements. *Journal of Police and Criminal Psychology, 27*, 167–178. doi:10.1007/s11896-011-9098-7

Megreya, A.M., & Burton, A.M. (2006). Unfamiliar faces are not faces: Evidence from a matching task. *Memory & Cognition, 34*, 865–876. doi:10.3758/BF03193433

Megreya, A.M., & Burton, A.M. (2007). Hits and false positives in face matching: A familiarity-based dissociation. *Perception and Psychophysics, 69*, 1175–1184. doi:10.3758/BF03193954

Megreya, A.M., & Burton, A.M. (2008). Matching faces to photographs: Poor performance in eyewitness memory (without the memory). *Journal of Experimental Psychology: Applied, 14*, 364–372. doi:10.1037/a0013464

Megreya, A.M., Sandford, A., & Burton, A.M. (2013). Matching face images taken on the same day or months apart: the limitations of photo ID. *Applied Cognitive Psychology, 27*, 700–706. doi:10.1002/acp.2965

Megreya, A.M., White, D., & Burton, A.M. (2011b). The other-race effect does not rely on memory: evidence from a matching task. *Quarterly Journal of Experimental Psychology, 64*, 1473–1483. doi:10.1080/17470218.2011.575228

Meissner, C.A., Susa, K.J., & Ross, A.B. (2013). Can I see your passport please? Perceptual discrimination of own- and other-race faces. *Visual Cognition, 21*, 1287–1305. doi:10.1080/13506285.2013.832451

Moore, R.M., & Johnston, R.A. (2013). Motivational incentives improve unfamiliar face matching accuracy. *Applied Cognitive Psychology, 27*, 754–760. doi:10.1002/acp.2964

Munsterberg, H. (1908/1925). *On the Witness Stand: Essays on Psychology and Crime*. Retrieved from http://psychclassics.yorku.ca/Munster/Witness1

Murphy, T. (1999). The admissibility of CCTV evidence in criminal proceedings. *International Review of Law and Computers, 13*, 383–404. doi:10.1080/13600869955044

O'Toole, A.J., Phillips, P.J., Jiang, F., Ayyad, J., Penard, N., & Abdi, H. (2007). Face recognition algorithms surpass humans matching faces across changes in illumination. *IEEE: Transactions on Pattern Analysis and Machine Intelligence, 29,* 1642–1646. doi:10.1109/TPAMI.2007.1107

Özbek, M., & Bindemann, M. (2011). Exploring the time course of face matching: Temporal constraints impair unfamiliar face identification under temporally unconstrained viewing. *Vision Research, 51,* 2145–2155. doi:10.1016/j.visres.2011.08.009

Papesh, M.H., & Goldinger, S.D. (2014). Infrequent identity mismatches are frequently undetected. *Attention, Perception, & Psychophysics, 76,* 1335–1349. doi:10.3758/s13414-014-0630-6

Police and Criminal Evidence Act 1984 Codes of Practice (2011). Retrieved from http://www.homeoffice.gov.uk/publications/police/operational-policing/pace-codes/pace-code-d-2011

R v. Caldwell and Dixon (1993) CLR 862, UK

R v. Clare and Peach (1995) 2 Cr App R 333, UK

R v. Clarke (1995) 2 Cr App R 425, UK

R v. Dodson and Williams (1984) 79 Cr App R 220, UK

R v. Fowden and White (1982) Crim LR 588, UK

R v. Grimer (1982) Crim LR 674, UK

Rice, A., Phillips, P.J., & O'Toole, A. (2013). The role of the face and body in unfamiliar person identification. *Applied Cognitive Psychology, 27,* 761–768. doi:10.1002/acp.2969

Rossion, B., Schiltz, C., & Crommelinck, M. (2003). The functionally defined right occipital and fusiform "face areas" discriminate novel from visually familiar faces. *Neuroimage, 19,* 877–883. doi:10.1016/S1053-8119(03)00105-8

Russell, R., Duchaine, B., & Nakayama, K. (2009). Super-recognizers: People with extraordinary face recognition ability. *Psychonomic Bulletin & Review, 16,* 252–257. doi:10.3758/PBR.16.2.252

Smith v. The Queen (2001). HCA 50. Australia

Stainer, M.J., Scott-Brown, K.C., & Tatler, B. (2013). Expertise and spatial selection in the CCTV control room. *Frontiers in Human Neuroscience, 7,* 1–9. doi:10.3389/fnhum.2013.00615

Strathie, A., McNeill, A., & White, D. (2012). In the dock: Chimeric image composites reduce identification accuracy. *Applied Cognitive Psychology, 26,* 140–148. doi:10.1002/acp.1806

Strauss v. the Police (2013). SASC3, South Australia

Tanaka, J.W., & Farah, M.J. (1993). Parts and wholes in face recognition. *Quarterly Journal of Experimental Psychology: Human Experimental Psychology, 46A,* 225–245. doi:10.1080/14640749308401045

Tanaka, J.W., & Sengco, J.A. (1997). Features and their configuration in face recognition. *Memory & Cognition, 25,* 583–592. doi:10.3758/BF03211301

Taylor v. The Chief Constable of Cheshire (1987). 84 CR.APP.R. 191, UK.

Taylor, M. (2013). Police 'super recognisers' to keep watch over Notting Hill carnival. *The Guardian,* August 24. Retrieved from http://www.theguardian.com/uk-news/2013/aug/23/police-super-recognisers-notting-hill-carnival

Thompson, B., Dunkelberger, N., & Vescio, S. (2013). *Juror face matching accuracy: Do judicial instructions help?* Poster presented at the 25th Annual Convention of the Association for Psychological Science, Washington, DC, May 2013.

Thompson, R., & Gerrard, G. (2011). Two million cameras in the UK. *CCTV Image, 42,* 10–12.

Thompson, W.B., Grattan, J., Rawding, J., & Buchholz, L. (2010). Identifying unfamiliar faces from overhead surveillance photos. *American Journal of Forensic Psychology*, *28*, 71–78.

Towler, A, White, D, & Kemp, R.I. (2014). Evaluating training methods for facial image comparison: The face shape strategy does not work. *Perception*, *43*, 214–218. doi:10.1068/p7676 ‑

Troscianko, T., Holmes, A., Stillman, J., Mirmehdi, M., Wright, D., & Wilson, A. (2004). What happens next? The predictability of natural behaviour viewed through CCTV cameras. *Perception*, *33*, 87–101. doi:10.1068/p3402

Valentine, T., & Mesout, J. (2009). Eyewitness identification under stress in the London Dungeon. *Applied Cognitive Psychology*, *23*, 151–161. doi:10.1002/acp.1463

Vokey, J.R., & Read, J.D. (1992). Familiarity, memorability, and the effect of typicality on the recognition of faces. *Memory & Cognition*, *20*, 291–302. doi:10.3758/BF03199666

White, D., Burton, A.M., Kemp, R.I., & Jenkins, R. (2013). Crowd effects in unfamiliar face matching. *Applied Cognitive Psychology*, *27*, 769–777. doi:10.1002/acp.2971

White, D., Kemp, R.I., Jenkins, R., & Burton, A.M. (2014). Feedback training for facial image comparison. *Psychonomic Bulletin & Review*, *21*, 100–106. doi:10.3758/s13423-013-0475-3

Wright, D.B., & Sladden, B. (2003). An own gender bias and the importance of hair in face recognition. *Acta Psychologica*, *114*, 101–114. doi:10.1016/S0001-6918(03)00052-0

Young, A.W., Hay, D.C., McWeeny, K.H., Flude, B.M., & Ellis, A.W. (1985). Matching familiar and unfamiliar faces on internal and external features. *Perception*, *14*, 737–746. doi:10.1068/p140737

10

Expert Analysis: Facial Image Comparison

GARY EDMOND, JOSH P. DAVIS, AND TIM VALENTINE

INTRODUCTION

Photographs and moving visual images have been presented as evidence in courts for at least 150 years (*R v. Tolson,* 1864; Feigenson & Spiesel, 2009; Finn, 2009), with the first use of CCTV images for criminal proceedings in the UK appearing in *R v. Fowden and White* (1982). There were early concerns about the reliability and veracity of photographs, particularly in the second half of the 19th century (Mnookin, 1998). Nowadays, however, courts in most common law jurisdictions accept photography as a trustworthy technology and resource because of its "mechanical objectivity" and democratic legibility (Daston & Galison, 2007). Consequently, *most* images relevant to a crime or cause of action are presumptively admissible. Those most likely to be excluded, as unfairly prejudicial to the defendant, are gruesome crime scene images. In recent decades, technological advances (notably digitization) have substantially reduced the cost of cameras and the recording and reproduction of images. Technological innovation has not

Forensic Facial Identification: Theory and Practice of Identification from Eyewitnesses, Composites and CCTV, First Edition. Edited by Tim Valentine and Josh P. Davis.
© 2015 John Wiley & Sons, Ltd. Published 2015 by John Wiley & Sons, Ltd.

Case study: R v. Tang (2006) 65 NSWLR 681
(New South Wales, Australia)

Three armed robbers targeted a convenience store in Ultimo, Sydney, at about 3.55 am on March 14, 2003, and were recorded on poor-quality surveillance video. Two of the robbers were arrested approximately 40 minutes later as the car in which they were travelling was found to contain property similar to that stolen from the store. DNA tests also linked items in their vehicle to the crime scene. Both confessed.

Approximately eight months later Tang came to the attention of the police as being potentially the third robber as his fingerprint matched a print recovered on the stolen goods. An anatomist was asked to compare the images of the robbery with images of Tang. In court, providing opinion evidence as an expert witness, the anatomist concluded that the offender and the defendant were "one and the same". Specifically she argued that: (1) the two photographs depicted the same person; (2) there was a level of support to this conclusion by application of a six-point scale (e.g., see Table 10.1); and (3) certain characteristics were "unique identifiers".

Tang was found guilty and the admissibility of this evidence was challenged on appeal. In its ruling, the New South Wales Court of Criminal Appeal noted that the anatomist had based her conclusion on the comparison of facial and body features, respectively – "facial mapping" and "body mapping". The Court did not accept that there was a field of body mapping but accepted the existence of expertise in facial mapping, although doubts were raised that the field was sufficiently developed to facilitate a *positive* identification. Therefore, in the absence of evidence to the contrary, the Court ruled that image analysts were not to positively identify those appearing in images. Nevertheless, because the anatomist had spent time looking at the images of the robbery and the defendant, the Court considered that she had become an *ad hoc expert*. She was, therefore, entitled to express her opinion about similarities between the defendant and the person of interest. For the Court, the fact that this was perceived as a difficult task for the jury made it all the more important to have the assistance of an expert.

The appeal was allowed primarily because the anatomist had positively identified the person of interest as Tang. The Court accepted that the evidence of the anatomist would be admissible at the re-trial. However it would be limited to describing similarities between the facial features of the defendant and the individual in the CCTV footage of the robbery. In *Tang*, the Court explicitly rejected the need for expert opinion based on "specialized knowledge" (required under the uniform evidence law) to be reliable.

At the re-trial the prosecutor did not adduce the "expert" image evidence and Tang was, nonetheless, convicted.

Case study: *Morgan v. R* (2011) NSWCCA 257 (New South Wales, Australia)

On January 11, 2008, a red Audi vehicle was stolen from a residence in Sydney, and six days later two hotels were robbed by two armed men clothed from head to toe, including balaclavas. One of the robbers carried a sledgehammer. A red Audi car had been parked close to each hotel at about the time of the robberies. Three months later a key to the missing Audi was found in Morgan's possession. The prosecution case was that Morgan was the robber wielding the sledgehammer.

Morgan was more than 6 foot tall, whereas four witnesses described the robber holding the sledgehammer as between 5 foot 5 inches and 5 foot 9 inches tall (165–176 cm). Nevertheless, based on poor-quality CCTV footage and still images from both hotels, as well as moving and still images of Morgan taken at the time of his arrest, an anatomist provided expert opinion evidence that the robber holding the sledgehammer was very likely to be Morgan. The anatomist generated an indication of the frequency of points of similarity using figures he claimed to be favourable to the defendant (i.e. conservative) and provided the following summary: "I am of the opinion that there is a high level of anatomical similarity between the offender and the suspect. My opinion is strengthened by the fact that I could not observe on the suspect any anatomical detail different from those I could discern from the CCTV images of the offender."

Three additional experts, called by the defendant (so-called rebuttal witnesses), offered different perspectives. The first, a forensic psychologist, observed that by employing a morphological approach to evaluating the evidence, the prosecution expert had not used an established scientifically valid or reliable method. No anthropometric data, statistical likelihood of error, or proportion of members of the population who may possess similar anatomy had been provided. He also noted that the offender was entirely obscured by clothing, reducing the reliability of any anatomical analysis. The second expert, a forensic photographer, additionally focused on the effects of the CCTV camera lens above head height, distorting the appearance of the depicted offender. The final expert, the forensic anatomist who testified in *R v. Tang*, supported the opinions of those above, additionally pointing out that no scientifically standardized quantitative or qualitative analysis had been conducted.

The Court of Appeal found the prosecution expert's opinion to be inadmissible, quashed the guilty verdict and ordered a new trial. According to the Court, the expression used by the anatomist went beyond the mere description of similarities. Moreover, it was unclear how the anatomist's "training, study or experience" provided "specialized knowledge" that enabled him to compare low-quality images with police reference images, especially where the person of interest's body was covered.

been restricted to terrestrial systems, with the capabilities of satellites, planes and drones improving dramatically. All of the derivative images are potentially available to assist investigations and prosecutions relating to issues as varied as car accidents, bank robberies, the activities of armies and militias (for proceedings in the International Criminal Court and tribunals), the production of narcotics, and the illegal clearing of protected vegetation. Whether as part of state security organizations, private security systems or personal communication devices, cameras and images are now ubiquitous.

With the increased availability of images, police in many jurisdictions have become obliged to trawl through crime-related recordings, although investigations often extend to exploring relationships and activities recorded on social media (such as Facebook) and the metadata generated by digital devices. Images can help investigators and others to understand the sequence and timing of events, such as who delivered the first punch in a bar fight, the nature of activities and/or the number of people involved, as well as details such as vehicle registrations, whether a ship or road vehicle had its lights on, whether clothing worn by a bank robber matched clothes owned by the suspect, the relative heights of persons, and many other issues of interest. Imagery has been used to reconstruct the background to terrorist events (e.g. the 2005 London bombings), and UK investigators have even relied on a lip-reader's interpretation of a conversation partially captured on poor-quality CCTV (*R v. Luttrell*, 2004). Although such images can often aid investigations, assistance is often constrained because of limited information (e.g., missing frames, events taking place off-screen, low-quality storage, and serious interpretive obstacles; *R v. Drollett*, 2005). These sorts of limitations have emerged most conspicuously in relation to the use of images to identify persons of interest – usually unknown offenders.

The prevalence of cameras and images has meant that courts in most advanced jurisdictions are routinely called upon to decide upon the identity of offenders, and/or those who are suspected on the basis of their proximity to a crime, at least in part relying on images. This chapter describes the manner in which courts, across a number of different jurisdictions, have responded to the use of images for the purposes of identification. The primary focus is on facial comparison or facial "mapping" analysts. These analysts have been recognized by courts as experts: deemed to possess specialized knowledge and able to assist the tribunal of fact (e.g. a jury) with opinions pertaining to identity. Regardless of whether they express opinions about the identity of the person of interest, or purport to describe similarities and differences between the defendant and the person of interest, the aim is to help establish that it is the defendant depicted in the crime scene imagery (or to eliminate them as the offender). In some cases analysts employing similar techniques have provided conflicting opinions (e.g., *Honeysett v. R*, 2013; *Morgan v. R*, 2011; *Murdoch v. The Queen*, 2007; *R v. Clarke*, 1995; *R v. Gardner*, 2004; *R v. Gray*, 2003).

Notwithstanding the participation of one or more analysts, judges and juries may be invited, by the prosecutor, to compare persons appearing in crime-related images with a defendant disputing the identification, in order to make up their own minds (e.g., *Morgan v. R*, 2011; *R v. Dodson and Williams*, 1984; *Smith v. The Queen*, 2001). Judges and juries will, of necessity, be unfamiliar with the defendant. Unfamiliar face identification tends to be error prone even if the quality of the images being compared is very high and there are no memory demands or restrictions on viewing time (Bruce, Henderson, Newman, & Burton, 2001; Bruce *et al.*, 1999; Henderson, Bruce, & Burton, 2001; see Chapter 9 for a review of this literature). Rates of both false negatives and false positives tend to be substantial. There is no advantage if the target is present in person (Davis & Valentine, 2009; Kemp, Towell, & Pike, 1997). Differences in facial expressions or angle of view increase errors (Bruce *et al.*, 1999), particularly if taken from angles and elevations typical of street surveillance cameras (Davies & Thasen, 2000).

Simultaneously, empirical research has demonstrated the contrasting finding that even with poor-quality images, face comparison and recognition tends to be reliable when performed by those who are familiar with the person of interest (Bruce *et al.*, 2001; Burton, Wilson, Cowan, & Bruce, 1999; see Chapter 9 for a review), and therefore most jurisdictions allow those who are familiar with the defendant to express an opinion as to whether the defendant appears in incriminating images (e.g., *Attorney-General's Reference*, 2003). An obvious difficulty is that those who are most familiar with those suspected of offending (i.e., family and acquaintances) are often reluctant to testify against them (although see *Murdoch v. The Queen,* 2007; *R v. Marsh*, 2005; *R v. Rix*, 2005). Both the level of familiarity as well as the reliability of any identification may be questioned—particularly if the identification is made by someone perceived as potentially hostile to the defendant (e.g., police officer or estranged partner, see *Smith v. The Queen*, 2001).

In England and Wales, police officers purporting to recognize offenders, usually on the basis of prior exposure, may positively identify them. A similar approach is followed in Scotland (*Her Majesty's Advocate v. Henry,* 2012). In addition, if familiarity is obtained through the course of an investigation from repeated exposure to images, English and Welsh police officers may be allowed to proffer their opinions on identification at trial as "ad-hoc" experts (e.g., *Attorney General's Reference*, 2003; *R v. Clare and Peach*, 1995; cf. *R v. Flynn*, 2008; Edmond & San Roque, 2012). Such judgments are highly susceptible to confirmation bias (see Expert Working Group, 2012). Indeed, expert interpretation of evidence using other techniques known to be basically reliable (e.g., latent fingerprint comparison) can be influenced by the provision of extraneous information pointing towards guilt or innocence (Dror, Charlton, & Peron, 2006; Dror & Rosenthal, 2008). Information about other investigators' opinions or a suspect's background can be highly influential. If evidence is ambiguous, which is often the case with disputed crime scene images, professed *independent* opinions of identity may inadvertently be prejudiced. Regardless of status, all involved in assessing evidence (e.g., judge, jury, lawyers, police and analysts) may be highly susceptible to the influence of cognitive biases.

Canadian courts allow judges and jurors to interpret images (*R v. Nikolovski,* 1996), but also allow those with familiarity to express their opinions. However, only police officers with considerable familiarity with defendants are eligible to testify (*R v. Leaney*, 1989). In practice, Canadian investigators and prosecutors have preferred probation officers and prison guards to act as witnesses because they can be portrayed as independent from the investigation. Officials in these roles frequently have sustained exposure to parolees and prisoners, and the reason for their familiarity is typically revealed in court in ways that tend to be adverse to the defendant.

In the US, there have been relatively few reported controversial cases around the use of images for identification (Vorder Bruegge, 1999; cf. *Wisconsin v. Avery,* 2012). US investigators have tended to rely on photogrammetry to assist with identification through estimations of height and/or shoe size (*United States v. Smithers*, 2000). Following reforms to the Federal Rules of Evidence (1975) and rulings on the use of expert evidence (e.g. *Daubert v. Merrell Dow Pharmaceuticals Inc.*, 1993), in theory techniques should have been tested and gained scientific acceptance, with assessments of the statistical likelihood of error published in peer-reviewed journals, prior to admission.

In Australia the opinions of police officers on the identity of those in images have been deemed inadmissible since *Smith v. The Queen* (2001). In *Smith* their evidence was thought to add nothing beyond what the jurors could do for themselves, because they develop familiarity with the defendant during the course of proceedings. The exception is in cases in which the appearance of the defendant has changed significantly (e.g., from weight change, beard or hair loss, or cosmetic surgery). However, because of concerns about jury capabilities, this exclusionary approach prompted a rise in the use of purported experts in image analysis and facial comparison. Even so, some Australian judges have expressed disquiet about the use of body shape (morphology) to assist with identification (e.g., *R v. Tang*, 2006: see box), especially where offenders are disguised (*Morgan v. R*, 2011: see box). Anxieties led judges to restrict the opinions of analysts to descriptions of similarities and differences between the features discerned from the person of interest and those of the defendant (Edmond & San Roque, 2014). A recent appeal to the High Court of Australia may have rendered 'expert' opinions about body shape inadmissible (R v. Honeysett, 2014).

In South Africa, police with limited training and experience, derived from their participation in earlier investigations and trials, are allowed to positively identify persons of interest (Edmond & Meintjes-van der Walt, 2014). South African courts do not use juries but the practice in relation to *expert* image comparison evidence is similar to the accommodating approach adopted in the UK (Edmond, Cole, Cunliffe, & Roberts, 2013).

PHOTOGRAPHIC FACIAL COMPARISON ANALYSIS

All advanced adversarial systems have admitted the opinions of various kinds of analysts – recognized as experts – to assist with the identification of persons appearing in images. From the very first use of surveillance and security cameras in England (*R v. Stockwell*, 1993), and following *Smith v. The Queen* (2001) in Australia, a range of individuals have been allowed to express their opinions about identity on the *assumption* that they possessed abilities beyond those of lay jurors and judges. These analysts have provided opinions about clothing, gait (Larsen, Simonsen, & Lynnerup, 2008), or body size (e.g., Bridge, 2009;

De Angelis *et al.*, 2007; see Scoleri, Lucas, & Henneberg, 2014, for the difficulty in estimating stature through different clothing). However, using one or more undisputed comparison images of the defendant as a reference, identity evidence often involves facial structure and feature comparisons. In England and Wales, where there may be as many as 600 such cases per annum (Bromby, 2003), a reference from the Attorney General produced guidelines on the use of such techniques, explaining that:

> A suitably qualified expert with facial mapping skills can give opinion evidence of identification based on a comparison between images from the scene (whether expertly enhanced or not), and a reasonably contemporary photograph of the defendant, provided the images and the photographs are available for the jury (Attorney General's Reference, 2003).

The analysts comparing images originate from a variety of professional backgrounds including visual image analytics, military intelligence and surveillance, psychology, IT and computer engineering, art, forensic anthropology and medicine (e.g., anatomists, dentists and podiatrists). However, it is worth noting that few, if any, of these fields routinely involve members comparing a person of interest, in a low-quality image, to a reference photograph of a known person. There is, in consequence, a serious and unanswered question about whether the various individuals allowed to express opinions actually possess expertise in relation to image comparison and identification. This applies to the ability to make assertions about identity as well as to discern the features of a person of interest and attach significance to them. In England and Wales, the Association of Chief Police Officers and the National Policing Improvement Agency guidance (NPIA, 2009, p. 17) expects "experts" to possess the following skills, although these are not admissibility rules, and no court has required evidence of formal evaluation.

- Sound knowledge of human facial anatomy, anthropometry, physiology together with an in-depth knowledge of photo interpretation and image analysis techniques, including capture, process and output media.
- Be able to demonstrate an ability to compare facial morphology and facial proportions, observing the spatial relationships of facial features and facial landmarks between images, from more than one source.
- Be aware of the significance of probability factors, likelihood of repetition, and likely range of variation in images, thus demonstrating awareness and an ability to analyse the effects of distortion caused

by perspective, camera angle, motion blur, lighting and transfer of data formats.
* Be familiar with relevant Home Office guidelines and current research in this field.

Regardless of their technique, all analysts must address the issue that a two-dimensional (2D) image is a representation of a three-dimensional (3D) reality, so that the distance between features, and the curvature or perceived depth of features, will be distorted (see Figure 10.1). These distortions can be exaggerated by comparing images captured at different distances and through different lenses (Edmond, Biber, Kemp, & Porter, 2009; Harper & Latto, 2001). The recording and compression of digital images may also decrease fine detail and introduce distortion. The risk of error may be reduced if high-quality, close-up images are compared. Nevertheless, even under optimal conditions, proof of identity may not be feasible, for it is always possible that one or more individuals photographed under similar conditions will generate analytics that are indistinguishable from those of the person of interest (Davis, Valentine, & Davis, 2010). Conversely, a single reliable difference, not caused by camera or image irregularities, or natural changes to appearance (e.g., expression or ageing), may provide strong evidence that two different people are depicted (Bogan & Roberts, 2011). Analysts, however,

(a)   (b)   (c)

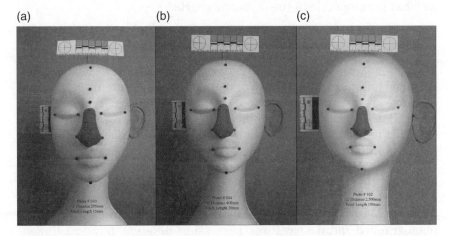

Figure 10.1 Image distortion in high-quality rectilinear photographs. What do the "head" and facial features actually look like? What is the shape of the actual "head" and is the "ear" larger than the "nose"? From the left the photographs were taken from (a) a distance of 295 mm, with a focal length of 15 mm; (b) a distance of 400 mm and a focal length of 20 mm; and (c) a distance of 2500 mm with a focal length of 100 mm. (Images courtesy of Dr Glenn Porter, 2009)

are typically asked to apply their techniques to poor-quality images where targets are some distance from the camera, with features obscured or indistinct due to disguises, movement or shadow effects produced by competing light sources (especially at night), and with differences in the perspective of the images to be compared.

In addition to the analysis and comparison of images by humans, for several decades researchers have been developing computer-based algorithms (Porikli *et al.*, 2013). These systems convert a facial image into a biometric or digital signature, which allows comparison against a database. Under ideal conditions with posed close-up images and good lighting, algorithms can be reasonably accurate and outperform humans. However, performance is far worse in environmentally unconstrained conditions (Burton, Miller, Bruce, Hancock, & Henderson, 2001; see Chapter 11). Over time, biometric systems may become increasingly efficient at profiling or short-listing potential targets from a database. However, in the foreseeable future final decisions about identity are likely to be made by humans, whether from visual inspection or by the use of facial comparison techniques.

The analysts recognized by courts as experts have tended to rely upon three broad techniques: *photo-anthropometric analysis, morphological comparison* and *photographic superimposition*. The actual methodology or combination of techniques selected tends to depend upon the particular analyst, image quality and characteristics, as well as what is acceptable in the domestic courts.

Photo-anthropometry (or Photogrammetry)

With photo-anthropometry, the distances and angles between anatomical facial landmark sites on two or more photographs are measured and compared to demonstrate a match or a mismatch in their facial dimensions. It is difficult to determine absolute distances in photographs, even if the focal lens of the camera and the exact distance from the target is known. For this reason, the normalized proportional indices between facial features using a standardized visual reference are employed (e.g., the distance between the corners of the eyes). Nevertheless, the comparison of images captured from cameras with different lenses, even if taken from the same viewpoint, will result in photographed facial structures possessing different physical dimensions (see Figure 10.1).

Figure 10.2 illustrates an attempt to approximate facial size and angle. When presented as evidence in court, photo-anthropometrical analyses will often be supported by diagrams depicting grids superimposed over the images to assist with measurements or proportions

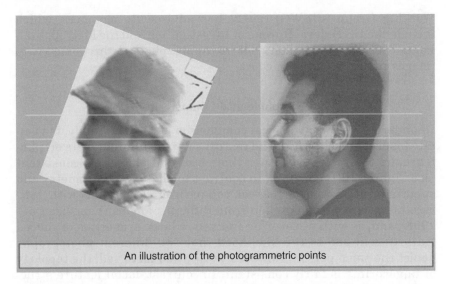

An illustration of the photogrammetric points

Figure 10.2 An example of anthropometry from an investigation in New Zealand. (images courtesy of Rod McCourt)

(Bromby, 2003). Grids and other aids may also bias decision-making as they emphasize the consistencies between facial images, without addressing image variation and distortion or the frequency of similar measurements among relevant populations.

Case studies of the kinds of photo-anthropometric techniques used in court have been published (Halberstein, 2001; Porter & Doran, 2000), as have empirical tests of the technique against a variety of facial image databases with images taken from different distances and angles, incorporating variation in the demographic and physical homogeneity of the individuals included (Catterick, 1992; Davis *et al.*, 2010; Kleinberg, Vanezis, & Burton, 2007; Mardia, Coombs, Kirkbride, Linney, & Bowie, 1996; Moreton & Morley, 2011; Roelofse, Steyn, & Becker, 2008). Few crime scene images are of high quality and taken with the same camera and from exactly the same angle, as has been the primary stimuli employed in much of this research. Variations in viewpoint, which may appear deceptively minor, add substantially to the likelihood of error. In large part this seems to be a consequence of the frequency of highly similar facial measurements belonging to different people. Even with high-quality images taken from carefully posed, closely aligned viewpoints, this body of research has consistently demonstrated that photo-anthropometry is not suitable for identification or for elimination (Moreton & Morley, 2011). For this reason the Facial Identification Scientific

Working Group (FISWG) (2012) has advised its members, which include the US Federal Bureau of Investigation and the Metropolitan Police Service in London, not to apply photo-anthropometry to images to be presented in court.

Morphological Comparison

In undertaking morphological comparison of the face, analysts visually inspect and classify facial features in two different (sets of) photographs to examine whether their size and shape are consistent (see Figures 10.1 and 10.2). In contrast to photo-anthropometry and superimposition, morphological comparison is possible with low-resolution photographs taken from different angles (Vanezis et al., 1996), and, as with fingerprint analysis, a large proportion of shared features will add to the likelihood that two different photographs depict the same person. However, even when distorted, the topology of fingerprints is fairly consistent. In contrast, facial feature structure may be dramatically altered by changes in facial expressions, lighting, the focal length of the lens, camera angle, and so forth (Mardia et al., 1996).

As a guide to analysts, FISWG (2013) provided a list of the primary facial features that they recommend be included in a court report. Other morphological comparison techniques have also been published, tested against databases of various sizes and demographic homogeneity (Ritz-Timme et al., 2011a, 2011b; Roelofse et al., 2008; Vanezis et al., 1996). Ventura, Zacheo, Ventura, and Pala (2004) described how the use of the technique assisted a US court in a single case study. An international group of researchers have developed a morphological "face atlas" (Ritz-Timme et al., 2011a; cf. Ellenbogen, 2013), which requires analysts to classify 43 facial features into 136 categories. The atlas has been tested using a database of at least 900 people from different European countries (Germany, Italy and Lithuania). Significantly, due to high levels of common features, more than one person was sometimes classified into exactly the same subcategories (Ritz-Timme et al., 2011b). This limits the use of such classification for purposes of individuation. An additional problem with any system that requires classification is that a facial feature may possess properties that are hard to classify into a single category. Different analysts may classify the same features differently and the same analyst might be inconsistent over time (e.g., Dror et al., 2011). This problem of poor reliability is likely to increase with the use of multiple photographs of the same person.

Photographic Superimposition

With photographic superimposition, one image is superimposed over a second, for visual inspection of the combined image to identify similarities or discrepancies. Analysts can employ *visual flicker*, by rapidly switching between the superimposed images to expose differences through apparent motion (e.g., Ramachandran & Anstis, 1986); *visual fading*, a similar but very much more gradual process; and *visual wiping*, in which the lower image is systematically vertically, horizontally or diagonally exposed. Wipe speed is variable, although slower wipes will tend to be used when there is fine detail.

Vanezis and Brierley (1996) described the use of superimposition to provide opinion evidence in the identification of 51 individuals in 46 UK criminal cases. They claimed to provide evidence of 11 "reliable", 16 "probable", and 8 "possible" matches, as well as three "exclusions". The authors proposed that the technique is most useful for the matching of facial marks such as scars, moles or ear structure on two photos of the same person. However, an analyst's report that includes observations concluding that such marks can be seen in the same location on two images, purportedly of the same person, will not include the statistical probability of different individuals possessing similar marks. No database exists as to the rarity of such features. Vanezis and Brierley additionally argued that minor viewpoint differences can be overlooked, as "what is acceptable depends on the experience of the examiner who should be aware of the various possible positional changes of the head" (p. 28). In contrast, İşcan (1993) argued that superimposition is really only possible on perfectly aligned images, and that wiping or fading between superimposed images at extremely slow speeds can induce a bias towards believing that images of two different people depict the same person. Consequently, if an analyst is asked to demonstrate superimposition evidence in court, the manner in which this is conducted may unduly influence those required to evaluate the evidence.

OTHER TECHNICAL AND METHODOLOGICAL ISSUES

There are a range of additional technical and methodological issues associated with image comparison evidence, including contextual bias, the possibility of increased performance using 3D imaging, and what might be described as ageing effects.

Contextual Bias and Contamination

The way in which investigators solicit the opinions of analysts and the way analyses are normally undertaken unnecessarily introduces non-trivial risks of cognitive contamination and error. The process of comparison used by anatomists (and many other forensic analysts) often involves exposure to domain-irrelevant information, and appears vulnerable to a range of insidious influences, such as suggestion and confirmation bias. The anatomists appearing in *R v. Tang* (2006) and *Morgan v. R* (2011) (see case studies), for example, were only asked to compare one set of images and appear to have known about the existence of the fingerprint and DNA "matches". That is, they undertook a difficult interpretive exercise in conditions where they knew the police believed the person of interest and the suspect were the same, and that other, more powerful forensic techniques supported that conclusion. The fact that analysts are routinely exposed to other incriminating evidence has not prevented their opinions being represented as "independent" corroboration. Such representations misrepresent the value of opinions developed in conditions where the analyst was not shielded from gratuitous information or a process that suggests the desired answer (Edmond, Searston, Tangen, & Dror, 2014).

Three-Dimensional Images

Due to the high commonality of facial measurements possessed by different faces, it may not be possible to reliably individuate even carefully posed 2D photographs. Employing multiple images taken from alternative angles may assist (Davis *et al.*, 2010), as might three-dimensional technology (e.g., laser surface scanning, 3D stereo-photogrammetry; Cattaneo *et al.*, 2009). Research using high-quality images taken in optimum environmental conditions has demonstrated that it is feasible to extract a 2D image from a 3D scan and superimpose that image over a photograph from a normal 2D camera, so that anthropometric landmarks can be located on both 2D images with sub-millimetre accuracy (De Angelis, Sala, Cantatore, Grandi, & Cattaneo, 2009; Fourie, Damstra, Gerrits, & Ren, 2011; Yoshino, Matsuda, Kubota, Imaizumi, & Miyasaka, 2000; Yoshino *et al.*, 2002). The suggestion from this stream of research is that the police could routinely collect 3D images, in the same manner as most forces currently collect mugshot images (Yoshino *et al.*, 2002). However, despite some experimental successes, 3D images are often accompanied with distortions caused by lighting anomalies and inadvertent movement. Furthermore, anthropometric techniques using 3D images suffer from reliability problems similar to those encountered with 2D images (Evison *et al.*, 2010).

Ageing Effects

Analysts may be asked to apply facial comparison methods to images taken some time apart. Indeed, the first editor of this volume (Valentine, ND)[1] describes a case in which a series of undisputed photographs taken over a number of years of a prisoner held in Guantanamo Bay were compared with a photograph that was alleged by his US captors to provide evidence that the prisoner was a member of the terrorist organization, Al Qaeda. Analysis of the images by Valentine contributed to the decision by the US security forces to release the prisoner. The former prisoner was not charged on his return to the UK.

If images are taken some time apart, age-related changes to facial structure will occur (Gonzalez-Ulloa & Flores, 1965; Khalil, Kubota, Tawara, & Inomata, 1996; Shaw, McIntyre, & Mace, 1974; Takema, Yorimoto, Kawai, & Imokawa, 1994). Even minor changes to hairstyle and facial hair may further impede the reliability of facial comparison methods. Due to genetic and environmental factors (e.g., alcohol, smoking, accidents, sleeping position, cosmetic interventions, sun damage, medication, diet and illness), individual rates of change are not predictable. Changes to facial structure are most dramatic in the first few years of life. This may be a particular problem when attempting to identify child victims of sexual abuse from images in cases of child pornography (Cattaneo et al., 2009).

PROBATIVE VALUE, VALIDITY AND RELIABILITY

One issue associated with all the techniques described above is that analysts are unable to provide the courts with information about the margin of error tested against a large database of faces, as is the case with some other biometrics (e.g., DNA). Facial databases do exist (e.g., passports, driving licences, police files), although as these images are normally taken directly from the front or in profile, their use is limited if crime scene images are captured from alternative viewpoints. Indeed, no standardized valid or reliable methodology exists with any facial comparison analysis technique, and as a consequence the value of interpretations are unknown, and analyst susceptibility to cognitive bias would seem to be considerable (Dror et al., 2006). As such, regardless of whether 2D or 3D images are acquired, facial comparison techniques would seem to be better suited to assisting a police investigation by creating a profile and limiting the pool of potential suspects, rather than for providing "identification" evidence for a court (Ritz-Timme et al., 2011b).

[1]Available at www.valentinemoore.co.uk/recent.htm

Where called as expert witnesses, those analysing images have been subjected to challenges and sustained criticism (e.g., Edmond et al., 2009; Honeysett v. R, 2013; Morgan v. R, 2011; R v. Gray, 2003; R v. Tang, 2006). As a consequence, over time courts and analysts have gradually refined the shape and scope of testimony. These responses appear to have been driven by concerns to circumvent recurrent problems through compromises and qualifications to interpretations and opinions, rather than by conducting or requiring evaluative experimental research.

We can observe changes in the way analysts proffering opinions pertaining to identity expressed their conclusions. Analysts in England and Australia initially presented anthropometric evidence and used superimposition to support positive claims. As a response to the measurement problems associated with anthropometry, analysts switched to morphological approaches and tended to refrain from positively identifying the person of interest. In Australia, analysts are required to restrict themselves to describing similarities and differences (based on morphological style approaches) between persons of interest and known persons (Morgan v. R, 2011; R v. Tang, 2006). Analysts may use highly suggestive language and terminology (e.g., "no differences" in Honeysett v. R, 2013), and in England, analysts now tend to use verbal formulations based loosely on the reporting scales developed for quantitative forensic sciences by the Forensic Science Service (see Bromby, 2003). They might say, for example, that "the analysis lends strong support to the contention that the person in the crime scene imagery and the suspect are the same person". The example in Table 10.1, taken from R v. Atkins (2009), a case with a single low-quality image, illustrates how potentially forceful though simultaneously vague such subjective conclusions might be (i.e. two whole points on a six-point scale). Confronted with the obligation to limit testimony to describing similarities (and differences), lawyers and judges in Australia have struggled to prevent analysts from generating highly prejudicial numbers or suggesting that a few apparent similarities in what is often a badly distorted image constitute "a high level of anatomical similarity" (e.g., Morgan v. R, 2011; R v. Dastagir, 2013).

In England, image analysts and investigators are entitled to positively identify an individual in low-quality images provided that they acknowledge weaknesses such as the fact that there is no database behind the assertion (Attorney-General's Reference, 2003; R v. Atkins, 2009). In practice they tend to present weaker conclusions, along the lines that the evidence "lends powerful support" (Otway v. The Queen, 2011; R v. Atkins, 2009; see also Edmond et al., 2010; R v. T, 2010).

Table 10.1 An example of a verbal scale often adopted by image analysts in England and Wales. This version is taken from the analyst's report in *R v. Atkins* (2009)

Level	Description
0	Lends no support
1	Lends limited support
2	Lends moderate support
3	**Lends support**
4	**Lends strong support**
5	Lends strong support

The revelation of limitations in Australia tends to be more serendipitous, depending on the resourcing and abilities of defence lawyers.

Qualifications to conclusions have been promoted primarily by judges responding to occasional defence concerns. They have not been driven by analysts, and are not the result of analysts attending to sustained scholarly criticisms. The provision of conclusions that are weaker than positive identification (i.e. individualization) effectively insulates image analysts from some of the methodological criticisms they might otherwise confront. They do not, as we explain, make weaker forms of opinion reliable or even better suited to the limits of legal institutions and the capabilities of trial personnel. It is revealing that, notwithstanding the Australian proscription on positive identification, the actual "expert" reports and sometimes testimony continue to embody the analyst's belief in their ability to positively identify persons of interest.

Several image analysts have been discredited by mistakes or criticized for questionable practices, performances and conclusions (e.g., *Morgan v. R,* 2011; *R v. Gray,* 2003; *R v. Tang,* 2006). Somewhat curiously, these problems have been interpreted as limited to the case or the individual analysts and any wider implications for image interpretation and identification have been dismissed (e.g., *R v. Atkins,* 2009; *Honeysett v. R,* 2013). Authoritative legal criticism has led to some analysts being "dropped" by investigators and prosecutors and replaced by others using remarkably similar techniques and drawing similar conclusions. The failure to have formally evaluated techniques and standardized practices is typically treated, like the absence of a database of face and body features, as issues for the jury to somehow consider as part of their evaluation of the evidence, in the context of the overall case (*Morgan v. R*, 2011; *R v. Gray,* 2003; *R v. Tang,* 2006).

JURY INTERPRETATION OF FORENSIC EVIDENCE

Image evidence, the opinions of putative experts and the images themselves are often admitted in criminal proceedings because judges maintain inordinate confidence in the effectiveness of adversarial trials (and appeals) to identify, explain and convey any problems with the evidence to the tribunal of fact – very often a jury. Anyone who follows trials and appeals (or reads some of the judgments cited in this chapter) might come to a less sanguine view about the capabilities of lawyers and judges. Very often cross-examination is perfunctory and judicial understandings, as manifested in admissibility determinations, directions and warnings, do not consistently identify serious methodological limitations (e.g., no validation testing, lack of standards and inattention to contextual bias), relevant scientific literatures (such as those discussed above), or provide means of rationally evaluating the opinions of analysts. The judges themselves do not seem to have appreciated the magnitude of problems, and often compound risks by ignoring the effects of combining the opinions of analysts, recognized by the courts as experts, with jury access to the images.

In too many cases, serious problems with images (and many other kinds of expert evidence, purporting to be scientific and technical) are not identified or explained to the jury by lawyers or the trial judge. There are, for example, very few cases where trial judges provide assistance with the kind of issues raised in this chapter. In England, for example, jurors will be told that the analyst did not use a database in developing their incriminating opinion about the significance of the alleged similarities. In Australia, the jury will be presented with a list of similarities and, perhaps, no more. In both jurisdictions, jurors are expected to interpret this "expert" evidence, in conjunction with the images and any other incriminating evidence, in the absence of validation studies, error rates, databases, insights into the dangers posed by contextual biases, and the extensive literature on the difficulties of unfamiliar face-matching.

There is a need for genuine caution before accepting legal claims of interrogation and critical engagement at face value. Legal safeguards can work, particularly where the defendant is well resourced. In the vast majority of cases, however, admissibility rules and safeguards appear to be far from effective (Edmond & San Roque, 2012; Law Commission, 2011).

ANAMORPHIC LAW

Legal use of image analysts to proffer evidence pertaining to identity raises difficult ethical dilemmas for psychologists capable of providing courts with rebuttal testimony and, more importantly, advice.

Embodying concerns expressed in *R v. Turner* (1975), trial and appellate courts have not been responsive to the methodological criticisms and the serious problems highlighted by psychological research occasionally raised by lawyers in cross-examination or via rebuttal experts.

It is doubtful that explaining interpretive and methodological problems, such as the lack of validation studies, to juries after they have been allowed to compare the images with the defendant, usually in conjunction with the opinion of an "expert", will counteract suggestive interpretations of the images *even if mistaken*. If a lay person or jury is not explicitly encouraged to deduce the identity of those depicted in images, they are likely to implicitly judge evidence from "experts" on the basis of their own opinion. There is probably little a court could do in forewarning them about the high risks of error when performing face-matching judgements. When it comes to the comparison and interpretation of images, jurors and judges are rarely placed in a position that is conducive to the rational assessment of the images or the opinions of those presented as experts.

By participating in such proceedings, where the problems are unlikely to be fully explained or taken seriously by fact-finders or appellate courts, psychological researchers would seem to be lending legitimacy to a process that does not appropriately value their knowledge or contributions. Courts have been far too accommodating of image analysts and far too ready to recognize, but in effect create, "fields". Courts have accepted face and body mapping, and identification via gait analysis (*Otway v. The Queen*, 2011; *R v. Aitken*, 2012), as reliable and widely accepted and valuable practices. As this chapter has endeavoured to explain, this is not a reasonable response to what is *known* beyond the courts.

The question arises of whether psychologists should participate in legal proceedings, in an attempt to assist those accused and prosecuted with questionable evidence. Alternatively, should they criticize legal ignorance and obduracy from the outside, where there is no need for deference to traditions that do not engage seriously with scientific knowledge or credibly review their own performances? Or should they do both, in more creative and strategic ways? Recently, the US National Academy of Sciences (2009), as one example, adopted a conspicuously critical and perhaps contemptuous approach to American legal practice in its attempt to inaugurate the reform of forensic science.

In their approaches to image comparison evidence, courts in most jurisdictions have been remarkably insensitive to the difficulty of interpreting images and comparing the faces of unfamiliar persons. Instead of directing their attention to a substantial, though largely critical, scientific literature that has repeatedly identified the difficulty and error-prone nature of image interpretation, courts have allowed highly credentialed analysts to express their incriminating opinions

material. *Forensic Science International*, *183*, e21–e24. doi:10.1016/j. forsciint.2008.09.005

Catterick, T. (1992). Facial measurements as an aid to recognition. *Forensic Science International*, *56*, 23–27. doi:10.1016/0379-0738(92)90142-J

Daston, L., & Galison, P. (2007). *Objectivity*. Boston: Zone Books.

Daubert v. Merrell Dow Pharmaceuticals Inc. (1993) 509 U.S. 579.

Davies, G., & Thasen, S. (2000). Closed-circuit television: How effective an identification aid? *British Journal of Psychology*, *91*, 411–426. doi:10.1348/000712600161907

Davis, J.P., & Valentine, T. (2009). CCTV on trial: Matching video images with the defendant in the dock. *Applied Cognitive Psychology*, *23*, 482–505. doi:10.1002/acp.1490

Davis, J.P., Valentine, T., & Davis, R.E. (2010). Computer assisted photo-anthropometric analysis of full-face and profile facial images. *Forensic Science International*, *200*, 165–176. doi:10.1016/j.forsciint.2010.04.012

De Angelis, D., Sala, R., Cantatore, A., Grandi, M., & Cattaneo, C. (2009). A new computer-assisted technique to aid personal identification. *International Journal of Legal Medicine*, *123*, 351–356. doi:10.1007/s00414-008-0311-x

De Angelis, D., Sala, R., Cantore, A., Poppa, P., Dufour, M., Gandi, M., & Cattaneo, C. (2007). New method for height estimation of subjects represented in photograms taken from video surveillance systems. *International Journal of Legal Medicine*, *121*, 489–492. doi:10.1007/s00414-007-0176-4

Dror, I.E., Champod, C., Langenburg, G., Charlton, D., Hunt, H., & Rosenthal, R. (2011). Cognitive issues in fingerprint analysis: Inter- and intra-expert consistency and the effect of a 'target' comparison. *Forensic Science International*, *208*, 10–17. doi:10.1016/j.forsciint.2010.10.013

Dror, I.E., Charlton, D., & Peron, A.E. (2006). Contextual information renders experts vulnerable to making erroneous identifications. *Forensic Science International*, *156*, 74–78. doi:10.1016/j.forsciint.2005.10.017

Dror, I.E., & Rosenthal, R. (2008). Meta-analytically quantifying the reliability and biasability of forensic experts. *Journal of Forensic Sciences*, *53*, 900–903. doi:10.1111/j.1556-4029.2008.00762.x

Edmond, G. (2008). Specialised knowledge, the exclusionary discretions and reliability: Reassessing incriminating expert opinion evidence. *UNSW Law Journal*, *31*, 1–55.

Edmond, G., Biber, K., Kemp, R., & Porter, G. (2009). Law's looking glass: Expert identification evidence derived from photographic and video image. *Current Issues in Criminal Justice*, *20*, 337–377.

Edmond, G., Cole, S., Cunliffe, E., & Roberts, A. (2013). The reception of incriminating expert evidence (i.e., forensic science) in four adversarial jurisdictions. *University of Denver Criminal Law Review*, *3*, 31–109.

Edmond, G., Kemp, R., Porter, G., Hamer, D., Burton, M., Biber, K., & San Roque, M. (2010). *Atkins v. The Emperor*: The "cautious" use of unreliable "expert" evidence. *International Journal of Evidence & Proof*, *14*, 146–166.

Edmond, G., & Meintjes-van der Walt, L. (2014). Blind justice? Forensic science and the use of CCTV images as identification evidence in South Africa. *South African Law Journal*, *131*, 109–148.

Edmond, G., & San Roque, M. (2012). The cool crucible: forensic science and the frailty of the criminal trial. *Current Issues in Criminal Justice*, *24*, 51–66.

Edmond, G., & San Roque, M. (2014). *Honeysett v. The Queen*: Forensic science, 'specialised knowledge' and the Uniform Evidence Law. *Sydney Law Review*, *36*, 323–344.

Edmond, G., Searston, R., Tangen, J., & Dror, I. (2014). Contextual bias and cross-contamination in the forensic sciences: The corrosive implications for investigations, plea bargains, trials and appeals. *Law, Probability & Risk* (online only). doi:10.1093/lpr/mgu018

Ellenbogen, J. (2013). *Reasoned and Unreasoned Images: The Photography of Bertillon, Galton, and Marey*. Philadelphia: Penn State University Press.

Evison, M., Dryden, I., Fieller, N., Mallett, X., Morecroft, L., Schofield, D., & Vorder-Bruegge, R. (2010). Key parameters of face shape variation in 3D in a large sample. *Journal of Forensic Sciences,55*,159–162.doi:10.1111/j.1556-4029.2009.01213.x

Expert Working Group on Human Factors in Latent Print Analysis. (2012). *Latent Print Examination and Human Factors: Improving the Practice through a Systems Approach*. Washington, DC: Department of Commerce, National Institute of Standards and Technology, National Institute of Justice. Retrieved from http://www.nist.gov/manuscript-publication-search.cfm?pub_id=910745

Facial Identification Scientific Working Group (FISWG) (2012). *Guidelines for Facial Comparison* Methods. Retrieved from https://www.fiswg.org/doc/pdf/FISWG_GuidelinesforFacialComparisonMethods_v1.0_2012_02_02.pdf

Facial Identification Scientific Working Group (FISWG) (2013). *Facial Image Comparison Feature List for Morphological Analysis*. Retrieved from https://www.fiswg.org/document/viewDocument?id=29

Federal Rules of Evidence (1975). Available at http://www.law.cornell.edu/rules/fre

Feigenson, N., & Spiesel, C. (2009). *Law on Display: The Digital Transformation of Legal Persuasion and Judgment*. New York: New York University Press.

Finn, J. (2009). *Capturing the Criminal Image: From Mug Shot to Surveillance Society*. Minneapolis: University of Minneapolis Press.

Fourie, Z., Damstra, J., Gerrits, P.O., & Ren, Y. (2011). Evaluation of anthropometric accuracy and reliability using different three-dimensional scanning systems. *Forensic Science International*, *207*, 127–133. doi:10.1016/j.forsciint.2010.09.018

Gonzalez-Ulloa, M., & Flores, E.S. (1965). Senility of the face: Basic study to understand its causes and effects. *Plastic and Reconstructive Surgery*, *36*, 239–246.

Halberstein, R.A. (2001). The application of anthropometric indices in forensic photography: Three case studies. *Journal of Forensic Sciences*, *46*, 1438–1441. doi:10.1520/JFS15167J

Harper, B., & Latto, R. (2001). Cyclopean vision, size estimation, and presence in orthostereoscopic images. *Presence*, *10*, 312–330. doi:10.1162/105474601300343630

Henderson, Z., Bruce, V., & Burton, A.M. (2001). Matching the faces of robbers captured on video. *Applied Cognitive Psychology*, *15*, 445–464. doi:10.1002/acp.718

Her Majesty's Advocate v. Henry (2012) HCJAC 128 (Scotland).

Honeysett v. R (2013) NSWCCA 135 (New South Wales, Australia).

İşcan, M.Y. (1993). Introduction to techniques for photographic comparison: Potentials and problems. In M.Y. İşcan, & R.P. Helmer (Eds.), *Forensic Analysis of the Skull* (pp. 57–70). New York: Wiley-Liss.

Kemp, R., Towell, N., & Pike, G. (1997). When seeing should not be believing: Photographs, credit cards and fraud. *Applied Cognitive Psychology*, *11*, 211–222. doi:10.1002/(SICI)1099-0720(199706)11:3<211::AID-ACP430>3.0.CO;2-O

Khalil, A.K., Kubota, T., Tawara, A., & Inomata, H. (1996). Ultrastructural age-related changes on the posterior iris surface. A possible relationship to the pathogenesis of exfoliation. *Archives of Ophthalmology, 114*, 721–725. doi:10.1001/archopht.1996.01100130713013

Kleinberg, K.F., Vanezis, P., & Burton, A.M. (2007). Failure of anthropometry as a facial identification technique using high-quality photographs. *Journal of Forensic Science, 52*, 779–783. doi:10.1111/j.1556-4029.2007.00458.x

Larsen, P.K., Simonsen, E.B., & Lynnerup, N. (2008). Gait analysis in forensic medicine. *Journal of Forensic Science, 53*, 1149–1153. doi:10.1111/j.1556-4029.2008.00807.x

Law Commission. (2011). *Expert Evidence in Criminal Proceedings in England and Wales*. London: Report No. 235. Retrieved from http://lawcommission. justice.gov.uk/docs/lc325_Expert_Evidence_Report.pdf

Mardia, K.V., Coombs, A., Kirkbride, J., Linney, A., & Bowie, J.L. (1996). On statistical problems with face identification from photographs. *Journal of Applied Statistics, 23*, 655–675. doi:10.1080/02664769624008

Mnookin, J. (1998). The image of truth: Photographic evidence and the power of analogy. *Yale Journal of Law & the Humanities, 10*, 1–74.

Moreton, R., & Morley, J. (2011). Investigation into the use of photoanthropometry in facial image comparison. *Forensic Science International, 212*, 231–237. doi:10.1016/j.forsciint.2011.06.023

Morgan v. R (2011) NSWCCA 257 (New South Wales, Australia)

Murdoch v. The Queen (2007) NTCCA 1 (Northern Territory, Australia)

National Academy of Sciences (US). (2009). *Strengthening the Forensic Sciences in the United States: A Path Forward*. Washington, DC: The National Academies Press.

National Policing Improvement Agency (2009). *Facial Identification Guidance 2009*. Retrieved from http://www.acpo.police.uk/documents/crime/2009/200911CRIFIG01.pdf

Otway v. The Queen (2011) EWCA Crim 3 (England and Wales)

Porikli, F., Bremond, F., Dockstader, S.L., Ferryman, J., Hoogs, A., Lovell, B.C., ...Venetianer, P.L. (2013). Video surveillance: Past, present, and now the future. *IEEE Signal Processing Magazine, 30*, 190–198.

Porter G. (2009). CCTV images as Evidence. *Australian Journal of Forensic Sciences, 41*, 11–25.

Porter, G., & Doran, G. (2000). An anatomical and photographic technique for forensic facial identification. *Forensic Science International, 114*, 97–105. doi:10.1016/S0379-0738(00)00290-5

Ramachandran, V.S., & Anstis, S.M. (1986). The perception of apparent motion. *Scientific American, 254*, 102–109.

R v. Aitken (2012) BCCA 134 (British Columbia, Canada)

R v. Atkins (2009) EWCA Crim 1876 (England and Wales)

R v. Clare and Peach (1995) 2 Cr App R 333 (England and Wales)

R v. Clarke (1995) 2 Cr App R 425 (England and Wales)

R v. Dastagir (2013) SASC 26 (South Australia)

R v. Dodson and Williams (1984) 79 Cr App R 220 (England and Wales)

R v. Drollett (2005) NSWCCA 356 (New South Wales, Australia)

R v. Flynn (2008) EWCA Crim 970 (England and Wales)

R v. Fowden and White (1982) Crim LR 588 (England and Wales)

R v. Gardner (2004) EWCA Crim 1639 (England and Wales)

R v. Gray (2003) EWCA Crim 1001 (England and Wales)

R v. Honeysett (2014) HCA 29 (High Court of Australia)

R v. Leaney (1989) 2 S.C.R. 393 (Canada)

R v. Luttrell (2004) EWCA Crim 1344 (England and Wales)

R v. Marsh (2005) NSWCCA 331 (New South Wales, Australia)

R v. Nikolovski (1996) 3 S.C.R. 1197 (Canada)

R v. Rix (2005) NSWCCA 31 (New South Wales, Australia)

R v. Stockwell (1993) 97 Cr App R 260 (England and Wales)

R v. T (2010) EWCA Crim 2439 (England and Wales)

R v. Tang (2006) 65 NSWLR 681 (New South Wales, Australia)

R v. Tolson (1864) 4 F & F 103 (England and Wales)

R v. Turner (1975) QB 834 (England and Wales)

Ritz-Timme, S., Gabriel, P., Obertova, Z., Boguslavsky, M., Mayer, F., Drabik, A., ... Cattaneo, C. (2011a). A new atlas for the evaluation of facial features: Advantages, limits and applicability. *International Journal of Legal Medicine*, *125*, 301–306. doi:10.1007/s00414-010-0446-4.

Ritz-Timme, S., Gabriel, P., Tutkuviene, J., Poppa, P., Obertova, Z., Gibelli, D., ... Cattaneo, C. (2011b). Metric and morphological assessment of facial features: A study on three European populations. *Forensic Science International*, *207*, 239e1–239e8. doi:10.1016/j.forsciint.2011.01.035

Roelofse, M.M., Steyn, M., & Becker, P.J. (2008). Photo identification: Facial metrical and morphological features in South African males. *Forensic Science International*, *177*, 168–175. doi:10.1016/j.forsciint.2007.12.003

Scoleri, T., Lucas, T., & Henneberg, M. (2014). Effects of garments on photoanthropometry of body parts: Application to stature estimation. *Forensic Science International*, *237*, 148.e1–148.e12. doi:10.1016/j.forsciint.2013.12.038

Shaw, R.E., McIntyre, M., & Mace, W. (1974). The role of symmetry in event perception. In R.O.B. Macleod, & H.L. Pick (Eds.), *Perception: Essays in Honour of James J. Gibson* (pp. 276–310) Ithaca, NY: Cornell University Press.

Smith v. The Queen (2001) 206 CLR 650 (Australia)

Takema, Y., Yorimoto, Y., Kawai, M., & Imokawa, G. (1994). Age-related changes in the elastic properties and thickness of human facial skin. *British Journal of Dermatology*, *131*, 641–648. doi:10.1111/j.1365-2133.1994.tb04975.x

United States v. Smithers, 212 F.3d 306 (6th Cir. 2000) (USA)

Vanezis, P., & Brierley, C. (1996). Facial image comparison of crime suspects using video superimposition. *Science & Justice*, *36*, 27–33. doi:10.1016/S1355-0306(96)72551-0

Vanezis, P., Lu, D., Cockburn, J., Gonzalez, A., McCombe, G., Trujillo, O., & Vanezis, M. (1996). Morphological classification of facial features in adult Caucasian males based on an assessment of photographs. *Journal of Forensic Sciences*, *41*, 786–791. doi:10.1520/JFS13997J

Ventura, F., Zacheo, A., Ventura, A., & Pala, A. (2004). Computerized anthropomorphometric analysis of images: case report. *Forensic Science International*, *146*, S211–S213. doi:10.1016/j.forsciint.2004.09.065

Vorder Bruegge, R. (1999). Photographic identification of denim trousers from bank surveillance film. *Journal of Forensic Science*, *44*, 613–622.

Wisconsin v. Avery, N.W.2d 221 (Wis. Ct. App. 2012) (USA).

Yoshino, M., Matsuda, H., Kubota, S., Imaizumi, K., & Miyasaka, S. (2000). Computer-assisted facial image identification system using a 3D physiognomic range finder. *Forensic Science International*, *109*, 225–237. doi:10.1016/S0379-0738(00)00149-3

Yoshino, M., Noguchi, K., Atsuchi, M., Kubota, S., Imaizumi, K., Thomas, C.D.L., & Clement, J.G. (2002). Individual identification of disguised faces by morphometrical matching. *Forensic Science International*, *127*, 97–103. doi:10.1016/S0379-0738(02)00115-9

11

Evaluating Automatic Face Recognition Systems with Human Benchmarks

ALICE O'TOOLE AND P. JONATHON PHILLIPS

Face recognition for humans seems an effortless part of our everyday experience. Psychological studies have documented human expertise at face recognition and have argued for the "special" nature of our ability to represent and remember fine-scale configural information about individuals (cf., McKone & Robbins, 2011). Human face recognition can also be considered impressive in its ability to operate robustly in photometrically challenging conditions (e.g., poor illumination, low resolution, pose changes). By any measure of information quality, face recognition under these circumstances is extremely challenging. A careful look at the human face recognition literature, however, suggests that robust face recognition may be limited to the relatively small set of individuals we know or have seen frequently (Burton, Wilson, Cowan, & Bruce, 1999). Unfortunately, most forensic and security applications require recognition of unfamiliar people after only a brief personal encounter, or after seeing them in a single photograph or clip of surveillance video. In these cases, human performance is far below optimum. Understanding the differences between human skills with

Forensic Facial Identification: Theory and Practice of Identification from Eyewitnesses, Composites and CCTV, First Edition. Edited by Tim Valentine and Josh P. Davis.
© 2015 John Wiley & Sons, Ltd. Published 2015 by John Wiley & Sons, Ltd.

Case study

A "case study" for an automatic face recognition system is not quite the same as a case study for a human eyewitness. Indeed, we can assume that a face identification error made by a particular human eyewitness at a given point in time (e.g., 2014) is representative of human error potential at other points in time (e.g., 2016 or 1999). Human abilities change on an evolutionary timescale, with major updates to our "programming" detectable only over time differences on this scale. Computer-based face recognition systems, on the other hand, are constantly undergoing revisions to the algorithms that determine their behaviour. Between 1993 and 2010, the error rate[1] for state-of-the-art face recognition systems for frontal faces acquired in mobile studio or mugshot environments has halved every two years (Phillips, 2011). As such, the quantity and quality of errors that characterize face recognition algorithms are constantly in flux, and so the value of a particular case study for an algorithm in the field may be short-lived. Moreover, to the best of our knowledge, there are no peer-reviewed papers that document a particular success or failure of individual face recognition algorithm in the detail one expects for a social science case study. There are, however, a limited number of semi-official reports and press releases from state government offices that offer a glimpse into internal studies of the performance of face recognition systems. Our goal here is to consider one of these reports, not so much as a case study, but as a broader look at the performance of a particular face recognition system "in the field".

Face recognition algorithms are now applied routinely in the US for a variety of applications, including driver's licence registries. A *Washington Post* article published in 2013 reported that 37 of the 50 states have facial recognition software for use with their state driver's licence registries (Timber & Nakashima, 2013). They report that at least 26 of these states now allow state, local, or federal law enforcement officials to search or "request to search" these databases to find the identities of people "considered relevant to investigations". Given this widespread use, reports of successes and failures of computer-based face recognition systems are appearing with increasing regularity in the media. Here, we consider a report pre-

---

[1]Specifically, the error rate referred to is the false reject rate at a false accept rate of 1 in 1000.

pared about the performance of face recognition software used by that state's Department of Motor Vehicles (DMV).[2] The findings of this report are widely available in the form of a press release from the New York State Governor's office.[3] The report was generated by the DMV in collaboration with the University at Albany's Institute for Traffic Safety Management and Research (ITSMR).

The findings of the study paint a picture of how law enforcement makes active use of face recognition software, both incidentally and by design. According to Governor Cuomo's press release, the New York DMV began using facial recognition software in February 2010. The performance review included new photos taken continuously by the DMV in addition to the more than 20 million images already in the DMV's database. It is important to note that the main law enforcement application of the technology is to detect identity fraud, which commonly takes the form of an individual attempting to obtain multiple official identity documents (driver's licences) under different names. In the US, driver's licences are used routinely as official identity cards. Driver's licences are checked as a matter of course when a person opens a bank account, obtains a credit card, or withdraws money from existing accounts. Thus, assuring the validity of driver's licences can be important for preventing identity theft.

In the first three years following the introduction of face recognition technology, the DMV investigated more than 13,000 possible cases of identity fraud. Of these, over 2500 resulted in an arrest and more than 5000 cases resulted in administrative action. Among those individuals found by the software to have multiple drivers' licences, 70% had one or more other licences that had been suspended or revoked. In the majority of cases, the licences were revoked or suspended for reckless or impaired driving. The remaining 30% of cases involved people who had multiple valid licences, for unspecified reasons. Turning to the most serious crimes, the press report cites five cases where the face recognition technology identified people charged with felony-level crimes, including a school bus driver with a history of reckless driving and drug offences, as well as an individual accused of Social Security fraud for more than $500,000.

---

[2]*Face Recognition Program: Traffic Safety Implications, The First Three Years* (February 2010–January 2013), New York State, DMV and the University of Albany, State University of New York.
[3]Governor Cuomo announces 13,000 identity fraud cases investigated by DMV using facial recognition technology, Albany NY (March 5, 2013). Retrieved from https://www.governor.ny.gov/press/03042013-dmv-cuomo-faces

Although anecdotal reports of success and failure in solving crimes make for interesting reading in the media (e.g., Stanley, 2009), the widespread and routine use of face recognition systems in driver databases strongly suggests the need to assess the accuracy of these systems using systematic, scientific methods. These government commissioned reports, conducted in collaboration with universities, are a good start. Unfortunately, similar accurate and comprehensive data on the number of searches conducted and/or number of successful and failed searches are not available for most face recognition technology applications. The wealth of real-world data produced by these systems can now provide us with an informative and intriguing look at the current state-of-the-art in computer-based face recognition. These data could provide a treasure trove of information for operational and social science researchers.

familiar and unfamiliar faces may be the key to advancing the next generation of computer-based face recognition systems.

Notwithstanding the differences between familiar and unfamiliar face recognition skills, human performance is often considered the gold standard against which machines must compete. Over the last two decades, however, international tests of computer-based face recognition algorithms have shown steady improvements in accuracy with increasingly challenging photometric conditions. Indeed, the most recent comparisons between humans and algorithms show that the best algorithms compete favourably with humans when recognizing frontal images of faces – even across substantial changes in illumination, facial expression and appearance. We review these comparisons considering both quantitative and qualitative benchmarks for evaluating performance on identification tasks. In this chapter, we will argue that machine-based face recognition of frontal faces, taken with digital single lens reflex cameras, is now at the same level as human recognition of unfamiliar people. It is from this perspective that human benchmarks are relevant for measuring the performance of face recognition algorithms. One commonly applied criterion states that, to be useful in real-world applications, machines must be able to perform at or above the level of humans on the task of unfamiliar face recognition. Although we commonly compare face recognition algorithms with each other, only recently have we undertaken systematic comparisons between humans and machines on identical problems and with identical stimulus sets. Our goal here is to review a series of comparisons between humans and state-of-the-art face recognition algorithms from international competitions conducted over the last decade. The studies we present offer both quantitative and qualitative benchmarks for algorithms. The quantitative benchmarks consist of head-to-head comparisons of humans and machines on the same set of stimuli. The qualitative benchmarks include comparisons based on variable demographics (e.g., consistency of performance over different ethnicities of faces) and on the nature of the information that contributes to recognition. Combined, the goal is to understand the strengths and weakness of humans and machines across a variety of operating conditions.

The chapter is organized as follows. First, we begin with a brief background on the face recognition competitions that are the source of data for these comparisons. Second, we detail human–machine comparisons over the time period from 2005 to present. At the outset, we note that the state-of-the-art for algorithms over this time-span is fluid, as algorithms have continued to improve on a variety of face and person recognition tasks. We trace these improvements as algorithms have taken on increasingly difficult identification problems. *Difficulty* in these tests is defined operationally by the test images, which have become progressively more challenging over the years by using increased variability in illumination, expression, distance, and resolution.

Third, we discuss a technique for statistically combining (or fusing) human and machine judgments to achieve better performance than that achievable with either "system" operating alone. For one set of applications, humans and machines will work together on face recognition tasks, and so it is important to consider how to combine uncertain identity judgments and how to resolve disagreements between humans and machines when they arise. Fourth, we look at how qualitative factors, such as the demographic diversity of the target population, can impact upon the performance of algorithms. This factor is highly relevant in predicting how well machines will perform in any given application. In the final section of the paper, we consider the next step for algorithms to meet the challenges of current and future applications.

INTRODUCTION TO INTERNATIONAL TESTS OF FACE RECOGNITION ALGORITHMS

Over the last two decades, the US government has organized international competitions for face recognition algorithms with the stated goal of pushing algorithm developers to take on progressively more difficult problems. Since 2002, the tests have been organized and implemented at the National Institute of Standards and Technology (NIST). These competitions began with the Facial Recognition Technology (FERET) evaluations between 1993 and 1996 (Phillips, Moon, Rizvi, & Rauss, 2000), and have continued with the Face Recognition Vendor Test (FRVT) 2000 (Blackburn, Bone, & Phillips, 2001), the FRVT 2002 (Phillips *et al.*, 2003), the Face Recognition Grand Challenge 2005 (Phillips, Flynn, Scruggs, Bowyer & Worek, 2006), the FRVT 2006 (Phillips *et al.*, 2010b), the Multiple Biometrics Grand Challenge 2008–2009 (Phillips *et al.*, 2009), and the Multiple Biometric Evaluation (MBE) 2010 (Grother, Quinn, & Phillips, 2010). The test that is currently underway is the Point and Shoot Challenge (PaSC), which began in mid-2013 (Beveridge *et al.*, 2013). This most recent challenge is aimed at evaluating algorithm performance on images and videos from hand-held smartphone cameras.

In all but the FERET test, the competitions have been open to algorithm developers internationally and have typically garnered participation from the best algorithms available at the time of each test. Although the earlier tests consisted mostly of competitors in academia, the more recent participants are mostly commercial algorithms. It is worth noting that to accommodate the need to protect proprietary software in commercial systems, the test protocol has involved installing executable code on computers at the NIST. In other words, the organizers of the tests do not have direct access to the source code for the algorithms. Thus, although the performance of the algorithms in the competition has been studied intensively, the algorithms themselves are black boxes. On the good side, the need to accommodate proprietary algorithms indicates that automatic face recognition technology now supports viable commercial products. On the down side, from the point of view of psychologists and computer vision researchers, clear knowledge of precisely *how* image processing has improved over the years of these competitions cannot be ascertained directly from the results of the competitions.

In all of the tests we consider in this chapter, the test protocol is straightforward. We outline this protocol here and fill in relevant details for the individual tests as we proceed. The NIST face-recognition tests report performance on a wide variety of data-sets, which include both operational and laboratory-collected databases. We provide information on the data-sets used in results reported in this chapter. The first step in preparing a test is for NIST to assemble a very large dataset (usually in excess of 20,000 images), taken under conditions specified by the test (e.g., passport-style images, images with uncontrolled indoor illumination, etc.). These data-sets always include multiple images of each person, taken over weeks, months, and sometimes up to a year. This allows for natural variation in appearance (e.g., due to changes in hairstyle, clothing, etc.). Second, the task of the algorithm is to determine whether two images show the *same person* or *different people*. This identity-matching task is highly relevant for applications in processing visas, making comparisons with images from watch lists of crime suspects, and for a host of other common forensic and security tasks.

The identity-matching task is implemented for algorithms as follows. Each algorithm computes a similarity matrix, s, consisting of an algorithm-computed similarity between all possible pairs of faces in the dataset. Most of these pairs show different identities, but many of the paired images show the same person. In the similarity matrix, the entry $s_{i,j}$ contains an algorithm's rating of similarity of the people in the ith and jth image. Higher scores indicate a greater likelihood that two images show the same person. This yields a distribution of similarity scores for same-identity image pairs and a distribution of similarity scores for different-identity image pairs for each algorithm. The machine's overall accuracy is assessed by looking at how "separable" the similarity scores are for the pairs of images with the same identity and the pairs of images with different identities. When there is good performance, the similarity scores for same-identity pairs are generally higher than the similarity scores for different-identity pairs. More formally, the performance of the algorithm can be summarized in signal detection terms (Green & Swets, 1966). Specifically, a d' is computed as the distance between the means of the same- and different-identity distributions. A large d' indicates that the same-identity pairs are assigned much higher similarity scores than the different-identity pairs. A d' of zero indicates chance performance with similarity scores for the same- and different-identity pairs roughly described by the same distribution. To compute d' for a machine, one first sets a threshold similarity score. Pairs with similarity scores greater than the threshold are judged to be the same identity and pairs with scores lower than the threshold are judged to be different identities. Next one computes a hit rate and false alarm rate. The hit rate is the proportion of same-identity image pairs with similarity scores greater than the threshold. These are *correct* answers for same-identity pairs. The false alarm rate is the proportion of different-identity image pairs with similarity scores greater than the threshold. These are *incorrect* answers for different-identity pairs.

The final step in the process is to characterize performance across all possible thresholds. This is possible because the entire distribution of similarity scores is available from the algorithm. The common way to do this is with a *receiver operating characteristic* (ROC) curve. This shows the performance across the full range of threshold values. We will illustrate these kinds of curves in different places in this chapter and will describe and interpret these graphs in more detail when we present them.

Testing humans in a way that produces data that can be compared directly with the algorithm data is straightforward. To obtain a human-generated similarity score, participants view pairs of images, side-by-side, on a computer screen and are asked to respond, on a 5-point rating scale that ranges from "1: sure they are the same person" to "5: sure they are different people". In this way, humans produce a similarity score for each pair of images. In this case, low ratings indicate high-rated similarities. These data are identical in form to the data produced by the algorithms, with a distribution of similarity scores for same-identity pairs and a distribution for different-identity pairs. An ROC curve can therefore be used to summarize human performance on a subset of the image pairs scored by the algorithms. This gives us the same kind of format to compare the performance of humans and machines.

COMPARING THE PERFORMANCE OF HUMANS AND FACE RECOGNITION ALGORITHMS

Starting with the Face Recognition Grand Challenge (FRGC) in 2005, we conducted a series of head-to-head comparisons between humans and machines. In the first study, we started with the most challenging FRGC test, a comparison of identity between image pairs with one image taken under controlled illumination (e.g., a passport-style picture) and the other image taken indoors in a corridor under uncontrolled illumination (O'Toole et al., 2007b). Two example image pairs appear in Figure 11.1. It is worth noting that the image pairs differ strongly in illumination, but also (potentially) in expression. In all cases, however, the face is viewed from the front. In the experiments we present, paired images of the same person were always taken on different days. Thus, there were no clothing or accessory cues as to identity.

Algorithms in the FRCG were tested on all possible pairs of 16,028 controlled illumination images and 8014 uncontrolled illumination images, for a total of 128,424,350 comparisons.[4] Seven algorithms were tested on this challenge problem. For the experiments with human participants, we prescreened two sets of image comparisons based on their difficulty for a baseline algorithm. *Difficult* same-identity image pairs had similarity scores less than two standard deviations below the average score for the same-person match pairs (i.e., dissimilar images

---

[4]This was FRCG Experiment 4.

(a)

(b)

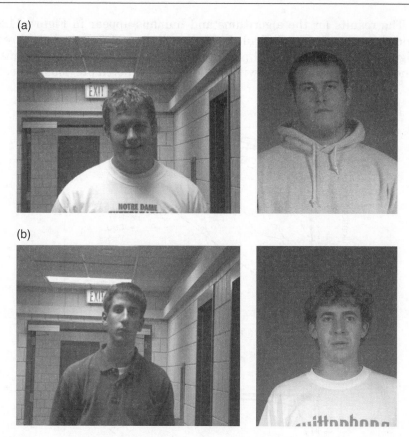

Figure 11.1 Two example pairs of images from the human–machine comparisons in O'Toole *et al.* (2007b) are shown. The images on the left are taken under uncontrolled illumination and the images on the right are taken in controlled illumination. Humans are asked whether the people in each pair are the same person or different people. From O'Toole, Phillips, Jiang, Ayyad, Pénard, and Abdi (2007b). Reproduced with permission from IEEE.

of the same person). *Easy* same-identity pairs were image pairs of the same person with similarity scores greater than two standard deviations above the mean similarity score for the same-person pairs (i.e., highly similar images of the same person). Difficult and easy different-identity pairs were chosen analogously to yield similar pictures of different people and dissimilar pictures of different people, respectively. In the experiment, participants judged 240 pairs of images, half in the easy condition and half in the difficult condition. The algorithms' similarity scores for these 240 pairs of images were extracted from the overall similarity matrix they produced.

because the task was seen as beyond the abilities of lay jurors and judges. In so doing, our courts have allowed those without demonstrated expertise, and who have not tested their techniques, to provide opinions about the identity of persons in images. These analysts frequently identify, or suggest the identity of, individuals accused of the most serious crimes, and the courts have gradually developed a range of naïve responses to some of the most obvious criticisms. They have consistently demonstrated their inability to understand the importance of validation studies, measuring error rates, and the desirability of shielding analysts from suggestive information or environments. Instead of relying upon experimental evidence to develop reliable standards and practices that should be in place as a condition of admissibility, courts around the world have preferred to rely upon cross-examination and witness demeanour, the occasional use of rebuttal witnesses, and judicial directions as a means of overcoming the lack of rigorous scientific research. Legal responses to identification evidence of offenders from images reinforce the need to require expert evidence in criminal proceedings to be demonstrably reliable as a condition of admissibility (*Daubert v. Merrell Dow Pharamaceuticals Inc.*, 1993; Edmond, 2008; Law Commission, 2011). Given the current situation, courts should be cautious about the admission and use of the opinions of analysts presented as facial comparison experts.

REFERENCES

Attorney-General's Reference (2003) *No 2 of 2002*. EWCA Crim 2373 (England and Wales).

Bogan, P., & Roberts, A. (2011). *Identification: Investigation, Trial and Scientific Evidence*. Bristol: Jordan Publishing.

Bridge, R. (2009). Technique maps crash suspect. *BBC News*, October 21 2009. Retrieved from http://news.bbc.co.uk/1/hi/uk/8317887.stm

Bromby, M.C. (2003). At face value? *New Law Journal Expert Witness Supplement*, *28*, 302–303.

Bruce, V., Henderson, Z., Greenwood, K., Hancock, P.J.B., Burton, A.M., & Miller, P. (1999). Verification of face identities from images captured on video. *Journal of Experimental Psychology: Applied*, *5*, 339–360. doi:10.1037/1076-898X.5.4.339

Bruce V., Henderson, Z., Newman, C., & Burton, A.M. (2001). Matching identities of familiar and unfamiliar faces caught on CCTV images. *Journal of Experimental Psychology: Applied*, *73*, 207–218. doi:10.1037/1076-898X.7.3.207

Burton, A.M., Miller, P., Bruce V., Hancock, P.J.B., & Henderson Z. (2001). Human and automatic face recognition: a comparison across image formats. *Vision Research*, *41*, 3185–3195. doi:10.1016/S0042-6989(01)00186-9

Burton, A.M., Wilson, S., Cowan, M., & Bruce, V. (1999). Face recognition in poor-quality video: Evidence from security surveillance. *Psychological Science*, *10*, 243–248. doi:10.1111/1467-9280.00144

Cattaneo, C., Ritz-Timme, S., Gabriel, P., Gibelli, D., Giudici, E., Poppa, P., ... Grandi, M. (2009). The difficult issue of age assessment on pedo-pornographic

The results for the algorithms and humans appear in Figure 11.2 and show that for the difficult face pairs (Figure 11.2a), the best three algorithms from the FRCG performed more accurately than humans. The results are illustrated with ROC curves. As noted previously, these

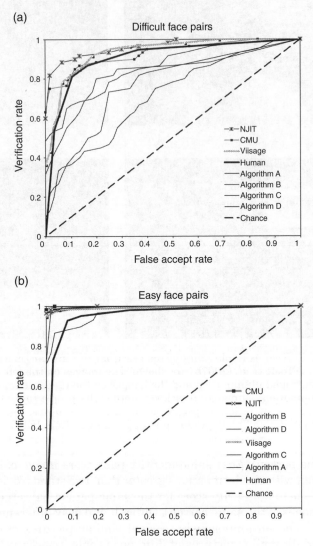

Figure 11.2 The results of the human–machine comparisons for (a) the difficult face pairs and (b) the easy face pairs from O'Toole *et al.* (2007b). The best three algorithms are more accurate than humans on the difficult face pairs, and all but one algorithm is more accurate on the easy pairs. From O'Toole, Phillips, Jiang, Ayyad, Pénard, and Abdi (2007b). Reproduced with permission from IEEE.

curves plot the proportion of hits and false alarms across a range of thresholds. Chance performance is indicated with a dotted diagonal line across the graph. The closer the curves are to the top left corner, the better the performance. As can be seen, for the difficult face pairs, humans are less accurate than three algorithms and more accurate than four other algorithms. For the easy pairs, all but one algorithm surpassed humans (Figure 11.2b). At the time, the results of O'Toole *et al.* (2007b) were somewhat surprising. They indicated that the best face recognition algorithms, circa 2005, were competitive with humans on a task that neither humans nor machines performed at ceiling. We replicated this result with a new set of images and algorithms in the FRVT 2006 test (O'Toole, Phillips, & Narvekar, 2008). Again, the best algorithms surpassed humans on this challenging task.

Moving the clock forward to 2010, the difficulty of the problem was increased for face recognition algorithms by introducing more variation into the image pairs. Notably, the NIST test included images taken outdoors under highly variable illumination conditions. Indoor images with both controlled and uncontrolled illumination were included. One goal was to dissect the performance of algorithms according to levels of difficulty. These levels were labelled by NIST as the "Good, Bad, and Ugly" of face recognition algorithm performance (Phillips *et al.*, 2011). To define difficulty for computer-based face recognition at a level of abstraction beyond a single algorithm, Phillips *et al.* (2011) statistically fused the similarity scores from three top-performing algorithms to create performance stratifications for the fused algorithm. This fused algorithm was used to select stimulus sets for which the algorithm identified people with good, moderate and poor accuracy.

More concretely, the stratification process was implemented as follows. The data-set contained hundreds of pictures of each person. Thus, each of the many pairings of a person with himself/herself produced a similarity score. These scores were ranked for each person and the rankings were partitioned into three parts: the *good* (the top performance partition), the *moderate* (the middle performance partition), and the *poor* (the lowest performance partition) image pairs. Figure 11.3 shows six images of the same person: column 1 shows a pair from the good condition; column 2 shows a pair from the moderate condition; and column 3 shows a pair from the poor condition.

To test the extent to which the algorithm stratifications were relevant for predicting the difficulty of these images for humans, O'Toole, An, Dunlop, Natu, and Phillips (2012b) tested humans using a subset of image pairs from these stratifications. The results showed, first, that the algorithm-based stratifications were relevant for humans. Second, O'Toole *et al.* (2012b) compared the performance of humans and

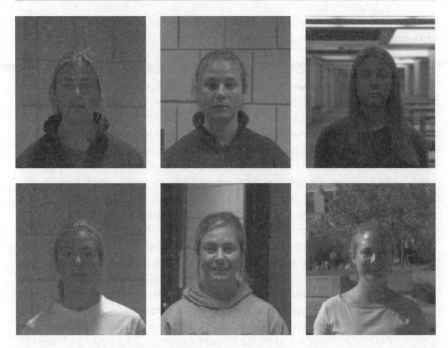

Figure 11.3 Six images of the same person are shown. Pairs of images are arranged in columns (left to right), according to algorithm performance, (left: good, middle: moderate, right: difficult) (cf. O'Toole *et al.*, 2012b).

algorithms on the three levels of difficulty. Algorithms were more accurate than humans in the good and moderate conditions, but were comparable to humans in the poor accuracy conditions. It is also worth noting that even though the algorithms performed with low accuracy on the "poor" image pairs, the performance of humans was not more accurate than the performance of algorithms.

The finding that machines were never less accurate than humans on these challenging frontal images suggested that face recognition systems may be ready for applications with comparable difficulty – specifically matching unfamiliar identities in frontal facial images that vary in illumination. However, a more recent study suggests that this conclusion is premature. Rice, Phillips, Natu, An, and O'Toole (2013) examined the worst-case scenario for the algorithms, using the following method. As noted, the fused algorithm produces a distribution of similarity scores for same-identity image pairs and a distribution of similarity scores for different-identity image pairs. A schematic of these distributions appears in Figure 11.4a. To find highly dissimilar images of the same person, Rice *et al.* (2013) sampled from the extreme left of the same-

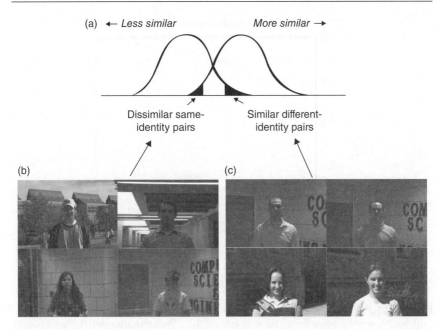

Figure 11.4 A schematic of the distribution of scores for the same- and different-identity pairs is shown (a). Sampling of dissimilar same-identities produces the example pairs on the left (b), and sampling of similar different identity pairs appears on the right (c) (cf. Rice *et al*., 2013).

identity distribution (e.g., Figure 11.4b). To find highly similar images of different people, they sampled pairs from the extreme right of the different-identity distribution (e.g., Figure 11.4c). Given the very large number of image pairs available (>1 million), it was possible to select a relatively large set of image pairs such that the similarity scores of the same-identity pairs are uniformly lower than the similarity scores of the different identity pairs. By definition, the algorithm is 100% *incorrect* at the task of identity matching with these image pairs.

Rice *et al*. (2013) asked whether humans would fare better than algorithms on these challenging stimuli. Although far from perfect, humans performed well above chance with these images (see Figure 11.5). One issue that complicates the simple interpretation of these results is that face recognition algorithms use only the face, ignoring other identity information in the external head (hair) as well as in the body (neck, shoulders, torso, etc.). The images presented to human participants by Rice *et al*. showed the upper body, torso and neck in most cases. To determine whether this extra non-facial information contributed to performance, Rice *et al*. tested new participants on the identity-matching

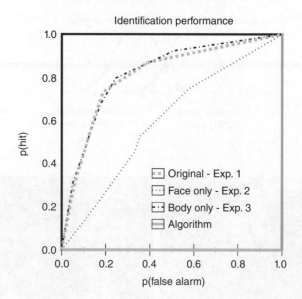

Identification performance

Figure 11.5 Human performance for the original images, face-only images, and body-only images from Rice *et al.* (2013). Performance with this special sample of images indicates that performance on the original images is due to the information in the body (see text).

task with images edited to present only the face or the body. The results were striking. Performance with only the body was nearly identical to performance with the entire image, whereas performance with only the face was barely above chance. Moreover, participants who performed the matching with the full images reported relying almost exclusively on the features in the internal face for their judgments. In a final experiment, Rice *et al.* (2013) used an item analysis to select image pairs that were matched more accurately with the face-only images than with the body-only images (i.e., *face-informative* stimuli) and pairs. Next they selected stimuli that were matched more accurately with the body-only than with the face-only images (i.e., *body-informative* stimuli). Eye tracking revealed a subtle, but measureable, shift in the proportion of fixations to the face, *toward the body* when the body was more informative.

The results of Rice *et al.* (2013) suggest that the accuracy advantage seen for people over the algorithm in these challenging cases came, not from information in the face, but rather from the information in the body. In fact, the use of the body accounted completely for performance with the original images. Notably, although people were not aware of using this information, eye movement patterns accurately reflected the human processing strategy.

It is perhaps worth noting briefly that despite the potential of the body and gait to offer useful information about a person's identity, there are only a handful of computer-based recognition systems that use this information. These systems are under development, and are currently research efforts rather than mature commercial systems.

Summary

In quantitative terms, the best face-recognition algorithms now compare favourably to humans across a range of viewing conditions. These conditions include variations in illumination between passport-style images (controlled indoor illumination) and uncontrolled indoor and outdoor illumination. Notably, commercial algorithms have not yet solved the problem of face recognition from viewpoints other than the frontal image. This has largely limited their application to controlled environments and cooperative subjects, willing to comply with instructions, while being photographed (e.g., points of entry at border crossings, mugshots, and applications where people can be asked to face toward a camera).

QUALITATIVE COMPARISONS BETWEEN HUMANS AND FACE RECOGNITION ALGORITHMS

Do machines and people use similar strategies to recognize faces? One approach to addressing this question is to determine whether humans and machines make the same kinds of errors. We used the similarity scores generated by humans and the seven FRGC algorithms compared in O'Toole et al. (2007b) to address this question. Specifically, in a follow-up on the human–machine comparison, O'Toole, Abdi, Jiang, and Phillips (2007a) used a statistical fusion approach to determine the extent to which the algorithms and humans generated similar patterns of errors. Statistical fusion is a method commonly used in biometrics for combining multiple, but imperfect, estimates of identity from different sources (e.g., fingerprints, iris, etc.). In general, the approach is to train a statistical learning algorithm to map estimates of identity generated by the different sources (e.g., fingerprints, iris, face) to the actual identity status of a person. Once the mapping formula is learned with training data, the formula can be evaluated for accuracy using novel data. In practical terms, fusion is considered successful when the combination of identity estimates performs better than any individual estimate from a single source. In more theoretical terms, fusion improves performance when the source estimates are based on information that is at least partially independent. Thus, O'Toole *et al.* (2007a) reasoned that fusion would improve performance if the strategies of algorithms and humans were sufficiently different to produce diverse patterns of errors.

The statistical fusion was first applied to combine the seven algorithms and succeeded in cutting the error rate of the fused system by comparison to the best performance algorithm. Specifically, the 6% error rate for the fusion of the seven algorithms was half that of the best-performing algorithm operating alone. Next, human similarity estimates were fused with the estimates of the seven algorithms. The performance of this fusion produced nearly perfect performance. These two fusion experiments suggest diversity of strategy both among the algorithms tested and across the algorithms and humans. The study further suggests that optimal combinations of human and machine decisions will result in performance that is more accurate than either the humans or machines operating alone.

Another way to approach qualitative differences for humans and machines is to consider some well-known characteristics of human memory for faces that seem to be particularly "human". One such phenomenon is the cross-ethnicity effect, whereby people recognize faces of their own ethnicity more accurately than faces of other ethnicities (Malpass & Kravitz, 1969). Although there are several possible explanations for the cross-ethnicity effect, most reference one's experience or learning history with own- versus other-ethnicity faces. This literature is complex and beyond the scope of this chapter. Suffice to say that contact with cross-ethnicity faces is an important prerequisite for the cross-ethnicity effect, but the timing of this contact may be crucial for producing the effect. In particular, most theories now suggest that limited contact with other-ethnicity faces early in development, when neural feature tuning is at its most plastic, is the best predictor of an own-ethnicity face recognition advantage in adulthood (cf. Nelson, 2001; O'Toole & Natu, 2013). Indeed, computational models of the cross-ethnicity effect endorse this perspective, showing that, in principle, an imbalance in the ethnicity of faces used to tune the feature selection for face recognition algorithms produces differences in the accuracy with which algorithms recognize faces of different ethnicities (Furl, Phillips, & O'Toole, 2002; O'Toole & Natu, 2013).

More recently, Phillips, Narvekar, Jiang, and O'Toole (2010a) examined face-recognition algorithms from the FRVT 2006 to determine whether they show a cross-ethnicity effect. In this case, the ethnicity of the algorithm was defined as the geographical origin of the algorithm (i.e., where it was developed). The FRVT 2006 included eight algorithms from Western countries (France, $n = 2$; Germany, $n = 4$; the US, $n = 2$) and five algorithms from countries in East Asia (China, $n = 2$; Japan, $n = 2$; Korea, $n = 1$). In order to get a general assessment of the problem, beyond specific algorithms, Phillips *et al.* (2010a) created a Western fusion algorithm by combining the similarity scores of the eight algorithms from Western countries, and an East Asian fusion algorithm by combining the similarity scores of the five algorithms from East Asian countries. The algorithms were then scored separately on their accuracy at matching pairs of Caucasian and East Asian faces. The results of this comparison yielded the classic cross-ethnicity effect, with the Western algorithms performing more accurately on the Caucasian faces and the East Asian algorithm performing more accurately on the East Asian faces.

As noted at the outset, the algorithm competitions have access only to executable versions of the programs. From these results, therefore, it is impossible to know precisely why an algorithm shows a cross-ethnicity effect. It is tempting to assume that most of these algorithms are "trained", or at least optimized, using available pre-existing data-sets of faces, and that there is a tendency to source these data-sets locally. This kind of biased training might produce a cross-ethnicity effect. However, in the context of the present study, it is not possible to know this for certain.

A recent study of computational models of the cross-ethnicity effect by Klare, Burge, Klontz, Vorder Bruegge, and Jain (2012) gets closer to the computational causes of the effect. They examined the effects of demographics on the performance of six face-recognition algorithms. Their strategy was to compare three commercial "off-the-shelf" (COTS) algorithms (Cognitec's FaceVACS v.8.2, PittPatt v.5.2.2, and Neurotechnology's MegaMatcher v.3.1) with algorithms implemented "in-house" by the researchers.[5] Although it is possible that the COTS make use of training regimes, Klare *et al.* (2012) were not able to alter that training. Two in-house algorithms consisted of a local binary pattern and a Gabor feature representation model. Both of these are "non-trainable" algorithms. Finally, a trainable algorithm developed in-house by Klare *et al.* (2012) was implemented. This was a spectrally sampled, structural subspace feature (4SF) algorithm. Klare *et al.* (2012) used this combination of controlled trainable and non-trainable algorithms to test hypotheses about the computational mechanisms that underlie the other-ethnicity effect. They used a large multi-ethnicity

---

[5]The identification of any commercial product or trade name does not imply endorsement or recommendation by NIST.

database of black, Hispanic and white faces, with males and females, of three age groups (18–30, 30–50 and 50–70 years). The COTS algorithms all performed less accurately on three demographic groups: females, blacks, and the youngest age subjects. This might suggest that these commercial algorithms had limited experience with faces from those demographic groups. Klare *et al.* (2012) then tested to see whether demographic-specific training could improve performance. They trained their 4SF algorithm with a multi-ethnic data-set and compared it with multiple versions of the algorithm that trained with specific demographic groups. In other words, these latter implementations were specialized for recognizing specific demographic groups of faces. Indeed, the results showed that specialized demographic-specific systems performed best with the faces that matched the training.

Although some of the results of the cross-ethnicity effect are predictable, the use of training regimes in pattern classifiers is common in published face-recognition algorithms. Thus, one would expect performance to be best when the stimuli are similar to the stimuli used to train the algorithm. In more pragmatic terms, however, developers of commercial face-recognition systems must create performance specifications (i.e., "specs") that tell the customer how well the algorithm will perform in various test scenarios. Imagine the test context for a face-recognition algorithm at any international airport – for example, Zurich, Switzerland. The demographic profile of people at the airport will change by time of day (e.g., flights from North America arrive in the morning, flights from the Far East arrive in the evening, etc.), the time of year (e.g., tourist season), and during special events (e.g., the Olympics).

Predicting the expected performance of an algorithm under arbitrary shifts in the demographic diversity of the population is a challenging and as yet unsolved problem (cf. O'Toole, Phillips, An, & Dunlop, 2012b, for experiments and an overview of the issue). One of the most difficult parts of this prediction issue comes from the fact that the performance of algorithms is measured using a signal detection approach whereby both hits (i.e., correct match of a same-identity pair of images) and false alarms (i.e., the incorrect match of a different-identity pair) contribute to a performance score. The diversity of the background population has a direct effect on the similarity scores in the different-identity distribution. This is because pairs of images that show people of different ethnicities, ages, or genders, are less similar, on average, than pairs of images that show people with matching demographics. Therefore, the overlap of the same- and different-identity distributions changes as a function of the assumptions made about image pairs in the *different-identity* distribution. The complexity of the problem requires rigorous field tests to get a handle on what to expect from any given algorithm, under particular test scenarios that involve changes in the representation of different demographic groups.

NEXT GENERATION ALGORITHMS: CHALLENGES AND PROMISE

In summary, we have argued that the performance of the best current algorithms compare favourably with humans identifying relatively unfamiliar faces. The caveats to this assertion are that these algorithms are strictly limited to face recognition from frontally facing images taken with a digital single lens reflex camera. Within that realm, algorithms can now cope with a range of illumination conditions and with appearance changes, including facial expression. Looking toward the future, the next generation of algorithms will have to begin to operate more like humans recognizing familiar faces. Perhaps it is possible to go even beyond this to the performance levels shown by putative "super-recognizers" (Russell, Duchaine, & Nakayama, 2009), who seem to score consistently higher on face recognition tasks than other people. These levels of performance may require more than just improvements in processing. Our best guess is that the most successful algorithms will use, not more processing, but more data. Part of the power of human recognition for familiar faces is that we have varied and diverse experience with familiar faces. We see familiar faces from many viewpoints, across a range of distances, and with occlusion. A study by Burton, Jenkins, Hancock, and White (2005) demonstrated the benefits of deriving a representation of a person based on averaged images, taken from a frontal viewpoint. This proved a powerful strategy for increasing recognition accuracy. How we harness this experience to build face representations that operate robustly across image variations (including viewpoint) is not well understood, even after two decades of psychological study. Both psychologists and computer vision researchers need to think about how data (many pictures and videos) can be used to create representations that generalize across viewing conditions. Only when machines can perform with generalization across challenging conditions will they compare to humans at their best.

REFERENCES

Beveridge, J.R., Phillips, P.J., Bolme, D., Draper, B.A., Givens, G.H., Lui, Y.M., ... Cheng, S. (2013). The challenge of face recognition from digital point-and-shoot cameras. In *Proceedings of the IEEE Sixth International Conference of Biometrics: Technology, Applications, and Systems*.

Blackburn, D., Bone, J.M., & Phillips, P.J. (2001). *FRVT 2000 Evaluation Report*, Tech. Report. Retrieved from http://face.nist.gov

Burton, A.M., Jenkins, R., Hancock, P.J.B., & White, D. (2005). Robust representations for face recognition: The power of averages. *Cognitive Psychology, 51*, 256–284. doi:10.1016/j.cogpsych.2005.06.003

Burton, A.M., Wilson, S., Cowan, M., & Bruce, V. (1999). Face recognition in poor-quality video. *Psychological Science, 10*, 243–248. doi: 10.1111/1467-9280.00144

Furl, N., Phillips, P.J., & O'Toole, A.J. (2002). Face recognition algorithms as models of the other-race effect. *Cognitive Science, 96*, 1–19. doi:10.1207/s15516709cog2606_4

Green, D.M., & Swets, J.A. (1966). *Signal Detection Theory and Psychophysics*. New York: John Wiley & Sons, Ltd.

Grother, P. Quinn, G.W., & Phillips, P.J. (2010). Multiple Biometric Evaluation (MBE) 2010: report of the evaluation of 2D still image face recognition algorithms. *National Institute of Standards and Technology Report, NISTIR 7709*. Retrieved from http://face.nist.gov.

Klare, B.F., Burge, M., Klontz, J., Vorder Bruegge, R.W., & Jain, A.K. (2012) Face recognition performance: Role of demographic information. *IEEE Transactions on Information Forensics and Security, 7*, 1789–1801.

Malpass, R.S., & Kravitz, J. (1969). Recognition for faces of own and other race. *Journal of Personality and Social Psychology, 13*, 330–334.

McKone, E. & Robbins, R. (2011). Are faces special? In A. Calder, G. Rhodes, M. Johnson, & J.V. Haxby (Eds.), *Oxford Handbook of Face Perception* (pp. 149–176). Oxford: Oxford University Press:

Nelson, C.A. (2001). The development and neural bases of face recognition. *Infant and Child Development, 10*, 3–18. doi:10.1002/icd.239

O'Toole, A.J., Abdi, H., Jiang, F., & Phillips, P.J. (2007a). Fusing face recognition algorithms and humans. *IEEE: Transactions on Systems, Man & Cybernetics, 37*, 1149–1155.

O'Toole, A.J., An, X., Dunlop, J., Natu, V., & Phillips, P.J. (2012a) Comparing face recognition algorithms to humans on challenging tasks. *ACM Transactions on Applied Perception, 9*, 1–13.

O'Toole, A.J., & Natu, V. (2013). Computational perspectives on the other race effect. *Visual Cognition, 9–10*, 1121–1137. doi:10.1080/13506285.2013.803505

O'Toole, A.J., Phillips, P.J., An, X., & Dunlop, J. (2012b). Demographic effects on estimates of automatic face recognition. *Image & Vision Computing, 30*, 169–176. doi:10.1016/j.imavis.2011.12.007

O'Toole, A.J., Phillips, P.J., Jiang, F., Ayyad, J., Pénard, N., & Abdi, H. (2007b). Face recognition algorithms surpass humans matching faces across changes in illumination. *IEEE: Transactions on Pattern Analysis and Machine Intelligence, 29*, 1642–1646.

O'Toole, A.J., Phillips, P.J., & Narvekar, A. (2008). Humans versus algorithms: Comparisons from the Face Recognition Vendor Test 2006. In *Proceedings of the 8th IEEE International Conference on Automatic Face and Gesture Recognition*.

Phillips, P.J. (2011). *Improving face recognition technology*. IEEE Computer, March, 84–86.

Phillips, P.J., Beveridge, J.R, Draper, B.A., Givens, G., O'Toole, A.J., Bolme, D.S., ... Weimer, S. (2011). An introduction to the Good, the Bad, and the Ugly Face

Recognition Challenge problem. In *Proceedings of the Ninth IEEE International Conference on Automatic Face and Gesture Recognition.*

Phillips, P.J., Flynn, P.J., Beveridge, J.R., Scruggs, W.T., O'Toole, A.J., Bolme, D., … Weimer, S. (2009). Overview of the Multiple Biometrics Grand Challenge. In *Proceedings Third IAPR International Conference on Biometrics.*

Phillips, P.J., Flynn, P.J., Scruggs, T., Bowyer, K.W., & Worek, W. (2006). Preliminary Face Recognition Grand Challenge results. In *Proceedings of the Seventh International Conference on Automatic Face and Gesture Recognition,* pp. 15–24.

Phillips, P.J., Grother, P., Micheals, R., Blackburn, D.M., Tabassi, E., & Bone, M. (2003). Face Recognition Vendor Test 2002. *IEEE International Workshop on Analysis and Modeling of Faces and Gestures 2003,* 44. doi:10.1109/AMFG.2003.1240822

Phillips, P.J., Moon, H., Rizvi, S.A., & Rauss, P.J. (2000). The FERET evaluation methodology for face-recognition algorithms. *IEEE Transactions on Pattern Analysis and Machine Intelligence, 22.* doi:10.1109/34.879790

Phillips, P.J., Narvekar, A., Jiang, F., & O'Toole, A.J. (2010a). An other-race effect for face recognition algorithms. *ACM Transactions on Applied Perception, 8,* ART 14.

Phillips, P.J., Scruggs, W.T., O'Toole, A.J., Flynn, P.J., Bowyer, K.W., Schott, C.L., & Sharpe, M. (2010b). FRVT 2006 and ICE 2006 large-scale results. *IEEE Transactions on Pattern Analysis and Machine Intelligence, 32,* 831–846.

Rice, A., Phillips, P.J., Natu, V., An, X., & O'Toole, A.J. (2013). Unaware person recognition from the body when face identification fails. *Psychological Science, 24*(11), 2235–2243. doi:10.1177/0956797613492986.

Russell, R., Duchaine, B., & Nakayama, K. (2009). Super-recognizers: People with extraordinary face recognition ability. *Psychonomic Bulletin & Review, 16,* 252–257. doi:10.3758/PBR.16.2.252

Stanley, K. (2009). Facial recognition technology proving effective for Pinellas deputies. Tampa Bay Times, July 23.

Timber, C., & Nakashima, E. (2013). State photo-ID databases become troves for police. *Washington Post,* June 16.

Part 5

Implications for Criminal Justice

12

Eyewitness Identification and Facial Image Comparison Evidence in Common Law Jurisdictions

Andrew Roberts

Reliance in criminal trials upon eyewitness identification evidence is both commonplace and problematic. It is problematic because psychological research has demonstrated that the accuracy of our attempts to identify others, particularly those with whom we have no prior familiarity, is affected by a broad range of variables (see Chapter 7). This is a matter that appears to be appreciated but not always acted upon by those responsible for the administration of criminal justice. In R v. Fergus (1994) the English Court of Appeal observed that:

> [t]he issue of identification of an offender is possibly one of the commonest facts that juries have to consider. It is also one of the issues most susceptible to error. Visual identification of an offender not known to the observer is a particularly fallible process.

In most jurisdictions it is possible to point to various procedures that are intended to address the risk of error and to provide those suspected of wrongdoing with safeguards against wrongful conviction on the

Forensic Facial Identification: Theory and Practice of Identification from Eyewitnesses, Composites and CCTV, First Edition. Edited by Tim Valentine and Josh P. Davis.
© 2015 John Wiley & Sons, Ltd. Published 2015 by John Wiley & Sons, Ltd.

basis of mistaken identification (on the law in England & Wales, see Bogan & Roberts, 2011). But we will see that the procedural response to the problem of mistaken identification varies considerably across juris- dictions. In some, it seems that concern over the risks associated with eyewitness identification evidence is reflected in the adoption of rela- tively sophisticated procedures. In others, procedure falls some way short of what might be considered "ideal procedures" or "best practice".

This chapter is concerned not only with the manner in which eye- witness identification evidence is dealt with by the criminal justice system, but also with the way in which images of offenders are used to generate identification evidence. On the one hand, we will see here a sharp contrast between long-standing judicial acknowledgement of the fallibility of eyewitness identification, and on the other, a general inattentiveness to the problems associated with the use of images of offenders. While the procedural framework that regulates eyewit- nesses' attempts at identification can be relatively sophisticated, procedure governing identification from images, where it exists, tends to be rudimentary. The aim in the sections that follow is not to provide detailed or comprehensive exposition of the relevant law in any par- ticular jurisdiction; rather, it is to consider the adequacy of the law generally, using the law in various jurisdictions as exemplars. But in order to engage in this kind of evaluative inquiry, it will be necessary to identify some criteria against which prevailing practice and proce- dure can be evaluated. One measure of the adequacy of the response to the problem of mistaken identification in any jurisdiction might be to examine the extent to which the procedures that have been adopted reflect what psychological research suggests is the most accurate pro- cedure for obtaining identification evidence. However, as Twining (1990) has pointed out, an inquiry into how the law might reduce the risk of wrongful conviction on the basis of mistaken identification (and the extent to which the law in any jurisdiction adequately addresses this risk) requires a broader perspective: one that is concerned not only with the cognitive processes of the particular witness, but with the decision-making of other actors involved in the process, and with "the interactive aspects of legal processes". The High Court of Australia observed in *Alexander v. R* (1981, p. 426), that:

> The problems which afflict identification evidence have their origin in four principal sources: (a) the variable quality of the evidence, much of which is inherently fragile; (b) the use by the police of meth- ods of identification which, although well suited to the investigation and detection of crime, are not calculated to yield evidence of high probative value in a criminal trial; (c) the consequential need to balance interests of the accused in securing a fair trial against the

interests of the State in the efficient investigation and detection of crime by the police; and (d) the difficulty of accommodating the reception of certain types of identification testimony to accepted principles of the law or evidence.

The issues identified here are interrelated. The form of procedure that the police use to obtain identification evidence from witnesses may have a significant adverse effect on its quality. The suggestion that the police might resort to procedures that are not likely to produce reliable identification evidence can be understood as a manifestation of the distorting effect of the adversarial nature of criminal proceedings. Although ascertaining the truth of the allegations of wrongdoing is widely considered to be the overriding objective of a criminal trial, a credible alternative view is that the criminal trial is not so much a search for the truth as a contest to determine a winner (Summers, 1999). In this contest, the jury has a largely passive role, unable to influence the course of the criminal trial or to make enquiries of witnesses or the parties. The parties are left to determine what evidence the jury will hear and the form in which it will be presented. The criminal trial should not be thought of as a quasi-scientific inquiry. Prevailing in the adversarial contest may lead parties to decide, for strategic reasons, not to call witnesses who might be able to provide relevant and probative evidence. They may seek an advantage by concealing or withholding evidence that might assist the other's case, or by failing to secure or declining to procure such evidence. In the context with which we are concerned, identification procedures may be used that increase the likelihood of the witness identifying a suspect at the expense of reliability. These tendencies compound difficulties that arise as a consequence of uncertainty that is inherent in attempts to reconstruct past events, and the forensic limitations of the criminal trial. There is some elaboration of these issues in the first two sections of the chapter, the first dealing with uncertainty, and the second with the forensic shortcomings of the criminal trial. These provide the general background to the discussion of the way in which the legal system deals with eyewitness identification evidence and identification of persons depicted in images that is undertaken later in this chapter.

UNCERTAINTY IN FACT-FINDING AND THE DISTORTING EFFECTS OF THE ADVERSARIAL CRIMINAL PROCESS

Those who, over the course of a criminal trial, are required to determine the truth of past events undertake a difficult task. Fact-finding inevitably involves the negotiation of uncertainty. The evidence offered in support of a proposition that a party seeks to establish may be direct or circumstantial. Direct evidence is evidence that, were it to be accepted by the jury or other fact-finder,[1] would prove the proposition that it is relied upon to support. Circumstantial evidence, on the other hand, is evidence that provides the foundation for an inference to be drawn regarding the existence of the proposition in support of which it is adduced.

Suppose in a murder trial, for example, the prosecution's contention is that the defendant caused the victim's death by beating him about the head with a wooden club. The evidence of a witness, who testified that he observed the defendant take a club from his jacket and hit the victim over the head with it, would be direct evidence that supports the proposition that the prosecution seeks to establish. If the jury were to accept the witness's testimony to be truthful and reliable, the proposition would be established. Suppose, however, there were no witnesses to the event, and the prosecution, in order to prove the proposition, adduced evidence that a wooden club recovered from the scene shortly after the incident in question was found to have traces of both the defendant's and the victim's DNA. Further to this they will also call a pathologist who states that, in his opinion, the victim died as a consequence of brain injury caused by blunt force trauma. If the proposition that the victim died as a result of the defendant beating him about the head with the club is to be established, the jury will have to draw on a number of inferences: an inference that because the victim's DNA was found on the club, it had probably been in contact with him; an inference from the fact that the defendant's DNA was found on the club that he had held the club; an inference from the pathologist's opinion regarding the cause of the victim's injuries, that a club could have been used to cause the victim's death. All of these lines of inferential reasoning could be used to support a finding that the defendant used the club to inflict the fatal injuries. The tribunal of fact, whether it is considering direct or circumstantial evidence, will have to engage in probabilistic reasoning. While direct evidence does not require the inferential reasoning that must be undertaken in respect of circumstantial evidence, even in respect of direct evidence, as the caveat "if accepted" suggests, the jury will be required to consider whether the witness is credible and his or her testimony reliable. The criteria by which this might be

---

[1]The terms "jury", "fact-finder" and "tribunal of fact" will be used interchangeably in this chapter. "Fact-finder" and "tribunal of fact" are generic descriptors that apply to those who are required to determine the facts for the purposes of adjudication in legal proceedings. The jury is a fact-finder, but so too are magistrates and judges sitting alone (without a jury) in proceedings.

judged – whether the witness has been untruthful in the past, has good eyesight, has an interest in the outcome of the case – all require the jury to engage in probabilistic inferential reasoning. In this sense, all evidence is to a greater or lesser extent *qualitatively* deficient; it will not offer conclusive proof.

In addition to qualitative deficiencies, the evidence presented to the jury will almost certainly suffer from *quantitative* deficiencies. While the prosecution must prove the elements of the offence with which the defendant is charged beyond reasonable doubt, the trier of fact will seldom be presented with all of the evidence that could have been obtained. Finite resources might mean that the scope of a police investigation is limited. It may not be possible to pursue all lines of inquiry. Some pieces of evidence may never be discovered, and others are lost or destroyed before any trial. The difficulties that these truisms present may be exacerbated by the distorting effect of the adversarial nature of the process. While the parties' interests in the outcome of the trial might motivate each to seek as much evidence as possible in support of its case, it has also been suggested that the desire to prevail may be:

> ...motivated to present only such evidence as is favorable to its position: if an item of evidence appears unfavorable to it, the party tries to keep it out of court, even if the item's value in the quest for truth is beyond dispute. (Damaška, 1997, p. 99)

In light of this we might say that the adequacy of those aspects of criminal procedure and the law of evidence that relate to facial identification ought to be measured by two things. The first is the extent to which it ensures that fact-finders are presented with as much relevant evidence as it is possible for the parties to obtain through reasonable efforts. The second is the extent to which it mitigates the risk of any evidence presented to fact-finders being unreliable. The first of these measures will be touched upon in the sections that follow, but the emphasis will be on the second – the way in which the law deals with the issue of reliability. I want to take the criminal trial as the starting point of consideration of the issue of reliability.

THE FORENSIC LIMITATIONS OF THE ADVERSARIAL CRIMINAL TRIAL

Not only do juries and other fact-finders have to meet the challenge of evidential shortcomings – the structure of the adversarial process itself constitutes a serious obstacle to accurate fact-finding.

One of the characteristics of adversarial proceedings that is said to distinguish it from inquisitorial proceedings found in continental Europe is the trial-centred and concentrated nature of fact-determination. It has been said that the adversarial trial overshadows pre-trial procedure as the source of information for the jury (Damaška, 1997). Although witnesses will provide information to investigators, and may be asked to take part in pre-trial identification procedures, their testimony at trial is considered to be the primary source of information about disputed issues. The problem that this presents for fact-finders is, as Simon (2012, p. 168) pointed out, that:

> ...[c]ourtroom testimony is usually proffered months, sometimes years following the criminal event, a period during which witnesses repeatedly interact with the criminal process and are subject to a variety of contaminating sources. As a result, the "raw evidence" perceived by the witness at the criminal event often undergoes editing, embellishment, and alteration.

Awareness of the manner in which memory functions and of its frailties among those responsible for the administration of criminal justice is illustrated in a remarkably perceptive analysis undertaken by the High Court of Australia in *Craig v. R* (1933, p. 446):

> An honest witness who says "the prisoner is the man who drove the car" whilst appearing to affirm a simple, clear and impressive proposition, is really asserting: (i) that he observed the driver; (ii) that the observation became impressed upon his mind; (iii) that he still retained the original impression; (iv) that such impression has not been affected, altered, or replaced... and; (v) that the resemblance between the original impression, and the prisoner is sufficient to base a judgment not of resemblance, but of identity.

This passage demonstrates an understanding of memory function that will be familiar to cognitive psychologists – perception, encoding, retrieval and comparison. But implicit in it is an awareness that memory deteriorates over time, is malleable and can be reconstructed, and that it is inevitable that a witness' memory of the appearance of a person with whom he or she is unfamiliar will be incomplete. The courts, or at least some courts, also appreciate that there is no strong correlation between confidence and accuracy, and that a witness' confidence in the accuracy of a mistaken identification can be subsequently inflated or reinforced (see Chapter 8). For example, in *R v. Johnson* (2000) the English Court of Appeal noted:

> ...it has been the courts' experience that identification evidence should be subject to particularly careful scrutiny. The reason for that is because a perfectly honest witness could believe, *and become increasingly convinced* that they were right in so believing that they had identified the right person when subsequently it could be shown in other ways that they had in fact made a mistake and identified the wrong person [emphasis added].

The Court has also acknowledged the impracticability of any attempt to prevent the "quality" of a witness's identification being affected by the acquisition of information in the period between identification of a suspect in a pre-trial procedure and the point at which he or she testifies at trial (*R v. Callum*, 2010).

The problem generally is not so much that actors involved in the criminal trial are unaware of the way in which memory functions and the ways in which it may be compromised. Rather, it is that too much faith is placed in the capacity of the forensic processes of the criminal trial to reveal unreliable and inaccurate identification evidence, and a belief that problems associated with such evidence can be dealt with effectively by issuing warnings and directions to the jury. Nowhere is this more evident than in the decision of the Judicial Committee of the Privy Council in *Holland v. HM Advocate* (2005). The courts have long acknowledged that the identification of an accused in the dock during the trial is of "very little value" (*Alexander v. R*, 1981; *Davies v. R*, 1937); however, there is no absolute prohibition on an accused being identified in this way. In *Holland v. HM Advocate*, the appellant had been convicted of assault and robbery following a trial in the High Court in Scotland. The trial judge had permitted two witnesses, who had failed to identify the defendant in pre-trial identification parades, to identify him in the dock. On appeal, he argued that the risk of misidentification inherent in this procedure was such as to violate his right to a fair trial under Article 6 of the European Convention on Human Rights. Although the Privy Council conceded that in some cases permitting a witness to identify an accused in the dock might deprive him of a fair trial, the identification of Holland in this way did not render the proceedings unfair. The Committee reached this conclusion on the grounds that Holland was legally represented and able to challenge the admissibility of the evidence, was able to cross-examine the witnesses and address the jury on the weaknesses of the evidence, and the trial judge had also directed the jury on those weaknesses. But we might ask, just how effective are these "safeguards"?

Cross-examination

Few now subscribe to the view that a witness's demeanour is a reliable indicator of the truthfulness of his testimony (Bingham, 2006). But the greatest challenge is not the witness who provides fabricated identification evidence, but the honest witness who has confidently but mistakenly identified the defendant. Empirical research suggests that cross-examination does little to assist the jury to distinguish reliable from unreliable eyewitness identification evidence (Devenport, Stinson, Cutler, & Kravitz, 2002; Lindsay, Wells, & O'Connor, 1989; Valentine & Maras, 2011; Wells, Lindsay, & Ferguson, 1979). Cross-examination might reveal circumstances that could cast doubt on the reliability of a witness's identification of the defendant, for example, that the light was poor, or the witness had consumed alcohol, or found the event stressful. But it cannot establish how, if at all, any of these things did in fact affect the reliability of a witness' identification of an accused. The Devlin Report, which in the 1970s undertook a review of the way in which evidence was dealt with in England and Wales, concluded that while cross-examination might reveal inconsistencies in a narrative of events provided by a witness, eyewitness identification evidence is impervious to this kind of testing:

> A witness says he recognizes the man, and that is that or almost that. There is no story to dissect, just a simple assertion to be accepted or rejected... the issue rests on a single piece of observation. The state of the light, the point of observation and the distance from the object are useful if they can show that the witness must be using his imagination; but otherwise where there is a credible and confident assertion, they are of little use in evaluating it. (Devlin, 1976, paras. 1.24 & 1.45)

The forensic limitations of cross-examination have also been judicially acknowledged. In *United States v. Downing* (1985, p.1231 fn.6), for example, it was suggested that "[t]o the extent that a mistaken witness may retain great confidence in an inaccurate identification, cross-examination can hardly be seen as an effective way to reveal weaknesses in a witness's recollection of an event.

Judicial Warnings

Are jury warnings an effective safeguard against the risk of wrongful conviction on the basis of mistaken identification? The form of such warnings may vary, but trial judges are generally required to warn the jury of the need to approach eyewitness identification evidence, as a class of evidence, with caution. In some jurisdictions there is an additional duty to highlight weaknesses in the identification evidence adduced by the prosecution, that is, to draw to the jury's attention circumstances or facts that indicate that the identification evidence might be unreliable. Just as empirical research suggests that cross-examination does not generally assist fact-finders to distinguish reliable eyewitness identification evidence from that which is not, the available research also suggests that judicial directions may have little or no effect on the manner in which juries evaluate eyewitness identification evidence (Ramirez, Zemba, & Geiselman, 1996). The formal requirements of such warnings in various jurisdictions have been the subject of comparative study (Bromby, MacMillan, & McKellar, 2007), and the judgments handed down by the appellate courts provide examples of some of the content of such warnings. However, there is a paucity of systematic empirical research on the adequacy of judicial warnings that are delivered routinely in criminal trials. In the absence of such studies, some have suggested that as judges' knowledge of the factors that might affect the accuracy of identification evidence will be limited, warnings are likely to be "inadequate and insufficient" in drawing the jury's attention to matters that might give rise to concerns over the reliability of identification evidence that implicates an accused (Holdenson, 1988). Even if warnings were generally adequate and sufficient in this respect, we know little about whether, having had these matters drawn to their attention and warned of the need for caution generally, juries understand how they ought use this information, and what affect that it has on their reasoning, if any (Davis & Loftus, 2012a; Simon, 2012).

(Non-)Exclusion of Weak Identification Evidence

One of the consequences of faith in the effectiveness of these trial "safeguards" is, as the Australian Law Reform Commission (1985, para. 424) has observed, that judges are "reluctant to exclude eyewitness identification evidence, however unreliable or weak it may seem". The Commission suggested that the view generally taken by Australian courts was that "even evidence of identification which is so liable to being mistaken that it would be extremely dangerous for a jury to assign any probative value to it may be properly admitted as long as a jury is given a warning in such terms". However, this is a tendency that was not peculiar to Australia during the period in which the Commission made this observation; it is evident in other jurisdictions (Garrett, 2011; Wells & Quinlivan, 2009) including England and Wales.

In *R v. Williams* (2003) – an English case – the witness, who had been waiting for a bus, was threatened with a hypodermic needle by a man who demanded that she hand over her jewellery. She managed to get away and went to a nearby house. She telephoned the police and provided a description of the offender, which was circulated over the police radio system. While officers responding to the victim's emergency call were making their way to the scene of the robbery, bystanders pointed out a suspect. Following a short pursuit, the suspect was detained. Because the culprit had used a hypodermic needle to threaten the victim, the suspect was handcuffed and led to the street where he stood in the company of uniformed officers. The victim had been conveyed to the place where the suspect had been detained, was invited to identify him, and duly obliged. The victim's identification of the suspect was the only evidence presented by the prosecution at the subsequent trial, at which his submission that the evidence should be excluded was rejected. He appealed his conviction on the grounds that the trial judge had been wrong to allow the prosecution to adduce evidence of the witness's identification of him because it was manifestly unreliable. The Court of Appeal noted that there were significant discrepancies in the description of the culprit provided by the victim and the defendant's appearance at the time of his arrest. The culprit had been described as a clean-shaven man with a local London accent, who wore brown shoes. The defendant, however, had a very distinctive Scottish accent, two to three days stubble, and had been wearing black shoes when he was detained. The Court acknowledged that various provisions of the statutory code governing the use of pre-trial identification procedures had been breached, and concluded that:

> ...the identification took place in circumstances which were clearly capable of resulting in the victim ... being, in effect, by the circumstances, told that this was the person who had attempted to rob her, that is by reason of the fact that it was clear that he had been apprehended, was in handcuffs and was surrounded by police officers. A clearer way of pointing out to her who it was that the police sought her to identify could not have been imagined. (*R v. Williams*, 2003, para. 12)

Nevertheless, it was satisfied that the evidence had been properly admitted, concluding that, as the witness had an opportunity to observe the offender at close quarters for some time, and the jury had been adequately warned of the need for caution in convicting on the basis of the witness's identification evidence, it could not be said that the jury's verdict was unsafe.

Notwithstanding judicial sentiments to the contrary, the forensic limitations of the criminal trial provide good grounds for thinking that regulation of the pre-trial procedures through which identification evidence is obtained provides the most effective safeguard against the risk of wrongful conviction on the basis of mistaken identification. If ascertaining the reliability of an identification at trial is problematic, it would seem to be imperative that all reasonable steps are taken to ensure that the identification evidence that is presented to juries is reliable. We now turn to consider, in relation to eyewitness identification evidence and evidence of identification from images, the extent to which the law meets this objective.

Eyewitness Identification Evidence

Perhaps the first requirement of any pre-trial procedure used to obtain identification evidence from a witness is that it should be conducted as soon as possible after he or she has observed the culprit. Not only will a witness' memory of the culprit begin to decay soon after observing him – the sooner an identification procedure is conducted, the less likely it is that the witness will be exposed to information from third parties that may compromise his or her recollections. Pre-trial identification procedures in England and Wales are governed by a statutory code: Code D of the Codes of Practice issued under section 66 of the Police and Criminal Evidence Act 1984 (Code D or "the Code"). The Code, "in the interests of fairness to suspects and witnesses", imposes on the police a duty to hold procedures as soon as practicable (Code D, para. 3.11).

Because the witness will be aware that at least one of the persons presented to them is someone who the police reasonably believe to be the offender, identification procedures are inherently suggestive. The Code, the first version of which came into effect in 1986 and has been subject to a number of revisions, establishes a hierarchy of permissible identification procedures, and prescribes in some detail how each should be conducted. The procedure of first resort is a *video identification* or video lineup. This involves the use of moving images of the suspect in a compilation of similar images of at least eight other people who must "resemble the suspect in age, general appearance and position in life" (Code D, Annex A, para. 2). The officer conducting the procedure must ensure that witnesses are not able to communicate with each other about the case or overhear a witness who has already taken part in the procedure (Code D, Annex A, para. 10). The officer is prohibited from discussing the composition of the video with the witness, or the outcome of an attempt at identification by another witness (Code D, Annex A,

para. 10). Only one witness at a time is permitted to take part in a procedure, and before any attempt at an identification, the officer conducting the procedure is required to inform the witness that the person seen committing the offence may, or may not, appear in the procedure and if the witness cannot make a positive identification he or she should say so (Code D, Annex A, para. 11). If a witness has previously viewed any photograph, or computerized/artist's impression, he or she is not to be reminded of doing so (Code D, Annex A, para. 13), and in any case the witness is to be asked after taking part in the procedure whether he or she has seen any broadcast of published images or descriptions of individuals suspected of committing the offence (Code D, Annex A, para. 14). The Code imposes detailed recording requirements. Among the matters that must be recorded are (1) the first description of the culprit provided by the witness (Code D, para. 3.1), (2) the grounds of any objection by the suspect to the proposed procedures and, if necessary, the reasons why it was not possible to overcome the grounds of the objection (Code D, Annex A, para. 7), and (3) anything said by the witness about any identifications or the conduct of the procedure (Code D, Annex A, para. 18). There is also a requirement that the conduct of the procedure itself be video-recorded (Code D, Annex B, para. 23). However, the Code, in common with other procedural codes around the common law world, does not provide suspects with all of the procedural measures that researchers suggest will significantly reduce the risk of wrongful conviction on the basis of mistaken identification, most notably, blind administration of procedures, and the recording of a statement of the witness' certainty or confidence in the accuracy of his or her identification of a suspect.

Sequential procedures There have been persistent calls for the use of sequential lineups, on the grounds that studies suggest that the rate of false positive identifications is lower where subjects are presented sequentially rather than simultaneously and that there is no corresponding reduction in the rate of accurate identification of offenders. However, recent research has cast doubt on these claims (see Chapter 6). It appears that the use of sequential procedures might lead to a reduction not only in the incidence of mistaken identification of innocent suspects, but also the rate of correct identification of factually guilty suspects.

The response of law reform bodies and appellate courts to proposals for the adoption of sequential procedures has in many instances been suitably cautious. Guidelines for conducting eyewitness identification procedures that were promulgated by the US Department of Justice, National Institute of Justice (1999) (referred to hereafter as the NIJ

Guide) contain both model simultaneous and sequential procedures. However, while both forms of procedure are included in the guide, the inclusion of sequential procedures does not indicate a preference for this type of procedure.

Appellate courts have been similarly reluctant to prescribe or endorse the use of strict sequential procedures. One of the difficulties for courts faced with claims that a particular practice or procedure was suggestive or was in some other way unsatisfactory or deficient, and that another form of procedure ought to be used, is that they do not generally have the resources required to ascertain the extent of any empirical support for such claims. The courts will usually have to rely on the material provided by the parties, and the limited resources available to the defence will often preclude any meaningful inquiry into practices and procedures used by the police and other law enforcement agencies. There are, however, a few notable examples of proceedings in which the courts have been willing to undertake an inquiry into the state of relevant empirical knowledge. In *New Jersey v. Henderson* (2011), the New Jersey Supreme Court appointed a Special Master to evaluate the available scientific research on eyewitness identification. The issues for the Court were (i) whether the extant test for determining whether evidence was obtained using identification procedures so suggestive that it should not be admitted at trial was satisfactory, and (ii) whether enhanced jury warnings ought to be developed. In relation to the first issue, the Court held that trial judges should consider various system variables to ascertain whether there is sufficient evidence of suggestiveness to warrant a hearing into the admissibility of the eyewitness's identification of the defendant. It suggested that among the matters that the trial judge ought to take into account are: whether the procedure used was subject to blind administration; whether the instructions given to the witness prior to the procedure were "neutral"; whether there were at least five foils who resembled the suspect; whether witnesses were provided with any information or feedback about the suspect or crime, either before, during or after the procedure; whether a record was made of the witness' confidence immediately after the procedure; and whether the witness had viewed the suspect in multiple procedures. However, having noted what it perceived to be an absence of consensus among researchers on the advantages of sequential over simultaneous procedures, the Court concluded that "there is insufficient, authoritative evidence accepted by scientific experts for a court to make a finding in favor of either procedure".

Likewise, in *Winmar v. Western Australia* (2007), the Western Australian Court of Appeal noted that while there is "some support" for the view that the use of a sequential lineup is preferable to simultaneous presentation, there appear to be drawbacks with the former, in particular that "it appears that sequential methods may lead a witness not to identify the offender when the offender is present, an inaccuracy favourable to an offender, but unfavourable to the community" (*Winmar v. Western Australia*, 2007, para. 58). It concluded that having regard to the state of the research "the question of whether an identification is performed by showing images of persons sequentially, or all at once, is not of such critical importance as to require a warning [about the dangers of relative judgments]" (*Winmar v. Western Australia*, 2007, para. 62). Judicial reluctance to make rulings, the effect of which would be to require the police to adopt particular procedures, is understandable. If it were to be demonstrated that particular procedures would result in fewer innocent defendants being convicted and that there would be no costs involved, then a failure on the part of the courts to insist that they be used would be indefensible. However, where there are a range of procedural options, the choice to adopt any one of them invariably involves some form of trade-off. The courts might reasonably take the view that a politically accountable and better resourced institution such as the legislature or executive is better placed to make the judgments involved in evaluation of the benefits and burdens associated with the various alternatives.

Blind administration Unfortunately, where eyewitness identification procedures have been reviewed by governmental and government-sponsored bodies for the purposes of law reform, it seems that scientifically informed proposals have sometimes been rejected on rather flimsy grounds. Very few jurisdictions, for example, require "blind administration" of identification procedures. Research suggests that where the person administering an identification procedure knows the identity of the suspect, he or she may inadvertently provide cues that indicate to the witness who that person is (Garrioch & Brimacombe, 2001; Phillips, McAuliff, Kovera, & Cutler, 1999). It has been pointed out that a process of blind administration would be "cost-free" in terms of acquittal of the factually guilty (Risinger, 2007), and that the only justifiable ground for failure to adopt it is that it would impose unreasonable financial costs. It has been claimed that this procedure might give rise to some "logistical problems", although there are various ways in which these might be circumvented (see e.g., Wilcock, Bull, & Milne, 2008, pp. 131–133). Blind administration procedures adopted by the Ohio legislature (Ohio Code, §2933.83) provide an example of how this might be done. These require the administrator to use photographs of the suspect and five fillers. The procedure requires a photograph of a filler to be placed in the first folder. The remaining five photographs including the photograph of the suspect are placed in separate folders, which are then shuffled so that the administrator does not know which folder contains the photograph of the suspect. Folders that are placed in positions 7–10 in the sequence contain "blank" photographs – cards that do not depict anyone's image. The shuffling of the photographs that appear at positions 2–6 in the sequence ensures that the administrator does not know where in the sequence the image of the suspect appears. The use of blanks ensures that the image of the suspect does not appear towards the end of the sequence. Presumably, this is intended to address the risk of mistaken identification that arises in respect of those witnesses who will be more inclined to make a positive identification as they approach the end of the sequence of images. The folders are presented to the witness who is told that the administrator does not know which, if any, of the folders contains a photograph of the alleged perpetrator; does not want to, and will not, view any of the photographs; and may not be shown any of the photographs by the witness. The witness is required to make a decision as to whether a photograph is of the perpetrator before viewing the next photograph in the sequence. After the sequence of folders has been viewed for the first time, a record must be made of the result of the procedure. Once the result has been recorded the witness may view the photographs once more and in the same sequence. Where a witness makes an identification, whether during the first or the second viewing of the sequence of images, the officer conducting the procedure is required to take a statement of the witness's confidence in his or her identification.

Confidence statements The Ohio procedures perhaps most closely reflect what those engaged in empirical research might consider "ideal procedures" or "best practice". They are, for example, one of the few that require those who administer identification procedures to obtain a statement of confidence immediately after a witness identifies a suspect. This measure provides juries with some indication as to whether the degree of confidence that the witness expresses in the accuracy of his or her identification has been inflated in the period between the identification procedure and the trial. Inflation may occur, for example, as a consequence of investigators informing the witness that he or she identified the suspect, or the witness learning that other witnesses identified the same person in the procedure (see Chapter 8). We have already noted that cross-examination is largely ineffective in revealing an identification made by an honest, confident but mistaken witness to be inaccurate. Some calibration of the witness's confidence in his or her identification immediately after it was made – in the form of a confidence statement – might have a significant effect on the jury's evaluation of the testimony that the defendant is the person the witness saw engaged in the alleged wrongdoing. Such a statement would provide an indication of the extent to which the witness's confidence in the accuracy of his or her identification of the defendant had changed in the period leading up to trial. However, it appears that in most jurisdictions, including England and Wales, the police are under no obligation to make any such record during a pre-trial identification procedure.

Departure from, or failure to use, prescribed procedures Twining has suggested that so much attention has been focused on identification parades (lineups) that "it has sometimes appeared that the problem of identification is perceived as being co-extensive with some acknowledged defects of parades or lineup procedures and that the only, or at least the central, question is: How can the reliability of identification parades be improved?" (Twining, 1994, p. 162). It is a truism to say that procedures that are designed to produce more reliable identification evidence will mitigate the risk of wrongful conviction on the basis of mistaken identification only if they are used to obtain identification evidence from eyewitnesses. Although this point seems obvious, it is not uncommon to find examples of guidelines and statutory provisions that prescribe relatively sophisticated identification procedures yet say nothing about the circumstances in which they ought to be used. The Ohio procedures described above are a good example of this. While they incorporate most of the recommendations made by scientific researchers, the legislative Code in which they are set out does not prescribe the circumstances in which they are to be used. Wells (2006, p. 623) has lamented that, following publication of the NIJ Guide, "the vast majority of police departments have not changed their procedures even to the point of being consistent with [it]". As the Court in *Alexander v. R* (1981) noted, one of the sources of problems associated with identification evidence is use by the police of identification procedures that assist the investigation but are unlikely to yield reliable evidence.

To the detached observer, the use of a procedure that is likely to produce evidence of limited probative value, rather than an alternative procedure through which much more reliable evidence could have been procured, may seem irrational. However, police officers are not detached observers. The House of Lords observed in *R v. Forbes* (2000, 20) that police officers' primary concern "will (perfectly properly) be to promote the investigation and prosecution of crime rather than to protect the interests of the suspect". Partisan interest in the course of an investigation and the outcome of criminal proceedings might provide incentives to do things that are not conducive to accurate fact-finding (Roberts, 2008a). One of these might be to use informal, *ad hoc* procedures that can be arranged and conducted expeditiously, but do not provide the kind safeguards inherent in procedures that are designed to control various forms of bias and suggestiveness.

Particularly problematic is the use of street identifications (street confrontations or showups).[2] These usually occur shortly after the commission of an offence and in the vicinity in which it was committed. The witness will either be taken on a tour of the area to see whether the offender can be found, or where the police have stopped someone who resembles the person described by the witness, a confrontation between witness and suspect will be conducted. Street identifications are suggestive, particularly those in which a witness is asked to attempt to identify a person who has been stopped by the police. In a video identification procedure or some other form of lineup, the risk of a false positive identification is distributed across those who appear in the procedure. In a street identification, the suspect alone bears the risk (Valentine, 2006). Of course, there may be good reasons for conducting a street identification. In the absence of an identification of the suspect, there may be insufficient grounds ("reasonable suspicion" or "probable cause") to justify an arrest. But the expedience of a street identification may prove to be a powerful incentive to attempt to obtain identification evidence in this way rather than defer an attempt to obtain an identification of the suspect so that a formal procedure can be arranged.

In England and Wales, the use of a street identification is prohibited where the police have sufficient information to justify the arrest of a suspect. However, while the courts have drawn a line at allowing the police to conduct a street identification following a suspect's arrest, they have been criticized for allowing evidence of a street identification to be given in circumstances in which a formal identification procedure such as a lineup should have been used (see Wolchover & Heaton-Armstrong, 2006). In *R v. Toth* (2005), for example, Customs and Excise officials were pursuing a vehicle, the occupants of which were suspected of involvement in the illegal importation of drugs. The vehicle crashed and was abandoned, and when searched was found to contain a large quantity of cocaine. The defendant was the registered keeper of the vehicle, and one of the customs officers who had seen the person driving the vehicle before it had been abandoned, attended his address with the intention of establishing whether he was the driver. The trial judge and the Court of Appeal were satisfied that the fact that the defendant was the registered keeper of the vehicle did not constitute reasonable grounds for suspecting him of involvement in the offence.

---

[2] Equally problematic is the showing of a single photograph of a suspect to a witness, although in many jurisdictions the police are not permitted to use this form of procedure.

Consequently, identification of the defendant at his home address was necessary. But this seems disingenuous. Had the defendant been arrested without having been identified by the customs officer, it is doubtful that any court would have found that the police did not have reasonable grounds to suspect him of involvement in the offence, and the arrest to be unlawful. The reported cases suggest that where there is a question of whether a street identification was permissible, the courts appear too ready to defer to police assertions that such a procedure was necessary to justify the arrest of a suspect.

In the early stages of an investigation, the need to obtain *any* form of identification evidence in order to establish a *prima facie* case against a suspect might overshadow consideration of the probative value of the evidence that might be obtained. A notable and particularly egregious example of this is the English case of *R v. Marcus* (2004). Here the suspect was a man of unusual appearance and the police had difficulty in obtaining images of volunteers who bore a sufficient resemblance to the suspect for use in a video procedure. The images had, with the agreement of the defence, been masked so as to obscure any significant differences in appearance. However, after consulting the Crown Prosecution Service, the police compiled a second set of unmasked images, which would be shown to the witness if the suspect was not identified from the masked images. After failing to identify the suspect when shown the masked images, the witness perhaps unsurprisingly, picked him out when shown the unmasked set of images. At the subsequent trial, a police witness conceded that the suspect had stood out "quite blatantly", and that the procedure was unfair. It came to light that the decision to show the witness unmasked images was a consequence of police frustration at the "poor results" (presumably a low rate of suspect identification) that had been obtained generally when masked images had been used in identification procedures.

One way of deterring the use of informal identification procedures is to make the use of formal procedures a condition of the admissibility of identification evidence. This is the approach taken in Australian jurisdictions that have adopted Australian Uniform Evidence Legislation, and in New Zealand. In Australia, the prosecution cannot adduce evidence of "visual identification" unless an "identification parade" has been conducted prior to trial (Evidence Act (Cth), 1995, s. 114). The Act is based on proposals developed by the Australian Law Reform Commission (1985, 1987) as a response to concern over: (a) police practice of using photo-arrays comprising images of persons who had, at some time, been in police custody for other offences (police mugshots) in order to obtain identification in respect of a suspect detained as part of an ongoing investigation (the "rogues gallery"); and (b) the tendency of trial judges to admit weak identification evidence. However, the legislation may not be as effective in ensuring the use of procedures that are likely to produce reliable evidence as it might at first appear. What constitutes an "identification parade" is not defined or prescribed in the Act, which leaves open the possibility of evidence being admitted which has been obtained using a procedure that has the appearance of an "identification parade", and might reasonably be described as such, but which is conducted in manner that produces evidence of little probative value (Roberts, 2008b).

The approach adopted in the New Zealand Evidence Act (2006) is, on its face, more satisfactory in this respect. It requires visual identification evidence to be excluded where: (a) it was obtained through means other than a "formal procedure"; and (b) there was no "good reason" for not following such a procedure. There is an exhaustive list of circumstances that might constitute good reasons for not conducting a formal procedure: the suspect's refusal to participate in one; the "singular" appearance of the suspect; a substantial change in the suspect's appearance; the police involved in the investigation could not have been anticipated that identification would be an issue; an identification of the suspect was made to the police soon after the offence was reported and as part of the initial investigation (e.g., a street identification); or an identification was made following a chance encounter between the witness and the person alleged to have committed the offence. Where there was no good reason for failing to conduct a formal procedure, identification evidence may still be admitted if the prosecution can prove beyond reasonable doubt that it is reliable. This should be an onerous burden for the prosecution, although the effectiveness of the presumption in favour of exclusion of the evidence will rest, in part, on how trial judges approach the task of evaluating the quality of eyewitness identification evidence and the extent to which they are prepared to acknowledge their own limitations in this respect. The Act also requires an identification procedure to possess certain features in order to constitute a "formal procedure". These include that it be conducted as soon as practicable after the alleged offence, involve the use of at least seven fillers who resemble the suspect, and that the witness be told that the person who committed the offence may not be present. The requirements set out in the Act may be supplemented by further conditions issued in regulatory orders, but as yet, none appears to have been made. Consequently, the "formal procedure" required by the Act falls some way short of that which might be expected to produce the most reliable identification evidence. It has been pointed out that the legislative provisions do not preclude the possibility of more than one suspect being presented to a witness in a single procedure, nor do they say anything about the manner in which subjects should be presented to the witness (Mahoney, McDonald, Optican, & Tinsley, 2007). They neither require blind administration, nor that the procedure is administered by a police officer who is not involved with the investigation.

The Identification Procedure Administered as an "Impartial Service"

I suggested earlier that the adequacy of criminal procedure in any jurisdiction might be measured by the extent to which it minimizes deficiencies in the *quality* and *quantity* of evidence made available to the fact-finder. Although the police control the means of producing reliable identification evidence, identification procedures should not be thought of as a "police procedure", or solely a means of procuring identification evidence for the prosecution, where it chooses to rely on such evidence. Where, for example, the prosecution believes that it can prove identity without relying on the evidence of an eyewitness, it may take the view that there is little to be gained by conducting an identification procedure in the hope that an eyewitness will pick out the suspect, compared with the damage that might be caused to the prosecution case if the witness, having claimed that he would be able to identify the culprit, were to fail to identify the suspect. It has been suggested by the English Court of Appeal, however, that identification procedures ought to be viewed as a facility administered by the police for the benefit of *both* parties to proceedings:

> Despite what might at first be thought to be the purpose of an iden-
> tification parade, namely that it is a method or procedure by which
> the police seek to obtain evidence for the purposes of prosecuting
> suspects, as opposed to a service performed impartially for prosecu-
> tion and defence, this court in various of its previous decisions,
> leaned towards the latter view on the basis, it seems, that a parade
> may produce negative evidence favourable to an accused which the
> defence are incapable of generating for themselves. (*R v. Nicholson*,
> 1999, para. 28)

However, in some jurisdictions, the language used in provisions that regulate the use of identification procedures implies that they fulfil the more limited function of ensuring that evidence on which the prosecution intends to rely is reliable. In New Zealand, for example, the statutory definition of a formal identification procedure refers to the suspect as "the person to be identified" and the witness as "the person making the identification". These labels appear, respectively, to be inconsistent with a conception of witnesses as a source of evidence which might assist either of the parties, and formal procedures as the means through which the parties may obtain that evidence. It suggests, as Mahoney *et al.* (2007) have pointed out, that the purpose of the procedure is to have the witness confirm police suspicions as to who is the offender.

More satisfactory in this respect is the NIJ Guide which states that the function of identification parades (or lineups) is to provide for "accurate identification or non-identification" (NIJ, 1999, p. 29), and to this end recommends that witnesses be instructed before the procedure is conducted that absolving the innocent from suspicion and convicting the guilty are equally important objectives (NIJ, 1999, p. 32).

IDENTIFICATION FROM IMAGES

It should be clear from the preceding discussion that those involved in the administration of criminal justice are aware of the problems associated with eyewitness identification evidence, and that in most jurisdictions significant steps have been taken to address the risk of wrongful conviction on the basis of unreliable evidence provided by eyewitnesses – although in every jurisdiction more might be done. The position is very different in respect of evidence of identification from images and expert image comparison evidence, however. Most texts on the law of evidence have a chapter devoted to evidence of identification, much of which is concerned with the dangers associated with eyewitness identification and the law's response to those problems. Few have much more than a paragraph concerning the use of images to prove identity. This is due, in part, to the paucity of law and the absence of regulation of the means of obtaining this form of evidence. Reliance on eyewitness identification evidence is long-standing, the legal system is conscious of miscarriages of justice due to mistaken identification by eyewitness, and there is a substantial body of literature on the problems associated with this form of evidence that has seeped into the general stock of knowledge of the community at large. Routine use of images to prove identity, on the other hand, is a more recent phenomenon – a consequence of significant investment by states, commercial organizations and individuals in CCTV systems, and greater use of visual recording equipment by the police to gather evidence at public demonstrations, sporting events, and during covert surveillance operations (for an account of the development of CCTV systems for law enforcement purposes, see Norris, McCahill, & Wood, 2004). There is no catalogue of notorious cases of wrongful conviction on the basis of erroneous identification of persons depicted in images (however, for an example of wrongful conviction on the basis of flawed identification by a police officer of a person depicted in CCTV images, see *R v. Brady*, 2004), and we are probably less cognizant of the fallibility of our attempts to identify people in this way. Consequently, there is a disparity in the way that the law deals with eyewitness identification evidence and evidence of identification from images respectively.

Evidence of identification from images might take one of two forms. The first is a person's claim to be able to identify a person depicted in CCTV or other images as someone who is known to him or her – which is referred to here as "evidence of recognition". The second is a witness' testimony that, having compared an image of an alleged offender and an image of a "person of interest" or suspect, they have concluded that the persons are one and the same. This will be referred to below as "image comparison".

Recognition Evidence

Research suggests that our attempts to identify persons in images – even high-quality images – with whom we unfamiliar are particularly susceptible to error (see Chapter 9). How then, does – and should – the law deal with such evidence?

In England and Wales, a witness who knows the defendant "sufficiently well" to recognize him/her as the offender may testify that he or she is the person depicted in an image. While English courts have declined to identify criteria by which the question of whether the defendant is "well known" to a witness for the purposes of admissibility of this form of evidence, the Supreme Court of British Columbia suggested that the indicia for determining whether this threshold is met are: (a) the length of the prior relationship between the witness and the accused; (b) the circumstances of the prior relationship between the witness and the accused; and, (c) the recency of the contact between the witness and the accused prior to the event where the witness recognized the accused (*R v. Anderson*, 2005, para. 25).

In *R v. Smith* (2008), the English Court of Appeal acknowledged that a significant problem with this form of evidence is the absence of any objective means of testing the accuracy of the identification. It was noted earlier in respect of eyewitness identification evidence that while cross-examination might establish that a witness could not have seen what he or she claimed to have seen, in general it is an ineffective means of revealing that an honest and confident witness is mistaken. Where a witness has identified a person in an image, the difficulty will be in determining whether the circumstances in which the witness viewed the image were suggestive. While the risk of unreliability in identification evidence provided by an eyewitness can be controlled through regulation of the process through which it is obtained, the circumstances in which a person is identified in an image are much more difficult to control. Indeed, where the identification is made from images that have been published to the world at large, it may be impossible to acquire an adequate account of the circumstances in which the identification was made. An identification made by a member of the public following the release of an image of the offender might be the product of prompting or other forms of collaboration that may have influenced his or her perception, and it will be difficult at trial to establish whether any of these things occurred.

This problem is arising increasingly in circumstances other than those in which the police release an image of an offender. The publication of large numbers of photographs on social networking sites such as Facebook provides witnesses and victims of crimes with an opportunity to undertake their own investigations with a view to identifying offenders (for discussion of US cases that raise similar issues, see Davis & Loftus, 2012b). In one of the first reported cases concerning this form of identification in England and Wales, *R v. McCullough* (2011), the victim of a robbery was provided with the appellant's name by an acquaintance who suggested the robbery sounded like something that the appellant would do. In the company of his brother and the acquaintance, the victim used Facebook and viewed various photographs on the site, and identified the appellant in one of those photographs. It was suggested during the appellate hearing that the circumstance in which a witness or victim trawls Facebook looking for a photograph of a culprit is analogous to a street identification. However, O'Floinn & Ormerod (2011) have pointed out that where this is done without the knowledge of the police, it is likely to occur before the witness provides any description of the offender. Further, where a street identification is attempted, Code D prohibits any attempt to direct a witness' attention to a particular person. One might assume that an identification from a photograph posted on Facebook will in many cases have been prompted by the provision of some information or suggestion as to the identity of the offender. The volume of images published on social networking sites is such that, without some form of "lead", the task would be akin to the proverbial search for a needle in a haystack. However, the idea of a discreet interaction between the witness and another in which there is some prompt or suggestion may understate the extent of the problem that social networking sites present to those responsible for the administration of criminal justice. The South Australian Supreme Court has noted that:

...with Facebook comes the ever increasing social practice of groups of people having simultaneous electronic communications involving not just the two persons who might have a telephone conversation, or the number of people who might meet in a room, but an unlimited number of people at an unlimited number of physical locations... Thus the opportunities for witnesses to contact one another after the occurrence of a crime and to discuss their perceptions of the event and the appearance or identity of the offender are greatly increased. Such witnesses may also involve others who were not present at the scene and seek their opinion. (*Strauss v. Police*, 2013, paras. 31–32)

The unavailability of the material from which an identification is made is a significant problem for the defence and the tribunal of fact in cases in which a defendant has been identified from an image posted on a social networking site. In *R v. McCullough* (2011), the witness refused to provide details of the Facebook account from which the identification was made. In a more recent case, *R v. Alexander and McGill* (2012), the victim of a robbery viewed Facebook with his sister. She brought up Facebook accounts of two friends who lived in the area in which the robbery occurred. The victim stated that he recognized persons depicted in photographs published on these pages as those who had taken part in the robbery. The identification was subsequently reported to the police, and officers sat with the victim, his sister, and another family member, and viewed the Facebook pictures together. However, no record was made of what was said during this process, nor was any copy made of the Facebook pages from which the identification was made. The difficulty for the defence in such circumstances is establishing whether or not the Facebook pages on which the images were posted, or the trail of pages that led the witness to that page, provided any contextual information that gave rise to a significant risk of bias. Of course, there will be contextual cues that may prompt a witness to identify someone in a street identification – proximity, similarity of clothing, and so on – but these facts will be recorded and incontrovertible. Indeed, they may be probative evidence that the person identified is, in fact, the culprit. Contextual "facts" published on a social networking site, on the other hand, may be nothing more than a witches' brew of malicious gossip, speculation, innuendo or bravado, but capable of inducing an erroneous identification. Indeed, the Court that decided Strauss observed that "information [published on social networking sites] varies greatly in accuracy and reliability and it takes little imagination to see how these advances in technology together with concurrent changes in social behavior greatly magnify the traditional problems associated with identification evidence" (*Strauss v. Police*, 2013, para. 12).

To address the problems associated with identification on social networking sites, O'Floinn & Ormerod (2012) suggested that investigating officers take descriptions from eyewitnesses as soon as a crime is reported, and warn witnesses against attempting to identify offenders using social networking sites. Where a suspect is brought to the attention of a witness they recommend that the witness contact the police so that a formal identification procedure can be arranged. They also point out that where the witness has an opportunity to view images of a suspect on a social networking site over a considerable period, the risk of contamination of any subsequent formal identification procedure will be substantial.

The situations described above can be distinguished from those in which investigators present an image to a particular person who they believe may be able to identify the person depicted in the image. Here there is an opportunity to control the risk of suggestion. The first version of Code D was published in 1986 and it has been revised and reissued on a number of occasions. It has evolved over the years into a detailed and relatively sophisticated procedural regime for obtaining identification evidence from eyewitnesses. However, specific provisions concerning the showing of images to individuals who might be able to identify persons depicted in those images did not appear in the Code until 2011, although the English Court of Appeal issued some guidance in cases decided prior to this. If the police already have a suspect, then the Code requires the process of showing a witness an image to follow the principles governing the use of a video identification procedure, as far as it is possible to do so.

However, where an image is shown to a witness in order to identify a suspect (i.e. the police do not yet have a suspect), the only direction provided by the Code is that images should be shown to each witness alone to avoid the possibility of collusion. It does, however, impose detailed recording requirements. The matters to be recorded include: whether the person viewing the images knew or had been told who was suspected of committing the offence; what information the person had been told about the circumstances of the offence and the person depicted in the image; whether the person had viewed the image alone or with others; and whether the viewing of the image was controlled by anyone (Code D, para. 3.36). The recording requirements in respect of the showing of images to police officers may be of limited effect. It may often be the case that the only person present when an identification is made is the identifying officer. In such cases, or those in which the only persons other than the identifying officer are also police officers, it may be difficult to establish the veracity of any record that has been made.

Research suggests that we perform poorly when attempting to identify those depicted in images who we do not know well (Bruce et al., 1999; Davis & Valentine, 2009). Nevertheless, the jury in a criminal trial – as one might expect – is permitted to compare an image of the offender with the defendant where the images are considered to be sufficiently clear (Attorney-General's Reference, 2003). This principle might be a product, in various measures, of ignorance, pragmatism and principle. Whether the appellate court that held this to be the law appreciated the nature and extent of the risks associated with permitting the jury to compare images of the offender with the defendant sitting in the dock is open to doubt. Even if it did, a court might reasonably take the view that jurors would in any case compare the defendant with the person depicted in the image, notwithstanding a direction that they should not. Perhaps above all, directing a jury that it should not attempt a comparison or reach a view on whether the defendant is the person depicted an image would tend to undermine a fundamental principle of the jury system: that lay jurors have the capacity to evaluate the kind of information that they are likely to encounter in the course of everyday life, and examining images of people is part of that life.

It has been suggested that the problems associated with identification from images might be addressed by mandatory jury warnings and the provision of expert evidence regarding the frailties of this form of evidence (Costigan, 2007). These measures may do no harm, but their value is not at all obvious. How should a jury respond to being informed about the problems associated with a form of evidence? If the jury is provided with an image so that it can compare the person depicted in the image with the defendant, and is told that generally we are not accurate in our attempts to do this, how do we expect jurors to use this information in exercising its judgment? It seems to admonish jurors that they should be wary of trusting their own eyes, yet little thought has been given to how jurors might act upon this warning, if they are able to do so at all.

Image Comparison

Although the jury is permitted to examine images of the offender and draw its own conclusions as to whether the defendant is the person depicted, the courts allow expert witnesses to provide opinions on the identity of an offender on the basis of a comparison of images of the offender and the defendant. The various techniques and their limitations are described in Chapter 10. In some parts of the common law world – England and Wales, and the US, for example – police officers who have acquired "special knowledge" as a result of having spent a substantial amount of time viewing images are taken to possess a form of *ad hoc* expertise, and on this basis are permitted to express opinions about the identity of persons depicted in those images. In others, including Australia and Canada, such evidence is excluded on the grounds that it is superfluous: the jury being equally well-placed, having had an opportunity to observe the defendant during the course of the trial, to consider whether he or she is the person who appears in the image. However, in these jurisdictions, where a police officer is considered to have an advantage over the jury in this respect, for example where the defendant's appearance has changed in the period between the offence and the trial, he or she may be permitted to provide this form of evidence (Edmond & San Roque, 2009).

"Ad-hoc" or "quasi" expertise aside, image comparison ("facial mapping") evidence provided by a suitably qualified expert witness is generally admissible across common law jurisdictions (Edmond, Cole, Cunliffe, & Roberts, 2013). There is growing criticism of the failure of the legal system to require those offering facial mapping evidence (and other forms of forensic comparison evidence) both to demonstrate the validity and reliability of the methods used to compare images, and to justify opinions concerning the significance of similarities found in images.

Although facial mapping experts employ various methodologies, these all suffer from weaknesses that courts, despite the existence in some jurisdictions of seemingly rigorous admissibility standards governing the reception of expert evidence, have failed to properly address (Edmond et al., 2013). These problems are part of a broader malaise concerning the way in which the legal system deals with expert evidence generally. There is a general principle that witnesses should not offer opinions about the matters that are in issue in the proceedings. They are to provide evidence of fact. The rationale for the prohibition is that it is the jury's task to draw inferences (i.e. form opinions) from evidence of fact and, consequently, any opinion offered by a witness is superfluous. However, an exception exists in respect of opinion offered by someone who possesses "specialized knowledge" or expertise in matters that are the subject of dispute. Such witnesses are permitted to offer an opinion where the subject matter of the opinion is likely to be beyond the common knowledge and experience of the jury (R v. Turner, 1974).

The justification for allowing expert opinion is that, without the expert's testimony, the jury may have difficulty in interpreting factual evidence with which they are presented, and/or drawing appropriate inferences from those facts. The function of expert evidence generally might be thought of as educating the jury on matters about which they know little. However, it has been suggested that the idea that experts might be able, within the constraints of a criminal trial, to equip the jury with sufficient knowledge to engage in satisfactory evaluation of the subject matter of expert testimony is implausible (Edmond & Roberts, 2011). Even if we were to accept that a jury could be educated in this way, empirical studies suggest that cross-examination is largely ineffective in exposing the extent of any limitations in methodology and inflated opinion offered by expert witnesses (McQuiston-Surrett & Saks, 2009). The reality might be, therefore, that juries from their disadvantaged position can either defer to the opinion of the expert, or reject it on grounds that may not be entirely rational (Allen & Miller, 1993: Edmond & Roberts, 2011). The burden of preventing miscarriages of justice on the basis of flawed expert forensic testimony, therefore, falls primarily on the courts and the forensic science community.

In 2009, the National Research Council of the US National Academy of Sciences (NAS) published a report on the state of the forensic sciences, in which it observed:

> The degree of science in a forensic science method may have an important bearing on the reliability of forensic evidence in criminal cases. There are two very important questions that should underlie the law's admission of and reliance upon forensic evidence in criminal trials: (1) the extent to which a particular forensic science discipline is founded on a reliable scientific methodology that gives it the capacity to accurately analyze evidence and report findings, and (2) the extent to which practitioners in a particular forensic discipline rely on human interpretation that could be tainted by error, the threat of bias, or absence of sound operational procedures and robust performance standards. (NAS, 2009, p. 9)

If one considers these two questions in relation to facial image comparison evidence, the failings of the courts and the particular forensic discipline are all too evident. A challenge that those using these techniques have so far failed to overcome is "to produce a credible and reproducible technique for overcoming image distortions" (Edmond *et al.*, 2010, p. 150; for consideration of these issues, see Edmond, Biber, Kemp, & Porter, 2009). This and the failure to recognize and address other sources of potential error such as poor image resolution, they suggest, means that "we cannot be sure that any apparent similarities accurately represent the underlying reality".

But even if similarities were to be accepted to be such, determining their significance is another problematic issue. Unless the frequency of a particular type of facial feature or characteristic, or combination of features in the population, is known, it is difficult to say with any certainty what – if any – significance should be attached to the fact that the defendant and the offender both share those features. Those who provide opinions about identity based on facial image comparison must overcome a problem that confronts many of those involved in forensic comparison – the lack of a suitable database that can be used to generate reliable probability estimates. The multidisciplinary committee that drafted the NAS report noted that:

Among existing forensic methods, only nuclear DNA analysis has been rigorously shown to have the capacity to consistently, and with a high degree of certainty, demonstrate a connection between evidence and a specific individual or source. (NAS, 2009, p. 100)

Despite this, English courts have taken a notoriously laissez faire approach to the reception of expert evidence. Notwithstanding the problems described above, they have been willing to place faith in the trial processes and to trust that juries have the ability to evaluate facial mapping evidence appropriately.

The general position is that a witness who is "suitably qualified" in facial mapping may give expert opinion based on image comparison (Attorney-General's Reference, 2003; *R v. Clarke*, 1995; *R v. Stockwell*, 1993). An expert may express an opinion in positive terms – that is to say, to declare that the individual depicted in the images of the culprit and defendant are one and the same person. However, the common practice is to express a basic form of probabilistic opinion using a graded scale. The English Court of Appeal's decision in *R v. Grey* (2003) stands alone as an example of critical comment by an English appellate court on this form of evidence. In a notable passage, the Court observed that:

[The expert in the case], like some other facial imaging and mapping experts, said that comparison of the facial characteristics provided "strong support for the identification of the robber as the appellant". No evidence was led of the number of occasions on which any of the six facial characteristics identified by him as "the more unusual and thus individual" were present in the general population, nor as to the frequency of the occurrence in the general population, of combinations of these or any other facial characteristics. [The expert] did not suggest that there was any national database of facial characteristics or any accepted mathematical formula, as in the case of fingerprint comparison, from which conclusions as to the probability of occurrence of particular facial characteristics or combinations of facial characteristics could safely be drawn. This court is not aware of the existence of any such database or agreed formula. In their absence any estimate of probabilities and any expression of the degree of support provided by particular facial characteristics or combinations of facial characteristics must be only the subjective opinion of the facial imaging or mapping witness. There is no means of determining objectively whether or not such an opinion is justified. Consequently, unless and until a national database or agreed formula or some other such objective measure is established, this court doubts whether such opinions should ever be expressed by facial imaging or mapping witnesses. The evidence of such witnesses, including opinion evidence, is of course both admissible and frequently of value to demonstrate to a jury with, if necessary, enhancement techniques afforded by specialist equipment, particular facial characteristics or combinations of such characteristics so as to permit the jury to reach its own conclusion ... but on the state of the evidence in this case, and if this court's understanding of the current position is correct in other cases too, such evidence should stop there. (*R v. Grey*, 2003, para. 16)

Although the judgment in *Grey* appeared to mark the imposition of a significant constraint on the extent of the opinions that facial mapping experts are permitted to offer in English criminal proceedings, it was marginalized in subsequent judgments of the Court of Appeal. In *R v. Gardner* (2004), which was decided shortly after *Grey*, the observations made in *Grey* were described as a "note of caution" relating to new techniques, and it was said that there was no rule that prevented an expert, having identified similarities, from expressing an opinion as to the degree of probability of the images being the same. The expression of opinion in the form of a probability estimate was the subject of renewed challenge in *R v. Atkins* (2009). Here the expert utilized the following descriptors:

Level 0: Lends no support
Level 1: Lends limited support
Level 2: Lends moderate support
Level 3: Lends support
Level 4: Lends strong support
Level 5: Lends powerful support

His evidence was that the similarities found in images of the offender and the defendant provided a level of support to the proposition that they were the same person which was somewhere between the top of Level 3 and into Level 4 on this scale. There was no objection to the expert giving evidence of the examination and comparison of the images, or to evidence concerning the similarities that were found. But it was submitted that the absence of a database meant that there was no objective basis for the opinion regarding levels of support. Those engaged in this practice can and do claim that they draw upon considerable experience in the field to determine the appropriate point on the scale. However, as counsel for the defendant in *Atkins* suggested, the use of this kind of scale carries the risk that purely subjective evaluation will be invested with spurious scientific authority. The response of the Court of Appeal to this issue was consistent with the general approach of the English courts – the limitations of the evidence could be explored in cross-examination, and the basis upon which the opinion is advanced ought to be made clear to the jury. The fact that the jury is aware of these matters does not change a fact that is common to all forms of identification evidence: that where such evidence is based on nothing more than subjective judgment, its reliability cannot be determined effectively at trial. As Edmond *et al.* (2010) pointed out, concessions regarding the limitations of expert evidence are no substitute for validating and demonstrating the reliability of the technique.

CONCLUSION

What general conclusions might be drawn from the preceding discussion? We might think about three matters relating to the forms of evidence with which we have been concerned – eyewitness identification evidence, evidence of recognition from images, and image comparison evidence. The first is the extent of our knowledge of the risk of error associated with each form of evidence. The second is the extent to which procedures have been developed that might control these risks and produce reliable evidence. The third is the extent to which such procedures have been adopted by those responsible for the administration of the criminal process. A great deal is known about the sources of error that can adversely affect the accuracy of eyewitnesses' attempts to identify others, and the scientific literature contains a relatively sophisticated set of procedural recommendations that would do much to mitigate the risk of wrongful conviction on the basis of mistaken eyewitness identification evidence. However, few legal systems have procedures that are consistent with the more significant recommendations, such as blind administration and the recording of a witness' confidence. We know that people are not particularly accurate in their attempts to identify people from images where the subject is not well known to them, but courts seem less aware of the problems associated with this form of evidence than with eyewitness identification evidence. The question of how we might address the kind of problems considered above seems to have received less attention from researchers, and perhaps as a consequence of this, those responsible for the development of criminal procedure appear to have been slow to develop specific procedures to manage the risk of error. But of the three forms of evidence considered above, the manner in which the law deals with facial mapping evidence provides the greatest cause for concern. Although they are "knowable", we know little about the extent of the risks (error rates) associated with this form of evidence. There are weaknesses associated with all of the techniques that are commonly used by experts to compare images of an offender with one of a suspect (see Davis, Valentine, & Wilkinson, 2012). It might be that some experts who use these techniques are able to identify suspects correctly some of the time (perhaps even most of the time), but those who routinely provide this form of evidence have not been required by the courts to demonstrate the validity or reliability of their methods and techniques, which inevitably involve some form of subjective evaluation. The legal system has taken no significant steps to ensure that where this form of evidence is presented to juries it is reliable. We are acutely aware of the risk of miscarriage of justice as a result of flawed eyewitness identification evidence, but there are good grounds for thinking that the risk may be greater where a prosecution case relies on evidence of identification from images.

REFERENCES

Alexander v. R (1981). 145 CLR 395 (Australia)

Allen, R., & Miller, J. (1993). The common law theory of experts: Deference or education? *Northwestern University Law Review*, *87*, 1131–1147.

Attorney-General's Reference (2003). No. 2 of 2002. EWCA Crim 2373 (England and Wales)

Australian Law Reform Commission (1985). *Evidence*, Report No. 26. Interim, Canberra: ALRC.

Australian Law Reform Commission (1987). *Evidence*, Report No. 38. Canberra: ALRC.

Bingham, T. (2006). Assessing contentious eyewitness evidence: A judicial view. In A. Heaton-Armstrong, E. Shepherd, G. Gudjonsson, & D. Wolchover (Eds.), *Witness Testimony: Psychological, Investigative and Evidential Perspectives*. Oxford: Oxford University Press.

Bogan, P. & Roberts A. (2011). *Identification: Investigation, Trial and Scientific Evidence* (2nd Edn.). Bristol: Jordan.

Bromby, M., MacMillan, M., & McKellar, P. (2007). An examination of criminal jury directions in relation to eyewitness identification in Commonwealth jurisdictions. *Common Law World Review*, *36*, 303–336

Bruce, V., Henderson, Z., Greenwood, K., Hancock, P., Burton, A.M., & Miller, P. (1999). Verification of face identities from images captured on video. *Journal of Experimental Psychology: Applied*, *5*, 339–360. doi:10.1037/1076-898X.7.3.207

Costigan, R. (2007). Identification from CCTV: The risk of injustice. *Criminal Law Review*, 591–608.

Craig v. R (1933). 49 CLR 429 (Australia)

Damaška, M. (1997). *Evidence Law Adrift*. New Haven, CT: Yale University Press.

Davies v. R (1937). HCA 27; 57 CLR 170 (Australia)

Davis, D., & Loftus, E. (2012a). Inconsistencies between law and the limits of human cognition: The case of eyewitness identification. In L. Nadel, & W. Sinnott-Armstrong (Eds.), *Memory and the Law* (pp. 29–58). Oxford: Oxford University Press.

Davis, D., & Loftus, E. (2012b). The dangers of eyewitnesses for the innocent: learning from the past and projecting into the age of social media. *New England Law Review*, *46*, 769–809.

Davis, J.P., & Valentine, T. (2009). CCTV on trial: Matching video images with the defendant in the dock. *Applied Cognitive Psychology*, *23*, 482–505. doi:10.1002/acp.1490

Davis. J.P., Valentine, T., & Wilkinson, C. (2012). Facial image comparison. In C. Wilkinson, & C. Rynn (Eds.), *Craniofacial Identification* (pp. 136–153). Cambridge: Cambridge University Press.

Devenport, J., Stinson, V., Cutler, B., & Kravitz, D. (2002). How effective are the cross-examination and expert testimony safeguards? Jurors' perceptions of the suggestiveness and fairness of biased lineup procedures. *Journal of Applied Psychology*, *87*, 1042–1054. doi:10.1037/0021-9010.87.6.1042

Devlin, P. (1976). *Report to the Secretary of State for the Home Department of the Departmental Committee on Evidence of Identification in Criminal Cases*. London: HMSO.

Edmond, G., Biber, K., Kemp, R., & Porter, G. (2009). Law's looking glass: Expert identification evidence derived from photographic and video images. *Current Issues in Criminal Justice*, *20*, 337–377.

Edmond, G., Cole, S., Cunliffe, E., & Roberts, A. (2013). Admissibility compared: The reception of incriminating expert opinion (i.e. forensic science) evidence in four adversarial jurisdictions. *University of Denver Criminal Law Review*, *3*, 31–109.

Edmond, G., Kemp, R., Porter, G., Hamer, D., Burton, M., Biber, K., & San Roque, M. (2010). Atkins v. The Emperor: The "cautious" use of unreliable "expert" opinion. *International Journal of Evidence and Proof*, *14*, 146–166.

Edmond, G., & Roberts, A. (2011). Procedural fairness, the criminal trial, and forensic science and medicine. *Sydney Law Review*, *33*, 359–394.

Edmond, G., & San Roque, M. (2009). Quasi justice: *Ad hoc* experts and identification evidence. *Criminal Law Journal*, *33*, 8–33.

Garrett, B. (2011). *Convicting the Innocent: Where Criminal Prosecutions Go Wrong*. Cambridge, MA: Harvard University Press.

Garrioch, L., & Brimacombe, C. (2001). Lineup administrators expectations: Their impact on eyewitness confidence. *Law and Human Behavior*, *25*, 299–315. doi:10.1023/A:1010750028643

Holdenson, O. (1988). The admission of expert evidence of opinion as to the potential unreliability of evidence of visual identification. *Melbourne University Law Review*, *16*, 521–547.

Holland v. HM Advocate (2005) UKPC D1.

Lindsay, R., Wells, G., & O'Connor, F. (1989). Mock juror belief of accurate and inaccurate eyewitnesses: A replication and extension. *Law and Human Behavior*, *13*, 333–339. doi:10.1007/BF01067033

Mahoney, R., McDonald, E., Optican, S., & Tinsley, Y. (2007). *The Evidence Act 2006: Act and Analysis*. Wellington: Thomson Brookers.

McQuiston-Surrett, D., & Saks, M. (2009). The testimony of forensic identification science: What expert witnesses say and what fact-finders hear. *Law and Human Behavior*, *33*, 436–453. doi:10.1007/s10979-008-9169-1

National Academy of Sciences (US). (2009). *Strengthening the Forensic Sciences in the United States: A Path Forward.* Washington, DC: The National Academies Press.

New Jersey v. Henderson (2011) 27 A.3d 872.

Norris, C., McCahill, M., & Wood, D. (2004). The growth of CCTV: A global perspective on the international diffusion of video surveillance in publicly accessible space. *Surveillance and Society*, *2*, 110–135. Retrieved from http://www.surveillance-and-society.org/articles2(2)/editorial.pdf

O'Floinn, M., & Ormerod, D. (2012). Social networking material as criminal evidence. *Criminal Law Review*, 486–512.

Ohio Code (2010) §2933.83. Retrieved from http://codes.ohio.gov/orc/2933.83

Phillips, M., McAuliff, B., Kovera, M., & Cutler, B. (1999). Double-blind photoarray administration as a safeguard against investigator bias. *Journal of Applied Psychology*, *84*, 940–951. doi:10.1037/0021-9010.84.6.940

Police and Criminal Evidence Act (1984) Codes of Practice, Code D (2011). Retrieved from http://www.homeoffice.gov.uk/publications/police/operational-policing/pace-codes/pace-code-d-2011

R v. Alexander and McGill (2012) EWCA Crim 2768 (England and Wales)

R v. Anderson (2005) BCSC 1346 (CanLII) (Canada)

R v. Atkins (2009) EWCA Crim 1876 (England and Wales)

R v. Brady (2004) EWCA Crim 2230 (England and Wales)

R v. Callum (2010) EWCA Crim. 1325 (England and Wales)

R v. Clarke (1995) 2 Cr App R 425 (England and Wales)

R v. Fergus (1994) 98 Cr. App. R. 313, CA (England and Wales)

R v. Forbes (2000) All ER (D) 2291, 1 AC 473, UKHL40 (England and Wales)

R v. Gardner (2004) EWCA Crim 1639 (England and Wales)

R v. Grey (2003) EWCA Crim 1001 (England and Wales)

R v. Johnson (2000; unreported) 24th October 2000 (2000 WL 1675176) (England and Wales)

R v. Marcus (2004) EWCA Crim 3387; *The Times*, December 3, 2004 (England and Wales)

R v. McCullough (2011) EWCA Crim 1413 (England and Wales)

R v. Nicholson (1999) EWCA Crim 2101 (England and Wales)

R v. Smith (2008) EWCA Crim 1342 (England and Wales)

R v. Stockwell (1993) 97 Cr App R 260 (England and Wales)

R v. Toth (2005) EWCA Crim 754. (England and Wales)

R v. Turner (1974) 60 Cr. App. R. 80 (England and Wales)

R v. Williams (2003) EWCA Crim 3200 (England and Wales)

Ramirez, G., Zemba, D., & Geiselman, R. (1996). Judges' cautionary instructions on eyewitness testimony. *American Journal of Forensic Psychology*, *14*, 31–66.

Risinger, M. (2007). Innocents convicted: An empirically justified factual wrongful conviction rate. *Journal of Criminal Law and Criminology*, *97*, 761–806.

Roberts, A. (2008a). Pre-trial defence rights and the fair use of eyewitness identification procedures. *Modern Law Review*, *71*, 331–357.

Roberts, A. (2008b). Eyewitness identification evidence: Procedural developments and the ends of adjudicative accuracy. *International Commentary on Evidence*, *6*, Article 3.

Simon, D. (2012). More problems with criminal trials: The limited effectiveness of legal mechanisms. *Law and Contemporary Problems, 75*, 167–209.

Strauss v. Police (2013) SASC 3 (Australia)

Summers, R. (1999). Formal legal truth and substantive truth in judicial fact-finding: Their justified divergence in some particular cases. *Law and Philosophy, 18*, 497–511.

Twining, W. (1994). *Rethinking Evidence: Exploratory Essays*. Evanston: Northwestern University Press.

United States v. Downing (1985) 753 F.2d 1224 (United States)

United States Department of Justice, National Institute of Justice (1999). *Eyewitness Identification: A Guide for Law Enforcement*. Washington, DC: Department of Justice.

Valentine, T. (2006). Forensic facial identification. In A. Heaton-Armstrong, E. Shepherd, G. Gudjonsson, & D. Wolchover (Eds.), *Witness Testimony: Psychological, Investigative and Evidential Perspectives* (pp. 281–307). Oxford: Oxford University Press.

Valentine, T., & Maras, K. (2011). The effect of cross-examination on the accuracy of adult eyewitness testimony. *Applied Cognitive Psychology, 25*, 554–561. doi:10.1002/acp.1768

Wells, G. (2006). Eyewitness identifications: Systemic reforms. *Wisconsin Law Review*, 615–644.

Wells, G., Lindsay, R., & Ferguson, T. (1979). Accuracy, confidence and juror perceptions in eyewitness identifications. *Journal of Applied Psychology, 64*, 440–448.

Wells, G., & Quinlivan, D. (2009). Suggestive identification procedures and the Supreme Court's reliability test in light of eyewitness science: 30 years later. *Law and Human Behavior, 33*, 1–24. doi:10.1007/s10979-008-9130-3

Wilcock, R., Bull, R., & Milne, B. (2008). *Witness Identification in Criminal Cases: Psychology and Practice*. Oxford: Oxford University Press.

Winmar v. Western Australia (2007) WASCA 244.

Wolchover, D., & Heaton-Armstrong, A. (2006). Improving visual identification procedures under PACE Code D. In A. Heaton-Armstrong, E. Shepherd, G. Gudjonsson, & D. Wolchover (Eds.), *Witness Testimony: Psychological, Investigative and Evidential Perspectives*. Oxford: Oxford University Press.

13

Forensic Facial Identification: A Practical Guide to Best Practice

TIM VALENTINE AND JOSH P. DAVIS

The witness who has sincerely convinced himself and whose sincerity carried conviction is not infrequently mistaken. (Devlin, 1976, para. 8.1)

Identification evidence is a vital tool in the prosecution of offenders in the criminal justice system; it is often critical to the successful prosecution of criminals. But identification evidence carries a high risk of being unreliable. With identification evidence central to criminal prosecution, methods need to be developed that eliminate as much risk of mistaken identification as possible. The careful analysis of experimental science and archival case studies presented by leading researchers in the preceding chapters show that diligent attention to procedure, combined in some cases with technological developments, can reduce the risks of error.

It this chapter we make practical recommendations for best practice based on the current state of scientific knowledge and established procedure. Before considering the various procedures individually, we turn

Forensic Facial Identification: Theory and Practice of Identification from Eyewitnesses, Composites and CCTV, First Edition. Edited by Tim Valentine and Josh P. Davis.
© 2015 John Wiley & Sons, Ltd. Published 2015 by John Wiley & Sons, Ltd.

Case study: Identification in a case of historic sex abuse

Paul Cannon, 40, was suspected of multiple offences of child sexual abuse. Three offences were alleged to have taken place against different victims approximately 5, 10 and 15 years previously. The victims were aged between 7 and 12 years old at the time of the offences. The suspect denied the allegations and stated he was prepared to participate in an identification procedure. In these circumstances the code of practice in the UK requires that the suspect should be offered a video identification procedure using moving images, unless the suspect has an unusual physical feature that cannot be concealed or replicated on the other images available. The identification officer may then decide to use still images. A still image of the suspect taken approximately ten years previously was available. The appearance of the suspect had changed considerably in that time.

The identification officer sought advice on the best procedure to adopt. The officer proposed using a video lineup with moving images containing a contemporary image of the suspect. If the witness made no identification, a second procedure using still images including the old photograph of the suspect was proposed. The identification officer was aware of the dangers of repeated procedures and suggested inserting a delay of two weeks between procedures.

If two identification procedures were run, the suspect would be the only person included in both procedures. There was a risk of transference of familiarity between the procedures. A positive identification in the second procedure could be disputed on the grounds that his face was familiar from the first identification procedure and not from the alleged offence. A second procedure would only be carried out if the witness did not identify the suspect from the first procedure. Therefore there would be no "commitment effect" of a repeated identification (see Chapter 4). A delay of two weeks would help to reduce the familiarity induced by repeating the same person in a lineup. Nevertheless, if the suspect was identified in the second procedure, the defence could challenge the probative value of the identification in court. Psychological science would provide a basis for such a challenge. For these reasons, the advice offered was not to use repeated procedures, if at all avoidable.

Instead the identification officer was advised to use a single procedure using the old photograph in a lineup of still video images, taking care to ensure that the photograph of the suspect did not stand out in any way. The old photograph is likely to be a better representation of the appearance of the suspect at the time of the offence, especially for the two earlier offences. By the encoding specificity principle (Tulving & Thompson, 1973) an image that includes more of the facial cues present at the time of the offence is more likely to be recognized than an image of the suspect's appearance now. If his appearance had changed considerably, this could have a substantial effect. Equally, using the encoding specificity principle, one could argue that a moving image would contain more cues that were available at the time of the offence than a still image. A lineup format which contains "more" rather than "less" information (i.e., moving vs. still images) provides a more sensitive test, but the effect is relatively small (see Chapter 6). Using a single lineup of still images containing the old photograph could only be challenged on the grounds that moving images should have been used. The identification officer could justify his choice on the grounds that the suspect's appearance had changed since the crime. Ultimately, this would be a matter for the court to decide.

At the time the identification procedure was run, the defence solicitor did not challenge the use of still images in a lineup based on the old photograph. Three witnesses identified the suspect without hesitation. Paul Cannon subsequently made admissions at interview. At trial he admitted more than 30 offences and was sentenced to four years imprisonment.

first to a ubiquitous psychological bias that affects all of forensic science and other areas of human judgement.

CONFIRMATION BIAS

Confirmation bias (see Nickerson, 1998, for an extensive review) refers to a tendency to perceive and interpret information in such a way as to reinforce prior beliefs or expectations. Confirmation bias is well established in the scientific literature, and found in many areas of human judgement. The person affected by confirmation bias will often be entirely unaware of any selective or biased use of evidence, and may have no apparent motivation to interpret evidence in one way or another. Confirmation bias may take the form of failing to look for disconfirming evidence, placing too much weight on confirmatory evidence, a predisposition to see what one expects to see, and an over-reliance on habitual or familiar ways of interpreting ambiguous evidence.

A person called upon to make a judgement can avoid confirmation bias if they are kept "blind" to the relevant expectation or hypothesis. It is for this reason that the double-blind randomized controlled trial is accepted as the best method to study clinical interventions (Rajaopal, 2006). In a double-blind trial a drug administered in the form of a pill, for example, is tested against a placebo condition in which a pill with no active ingredient is taken. Both the patient and the person running the trial (the experimenter) do not know whether the patient is taking the drug or the placebo (hence *double-blind*). Knowledge of the experimental condition can increase or decrease reports of the efficacy of the treatment and/or reporting of side-effects, depending on the person's prior beliefs or motivations. For example, the experimenter may be keen to demonstrate that the medicine is effective and safe. The patient may be strongly motivated to find symptoms are relieved. Patients in the placebo condition show improvement compared with a control condition, and often report side-effects (Rajaopal, 2006).

Unfortunately, double-blind randomized controlled trials are rare in forensic science. And yet, confirmation bias has been shown to adversely affect the reliability of forensic science, in particular judgements made by fingerprint experts (Dror, Charlton, & Peron, 2006; Kassin, Dror, & Kukucka, 2013). Dror *et al.* (2006) investigated the reliability of identification of a latent fingerprint recovered from a crime scene when compared with records held on file. They used a covert procedure to present five experts from an international pool (who had a mean of 17 years experience) with a pair of fingerprints that he or she had previously judged to be a match. The experts were led to believe it was a fingerprint from a well-known case in which a fingerprint had been erroneously matched. Therefore the expectation was set up that the fingerprint presented would *not* be a match with the latent print recovered from the crime scene. Only one of the five experts judged the prints to be a match, consistent with their previous judgement. The remaining experts changed their decision demonstrating the effects of a confirmation bias.

The result of Dror *et al.*'s (2006) research was shocking. For more than 100 years courts have been led to accept that fingerprints are unique and that a positive match is undisputable. However, during the course of the investigation of the murder of Marion Ross in 1997, the Scottish Criminal Records Office (SCRO) incorrectly identified two fingerprints. As a consequence, David Ashbury was convicted for the murder of Ross, and Shirley McKie – a serving police officer – was charged with perjury. Following an appeal, Ashbury was acquitted. McKie was acquitted after international fingerprint experts testified at her trial that, contrary to the SCRO identification, a fingerprint found at the crime scene was not hers.[1]

If an expert judgement is reliable it should be consistent from one occasion to another, different experts should make the same judgement, and the judgement should not be affected by bias from the cognitive context. The problem of confirmation bias in forensic science has been demonstrated in subsequent studies (e.g., Dror & Rosenthal, 2008), and has been recognized in a report by the US National Research Academy (2009) on strengthening forensic science. Referring to forensic science in general, the report found that:

> A body of research is required to establish the limits and measures of performance and to address the impact of sources of variability and potential bias. Such research is sorely needed, but it seems to be lacking in most of the forensic disciplines that rely on subjective assessments of matching characteristics. ...
>
> The development of such research programs can benefit significantly from other areas, notably from the large body of research on the evaluation of observer performance in diagnostic medicine and from the findings of cognitive psychology on the potential for bias and error in human observers. (National Research Academy, 2009, p. 8)

The courts have an important role to play in demanding high-quality scientific evidence from the forensic sciences, as without such demands there is no incentive for forensic science labs to provide better quality work. An essential step is to require that forensic scientists adopt the standard of double-blind testing that is used in other scientific disciplines (Saks, Rislinger, Rosenthal, & Thompson, 2003).

The National Research Academy (2009) report expressed particular concern about the many areas of forensic science that rely on "subjective assessments of matching characteristics". Examples include identification of fingerprints, ballistics (marks on bullets used to identify the gun), bite marks, ear prints, and footwear impressions (see Kassin et al., 2013, for a review). In the same manner, judgements of facial identity can also be based on "subjective assessments of matching characteristics". Confirmation bias has been shown to affect similarity judgements in comparing facial photographs of adults and children (Bressan & Dal Martello, 2002), and comparing a facial composite and a suspect (Charman, Gregory, & Carlucci, 2009). Therefore, it is likely that judgements made by ordinary observers (such as police officers) and by experts in facial comparison who give expert testimony in court

[1]See www.shirleymckie.com

may be subject to confirmation bias. Facial comparison experts may be particularly susceptible to bias, as there is no reliable database of the frequency of facial characteristics in the population or any standard algorithm for determining a match (see chapters 10 and 12).

In addition to its influence on forensic science, confirmation bias can influence eyewitness identification evidence. For example, confirmation bias may underlie a propensity of a witness to select from a police lineup, rather than make no choice. A belief that there is a suspect in the lineup, who must have been arrested for a good reason, may induce a witness to choose from the lineup. Similarly, confirmation bias may induce witnesses to identify somebody from police photographs (mugshots) of people associated with similar criminal activity, or to identify a suspect in a street identification or showup. The risk of confirmation bias may be heightened if a witness, having identified a suspect in one identification procedure, is presented with the same suspect in a second procedure.

Confirmation bias can affect the criminal investigation as well as the evaluation of evidence. An investigation can become focused on building a case against a suspect, and neglect the need to search for and evaluate exculpatory evidence, for example to confirm an alibi. Williamson (2004, 2006) refers to this effect as "tunnel vision". Confirmation bias had a lethal effect in the investigation of the failed attempt to plant bombs in London on July 21, 2005. The police had identified Hussain Osman as a suspect and had a block of flats where he lived under surveillance. The officers had a photograph of Osman. When Jean Charles de Menezes, who was staying in the same block, left to go to work the following morning, a police officer made a radio call to say that he was worth "another look". This call appears to have initiated a sequence of events in which *confirmation bias* amongst the operations team led them to interpret the call and subsequent information as evidence that de Menezes had been identified as Osman (see Cole & Thompson, 2013). Evidence that might have pointed towards de Menezes' innocence was ignored or not collected, and innocent actions were readily interpreted as evidence of guilt. For example, de Menezes caught a bus from the block of flats to Brixton underground station where he alighted. On finding out that the station was closed due to the security alert caused by the attempted bombing the previous day, he got back on the same bus to travel to the next station at Stockwell. The plain clothes officers who were following him on the bus were unaware that Brixton station was closed and interpreted de Menezes' behaviour as an anti-surveillance technique. Police transcripts suggest that by the time de Menezes was shot dead on a London Underground train at Stockwell station, the police were confident that he had been identified as a terrorist. See the case study in Chapter 9 for more details of this case.

BEST PRACTICE IN FORENSIC FACIAL IDENTIFICATION

Any test used in forensic science must be valid (i.e., measure what it is claimed to measure) and reliable (i.e., results should be replicable by different scientists and on different samples). A valid forensic test should be sensitive (have a low false negative rate by detecting small traces) and fair (it should have a low false positive rate). To achieve these goals it is essential that physical samples of forensic significance must not become contaminated by the forensic scientist, other witnesses or other people involved in the investigation.

Procedures used to obtain eyewitness identification evidence need to meet the same criteria as any other forensic science test. The procedure used to obtain identification evidence – from first interview to the evidence presented in court – should maximize the likelihood of obtaining accurate identification evidence against guilty suspects (i.e., be as sensitive as possible), and minimize the possibility of mistaken identification (i.e., be as fair as possible). Equally it is essential that the eyewitness evidence obtained is not distorted by potentially misleading information. Anybody who talks to an eyewitness or runs any sort of identification procedure can distort the witness' memory (see Chapter 2). For this reason, procedures used to obtain eyewitness identification evidence need to be designed and conducted as carefully as any other forensic test. The eyewitness' memory is the key to the forensic evidence. As much care needs to be taken not to distort a witness' memory as a scenes-of-crime officer takes not to contaminate the crime scene.

The recommendations made below are intended to apply to adult witnesses, except where other witnesses (e.g., children) are specifically mentioned. Interview or identification procedures conducted with vulnerable or intimidated witnesses may require additional procedures. Good practice in investigative interviewing, including procedures for vulnerable and intimidated witnesses, are described in the guidance on achieving best evidence published by the UK Ministry of Justice (2011) and the National Institute for Child Health and Development (NICHD) interview protocol.[2] Vulnerable witnesses include all witnesses under 18 years old, and witnesses with a mental disorder, learning disability or a physical disability.

Interviewing

The aim of interviewing an eyewitness is to obtain information that is as accurate and as complete as possible. Errors in a witness' description can adversely affect the accuracy of any subsequent identification

[2]The NICHD interview protocol can be downloaded from: http://nichdprotocol.com/

procedure (see Chapter 2). Therefore, it is of paramount importance to avoid description errors. Human memory is malleable, often incomplete, and may be based on the witness' subjective interpretation of events. Therefore, unless conducted with great care, an investigative interview can produce information that is inaccurate and incomplete.

- *Investigators should take steps to prevent witnesses talking to each other:* Discussing the event with a co-witness can be a highly influential source of misleading information.
- *Prior to an interview or identification procedure, a record should be made of whether the witness has discussed the case with any co-witnesses. If so which witnesses have conferred should be recorded:* Information obtained from a co-witness can be a powerful source of memory distortion. Witnesses conferring can give a false impression of unanimity on a false detail. This recommendation is made by Memon, Dalton, Horry, Milne, and Wright (2012).
- *Interviews should be conducted as soon as possible after the event:* Memory decays rapidly at first. The rate of forgetting slows with increased delay. An early interview is likely to capture a more complete account. It also minimizes the opportunity for witnesses to encounter potentially misleading information that may distort their memory.
- *Interviewers should be trained to conduct a high-quality interview:* There is an extensive body of research on investigative interviewing and use of the cognitive interview. Interviewers should establish a good rapport with the witness, and transfer control of the interview to the witness by inviting an open recall of events in their own words and in their own time, without interruption. Witnesses should be encouraged to report every detail, no matter how unimportant it may seem, but to avoid guessing details of which they are unsure. The cognitive interview includes a procedure for the witness to mentally reinstate the context of the event prior to recall of the event. Interviewers' questions should be based on the structure of the witness' account. Interviewers should ask open questions and avoid inappropriate questioning including use of leading questions, complex and multiple questions, and forced choice questions (see Memon, Meissner, & Fraser, 2010; Wells, Memon, & Penrod, 2006; for more information on the cognitive interview).
- *If resources are not available to interview witnesses immediately, witnesses should be asked to complete a self-administered interview:* This is a questionnaire that the witness can complete in their own time. It is based on the principles of the cognitive interview.

The self-administered interview has been shown to promote recall that is as complete as that obtained from a cognitive interview and includes no additional errors than the cognitive interview (Gabbert, Hope, & Fisher, 2009). The self-administered interview also provides some resistance to accepting misleading information that is subsequently encountered (Gabbert, Hope, Fisher, & Jamieson, 2012).

Facial Composites

If there is an eyewitness available but the police do not know the identity of a suspect, the witness may be invited to compile a likeness of the culprit using a facial composite system under the guidance of an operator. Although facial composites are used in a relatively small proportion of crimes, a good composite can provide the vital lead in a stalled investigation. As a consequence of technological advancements partly based on psychological principles, the quality of composites has markedly improved in recent years (see Chapter 3). The purpose of producing a facial composite is to circulate the likeness to people who may be known to the perpetrator personally (e.g., police officers or members of the public). Therefore composites are always produced by somebody who is unfamiliar with the target person, but hopefully recognized by somebody who knows the target well. The following recommendations for best practice in the production and use of facial composites are based on the research literature reviewed in Chapter 3.

- *Use of a holistic composite system should be considered:* The modern systems that evolve a facial appearance produce better likenesses than older systems that rely solely on selecting individual features, and are generally easier and quicker for the witness to use.
- *Facial composite operators should be trained to use the system appropriately:* Operating a facial composite system and facilitating production of the best possible likeness is a skilled task. It requires good interviewing and interpersonal skills, and sound knowledge of the system being used. Some artistic skills are an advantage. Companies that produce facial composite systems provide training courses for operators.[3]
- *A holistic-cognitive interview should be used to interview a witness prior to production of a facial composite:* The witness should be carefully interviewed using this technique, which is designed to elicit a description that is as accurate and complete as possible, without introducing errors.

[3]See www.evofit.co.uk and www.visionmetric.com

- *The outer features should be blurred or covered during facial composite construction:* Blurring the outer features (hair and face shape) focuses attention on the internal features of the face. A facial composite is constructed by a witness who is unfamiliar with the culprit's face. The outer features are more salient than the inner features to people who are unfamiliar with a face. However, in familiar face recognition the inner features are relatively more important. The purpose of constructing a facial composite is that it will be recognized by somebody who is familiar with the target person. Therefore it is important that the inner features are constructed as accurately as possible. Blurring or even removing the outer features entirely during construction helps to achieve a more recognizable image.
- *Presenting the composite image using methods such as a perceptual stretch or an animated caricature should be considered:* Presenting a facial composite as an animated caricature has been found to enhance recognition by people who are familiar with the target person. Animated caricature requires the composite to be presented in video on television or on a website, for example. A perceptual stretch, which does not require video and so is more suitable for print media, has also been found to enhance recognition.
- *If multiple witnesses are available, a morph of the composite produced by each witness should be made and only the morph should be circulated to the media:* In morphed images produced by different witnesses, errors tend to be averaged out because different witnesses tend to make different errors. Features common to all of the images will be relatively unmodified by the morphing process. Morphs are at least as well recognized as the best of the constituent composites. Morphing avoids the difficult problem of determining which is the "best" composite produced by different witnesses (Bruce, Ness, Hancock, Newman, & Rarity, 2002).
- *If multiple witnesses are not available, and a holistic composite system is used, consideration should be given to asking the witness to produce more than one composite to enable a within-witness morph to be produced:* A morph of multiple (e.g. four) composites produced by the same witness is better recognized than the individual composites. The witness' rank order of the quality of the composites is used to weight the contributions to the morph, so that the best likeness is given most weight in producing the morph (Valentine, Davis, Thorner, Solomon, & Gibson, 2010).
- *Facial composites should not be presented as evidence in court:* A facial composite is a type-likeness of the witness' recollection. It is not an image of the offender. The purpose of constructing a composite is to facilitate the investigation. Specifically, a composite is produced to

find a suspect. If the identity of the suspect is already known, production of a composite is unnecessary. If a composite image has been produced, and a suspect has been identified and charged, the defendant may have been arrested solely on the basis of his or her resemblance to the composite image. Therefore the composite image does not provide independent inculpating evidence and should not be used as evidence in court. If the prosecution wish to rely on identification evidence, a formal video identification procedure, or other lineup procedure appropriate for the jurisdiction, should be carried out.

Mugshot Searches

If the police do not know the identity of a suspect and therefore he or she is not available to be placed in a lineup, a witness may be invited to search photographs of persons from the locality associated with the type of offence (known as mugshot searches or witness albums). The photographs should be selected to include only people who fit the general description of the offender. It is important to appreciate that all persons in the photographs are potential suspects. Any person identified will be investigated by the police. In this way a mugshot search is fundamentally different from a lineup.

- *Use of a mugshot search is not recommended as a method to identify an offender:* Recent fieldwork in the UK suggests that these searches are an ineffective method to identify offenders (Davis, Valentine, Memon, & Roberts, 2015). Showing of mugshots is reported in a number of the US exoneration cases caused by mistaken eyewitness identification, which suggests that mugshot searches may be associated with wrongful convictions (Innocence Project, n.d.).

If a mugshot search is used, the composition of the albums should be well-managed so that only relevant people are included (e.g., by excluding people who are currently in prison; images should be as contemporary as possible). Further research would be required to establish whether a well-managed collection of photographs of previously-arrested persons would improve the effectiveness of mugshot searches.

Street Identification and Showups

We use the term "street identification" to refer to a procedure carried out shortly after a street crime has occurred. Either the police arrange for a witness to view a single suspect in person or the witness is driven around the vicinity in the back of a police car so that a suspect can be pointed out if seen. In the UK a street identification can only be used if there is insufficient evidence to arrest a suspect without an identification. This procedure is known as a showup in the US, but the term showup can also refer to showing a single photograph of the suspect at any point in the investigation – including after arrest.

A street identification or showup is an inherently suggestive process. The procedure provides no means of falsifying any identification made, in the way that identification of a foil from a lineup discredits the witness' identification. Therefore, by definition, all mistaken identifications from a street identification are of the police suspect. Counter-intuitively, the evidence shows that people are somewhat less likely to make an identification from a street identification or showup than from a lineup. Despite this difference, street identifications are a less reliable means of identification than a lineup and do produce more mistaken identifications of an innocent suspect. However, street identifications are frequently used by the police to investigate crime. Nevertheless, an informal identification in the street can have the advantage of quickly excluding an innocent suspect without having the inconvenience of organizing a formal identification procedure. For these reasons it is impracticable to exclude all street identifications entirely.

- *Street identifications should only be used shortly after the report of a crime, and only when there are insufficient grounds for arrest without identification evidence:* We recommend this provision, which is current within English law.
- *Identification should never be made from showing a single photograph, regardless of whether the suspect is arrested or not:* If a photograph is available for an identification procedure it should always be shown in a well-designed and appropriately conducted lineup procedure.
- *A description should always be taken before a street identification procedure:* If a description is not recorded before the witness sees the suspect, there is a danger that the witness' recollection of the offender will be influenced by the appearance of the suspect – who may be innocent. If a mistaken identification was made at a street identification and a description or perpetrator is taken subsequently, the match in the appearance of the suspect to this description may artificially inflate the evidential value of the identification.
- *In a street identification, when the suspect is brought to a witness or vice versa (a confrontation), the witness should be instructed that the person shown may or may not be the perpetrator:* This issue is discussed below in relation to lineups.

Repeated Identification Procedures

Following an identification of a suspect from a mugshot or a street identification/showup, the police may wish to conduct a second (repeated) more formal identification procedure by way of a lineup, during which the same witness views the same suspect. The intention may be to "test" the evidence by ensuring that it is collected via a (normally) more robust procedure.

- *Repeated identification procedures involving the same suspect and the same witness should be avoided:* Repeating identification procedures has a strong influence on the outcome. Witnesses are highly likely to repeat the same identification made in the first procedure, even if they are mistaken. Research findings show that repeated identification has very little or no probative value (Valentine, Davis, Memon, & Roberts, 2012).
- *If a lineup is used as a second identification procedure involving the same suspect and the same witness, failure to identify the suspect is of evidential value; but if the suspect is identified again, only the first identification procedure should be presented in evidence:* Prosecutors often recommend or require a lineup is held if an identification has been made from a mugshot book or street identification. A failure to identify from a lineup does undermine the identification evidence because this will be the first falsifiable test of identification. However, if a second identification from a lineup is presented in evidence, the impression created is that the identification evidence is of better quality than it really is. The previous positive identification has a large effect on the outcome of the second procedure. Therefore, the important issue for the jury is to consider carefully the quality of the first identification procedure – the identification from a mugshot album or street identification.

Procedures for Conducting Live, Video or Photograph Lineups

Some eyewitness identification researchers have promoted the view that there are a number of lineup procedures that can reduce the number of mistaken identifications of innocent suspects, without any impact on the number of correct identifications of guilty suspects (Wells *et al.*, 1998). On this basis, procedural changes have been recommended, and in some jurisdictions in the US, changes have been made to identification procedures (American Bar Association, 2004; National Institute of Justice, 1999). Analysis by Clark (2012) showed that although all of the recommendations did reduce mistaken identifications of innocent suspects, all except one has the undesirable effect of also reducing the number of correct identifications of guilty suspects. The exception is the basis of our first recommendation.

- *If possible, a lineup procedure should always be used instead of a showup:* Whenever the police have a suspect available, and identification is disputed, a lineup should be used to obtain formal identification evidence. A lineup is a more reliable method of identification than allowing the witness to see a single suspect (Clark, 2012). Furthermore, a formal test of identification should be capable of falsifying the contention that the suspect is the culprit. The lineup procedure must include foils who are not suspected of committing the crime. If a witness identifies a foil, it can be deduced that the identification is mistaken and therefore the witness is unreliable. Note that a collection of individuals in which all members are potential suspects, such as a group street identification or a mugshot album, is not a lineup and is not capable of falsifying any identification that a witness makes.

Next, we address recommendations made by Wells *et al.* (1998) on the use of unbiased instructions, double-blind administration of lineups and the selection of the lineup members. These recommendations reduce the chances of mistaken identification. Wells (1993) promoted the view of a police lineup as an experimental test of the hypothesis that the suspect is the culprit, and as scientists we endorse these recommendations because they are based on principles of good experimental design. As citizens, we endorse them because in our view they provide reasonable protections that should be afforded to a suspect who may be innocent of any crime. A poorly designed and biased procedure, which produces evidence of low probative value, may enable the police to catch more criminals, at a cost to unfortunate individuals who may become suspects during an investigation. It is unfortunate, therefore, that as well as reducing mistaken identifications, these three recommendations are not cost-free because they have a similar size of effect in reducing correct identifications (Clark, 2012). We argue, however, that this potential disadvantage from adopting these recommendations is no reason to abandon the more important duty to avoid wrongfully prosecuting innocent suspects. Indeed, a mistaken identification may result in an investigation being terminated because an innocent person has been charged, leaving the guilty free to commit further offences. The justice obtained from maximizing the rate of suspect identifications from unfair procedures would give a false sense of security.

We therefore acknowledge that the following recommendations are not based unambiguously on science and involve a value judgement. Some of the recommendations have been varied from Wells *et al.* (1998) to take account of best practice from the UK.

- *Witnesses should be told that the perpetrator may or may not be in the lineup, and that the appropriate response may be not to make any identification:* Inviting a witness to attend an identification procedure may lead the witness to believe that the culprit is in the lineup and their job is to identify the right person. This belief would encourage the witness to identify somebody from the lineup rather than make no identification. The purpose of this instruction is to remind witnesses that the perpetrator may not be in the lineup if the police have arrested the wrong person. Generally, at least a fifth of all witnesses identify a foil, so there is strong propensity to make an identification even when memory strength is low (Horry, Memon, Wright, & Milne, 2012; Penrod & Bull Kovera, 2009; Valentine, Pickering, & Darling, 2003; see Chapter 1).
- *The person who conducts the lineup should not be involved in the investigation and should not be aware of which member of the lineup is the suspect:* If the person who administers the lineup knows which member is the suspect, he or she may inadvertently or deliberately influence the witness in their identification. For example, if the witness looked at the suspect and hesitated, saying: "It could be number 2 but I'm not sure", the lineup administrator may say "Take as much time as you need". But if the lineup administrator knows that number 2 is a foil, he or she may record the witness' comment as a non-identification in the paperwork and move on. Situations like these have been noted by the first author when advising on real cases. It is extremely difficult to stop our knowledge subtly influencing our behaviour. The most effective and easiest way of avoiding unintended influence is to keep the lineup administrator blind to the identity of the suspect. Clark (2012) found there were both fewer mistaken identifications of innocent suspects and fewer identifications of perpetrators when lineups were run double-blind. If lineups are conducted live, double-blind administration will often require additional personnel because the suspect will need to be processed separately from the volunteers who stand on the lineup (e.g., to be bailed or retained in custody). However, now almost all identification procedures conducted in the UK are run on video and the majority run in the US are photograph lineups. Therefore, simple cost-free procedures can be adopted to prevent the lineup administrator from seeing which image the witness is looking at. One strategy is to

automate the viewing of a lineup using a computer-controlled display of photographs or video. In the UK the approach has been to specify that an officer involved in the investigation cannot take part in the identification procedure, but not to require double-blind administration. We note that whilst this rule does not overcome the problem of non-blind administration, it is a good principle to separate the identification task from an investigating officer, who may be highly motivated to obtain an identification. Therefore we recommend both double-blind administration and a requirement that the lineup administrator is not involved in the investigation. These measures increase the integrity of identification evidence. If challenged in court, it can be demonstrated that the administration of the lineup could not have been influenced and the lineup administrator was independent of the investigation.

- *The foils in the lineup should be selected to ensure that the suspect does not stand out in comparison with the other lineup members, or in comparison with the witness' first recorded description:* Research shows that outcomes of lineups with foils who are highly similar to the suspect produce more reliable identifications (Fitzgerald, Price, Oriet, & Charman, 2013; see Chapter 6). Special attention should be paid to the witness' description to ensure that the suspect is not the only lineup member who matches some aspect of that description.

- *A clear statement of the witness' confidence should be recorded at the time of the identification, before the witness can receive any feedback on the outcome of the identification:* Feedback that a witness identified the right person, or identified the suspect, inflates witness confidence, making witnesses overconfident (Semmler, Brewer, & Wells, 2004). If the witness has received feedback before they give evidence in court, the evidence they give may be more indicative of the feedback than of their initial confidence at the identification procedure. Even if a witness does not receive explicit feedback, they may infer that they have identified the suspect by the time they give evidence. A confidence statement taken before feedback could have been received is most diagnostic of accuracy. The unique opportunity to obtain the confidence statement of highest probative value is while the witness is still at the identification procedure, where the statement can be recorded verbatim (preferably by video and audio), possibly in the presence of the suspect's legal representative, before any feedback could have been given.

- *Feedback should not be given to the witness:* It should be made clear that the lineup administrator does not know the identity of the suspect, and the reasons for withholding this information from the administrator and the witness should be explained. This recommendation is a further measure designed to ensure that the witness is fully informed in advance of what to expect during the identification procedure as well as to avoid distorting the witness' memory before any possible appearance in court.

The following three recommendations are derived from the current best practice in the UK. The measures are intended to provide an opportunity to resolve any disputes about the quality of the lineup before it is shown to the witness and to preserve the best possible record of the lineup and any identification made. High-quality video and audio recording will provide the court with an accurate record upon which to base the evaluation of the identification evidence.

- *The suspect and/or his/her solicitor should be allowed to inspect the lineup prior to the identification procedure and any objection to lineups members should be recorded. The police should endeavour to address any objection raised or state why it should not be addressed.*
- *A copy of the lineup should be available to be shown in court.*
- *The identification procedure should be video and audio recorded and the recording should be available for inspection in court.*

Our last recommendation concerns the widespread use in the UK of the term "positive identification" (including the Police and Criminal Evidence Act (1984) code of practice) to refer to an identification of the suspect. The interpretation of the word "positive" varies considerably amongst police officers (Hughes, 2005; cited in Valentine, Hughes and Munro, 2009).

- *The term "positive identification" should not be used in instructions to witnesses:* Some officers understand "positive identification" to apply to any identification of the suspect; others believe it means an identification made with 100% certainty. Witnesses are also likely to make different interpretations of the term. Therefore we recommend that the simple term "identification" should be used instead. The current code of practice gives the instruction to the witness as: "*If you are unable to make a positive identification you should say so*". We propose the instruction should be replaced with: "*If you are unable to make an identification you should say so*". A clear statement of confidence should be recorded immediately after the identification. Memon *et al.* (2012) make the same recommendation to remove the word "positive".

Lineups: Specialized Procedures

We have recommendations for the construction of specialized lineups in specific circumstances.

- A *wild-card should be included in the lineup if it is prepared for a child witness:* Children are more likely than adults to make a mistaken identification from a culprit-absent lineup (see Chapter 7). An effective protection is to include a wild-card in the lineup (a silhouette with a question mark to indicate an unknown person). This serves to remind the witness that the culprit may not be present and has been found to reduce mistaken identifications by children, without reducing correct identifications of the culprit.
- A *distinguishing mark on the suspect's face should be replicated on the faces of other lineup members, in preference to obscuring the area on all faces:* It is common practice for distinguishing facial marks of a suspect's face (e.g., a scar or tattoo) to be occluded. The same area on each lineup member's face is similarly occluded so that the suspect does not stand out. However, this procedure involves changing the appearance of the suspect. If instead the mark is replicated on all of the lineup members, with some minor variation (e.g., a slightly different scar should be displayed on all lineup members), the witness is more likely to identify a guilty suspect (see Chapter 6).

Human Face Matching

The research literature on human performance in face-matching tasks is reviewed in Chapter 9. The tasks considered include comparing two photographs, or a person physically present with a photograph, to determine whether they are the same person or not. In court cases the comparison may be to CCTV imagery. Availability of CCTV imagery allows a "witness" who was not present at the scene (often a police officer) to provide identification evidence from the imagery. Research shows that matching the identity of unfamiliar faces is more difficult than it is often assumed to be, even when the quality of images is good. Differences in aspects of specific images, such as lighting, expression, angle of view, and the optical characteristics of a camera, make comparison of images of unfamiliar faces difficult. Two images of the same person can look very different; two images of different people can look very similar. Averaged facial images, which are produced by morphing the visual texture to a standard face-shape and averaging the texture across images, perform well as comparison images (Burton, Jenkins, Hancock, & White, 2005). Training people to improve their ability to match faces has been unsuccessful, or had only limited success which has not been shown to improve performance over an extended period (Alenezi & Bindemann, 2013; White, Kemp, Jenkins, & Burton, 2013). However, there are large individual differences in unfamiliar face-matching performance: a few people perform much better than the average (Davis, Jansari, & Lander, 2013). Matching faces of familiar people, who are well-known to the observer, is substantially more reliable than is matching unfamiliar faces. Therefore we make the following recommendations:

- *Identification evidence from photographs should be collected using a controlled protocol and be carefully recorded:* Photographs should be viewed alone; no identification should be suggested by another person prior to the viewing. Records of the photographs viewed and instructions given, and any response by the witness, should be recorded. If an identification is made, a careful record should be made of how the person identified is known to the witness, including details of the number of times encountered, for how long, over what period, and so on. Identity-specific verifiable information of the person known to the witness should be elicited to help to establish how well the person is known to the witness (e.g., their name, where they live or work, their friends, family, etc.).
- *Consideration should be given to use of averaged images (in which the texture from several photographs of the same person are mapped to a standard face-shape) in passports and other identification documents:* Matching a person to an averaged image is likely to be more reliable than to a single passport-style image. Automatic recognition systems perform better when recognizing averaged images than single images.
- *Personnel whose work involves matching facial images (e.g., border guards) should be selected on the basis of their performance in a standardized test of face-matching ability:* The London Metropolitan Police noticed that a few officers were able to identify hundreds of rioters from CCTV imagery of the 2011 London riots. Super-recognizers have been identified from amongst their officers and are deployed to identify unknown suspects from CCTV images. There are a number of face recognition and face-processing tests available that might be used for formal selection of "super-recognizers", but there is a need for standardized selection tests to be developed for this purpose.

Facial Image Comparison by Experts

Several types of analysis are used by expert witnesses to provide opinion evidence in court on face matching from photographs and video imagery. The research reviewed in Chapter 10 shows that there is no effective method that is based on a substantial body of research evidence. Techniques based on measuring proportions and ratios of the position of facial features (known as photo-anthropometry) from even the best quality of images typically available in a criminal case have been found to be unreliable (Davis, Valentine, & Davis, 2010; Moreton & Morley, 2011). Morphological comparison (based on categorizing the properties of facial features) lacks an adequate scientific research base, especially when low-quality images are compared, but the method is less susceptible than photo-anthropometry to bias from small differences in viewpoint and the optical properties of the cameras. Therefore, we make the following recommendations:

- *Expert evidence purporting to match unfamiliar faces from similarity in the proportions, ratios, and angles of facial features should not be presented in court.*
- *Courts should exercise great caution if seeking to rely on expert facial image comparison using morphological comparison or any other method. The adequacy of the research base for the method used should be carefully examined.*

CONCLUDING REMARKS

Eyewitness identification evidence is an especially difficult type of evidence for a court to evaluate: confident eyewitnesses provide impressive testimony but are frequently mistaken. Eyewitness identification involves an active process of reconstructing an impression of a face from a few details that have been remembered. When making decisions under uncertainty, as eyewitnesses do, it is inevitable that errors will occur: guilty culprits will be missed and innocent suspects mistakenly identified. Collection and evaluation of eyewitness identification evidence is fundamentally a very difficult process to improve. The goal of most experimental psychologists working on eyewitness identification has been to reduce the rate of mistaken identification of innocent suspects, without decreasing the rate of identification of guilty culprits. Some methods have been promoted as achieving this goal: using sequential presentation instead of showing all of the faces together, as in a photograph lineup; instructing the witness that the person they saw may not be in the lineup; and running the procedure double-blind. In some jurisdictions these procedures have been adopted by the law enforcement agencies on this basis. It is now clear that the advice provided by experimental psychologists was misleading. The protection gained for innocent suspects was gained at a cost of identifying the guilty (Clark, 2012; Chapter 6).

A major problem in eyewitness research is that it has developed as an applied research area, with little basis in contemporary theoretical models of memory. A step towards addressing this deficit in the dominant research paradigm has been taken by developing a procedure that allows signal detection theory to be applied in eyewitness identification research (Mickes, Flowe, & Wixted, 2012). Memory models based on signal detection theory have two parameters: the *sensitivity* of the system and the decision *criterion* set. Sensitivity determines how easily a target face can be distinguished from other faces and be recognized. High sensitivity means the witness has a good memory to perform the identification task. The task of the experimental psychologist is to design an identification procedure that is as sensitive as possible by enabling a witness to access and utilize all the information available in memory. The decision criterion can be manipulated by the procedure. One may set a very strict criterion which will reduce the probability of a mistaken identification, but it will be at the cost of failing to identify more guilty culprits. Alternatively, if the criterion is less conservative, guilty culprits are more likely to be identified, but mistaken identification of innocent suspects is more likely too. Mickes *et al.* (2012) described a method of using signal detection theory to compare lineup procedures by plotting accuracy separately for witnesses who expressed different levels of confidence (known as a receiver operating characteristic, or ROC, curve). Recent use of ROC analysis has bought into question the claim of an advantage in terms of identification accuracy for sequentially-presented lineups. This issue is discussed in more detail in Chapter 6.

Another example of the effect of a lack of theoretical development in eyewitness memory comes from research on the relationship between accuracy and confidence. Up until the mid-1990s, most psychologists argued that the confidence of eyewitnesses was unrelated to the accuracy of their identification. As Sauer and Brewer point out in Chapter 8, this conclusion is both counter-intuitive and has no theoretical basis, because in theoretical models of meta-memory, confidence and memory performance are derived from the same source. It turns out that the problem was the way in which confidence was recorded and analysed, and for the courts a major problem was the influence of feedback. When recorded carefully and appropriately analysed, confidence is associated with the accuracy of witnesses who make an identification from a lineup.

There is now a new era in eyewitness identification research that will be more firmly rooted in the contemporary theories of the psychology of memory. The need for this development has been clear for a long time, and there have been some impressive efforts to develop a more theoretically-based approach (e.g., Clark, 2003; Meissner, Tredoux, Parker, & MacLin, 2005). However, theoretically-motivated experiments often comprise aspects of experimental procedure that make the research appear less applicable to real-world identification tasks. A practical methodology for use of ROC curves to compare between a control and experimental manipulation of an identification procedure could enable eyewitness research to develop in a more theoretically rigorous manner. Such experimental rigour is to be welcomed. If psychologists make recommendations for changes to legal procedures, which will have serious consequences for people's lives, the recommendations need to be based on sound science. It should not be denied that a powerful case for reform of procedure may be properly based on an appeal to civilized values rather than science in isolation, but it is important that science and values are clearly distinguished.

REFERENCES

Alenezi, H.M., & Bindemann, M. (2013). The effect of feedback on face-matching accuracy. *Applied Cognitive Psychology*, *27*, 735–753. doi:10.1002/acp.2968

American Bar Association (2004). *American Bar Association statement of best practices for promoting the accuracy of eyewitness identification procedures.* Washington, DC: American Bar Association. Retrieved from http://meetings.abanet.org/webupload/commupload/CR209700/relatedresources/ABAEyewitnessIDrecommendations.pdf

Bressan, P., & Dal Martello, M.F. (2002). 'Talis pater: talis filius': Perceived resemblance and belief in genetic relatedness. *Psychological Science*, *13*, 213–218. doi:10.1111/1467-9280.0040

Bruce, V., Ness, H., Hancock, P.J.B., Newman, C., & Rarity, J. (2002). Four heads are better than one: Combining face composites yields improvements in face likeness. *Journal of Applied Psychology*, *87*, 894–902. doi:10.1037/0021-9010.87.5.894

Burton, A.M., Jenkins, R., Hancock, P.J.B., & White, D. (2005). Robust representations for face recognition: The power of averages. *Cognitive Psychology*, *51*, 256–284. doi:10.1016/j.cogpsych.2005.06.003

Charman, S.D., Gregory, A.H., & Carlucci, M. (2009). Exploring the diagnostic utility of facial composites: Beliefs of guilt can bias perceived similarity between composite and suspect. *Journal of Experimental Psychology: Applied*, *15*, 76–90. doi:10.1037/a0014682

Clark, S.E. (2003). A memory and decision model for eyewitness identification. *Applied Cognitive Psychology*, *17*, 629–654. doi:10.1002/acp.891

Clark, S.E. (2012). Costs and benefits of eyewitness identification reform: Psychological science and public policy. *Perspectives on Psychological Science*, *7*, 238–259. doi:10.1177/1745691612439584

Cole, S.A., & Thompson, W.C. (2013). Forensic science and wrongful convictions. In C.R. Huff, & M. Killias (Eds.), *Wrongful Convictions & Miscarriages of Justice* (pp. 111–136). London: Routledge.

Davis, J.P., Jansari, A., & Lander, K. (2013). *I never forget a face! The Psychologist*, *26*, 726–729. Retrieved from http://www.thepsychologist.org.uk/archive/archive_home.cfm?volumeID=26&editionID=231

Davis, J.P., Valentine, T., & Davis, R.E. (2010). Computer assisted photo-anthropometric analyses of full-face and profile facial images. *Forensic Science International*, *200*, 165–176. doi:10.1016/j.forsciint.2010.04.012

Davis, J.P., Valentine, T., Memon, A., & Roberts, A. (2015). Identification on the street: A field comparison of police street identifications and video lineups in England. *Psychology, Crime and Law*, *21*, 9–27. doi:10.1080/1068316X.2014.915322

Devlin, P. (1976). *Report to the Secretary of State for the Home Department on the Departmental Committee on Evidence of Identification in Criminal Cases*. London: HMSO.

Dror, I.E., Charlton, D., & Peron, A. (2006). Contextual information renders experts vulnerable to making erroneous identifications. *Forensic Science International*, *156*, 74–78. doi:10.1016/j.forsciint.2005.10.017

Dror, I.E., & Rosenthal, R. (2008). Meta-analytically quantifying the reliability and biasability of forensic experts. *Journal of Forensic Sciences*, *53*, 900–903. doi:10.1111/j.1556-4029.2008.00762.x

Fitzgerald, R.J., Price, H.L., Oriet, C., & Charman, S.D. (2013). The effect of suspect-filler similarity on eyewitness identification decisions: A meta-analysis. *Psychology, Public Policy and Law*, *19*, 151–164. doi:10.1037/a0030618

Gabbert, F., Hope, L., & Fisher, R.P. (2009). Protecting eyewitness evidence: Examining the efficacy of a Self-Administered Interview tool. *Law & Human Behavior*, *33*, 298–307. doi:10.1007/s10979-008-9146-8

Gabbert, F., Hope, L., Fisher, R.P., & Jamieson, K. (2012). Protecting against susceptibility to misinformation with the use of a Self-Administered Interview. *Applied Cognitive Psychology*, *26*, 568–575. doi:10.1002/acp.2828

Horry, R., Memon, A., Wright, D.B., & Milne, R. (2012). Predictors of eyewitness identification decisions from video lineups in England: A field study. *Law and Human Behavior*, *36*, 257–265. doi:10.1037/h0093959

Hughes, C. (2005). *Making the best use of video film identification parades and providing a fair and consistent approach to witnesses* (unpublished MSc thesis). University of Portsmouth.

Innocence Project. (n.d.). Eyewitness Identification Reform. Retrieved from http://www.innocenceproject.org/understand/Eyewitness-Misidentification.php

Kassin, S.M., Dror, I.E., & Kukucka, J. (2013). The forensic confirmation bias: Problems, perspectives and proposed solutions. *Journal of Applied Research in Memory and Cognition*, *2*, 42–52. doi:10.1016/j.jarmac.2013.01.001

Meissner, C.A., Tredoux, C.G., Parker, J.F., & MacLin, O. (2005). Eyewitness decisions in simultaneous and sequential lineups: A dual-process signal detection theory analysis. *Memory & Cognition*, *33*, 783–792. doi:10.3758/BF03193074

Memon, A., Dalton, G., Horry, R., Milne, R., & Wright, D. (2012). Screen Test. *Journal of the Law Society of Scotland*, November 2012. Retrieved from http://www.journalonline.co.uk/Magazine/57-11/1011839.aspx

Memon, A., Meissner, C.A., & Fraser, J. (2010). The cognitive interview: A meta-analytic review and study space analysis of the past 25 years. *Public Policy, and Law*, *16*, 340–372. doi:10.1037/a0020518

Mickes, L., Flowe, H.D., & Wixted, J.T. (2012). Receiver operating characteristic analysis of eyewitness memory: comparing the diagnostic accuracy of simultaneous versus sequential lineups. *Journal of Experimental Psychology: Applied, 18,* 361–376. doi:10.1037/a0030609

Ministry of Justice (2011). *Achieving best evidence in criminal proceedings. Guidance on interviewing victims and witnesses, and guidance on using special measures.* Retrieved from http://www.justice.gov.uk/downloads/victims-and-witnesses/vulnerable-witnesses/achieving-best-evidence-criminal-proceedings.pdf

Moreton, R., & Morley, J. (2011). Investigation into the use of photoanthropometry in facial image comparison. *Forensic Science International, 212,* 231–237. doi:10.1016/j.forsciint.2011.06.023

National Institute of Justice (1999). *Eyewitness Evidence: A Guide for Law Enforcement.* Washington: US National Institute of Justice. Retrieved from http://www.ojp.usdoj.gov/nij/pubs-sum/178240.htm

National Research Academy (2009). Strengthening Forensic Science in the United States: A Path Forward. Downloaded from https://www.ncjrs.gov/pdffiles1/nij/grants/228091.pdf

Nickerson, R.S. (1998). Confirmation bias: A ubiquitous phenomenon in many guises. *Psychological Review, 2,* 175–220. doi:10.1037/1089-2680.2.2.175

Penrod, S.D., & Bull Kovera, M. (2009). Recent developments in North American identification science and practice. In R. Bull, T. Valentine, & T. Williamson (Eds.), *Handbook of Psychology of Investigative Interviewing* (pp. 257–283). Chichester: Wiley-Blackwell.

Rajaopal, S. (2006). The placebo effect. *The Psychiatrist, 30,* 185–188. doi:10.1192/pb.30.5.185

Saks, M.J., Rislinger, D.M., Rosenthal, R., & Thompson, W.C. (2003). Context effects in forensic science: A review and application of the science of science to crime laboratory practice in the United States. *Science & Justice, 43,* 77–90. doi:10.1016/S1355-0306(03)71747-X

Semmler, C., Brewer, N., & Wells, G.L. (2004). Effects of postidentification feedback on eyewitness identification and nonidentification confidence. *Journal of Applied Psychology, 89,* 334–346. doi:10.1037/0021-9010.89.2.334

Tulving, E., & Thompson, D.M. (1973). Encoding specificity and retrieval processes in episodic memory. *Psychological Review, 80,* 352–373. doi:10.1037/h0020071

Valentine, T., Davis, J.P, Memon, A., & Roberts A. (2012). Live showups and their influence on a subsequent video lineup. *Applied Cognitive Psychology, 26,* 1–23. doi:10.1002/acp.1796

Valentine, T., Davis, J.P., Thorner, K., Solomon, C., & Gibson, S. (2010). Evolving and combining facial composites: Between-witness and within-witness morphs compared. *Journal of Experimental Psychology:Applied, 61,* 72–86. doi:10.1037/a0018801

Valentine, T., Hughes, C., & Munro, R. (2009). Recent developments in eyewitness identification procedures in the United Kingdom. In R. Bull, T. Valentine, & T. Williamson (Eds.), *The Handbook of Psychology of Investigative Interviewing* (pp. 221–240). Chichester: John Wiley & Sons, Ltd.

Valentine, T., Pickering, A., & Darling, S. (2003). Characteristics of eyewitness identification that predict the outcome of real lineups. *Applied Cognitive Psychology, 17,* 969–993. doi:10.1002/acp.939

Wells, G.L. (1993). What do we know about eyewitness identification? *American Psychologist, 48,* 553–571. doi:10.1037/0003-066X.48.5.553

Wells, G.L., Memon, A., & Penrod, S.D. (2006). Eyewitness evidence: Improving its probative value. *Psychological Science in the Public Interest, 7,* 45–75. doi:10.1111/j.1529-1006.2006.00027.x

Wells, G.L., Small, M., Penrod, S., Malpass, R.S., Fulero, S.M., & Brimacombe, C.A.E. (1998). Eyewitness identification procedures: Recommendations for lineups and photospreads. *Law and Human Behavior*, *22*, 603–647. doi:10.1023/A:1025750605807

White, D., Kemp, R.I., Jenkins, R., & Burton, A.M. (2013). Feedback training for facial image comparison. *Psychonomic Bulletin & Review*, *21*, 100–106. doi:10.3758/s13423-013-0475-3

Williamson, T. (2004). USA and UK responses to miscarriages of justice. In Adler, J. (Ed.) *Forensic Psychology: Concepts, Debates & Practice* (pp. 39–57). Cullompton: Willan Publishing.

Williamson, T. (2006). Towards greater professionalism: minimizing miscarriages of justice. In T. Williamson (Ed.), *Investigative Interviewing: Rights, Research, Regulation* (pp. 147–166). Cullompton: Willan Publishing.

Index

*Forensic Facial Identification: Theory and Practice of Identification from Eyewitnesses,
Composites and CCTV*, First Edition. Edited by Tim Valentine and Josh P. Davis.
© 2015 John Wiley & Sons, Ltd. Published 2015 by John Wiley & Sons, Ltd.